International Law in World Politics

International Law in World Politics

AN INTRODUCTION

Shirley V. Scott

LYNNE
RIENNER
PUBLISHERS

BOULDER
LONDON

Published in the United States of America in 2004 by
Lynne Rienner Publishers, Inc.
1800 30th Street, Boulder, Colorado 80301
www.rienner.com

and in the United Kingdom by
Lynne Rienner Publishers, Inc.
3 Henrietta Street, Covent Garden, London WC2E 8LU

Library of Congress Cataloging-in-Publication Data
Scott, Shirley V.
    International law in world politics : an introduction / Shirley V. Scott.
    Includes bibliographical references and index.
    ISBN 1-58826-174-3 (hard : alk. paper)
    ISBN 1-58826-199- 9 (pbk. : alk. paper)
    1. International law.   I. Title.
    KZ3410.S38   3004
    341—dc22

                                                        2003019863

British Cataloguing in Publication Data
A Cataloguing in Publication record for this book
is available from the British Library.

Printed and bound in the United States of America

The paper used in this publication meets the requirements
of the American National Standard for Permanence of
Paper for Printed Library Materials Z39.48-1992.

5 4 3 2 1

Contents

Figures

1

International Law and World Politics Entwined

International law is a system of rules, principles, and concepts that governs relations among states and, increasingly, international organizations, individuals, and other actors in world politics. International law has grown and expanded at a rapid rate since World War II to encompass a diverse range of issues and topics, including the preservation of the marine environment, the right to use force against another state, territorial rights in Antarctica, the use of outer space, and the rights of children. There is now no aspect of world politics that can be fully understood without some knowledge of international law and an awareness of how it operates as an integral component of global affairs. International law is also having an impact on national legal systems to an unprecedented extent. National court cases may turn on a point of international, rather than municipal, law, and national decisionmakers must now consider a constantly increasing number of international law obligations in the policymaking process. Indeed, international law now affects the life of every individual. Even persons living in a remote village in a small island state may have their livelihoods affected by the terms of a global treaty on trade while relying on a treaty on climate change to ensure the very survival of their island state. Citizens of the former Yugoslavia are looking to international law to restore justice and hope after years of civil war and human rights atrocities, just as indigenous leaders are seeking avenues in international law by which to improve the lot of their peoples and to increase their voice in international affairs. As the world becomes more globalized, there is a need for all informed citizens to gain an appreciation of the mechanism by which so many interstate and transnational links are forged and maintained.

If we are to understand how this system operates within world politics we need to appreciate that international law, although an integral part of politics, is also to a large extent autonomous. International law has considerable cohesion as a system of interrelated rules, principles, and concepts that, although operating within the political milieu, are to some extent distinct from it. A political term such as "sovereignty" or "state" may also be used within the system of international law but with a different meaning. Chapters 1–4 in this book will consider further the entwining of international law with politics before we focus in Chapter 5 on the autonomy of the system of international law.

How Does International Law Compare with Law in the Domestic Context?

Whether we are aware of it or not, most of us approaching international law for the first time intuitively bring certain assumptions about law in a domestic situation and expect international law to be the equivalent at an international level. This can be an asset where there are similarities between the two, but there are some aspects of the system of law in most liberal democracies that do not have an obvious parallel at the international level. We will begin by making some comparisons between domestic (i.e., "municipal") law and international law. To those whose main interest is world politics, it may at first seem strange to realize that an understanding of international law is essential to understanding political dynamics. Let us then begin our brief comparison by considering how it is that law—whether domestic or international—can be considered integral to political processes.

A political system can be defined as "any persistent pattern of human relationships that involves, to a significant extent, control, influence, power, or authority."[1] We often think first of national political systems, such as those of the United States or of India, but we can also talk about the politics internal to a school, or even to a family. When we analyze the operation of a political system we find that not everyone has equivalent power. In other words, control over political resources—the means by which one person can influence the behavior of other persons—is not distributed evenly.[2] The study of politics is in large part the study of the process that determines who gets what and who can do what in a particular political unit. At a national level in a democracy, the legislature makes and implements political decisions by passing legislation. Legislation is law, and so we can see that law is one mechanism through which politics may be conducted. And of course another domestic arena in which decisions are made that impact the distribution of the benefits of society is the courtroom. A legal judgment can have an immediate impact, for example, on who receives a family's inheritance, or on whether indigenous peoples have the same rights to land as other members of society. Politics and law are thus intimately related.

In the same way that domestic politics is entwined with law, international law is integral to world politics and may impact the global distribution of power. A free trade agreement may benefit the exporting countries more than the importing countries. The International Court of Justice (ICJ) may delimit a maritime boundary between two states that then determines which country is able to exploit valuable oil resources. International law is integral to international structures of power, but the place of international law in world politics cannot be appreciated unless one has a basic understanding as to how the system of international law functions. As a first step toward this goal it may be useful to draw some more comparisons and contrasts between the legal and political systems of modern liberal democracies and those in the international arena.

A Legislature to Make the Law?

One of the most important distinctions between the domestic legal system of liberal democratic societies and the system of international law is that there is no international legislature to pass legislation and "make law." Although this difference is sometimes lamented, it is worth pondering a larger question: If there were to be a world government, of whom would we want it to be made up? The closest equivalent in world politics to a domestic legislature is the United Nations (UN) General Assembly. Every member state represented in the General Assembly gets one vote, but the resulting decision is not law in the same way that an act of parliament or congress is a law. A General Assembly resolution is a political decision that may indicate the direction law is likely to take but that most lawyers do not recognize as "law."

If international law is not created by legislation, from where, then, does international law come? To put it differently: If we wanted to find what the rules, principles, and concepts of international law had to say on a subject—for example, hijacking or maritime safety—where would we go to find out?

Treaties. The main source of international law today is treaties, also known as conventions. Treaties are agreements between states, between states and international organizations, or between international organizations. A *bilateral treaty* is an agreement between two parties. International organizations commonly make agreements with their host state or with a state in which they are conducting a conference. An example of one type of bilateral treaty between states is the extradition treaty, which governs the surrender of fugitives from justice by the fugitive's state of residence to another state claiming criminal jurisdiction. Another example of a bilateral treaty is a status of forces agreement (SOFA), which provides for the legal status of military forces and the conditions under which one state can station them in another state. A SOFA includes, for example, which state has the primary duty to investigate and prosecute members of the armed forces suspected of committing crimes in the receiving state. The United States has concluded SOFAs with more than fifty countries in which its troops are stationed or operating.[3] These have often been controversial in the domestic politics of the host countries. In the 1960s the proposed U.S.-Iran SOFA and the exemption it would grant U.S. military personnel from the jurisdiction of Iranian courts was held up by Ayatollah Ruhollah Khomeini as distastefully reminiscent of the colonial domination of Iran.[4] More recently, the North Atlantic Treaty Organization (NATO)'s 1951 SOFA[5] became the subject of controversy following an incident in which a U.S. Marine EA-6B Prowler on a low-level training flight in the Italian Alps severed a cable-car line, killing twenty people.[6] The U.S.-Japan SOFA came to the fore as an issue in 2002 in relation to rape and arson attacks by U.S. servicemen in Okinawa.[7] The revision of the U.S.-South Korea SOFA became an issue in June 2002 after two U.S. soldiers driving an armored mine-clearing vehicle in South Korea crushed two schoolgirls to death; the United States court-martialed the two service personnel, but they were acquitted and rapidly transferred out of the country. Following the terrorist attacks of September 11, 2001, in New York City and Washington, D.C., the United States quickly concluded a SOFA with the Kyrgyz Republic in Central Asia, prior to basing combat and combat support units at Manas as part of Operation Enduring Freedom.[8]

In the context of antiballistic missile (ABM) control, the 1972 Treaty on the Limitation of Anti-Ballistic Missile Systems (ABM Treaty) between the United States and the Soviet Union, another bilateral treaty, was designed to prevent either state from deploying a nationwide ABM system for defending its territory. The treaty was premised on the doctrine of "mutually assured destruction" (MAD) as a deterrent to the use of nuclear weapons. The U.S. administration under President Bill Clinton sought to modify the treaty to permit the deployment of a limited national missile defense system but failed to win the agreement of Russia. Although the ABM Treaty is of unlimited duration, its terms provide that each party has the right to withdraw, upon six months' notification, if it decides that extraordinary events related to the subject matter of the treaty have "jeopardized its supreme interests." In 2001 President George W. Bush decided to abandon the ABM Treaty. The 2002 Treaty Between the United States of America and the Russian Federation on Strategic Offensive Reductions, providing for the reduction and limitation of strategic nuclear warheads, is another example of a bilateral treaty relating to arms control.[9]

Multilateral treaties are agreements between three or more states. Those states may belong to one geographical region—it may be an African regional treaty on human rights, for example; or the treaty may aim at global participation in order, for example, to protect the global climate. Approximately 4,065 new multilateral treaties appeared between 1945 and 1995, an average of almost ninety per year.[10] The entwining of international law with world politics is evident in the realm of treaties insofar as treaties are the product of negotiations between states and states can be expected to approach negotiations— whether on trade or marine pollution—as a political exercise. Each state will bring its own political objectives and strategies to the negotiating table, and as the product of those negotiations, the resultant treaty text is likely to reflect the political compromises that were required to reach agreement.

A treaty is usually dated to the year there is agreement on the text. This may differ significantly from the date on which the treaty becomes law and the parties become bound by its terms. The text of the Third United Nations Convention on the Law of the Sea (UNCLOS III), for example, was agreed to in 1982, but the convention did not receive the necessary support to enter into force until 1994. The UN Charter requires members to register all new treaties with the UN Secretariat, which publishes them in the United Nations Treaty Series (UNTS), available in hard copy and on the Internet.[11] Other places in which to locate treaties are *International Legal Materials*, the *League of Nations Treaty Series,* the *United Kingdom Treaty Series*, and Internet collections including the Multilaterals Project at the Fletcher School of Law and Diplomacy at Tufts University, Massachusetts.[12]

A treaty is divided into articles and, within an article, into paragraphs and subparagraphs. "Article 48(4)(a)" refers to "article 48, paragraph 4, subparagraph (a)." In a long treaty articles may be grouped into chapters, sections, and parts. The treaty may include annexes, and there may be subsequent treaties that build on it, usually referred to as "protocols."

The earliest known treaty dates from around 3000 B.C., preserved on a border stone between Lagash and Umma in Mesopotamia.[13] The important contemporary principle of *pacta sunt servanda*—states are bound to carry out in good faith the obligations they have assumed by treaty—is thought to derive from the fact that early treaties were often considered sacred.[14] And though states are expected to carry out their treaty obligations in good faith, a state is not bound by treaties to which it is not a party. This is because a state is, by definition, *constitutionally independent*, which means that a state must *consent* to be bound by a treaty before it becomes bound, consent being another basic concept in the system of international law.

We will look at the concept of consent more fully in Chapter 5 and at multilateral treaties in more detail in Chapters 7 and 8.

Custom. The second most important source of international law today is custom. Custom is created by what states do, where that action is carried out with a view to the rules and principles of international law. Customary international law was at one time the most important source of international law. As an example, the rules on the treatment of diplomats evolved through custom. The treatment by one state of the representative of another may have been accepted as valid, or it may have been the subject of protest and discussion. Rules gradually evolved as to how states would treat diplomats, and those rules are termed "customary international law." Custom is in many cases codified into a treaty; when formulated into a written document, the rules, principles, and concepts naturally appear more precise and are less subject to change. The customary international law relating to the treatment of diplomats was to a large extent codified in the 1961 Vienna Convention on Diplomatic Relations.

Not everything that a state does or does not do contributes to customary international law. Certain habitual practices may emerge; all diplomatic stationery may be of a certain color, for example, for purely pragmatic or practical reasons. The practice of a state can be used as evidence of custom only if the *opinio juris* component is present (i.e., that the state has been choosing to act in that way for reasons of law). Custom can be quite a slow way of creating law, although that is not always the case. The law that the airspace superjacent to land territory, internal waters, and the territorial sea is a part of state territory, and that as a consequence other states may use such airspace for navigation or other purposes only with the agreement of the territorial sovereign, developed in a relatively short period with the development of aviation and the impact of World War I.[15]

The entwining of international law with world politics is evident in relation to custom in that it may well have been specific political goals that prompted a state to engage in a particular practice (or not to act). The U.S. response to the terrorist attacks of September 11 and the attitude of other states to that response appear to have confirmed an evolution of customary international law to include a right to use force in self-defense against a terrorist attack (see Figure 1.1).

There is usually some room for maneuver in arguing whether or not a particular rule of customary international law exists. Here we get another glimpse of where politics enters the equation. If one is representing a state before the International Court of Justice, one is likely to argue for or against the emergence of a particular principle or rule of customary international law on the basis of one's overall case and strategic goals. We will be looking at international customary law in more detail in Chapters 3 and 5.

A Police Force to Enforce the Law?

Apart from there not being an international legislature, another major difference between most domestic legal systems and the system of international law is that there is no international police force to enforce compliance. For many, this is a great deficiency of international law and the reason why international law is not more politically effective. It might seem that if states were compelled to respect international law on, say, the use of force, we would live in a much more peaceful and ordered world. The great hiccup here is the concept of *sovereignty* and the related concept of consent. International law operates in a state-based system that is anarchical, meaning that there is no overarching government, and international law is, at least theoretically, a horizontal system made up of sovereign equals. The same question that was posed in the context of a world government can be posed here: If there were a country or body tasked with enforcing international law, which would we want it to be?

We must also be careful not to push too far our domestic analogy of law enforcement by police. The police forces in a domestic system primarily enforce criminal law. The bulk of international law governing relations among states does not address the criminal behavior of states but is better compared to the civil law of rights and wrongs, claims and defenses, and in a municipal system the outcomes of these matters are usually negotiated or settled through courts, much as they are in international law.

There are some methods for enforcing international law, although when viewed as a whole the picture may still look patchy. Individual

**Figure 1.1   Customary International Law and the
Right to Use Force in Response to a Terrorist Attack**

The right of a state to defend itself is well established in customary
international law. It was also incorporated into treaty law as article
51 of the United Nations Charter. The type of attack on a state envisaged by the drafters of the Charter was, understandably, that of one
state against another. Debate began in the 1980s as to the right of a
state to respond with force to terrorism under article 51. When in
1986 the United States claimed that its bombing of military targets in
Libya in response to an explosion at the LaBelle disco in Berlin,
which killed two U.S. servicemen and wounded seventy-eight
Americans, was an act of self-defense, international reaction was
largely negative.[i] A draft UN Security Council resolution condemning the strike was supported by a majority of members of the
Security Council but was vetoed by France, the United States, and
the United Kingdom.[ii] A U.S. missile attack on June 26, 1993, which
destroyed the Iraqi intelligence headquarters in Baghdad, taken in
response to an alleged Iraqi plan to kill former U.S. president George
H. W. Bush was again justified as self-defense. This time the majority of Security Council members accepted the U.S. position that the
attack was a justified act of self-defense, although China and some
Islamic states voiced criticism.[iii]

On August 20, 1998, the United States launched seventy-nine
Tomahawk cruise missiles at targets associated with Osama bin
Laden's Al-Qaida network, including paramilitary training camps in
Afghanistan and a pharmaceutical factory in the Sudan that the
United States claimed had been providing or storing a precursor
chemical used in chemical weapons.[iv] Bin Laden had been linked to
the bombing on August 7, 1998, of U.S. embassies in Nairobi,
Kenya, and Dar es Salam, Tanzania. The United States argued that
the strikes were in self-defense consistent with Article 51 of the UN
Charter. Russia condemned the attacks, as did Pakistan and several
Arab countries. The Non-Aligned Movement condemned the U.S.
attack as "unilateral and unwarranted," and in September UN
Secretary-General Kofi Annan criticized "individual actions" against
terrorism, implying disapproval of the U.S. strikes.[v] Most U.S. allies

(continues)

Figure 1.1   continued

supported the attacks, although France and Italy issued only tepid statements of support.

Following the terrorist attacks of September 11, 2001, the United States constructed an extensive coalition. NATO and parties to the Inter-American Treaty of Reciprocal Assistance identified the terrorist attacks as "armed attacks," as referred to in Article 51, and the United States drew a strong link between the Taliban regime and Al-Qaida, thus implicating a state in the "armed attack" as would traditionally have been expected under article 51. In a letter to the Security Council dated October 7, the United States stated that it had initiated actions "in the exercise of its inherent right of individual and collective self-defense."[vi] Following Operation Enduring Freedom, and the wide support given to the U.S.-led coalition bombing in response to September 11, it could be said that customary international law has evolved such that the right of self-defense now includes military responses against states that actively support or willingly harbor terrorist groups.[vii]

Notes

i.   Alan D. Surchin, "Terror and the Law: The Unilateral Use of Force and the June 1993 Bombing of Baghdad," *Duke Journal of Comparative and International Law* 5 (1995): 457–497.

ii.   Draft text no. S/18016/Rev.1, S/PV.2682, April 21, 1986, p. 43.

iii.   Surchin, "Terror and the Law," 467–468.

iv.   Sean D. Murphy, "Contemporary Practice of the United States Relating to International Law," *American Journal of International Law* 93, no. 1 (1999): 161–194, 161.

v.   Jules Lobel, "The Use of Force to Respond to Terrorist Attacks: The Bombing of Sudan and Afghanistan," *Yale Journal of International Law* 24 (1999): 537–557, 538.

vi.   Letter to Security Council from the Permanent Representative of the United States of America to the United Nations, addressed to the President of the Security Council, dated October 7, 2001, UN Doc. S/2001/946 (October 7, 2001), www.un.int/usa/s-2001–946.htm.

vii.   Michael Byers, "Terrorism, the Use of Force, and International Law After 11 September," *International and Comparative Law Quarterly* 51, no. 2 (2002): 401–414, 410.

states can attempt to ensure that other states respect the rules of international law in mutual relations by measures of *retorsion*, unfriendly but legal acts, such as the severance of diplomatic relations, used to indicate displeasure with the policies or actions of another state. A second form of enforcement of international law by an individual state is that of *countermeasures*, acts that would be illegal except that they are carried out in response to an illegal act by the other party. Countermeasures must be proportional to the original breach and may not include the use of force.[16] One of the most important ways to ensure compliance with multilateral treaties is to write into the treaty verification measures—ways of checking that the other states that are party to that treaty are complying. Verification measures may include a system of inspections or of reporting. If the UN Security Council believes that there is a threat to international peace, breach of the peace, or act of aggression, it can impose sanctions of an economic, diplomatic, or military nature.[17] The Security Council also has the power to enforce a decision of the ICJ. Article 94(2) of the UN Charter provides that if any party to a case "fails to perform the obligations incumbent upon it under a judgment rendered by the Court, the other party may have recourse to the Security Council, which may, if it deems necessary, make recommendations or decide upon measures to be taken to give effect to the judgment."[18] This has never been asked of the Security Council.

Compliance with international law is sometimes promoted by the provision of assistance via an intergovernmental organization (IGO). The United Nations Environment Programme (UNEP), for example, provides technical assistance to help developing countries implement environmental treaty obligations. The United Nations Programme of Technical Cooperation assists with human rights–related activities such as training law enforcement personnel and members of national judiciaries.[19]

National courts sometimes enforce international law. The Alien Tort Claims Act of 1789[20] grants jurisdiction to U.S. federal courts over "any civil action by an alien [someone who is not a U.S. citizen] for a tort only, committed in violation of the law of nations or a treaty of the United States." The reason for the act is not certain, but it was likely intended either to secure the prosecution of pirates or to protect diplomats. The act rose to prominence and became a source of controversy in the early 1980s, since when it has been used to bring cases against both individuals and companies for claimed breaches of international human rights law committed outside the United States. The Torture Victim Protection Act of 1991[21] creates a right for victims, including aliens, of state-sponsored torture and summary execution in other countries to sue in federal courts.

A Judiciary?

Although there is no international legislature, there is a world court, situated in The Hague. The Permanent Court of International Justice operated from 1922 to 1946, then was replaced by the International Court of Justice, one of the six principal organs of the United Nations. The operation of the ICJ is underpinned by the principle of consent: the ICJ can hear a contentious case between states only if those states have consented to the Court doing so. Again, this may sound extraordinary on first hearing. But there is a fascinating entwining of law with politics evident in a state deciding whether or not to consent to the jurisdiction of the Court. The decision as to whether to be involved in a case before the Court may well be a political decision, but it will be made on the basis of the rules, principles, and concepts of international law and, no doubt, on the prospects of a successful outcome. In some cases, like that relating to Iran's holding of U.S. hostages in Tehran from 1979 to 1981, a state may decide that it is not in its interests to have the case heard by the Court, but the Court will find that the state concerned has, in fact, given its consent. To understand how this could come about requires understanding the relevant law and the political context in which it was functioning. We will be looking at this in more detail in Chapters 5 and 6.

Article 38(1) of the Statute of the International Court of Justice sets out the basis on which the Court is to reach a decision:

1. The Court, whose function is to decide in accordance with international law such disputes as are submitted to it, shall apply:
    a. International conventions, whether general or particular, establishing rules expressly recognised by the contesting States;
    b. international custom, as evidence of a general practice accepted as law;
    c. the general principles of law recognised by civilised nations;
    d. subject to the provisions of Article 59, judicial decisions and the teachings of the most highly qualified publicists of the various nations, as subsidiary means for the determination of rules of law.

We have already considered the first two of these: conventions (i.e., treaties), and customary international law. Although treaties and custom are the two most common sources of international law, it is important to consider also the rest of article 38(1) because, although in the narrow sense the article refers only to the sources of international law to be drawn on by the ICJ, it is widely held to be a statement of all of the current sources of international law.

The reference to "civilized nations" in article 38(1)(c) refers to the fact that being "civilized" used to be a criterion for participation in the system of international law. This is no longer the case, and it is widely accepted that the phrase "civilized nations" now means "states." The term "general principles" refers to general principles of law common to a representative majority of domestic legal orders, which includes "the main forms of civilization and the principle legal systems of the world."[22] "General principles of law" was included in the ICJ Statute in case gaps remained after the consideration of treaties and custom.[23] The ICJ has also drawn on general principles originating in international relations and general principles applicable to all kinds of legal relations.[24] The principle of good faith, for example, requires parties to deal honestly and fairly with each other.[25] Applied to treaties, this means that a treaty should be interpreted "in accordance with the ordinary meaning to be given to the terms of the treaty in their context and in the light of its object and purpose."[26] A state should not attempt to find unintended meanings in a treaty that would result in it gaining an unfair advantage over the other party.

Article 38(1)(d) refers to judgments of tribunals and courts as well as to the writings of distinguished international lawyers as "subsidiary means for the determination of rules of law." This means that "judicial decisions" such as the judgments of the International Court of Justice, and learned texts by famous international lawyers, can also be looked at to enhance understanding of what international law may have to say on a particular issue. The phrase "subsidiary means for the determination of rules of law" means that judges and the most highly qualified publicists of the various nations do not create law as such but clarify what that law has to say on a particular issue; judicial decisions and learned writings are subordinate to the first three sources.[27]

Although the ICJ is the only international court or tribunal with general jurisdiction, there has in recent years been a proliferation of judicial and quasijudicial bodies with subject-specific jurisdiction.[28] Notable examples include the Law of the Sea Tribunal, established in Hamburg, Germany, under the provisions of the 1982 Law of the Sea Convention, and the Appellate Body of the World Trade Organization. There have been calls for an international environment court.[29] There are also regional courts and tribunals. The oldest operating in Europe is the European Court of Justice of the European Communities, which began work in 1952 as the Court of Justice of the European Coal and Steel Community.

The Rule of Law

If we accept that law is a part of politics and that politics is about who gets what and how in a particular political order, the most important principle is the *rule of law*.[30] The essence of this principle is that everyone is equal before the law. It does not matter whether one is a wealthy professional, unemployed, or a member of the political bureaucracy; one is subject to the same laws on theft or on murder. Of course, there may well be cases in which individuals do not appear to be treated equally by the law. White-collar crime is less likely to lead to a jail sentence than breaking and entering. Although such examples seem at first glance to undercut the principle of the rule of law, that principle serves as a normative basis for law: It establishes what the law *should* do, even though it does not always do so.

Critics of a law or its implementation often seek to demonstrate its inadequacy by demonstrating that the law is not commensurate with the principle of the rule of law, and they use this as a basis for demanding change to the law or its improved implementation. Mandatory sentencing, which removes the discretion of a judge to vary punishments, has, for example, been criticized by those who believe that, despite purportedly treating all offenders equally, it tends to impact most on those segments of the community who are most likely to commit the type of crime in question. In the Northern Territory of Australia the crimes covered by a scheme of mandatory sentencing that operated between 1996 and 2001 were "crimes of poverty" most likely to have been committed by Indigenous offenders.[31] In 2002 some commentators claimed that the intervention of the Queen of England in the criminal trial of Princess Diana's butler, which led to the prosecution withdrawing the charge and the defendant being declared not guilty, "vividly demonstrated that not everyone is equal before British law."[32] The episode led to calls from inside the Labour Party to reform the Queen's immunity from giving evidence in civil and criminal proceedings.[33] In November 2002 India's human rights commission launched an investigation into the police shooting of alleged Pakistani terrorists who, it appeared, may have been framed by police. Kuldip Nayar, India's former high commissioner to the UK, who complained to the commission, was quoted as saying that

"India is a democracy and it is of vital importance that we uphold the rule of law."[34]

The principle of the rule of law also exists in the system of international law, where it gives rise to the principle of the *sovereign equality of states*.[35] States are the main actors in international law, and according to this fundamental principle all states are legally equal. Of course, just as the principle of the rule of law does not always match reality in a domestic legal system, so it does not do so in the system of international law. In the same way that members of society enjoy differing levels of wealth and opportunity, states differ drastically in terms of history, income, resources, and political systems.[36] There is therefore little prospect of all states carrying equivalent weight in international law. The perceived importance of the United States, as the world's greatest military power, signing the treaty to establish the International Criminal Court (ICC) meant that it could not fail but be more influential than a weak state in the negotiations.

Sometimes small states carry less weight at treaty negotiations simply because they do not have the staff, expertise, or knowledge to contribute; a small state that has only a handful of trained international lawyers cannot hope to match the input of a major power. At the ICC negotiations several sets of negotiations were held simultaneously on different issues, making it impossible for any one delegate to attend more than a small percentage of sessions.[37] It was also notable that the text was drafted only in English; it was several months after the finalization of the treaty that it was available in the other five languages that, according to the Rome Statute of the International Criminal Court itself, are "equally authentic."[38] The principle of the sovereign equality of states nevertheless plays a normative role within the system of international law and gives rise to specific rules regarding the operation of the system. Some states may carry more negotiating weight than others, but a state is not bound by a treaty if its consent was procured through the coercion of its representative, and a treaty is void if it has been procured by the threat or use of force.

International Law and Power

International law is closely related to the political context in which it operates. What is fascinating, however, is to try to discern the exact nature of the relationship between the two. It has been a mainstream assumption in the study of international relations since 1945 that international law has little impact on the "real world" of politics—at least when it comes to the hard-core issues of war and peace. It is a perspective closely related to the realist school of international relations theory, which focuses on states as the principal actors in world politics, and sees them as being in a constant struggle to compete for greater power (and thereby security). Realists have generally conceptualized power as emanating from tangible factors such as military and economic might. This leaves no room for an independent role for international law. Realism has a long tradition in the study of international relations; in fact it was in existence long before international relations emerged as a discipline. Although the discipline of international relations is usually dated from the early years after World War I, *The History of the Peloponnesian Wars*, written by Thucydides in about 400 B.C., is often considered an early realist work. Realist thinking continues to dominate government thinking, and its influence extends to most of those working for international organizations such as the United Nations.[39]

The empirical literature inspired by realist thought generally adopts a simplistic attitude toward international law, and assuming that the law has no important role to play, often leaves it out of the story altogether. Hence, the bulk of writing on what is generally regarded as having been the most serious crisis during the Cold War—the Cuban Missile Crisis—makes no mention of international law. The U.S. decision to impose a "quarantine" around Cuba, to prevent Soviet ships carrying nuclear missiles capable of targeting the United States from reaching Cuba, is often discussed with no reference to the legality of such a quarantine. This makes for a rather skewed historical account of the episode because the historical evidence points to international law as having featured strongly in the U.S. decisionmaking process. The United States was not prepared to take any action that was categorically illegal and settled for a way of proceeding that was at least of possible legality. Moreover, the United States went to great lengths to justify its actions in terms of international law.

Some realist writers acknowledge the existence of international law but do so in order to dismiss its impact on real world events. Dean Acheson, former U.S. secretary of state, commented in relation to the Cuban Missile Crisis that "the power, prestige and position of the United States had been challenged by another state; and . . . law simply does not deal with such questions of ultimate power. . . . The survival of states is not a matter of law."[40] Hans Morgenthau, the most famous realist thinker of the post–World War II years, was a lawyer by training. The inadequacies of international law were a disappointment to

Morgenthau. Morgenthau portrayed international law as a system seeking to constrain the powerful, and he found it lacking. He was highly
critical of what he perceived to be the absence of an effective international judicial system and of serious weaknesses in the system of
enforcement. Morgenthau considered that the primitive system of law
enforcement made it easy for the strong both to violate international law
and to enforce it, thereby putting the rights of the weak in jeopardy.[41]

There would appear to be a considerable element of truth in what
Morgenthau thought. Contrary to the ideal of the rule of law, international law has generally supported the powerful. This is perhaps most
clearly evidenced in relation to the general prohibition on the use of
force in international law; maintenance of peace supports the status
quo. Powerful states usually play a greater role than others do in creating the law, and they have a greater capacity to see that the law is
enforced against other states. But if this were the whole story, it would
be a sad and dull story indeed. And one would wonder why the decisionmakers in less powerful states were so gullible as to continue to
support a system designed solely for their exploitation.

International law may be generally supportive of the powerful, but
it does on occasion also help the less powerful, whether individually or
collectively. Nauru, one of the smallest countries in the world, was able
finally to bring Australia—which had administered Nauru under the
League of Nations Mandate System and the UN Trusteeship System—
to the negotiating table with respect to the rehabilitation of its mined-
out phosphate lands, when the proceedings that Nauru had initiated
against Australia in the ICJ appeared likely to result in an outcome
favorable to Nauru.[42] Consider another example. After World War II a
number of smaller states made what at the time seemed to be extraordinary claims to fisheries zones that gradually came to be regarded as part
of international law, albeit only when accepted by the powerful states.[43]
International law was, similarly, the mechanism by which many new
states of the third world emerged as independent entities during the
process of decolonization.

Not only does international law assist weaker states to survive in
the maelstrom of world politics; international law also serves to constrain, at least to a certain extent and on certain occasions, the actions of
the powerful. In his analysis of the functions that international law had
fulfilled during the Cuban Missile Crisis, Abram Chayes found that
international law had not only been a basis of justification or legitimation for action and provided organizational structures, procedures, and
forums; it had been a factor in constraining U.S. policy choices.[44] Other

writers have identified additional functions fulfilled by international law in world politics, including those of "providing rules of the game, fostering stable expectations, positing criteria by which national governments and others can act reasonably and justify their action, and providing a process of communication in a crisis."[45] It has been the concern of many international lawyers that, in the post–Cold War international order in which there is only one superpower, international law does not exert as powerful a constraining influence on the United States as it did in the days when the Soviet Union could more readily check any U.S. breaches of international law.

It is the complexity of the relationship between international law and world politics that is so fascinating. We will be better equipped to consider this complexity once we have a better understanding of the system of international law. We will now go on to look at the main actors in international law.

Notes

1. Robert A. Dahl, *Modern Political Analysis*, 4th ed. (Englewood Cliffs, NJ: Prentice-Hall, 1984), p. 10.

2. Ibid., p. 31.

3. *Treaties and Other International Acts Series of the Department of State* includes those with Antigua and Barbuda (TIAS number 9054), Ascension Island (3603), Australia (5349), Bahamas (11058), Bahrain (7263, 8208, 8632), Canada (2846, 3074), Denmark (2846, 4002), Diego Garcia (6196, 7481, 8230), Egypt (10238), Egypt (10238), France (2846), Germany (2846, 5351, 5352, 7759, 10367), Greece (2846, 3649), Honduras (10890, 11256), Iceland (2295), Italy (2846), Japan (4510), Jamaica (2105), Korea (6127), Luxembourg (2846), Marshall Islands (11671), Netherlands (3174), New Zealand (4151), Norway (2846, 2950), Panama (10032), Papua New Guinea (11612), Portugal (2846), St Lucia (2105), Saudi Arabia (2812, 5830, 7425), Spain (2846), Sudan (10322), Trinidad and Tobago (2105), Turkey (2846, 3020, 3337, 6582, 9901), Turks and Caicos Islands (9710, 9711), and the United Kingdom (2846, 11537). A full list of SOFAS or other agreements conferring legal status on U.S. forces and personnel overseas can be found at www.defenselink.mil/policy/isa/inra/list_of_sofas.html.

4. Gary Sick, *All Fall Down: America's Fateful Encounter with Iran* (London: I. B. Tauris, 1985), p. 10.

5. Agreement Between the Parties to the North Atlantic Treaty Organization Regarding the Status of Their Forces, June 19, 1951, 199 United Nations Treaty Series (UNTS) 67. For commentary, see Dieter Fleck, ed., *The Handbook of the Law of Visiting Forces* (Oxford: Oxford University Press, 2001).

6. W. Michael Reisman and Robert D. Sloane, "The Incident at Cavalese and Strategic Compensation," *American Journal of International Law (AJIL)* 94, no. 3 (July 2000): 505–515.

7. B. Norman, "The Rape Controversy: Is a Revision of the Status of Forces Agreement with Japan Necessary?," *Indiana International & Comparative Law Review* 6, no. 3 (1996): 717–740, esp. 731.

8. "Diplomatic Support for Operation Enduring Freedom," Fact Sheet, U.S. Department of State, August 19, 2002. www.state.gov/coalition/cr/fs/12805.htm, J. D. Crouch II, Assistant Secretary of Defense for International Security Policy, Office of the Secretary of Defense, U.S. Department of Defense, "Defense and Security Cooperation in Central Asia," Remarks Before the Subcommittee on Central Asia and the South Caucasus Committee on Foreign Relations, U.S. Senate, June 27, 2002.

9. 41 International Legal Materials (ILM) 799 (2002)

10. These figures were calculated from the information provided in Christian L. Wiktor, *Multilateral Treaty Calendar 1648–1995* (The Hague: Martinus Nijhoff, 1998).

11. Available at www.un.org/depts/treaty.

12. Available at www.tufts.edu/fletcher/multilaterals.html.

13. Treaty relations were more elaborate in ancient China and India. Christian L. Wiktor, *Multilateral Treaty Calendar 1648–1995* (The Hague: Martinus Nijhoff, 1998), p. ix.

14. Christian L. Wiktor, *Multilateral Treaty Calendar 1648–1995* (The Hague: Martinus Nijhoff, 1998), pp. ix–x.

15. Ian Brownlie, *Principles of Public International Law,* 4th ed. (Oxford: Clarendon, 1990), p. 119.

16. C. Tomuschat, "General Course on Public International Law," *Recueil des Cours* 281 (1999): 376.

17. See articles 39–42 of the UN Charter.

18. Charter of the United Nations, article 94(2), 1 UNTS xvi.

19. Ian Martin, "The High Commissioner's Field Operations," in Gudmundur Alfredsson, Jonas Grimheden, Bertram G. Ramcharan, and Alfred de Zayas, eds., *International Human Rights Monitoring Mechanisms: Essays in Honour of Jakob Th. Möller* (The Hague: Martinus Nijhoff, 2001), 403–414.

20. United States Code section 1350. See Ralph G. Steinhardt and Anthony D'Amato, eds., *The Alien Tort Claims Act: An Analytical Anthology* (Ardsley, NY: Transnational, 1999).

21. United States Code section 1359. See Craig Scott, ed., *Torture as Tort: Comparative Perspectives on the Development of Transnational Human Rights Litigation* (Oxford: Hart, 2001).

22. Hermann Mosler, "General Principles of Law," in *Encyclopedia of Public International Law* 2 (1995): 511–527, 516–517. On "general principles" see also, L. G. Lammers, "General Principles of Law Recognized by Civilized Nations," in Fritz Kalxhoven, Pieter Jan Kuyper, and Jahan G. Lammers, *Essays on the Development of the International Legal Order in Memory of H. F. van Panhuys* (The Netherlands: Alphen aan den Rijn, 1980), pp. 53–75; H. Mosler, "To what extent does the variety of legal systems of the world influence the application of the general principles of law within the meaning of article 38(1)(c) of the Statute of the International Court of Justice," in Hugo Grotius, *International Law and the Grotian Heritage* (The Hague: T. M. C. Asser Instituut, 1985), pp. 173–185; and M. C. Bassiouni, "A Functional

Approach to General Principles of International Law," *Michigan Journal of International Law* 11 (1990): 768–818.

23. Mosler, "General Principles of Law," p. 516.

24. Ibid., pp. 511–527.

25. Anthony D'Amato, "Good Faith," in *Encyclopedia of Public International Law* 2 (1995): 599–601, 599.

26. Vienna Convention on the Law of Treaties, article 31(1).

27. Peter Malanczuk, *Akehurst's Modern Introduction to International Law*, 7th rev. ed. (London and New York: Routledge, 1997), pp. 56–57.

28. For a table of international judicial bodies, quasijudicial, implementation control, and other dispute settlement bodies, see the Project on International Courts and Tribunals, Supplement to the *New York University Journal of International Law and Politics* 31, no. 4, available at http://www.pict-pcti.org/synoptic/ChartExpl.html.

29. For a discussion of the relevant issues, see Ellen Hey, *Reflections on an International Environmental Court* (The Hague: Kluwer, 2000), and Sean D. Murphy, "Does the World Need a New International Environmental Court?" *George Washington Journal of International Law and Economics* 32, no. 3 (2000): 351–365.

30. Hayek explained that the rule of law means that "government is bound in all its actions by rules fixed and announced beforehand so that it is possible to foresee with fair certainty how authority will use its coercive powers in given circumstances and to plan one's individual affairs on the basis of this knowledge." F. A. Hayek, *The Road to Serfdom* (London: G. Routledge, 1944), p. 39.

31. Berit Winge, "Mandatory Sentencing Laws and Their Effect on Australia's Indigenous Population," *Columbia Human Rights Law Review* 33 (2002): 693–732.

32. Peter Wilson, "Queen Tilts Crown, Puts Royals Before Court of Public Opinion," *The Australian* (November 4, 2002), p. 13.

33. See Peter Gould, "The Queen and the law," *BBC News Online,* November 4, 2002, http://news.bbc.co.uk/1/low/uk/2400003.stm, accessed November 8, 2002; and Patrick Wintour and Clare Dyer, "Queen Did Nothing Wrong, Says Blair," *The Guardian*, November 5, 2002, www.guardian.co.uk/Print/0,3858,4539522,00.html, accessed November 8, 2002.

34. Edward Luce, "Shooting of 'Terrorists' Leads to Indian Inquiry," *Financial Times*, November 8, 2002, http://news.ft.com/servlet/ContentServer?pagename=FT.com/StoryFT/FullStory&c=StoryFT&acid=1035873112796&p=1012471727169, accessed November 8, 2002.

35. See R. P. Anand, "Sovereign Equality of States in International Law," *Recueil des Courses* 197 (1986/III): 1–228; R. A. Klein, *Sovereign Equality Among States: The History of an Idea* (Toronto: University of Toronto Press, 1974); P. H. Koojimas, *The Doctrine of the Legal Equality of States: An Enquiry into the Foundations of International Law* (Leyden: Sijthoff, 1964).

36. Terms used to refer to different groups of states include "North/South" and "developing/developed."

37. Bartram S. Brown, "The Statute of the ICC: Past, Present, and

Future," in Sarah B. Sewall and Carl Kaysen, eds., *The United States and the International Criminal Court: National Security and International Law* (Lanham, MD: Rowman & Littlefield, 2000), pp. 61–84, 62.

38. Antonio Cassese, "The Statute of the International Criminal Court: Some Preliminary Reflections," *European Journal of International Law* 10 (1999): 144–171, 145.

39. Richard Falk, *Human Rights Horizons: The Pursuit of Justice in a Globalizing World* (New York: Routledge, 2000), p. 22.

40. Dean Acheson, "Remarks by the Honorable Dean Acheson, Former Secretary of State," *Proceedings of the American Society of International Law* 57, April 25–27, 1963, pp. 13–18, 14.

41. Hans J. Morgenthau, *Politics Among Nations: The Struggle for Power and Peace,* 5th ed. (New York: Alfred A. Knopf, 1973), p. 27.

42. V. S. Mani, "International Litigation and Peaceful Settlement of Disputes: A Case Study of *Certain Phosphate Lands in Nauru,*" in UN Office of Legal Affairs, *Collection of Essays by Legal Advisers of States, Legal Advisers of International Organizations, and Practitioners in the Field of International Law* (New York: United Nations, 1999), pp. 415–433. See also Antony Anghie, "'The Heart of My Home': Colonialism, Environmental Damage, and the Nauru Case," *Harvard International Law Journal* 34 (1993): 445–506.

43. A point made by Oscar Schachter, "The Role of Power in International Law," 93 *American Society of International Law Proceedings (ASIL Proc.)* 203 (2000).

44. A. Chayes, *The Cuban Missile Crisis* (New York: Oxford University Press, 1974), pp. 41–42.

45. For the full list, see Anne-Marie Slaughter Burley, "International Law and International Relations Theory: A Dual Agenda," *AJIL* 87 (1993): 205–239, 205.

2

States in International Law

There is a considerable overlap among the actors in world politics and those in international law. States, intergovernmental organizations, nongovernmental organizations (NGOs), and individuals are key players in both, although the influence of each actor may be greater in one system than in the other. We can designate as actors important to the system of international law those that help make, implement, monitor, and/or enforce international law, as well as those that make judicial decisions on the basis of international law. In this chapter we will look at states as actors in both international law and world politics.

States are the most important actor in the system of international law. As we have already seen, state practice gives rise to custom, and interstate negotiations produce treaties. When states negotiate treaties it is to them that the responsibilities, as well as the rights, primarily fall. Only states can take part in contentious proceedings before the International Court of Justice. And though states are not permitted to request an advisory opinion of the ICJ, they are permitted to make written and/or oral statements to the Court in such cases.

The state is also the principal actor in world politics. A state is defined according to the territory it encompasses; it is delineated by sharp frontiers.[1] The geopolitical principle of territorial exclusivity means that, once a portion of territory is designated a state, that territory and its inhabitants are to be governed independently of the populations of other portions of territory. It is easy to take for granted that the world be divided on a territorial basis into political-legal units, but this is not the only possible arrangement we could have; we could, for example, be governed by the head of our respective religions, no matter where on earth we each live.[2]

It is easy to see how international politics and international law are interrelated when we consider that a test of a state's domestic legal system is the basis for membership of the international political system. To belong to the international (i.e., political) system of states, a state must be sovereign—that is, it must have constitutional independence.[3] The question as to whether a state is or is not sovereign is determined by constitutional, rather than international, law.[4]

The fundamental importance of sovereignty to the system of international law was explained in a classic statement by Max Huber in the *Island of Palmas* case: "Sovereignty in the relations between States signifies independence. Independence in regard to a portion of the globe is the right to exercise therein, to the exclusion of any other State, the functions of a State."[5] It is because sovereignty signifies independence that states of the South have, in their diplomacy with those of the North, emphasized the importance of the sovereignty concept. Chinese diplomats have argued strongly that sovereignty must remain an inviolable principle to protect the weak.[6]

Because a state has constitutional independence, its domestic legal system has traditionally not been subject to scrutiny by international law but is what is referred to as the "reserved domain." As Huber explains:

> The development of the national organization of States during the last few centuries and, as a corollary, the development of international law, have established this principle of the exclusive competence of the State in regard to its own territory in such a way as to make it the point of departure in settling most questions that concern international relations.[7]

The sovereign independence of a state gives it the capacity to enter into relations with other states. This capacity is considered to be a key criterion of statehood. Others include a permanent population, a defined territory, and a government.[8] Although international lawyers continue to debate the precise definition of statehood, the reality in an anarchic state-based system is that a state is a political entity that other states accept as being a state. Thus, when it is said that there are now "about" 190 states, this is not just due to a lack of research precision. Different states may actually believe there to be different numbers of states, depending on which other political entities they have accepted as being states.

The distinction between a formal definition of statehood and what happens in practice has been debated in international law in terms of, on the one hand, *constitutive theory,* which holds that an entity becomes a state through recognition by other states—whether or not it meets suggested international standards for statehood—and, on the other, *declaratory theory*, which holds that an entity can become a state even if not recognized by other states if it meets the criteria for statehood required by international law.[9] The first instance of the recognition of a new state was the recognition by Spain of the United Netherlands in 1648.[10]

The Spread of the States System

The territorially defined state is generally regarded as having originated in Europe. Statelike entities, at least in the sense of political units, have existed in a number of parts of the world, including precolonial Africa, but the identification of a state primarily on the basis of exact geographical boundaries has been rare.[11] Precolonial Africa, for example, did not consist of states existing within fixed borders. Although the form of political organization varied among parts of Africa and over time, it is safe to generalize that the notion of a boundary was unknown. Various types of frontier existed, as did mutual separation zones such as deserts. Most African political-social units were identifiable according to their king or chief. Although these communities were regarded as having rights over the land they inhabited and utilized, this was not the factor by which the political unit was defined.[12]

There is some difference of opinion as to the exact date at which the modern state came into being, but confirmation of the territorially defined state as the basic unit at the international level is usually dated from the Treaty of Westphalia of 1648.[13] That treaty ended the Thirty Years' War and the political dominance of the Roman Catholic Church. It established a territorial baseline that was repeatedly referred to in treaties until 1789.[14] Even before the state system was firmly established in Europe, it was spreading through European states that were building empires to increase wealth, power, and prestige. The first round of empire in the sixteenth, seventeenth, and eighteenth centuries established empires in North America and South America. A second round of empire in the nineteenth century saw European states divide up Africa and much of the Middle East and Asia; the United States and Japan also acquired overseas colonial holdings. This second round of empire coincided with the first proliferation of states; between 1870 and 1930 the number of states in Europe expanded from about fifteen to thirty-five. The second proliferation of states took place between 1945 and 1990 as old colonial empires fell; the number of states increased from about fifty-four in 1945 to about 170 in 1990. A third proliferation of states has taken place since the end of the Cold War, as established states, including Czechoslovakia, the Soviet Union, and Yugoslavia, have dissolved.[15]

Much of the expansion of the states system over the last two centuries has come about because of the ideal of the nation-state. Although as in, for example, the Latin term *jus gentium* (law of nations), international lawyers sometimes use the term "nation" synonymously with that of "state," political scientists now distinguish among a nation, a state, and a nation-state. A *state* is a technical term for "country," but a *nation* is a group of people of the same nationality who speak the same language and share a culture. It is possible to have a nation without a state, as was the case with the Jews before 1947. But from the time of the revolutions in America and France in the late eighteenth century we have had the ideal that states should be nation-states (i.e., that each nation should have its own state). Japan is one of the purest examples of a *nation-state*; most states contain people of a number of nationalities. It is the tension between the ideal of every nation having its own state and the reality of the geographical intermixing of peoples that has underlain much bloodshed over the last two centuries

The legal principle that has supported the twentieth-century growth in the number of states has been that of *self-determination*: people living within a particular territory have the right to choose their own political system. The term gained prominence with its use by President Woodrow Wilson during and after World War I. Wilson announced that the new international order to be established after the war was to be based "upon justice and upon the rights of all people to determine for themselves their own governments."[16] "Theoretically, self-rule would minimise the thrust for territorial expansion and make war less likely."[17] Self-determination of peoples is listed in the UN Charter as a general purpose of the United Nations (article 1(2)) and as a specific purpose of the United Nations in the promotion of economic and social cooperation (article 55).

The International Covenant on Civil and Political Rights (ICCPR) and the International Covenant on Economic, Social, and Cultural Rights (ICESCR) share in common article 1(1), which proclaims that "All peoples have the right of self-determination. By virtue of that right, they freely determine their political status and freely pursue their economic, social and cultural development." "Peoples" is thus sometimes used in international law in a sense similar to that of "nation," to refer to an "ethnic group linked by common history," which also "must itself delineate the purview of its common existence and settle criteria for belonging to the group."[18] Self-determination may, as in the union of East and West Germany, lead to integration with an independent state[19] or to free association with an independent state; in the case of Puerto Rico the people opted for a special legal status within a state. A much more common meaning that "a people under colonial domination is entitled to create a new State where none existed before," whereas "people living within the framework of an extant State secede from it and establish [their] own independent country."[20] The right of peoples to self-determination is thus "loaded with political and psychological gun-powder,"[21] because the principle does not prohibit civil war as a means of attaining a favored political status, nor specify a means by which to resolve a conflict among overlapping rights to self-determination—as witnessed by Palestine, the Indian subcontinent, and Cyprus.[22]

State Succession
The questions as to how one state replaces another, and with what legal and political consequences, were important during the process of decolonization in the 1950s and 1960s. This is also true given the increase in the number of states since the end of the Cold War. Although two multilateral treaties relate to the subject—the Vienna Convention on the Succession of States in Respect of Treaties of 1978 and the Vienna Convention on State Succession in Respect of State Property, Archives, and Debts of April 8, 1983—the latter has not yet entered into force; there being little customary law on the subject, the law of state succession is one of the underdeveloped areas of international law.[23] There is not even widespread agreement as to whether the succeeding state automatically succeeds to all the treaty obligations of its predecessor. In the case of Yugoslavia, lawyers have differed as to whether the state dissolved, producing five equal successor states, or whether there is one continuator state from which the other four succeeded. The dissolution of the Soviet Union gave rise to three categories of states. The Baltic States have claimed to be identical to the three states that had existed on their territory until 1940 and hence are not successor states to the Soviet Union; the Russian Federation has claimed to be the continuing state of the Soviet Union and hence took its seat on the Security Council and declared that it would continue to honor treaties entered into by the Soviet Union; and the former republics of the Soviet Union other than the Baltics have been treated as successor states.[24]

Recognition of States

One of the first problems faced by a state is that of recognition. The act of *recognition*, by which one state recognizes that another exists, may be either *express*—via a formal statement recognizing the new state—or *implied* through actions such as, for example, the making of a bilateral treaty arranging for commercial relations.[25] The law regarding recognition has been one of the most controversial areas of international law.[26] This is so because decisions as to whether to recognize a state do not always hinge on whether the state meets the broad criteria of statehood but may turn on foreign policy objectives. States have sometimes used nonrecognition as a way to signify disapproval or have granted recognition almost in anticipation of statehood, as a means of helping establish the independence of the new state. In 1903 the United States recognized Panama only three days after its revolt from Colombia. More recently, Europe's recognition of Slovenia, Croatia, and Bosnia-Herzegovina was criticized by some observers as premature, as not waiting for the outcome of a civil war but "work[ing] actively to determine the outcome."[27]

Questions of recognition have traditionally arisen not only when a new state seeks to establish its independence but also when a new government assumes control, usually by force, and wants to engage in relations with other governments. This practice had its origins in the competing claims to succession of European monarchs.[28] In 1977 the U.S. State Department announced that, because twentieth-century policy had created the international impression that U.S. recognition or nonrecognition signified approval or disapproval of governments, the State Department would henceforth focus not on recognition but on whether the United States wished to establish or maintain diplomatic relations with new governments.[29] The U.S. government has continued to recognize new states as they become independent, but the question of recognition no longer arises for the United States when a new government comes to power through a means other than independence.[30] In 1977 the United Kingdom announced that it too had decided that it would no longer accord recognition to governments,[31] as did Australia in 1988.[32] The tendency to "exploit recognition [of states] for political purposes" means that it may "eventually suffer the same fate as that of recognition of governments."[33]

One act is an unequivocal statement of the full recognition of a state: the establishment of diplomatic recognition.[34] Diplomatic relations are established by mutual consent. The 1961 Vienna Convention on Diplomatic Relations listed the functions of a diplomatic mission as consisting, inter alia, of representing the sending state in the receiving state; protecting in the receiving state the interests of the sending state and of its nationals, within the limits permitted by international law; negotiating with the government of the receiving state; ascertaining by all lawful means the conditions and developments in the receiving state, and reporting thereon to the government of the sending state; promoting friendly relations between the sending state and the receiving state; and developing their economic, cultural, and scientific relations.[35] The ambassador to a state may be "recalled" as a mark of displeasure with another state. In May 1998 the United States recalled its ambassador to India in response to the Indian nuclear tests. A stronger political weapon is the severance of diplomatic relations. This is a unilateral act, although international organizations may, as a measure of collective sanction, resolve that their members sever diplomatic relations with a state.

The Jurisdiction of the State

Jurisdiction is legal authority and can relate to legislative, executive, and judicial action. A state has jurisdiction over all persons, property, and activities in its territory and its airspace and the waters subject to its sovereignty. According to the *active personality principle* a state may prosecute its nationals for crimes committed anywhere in the world. A state has jurisdiction over a ship, aircraft, or spacecraft registered in its state, as well as over all persons and property on board that ship, aircraft, or spacecraft. According to the *objective territorial principle,* or the *effects doctrine,* a state also has jurisdiction over a person whose behavior outside its territory causes injury within its territory, and according to the *protective principle* a state may punish acts that threaten its security even if committed by nonnationals outside the territory of the state. Although this much is uncontroversial, other aspects of international law relating to the jurisdiction of the state are not as clearcut. It is not completely clear, for example, as to whether a state may exercise jurisdiction only where there is a recognized basis for its exercise or in the absence of any prohibition on its exercise.

The so-called *passive personality* principle, by which some states assert the right to try a foreigner for injuring one of its nationals outside its territory, is not so widely accepted as a basis of state jurisdiction. The principle is invoked in some national legislation pertaining to terrorism. There are also some internationally defined criminal offenses for which a state has jurisdiction to arrest and try a person no matter where the offense occurred. Exactly which offenses are subject to universal jurisdiction is not agreed, but most states would agree that such obligations *erga omnes* include slavery, piracy, genocide, certain war crimes and crimes against humanity, and offenses covered by the various multilateral treaties on terrorism.[36] There has in recent years been an increasing amount of human rights litigation based on universal jurisdiction; proceedings on the basis of universal jurisdiction have, for example, been brought in Austria, France, the Netherlands, Senegal, Spain, and the United Kingdom with respect to crimes committed in Chad, Chile, Mauritania, Rwanda, Sudan, and Yugoslavia.[37]

The most fundamental prohibition on the jurisdiction of a state is that over another state. Because states enjoy, at least theoretically, sovereign equality, no state has the legal right to exercise its jurisdiction over another state. A state may not perform any governmental act or send its agents to arrest or restrain any person or property in the territory of another state without the latter's consent. State immunity comes into play particularly in relation to the exercising of judicial jurisdiction. Under the doctrine of *absolute state immunity* the courts in one state cannot hear any case brought against a foreign state—in relation, for example, to human rights violations or environmental damages—unless that state has waived its immunity and consented to the proceedings.[38] By the middle of the twentieth century the doctrine of absolute immunity was giving way to *restrictive immunity*, which imposes some limits on the immunity of the state.[39] The change to restrictive immunity came about, at least in part, because national courts did not agree that a state, when acting in a commercial capacity, should enjoy a privileged position as compared to private traders.[40] Although more states now appear to accept the doctrine of restrictive immunity rather than absolute immunity,[41] the exact nature of the limits is not yet agreed; in particular, the question has been raised as to whether immunity from jurisdiction should be denied to states that violate fundamental human rights.[42]

Closely related to state immunity is *head-of-state immunity*, by which a head of state enjoys immunity from the jurisdiction of a foreign court. In October 1998 Spain issued an international warrant for the arrest of Augusto Pinochet, the senator-for-life who was at that time receiving medical treatment in the United Kingdom. Pinochet was arrested on October 17, 1998. A second provisional warrant stated, inter alia, that Pinochet between January 1, 1988, and December 1992 "intentionally inflicted severe pain or suffering on another in the performance or purported performance of his official duties." On March

24, 1999, the House of Lords ruled that Pinochet was not entitled to immunity in relation to acts of torture.[43] The House of Lords was the most prominent court to date to hold that heads of state can under certain circumstances be held responsible for gross violations of human rights;[44] the decision was hailed as a great victory by the human rights movement.

Such excitement was tempered by subsequent events. Home Secretary Jack Straw ruled on March 2, 2000, that Pinochet would not be extradited because of his frail medical condition, and Pinochet was able to leave the United Kingdom for Chile. Three years later, in a case involving questions of universal jurisdiction as well as immunity, the ICJ decided that a serving minister for foreign affairs enjoys full immunity from criminal jurisdiction and inviolability.[45] In April 2000 a Belgian investigating magistrate had issued an arrest warrant against the foreign minister of the Democratic Republic of the Congo, Abdulaye Yerodia Ndombasi, pending a request for extradition to Belgium for alleged crimes constituting serious violations of international humanitarian law relating to his allegedly having provoked the continuation of massacres of Tutsi people in 1998.[46] The Congo had responded to the arrest warrant by bringing proceedings against Belgium before the ICJ. Disappointment with the judgment in the *Case Concerning the Arrest Warrant of 11 April 2000 (Democratic Republic of the Congo v. Belgium)* on the part of the human rights community was tempered only slightly by the insistence of the ICJ that immunity did not mean impunity.[47]

Just as one state is immune from the jurisdiction of another state, and heads of state enjoy immunity because of their functional relationship to the state, so is a state not able to exercise criminal and administrative jurisdiction in relation to accredited diplomats, as the representatives of other states.[48] Although required to respect the laws and regulations of the receiving state and not to interfere in the internal affairs of that state,[49] diplomatic agents are not liable to any form of arrest or detention.[50] Diplomatic immunity is sometimes controversial when it has been abused, in which instance the receiving state must receive an express waiver of immunity by the sending state before proceeding to prosecution. The receiving state can, at any time, declare a diplomatic agent persona non grata (unwelcome person) and expel him or her from the state; it has become standard in such circumstances for the sending state to then make a similar declaration regarding an equal number of the other state's envoys.

With the growth of environmental, human rights, and humanitarian law the principle of noninterference in the internal matters of a state is no longer absolute. But the extent to which this is the case, and to which the concept of sovereignty should or may change further, is not clear-cut but a subject of ongoing debate and contention. This is particularly apparent regarding relations between individual states and the United Nations. In the same way that a state is not meant to exercise its jurisdiction in relation to another state, so is the United Nations not, at least theoretically, to intervene in the internal affairs of states. Article 2(7) of the UN Charter states:

> Nothing contained in the present Charter shall authorise the United Nations to intervene in matters which are essentially within the domestic jurisdiction of any State or shall require the Members to submit such matters to settlement under the present Charter; but this principle shall not prejudice the application of enforcement measures under Chapter VII.

Chapter 3 will consider in more detail the operation of the United Nations and the role of intergovernmental organizations in general in the system of international law.

Notes

1. See K. Boulding, "National Images and International Systems," in R. E. Kasperson and J. V. Minghi, eds., *The Structure of Political Geography* (Chicago: Aldine, 1969), pp. 341–349, 344. Compare the conceptualization of variable space that existed in South-East Asian thought. See S. J. Tambiah, *Culture, Thought, and Social Action: An Anthropological Perspective* (Cambridge, MA: Harvard University Press, 1985), p. 260.

2. "A society is not inconceivable . . . and might even be desirable, in which nations governed people but not territories and claimed jurisdiction over a defined set of citizens, no matter where on the earth's surface they happened to live." Boulding, "National Images and International Systems," p. 344.

3. Alan James, *Sovereign Statehood: The Basis of International Society* (London: Allen & Unwin, 1986), p. 30.

4. Ibid., p. 40.

5. *Island of Palmas Case (Netherlands v. United States)* (1928) 2 *Reports of International Arbitral Awards (RIAA)* 829, 838.

6. Evan A. Feigenbaum, "China's Challenge to *Pax Americana*," *Washington Quarterly* (Summer 2001): 31–43, 33.

7. *Island of Palmas Case, RIAA* 829, 838.

8. Convention on the Rights and Duties of States, article 1, December 26, 1933, known as the "Montevideo Convention," 165 League of Nations Treaty Series (LNTS) 19, reprinted in 28 *American Journal of International Law (AJIL) Supp.* 75 (1934).

9. For summaries of the debate see Ian Brownlie, *Principles of Public*

International Law, 4th ed. (Oxford: Clarendon, 1979), pp. 16–23; James R. Crawford, *The Creation of States in International Law* (Oxford: Clarendon, 1979), pp. 16–23; John Dugard, *Recognition and the United Nations* (Cambridge: Grotius, 1989), pp. 7–9; and Hersch Lauterpacht, *Recognition in International Law* (Cambridge: Cambridge University Press, 1948), pp. 38–66. Such a debate is now likely to be "beside the point." Thomas D. Grant, *The Recognition of States: Law and Practice in Debate and Evolution* (London: Praeger, 1999), p. 123.

10. Jochen Abr. Frowein, "Recognition," *Encyclopedia of Public International Law* 9 (1986), p. 341. The U.S. Declaration of Independence gave rise to a dispute between France and Britain as to the possibility of recognizing the new state as a subject of international law. Ibid.

11. For discussion on defining the state see J. Genet, "Introduction: Which State Rises?" *Historical Research* 65, no. 157 (June 1992): 119–133.

12. M. Shaw, *Title to Territory in Africa* (Oxford: Clarendon, 1986), pp. 27–29.

13. See discussion in Kenneth Dyson, *The State Tradition in Western Europe: A Study of an Idea and Institution* (New York: M. Robertson, 1980), p. 28. See also G. R. Potter, "The Beginnings of the Modern State," *History* 31 (1946): 73–84. The treaty can be found at www.yale.edu/lawweb/avalon/westphal.htm.

14. Gottman has traced the evolution of the relationship between people and their space prior to the modern state. He distinguished three turning points: that reported by Homer and Aristotle when people gathered into communities constituted by several villages; the notion of the vast Hellenistic world that was then assimilated into the Roman Empire; and the change, around A.D. 1500, by which personal allegiance came to be replaced by the national allegiance of the people to the sovereign. J. Gottman, *The Significance of Territory* (Charlottesville: University Press of Virginia, 1973), pp. 123–127. Modelski believes the evidence supports 1500 as a suitable cut-off point. G. Modelski, "The Long Cycle of Global Politics and the Nation-State," *Comparative Studies in Society and History* 20 (1978): 214–235.

15. The information in this paragraph derives from Daniel S. Papp, *Contemporary International Relations: Frameworks for Understanding*, 5th ed. (Boston: Allyn and Bacon, 1997), pp. 33–43.

16. Charles L. Mee Jr. *The End of Order: Versailles 1919* (London: Secker & Warburg, 1981), p. 11.

17. Papp, *Contemporary International Relations,* p. 38.

18. Yoram Dinstein, "Collective Human Rights of Peoples and Minorities," *International and Comparative Law Quarterly (ICLQ)* 25 (January 1976): 102–120, 105.

19. Shelley Wright, "The Individual in International Human Rights: Québec, Canada, and the Nation-State," *Saskatchewan Law Review* 59, no. 2 (1995): 437–469, 459.

20. Dinstein, "Collective Human Rights of Peoples and Minorities," p. 108. Principle VI of General Assembly Resolution 1541(XV) states that a non-self-governing territory can be said to have reached a full measure of self-government by: (1) emergence as a sovereign independent state; (2) free association with an independent state; or (3) integration with an independent state.

21. Dinstein, "Collective Human Rights of Peoples and Minorities," p. 108.

22. See also M. Koskenniemi, "National Self-Determination Today: Problems of Legal Theory and Practice," *ICLQ* 43 (1994): 241; and R. McCorquodale, "Self-Determination: A Human Rights Approach," *ICLQ* 43 (1994): 857–885.

23. Wladyslaw Czaplinski, "Equity and Equitable Principles in the Law of State Succession," in M. Mrak, ed., *Succession of States* (The Hague: Martinus Nijhoff, 1999), p. 61.

24. Jan Klabbers, Martti Koskenniemi, Olivier Ribbelinhk, and Andreas Zimmermann, eds., *State Practice Regarding State Succession and Issues of Recognition: The Pilot Project of the Council of Europe* (The Hague and Boston: Kluwer Law International, 1999), pp. 92ff.

25. D. J. Harris, *Cases and Materials on International Law*, 5th ed. (London: Sweet & Maxwell, 1998), p. 147.

26. Hans Kelsen, "Recognition in International Law: Theoretical Observations," *AJIL* 35 (1941): 605–617, 605.

27. Alex N. Dragnich, "The West's Mismanagement of the Yugoslav Crisis," *World Affairs* 156, no. 2 (Fall 1993): 63–71. On the recognition of the republics of the former Yugoslavia by the European Community and later the European Union, see also Thomas D. Grant, *The Recognition of States: Law and Practice in Debate and Evolution* (London: Praeger, 1999), chap. 6.

28. Frowein, "Recognition," p. 341.

29. "Diplomatic Recognition," *U.S. Department of State Bulletin* 77 (1977): 462, in Harris, *Cases and Materials on International Law*, p. 159. This approach had its roots in the Estrada Doctrine employed by Mexico in the 1930s. See *AJIL* 25 (1931), supp. no. 203.

30. Mary Beth West and Sean D. Murphy, "The Impact on U.S. Litigation of Non-Recognition of Foreign Governments," *Stanford Journal of International Law* 26, no. 2 (1990): 435–478, 456.

31. Statement by the Foreign Secretary (Lord Carrington), Hansard, H. L., vol. 408, cols. 1121–1122, April 28, 1980, in Harris, *Cases and Materials on International Law*, pp. 155–156.

32. Minister for Foreign Affairs and Trade, Press Release, January 19, 1988, reprinted in *Australian International Law News* (1988), p. 49. Although Australia's change in recognition policy had been contemplated for some time, the immediate impetus seemed to be Australia's relations with Fiji following the coups of May and September 1987. Hilary Charlesworth, "The New Australian Recognition Policy in Comparative Perspective," *Melbourne University Law Review* 18 (June 1991): 1–25, pp. 1–2.

33. Matthew C. R. Craven, "What's in a Name? The Former Yugoslav Republic of Macedonia and Issues of Statehood," *Australian Year Book of International Law* 16 (1995), pp. 199–239, 217–218.

34. Frowein asserts that the establishment of full diplomatic relations is the only act from which full recognition can always be deduced. Frowein, "Recognition," p. 342. See generally P. K. Menon, *The Law of Recognition in International Law: Basic Principles* (Lewiston, NY: Edwin Mellen, 1994).

35. Vienna Convention on Diplomatic Relations, article 3 (April 18, 1961), 500 United Nations Treaty Series (UNTS) 95–221.

36. See discussion in M. Cherif Bassiouni, "Universal Jurisdiction for International Crimes: Historical Perspectives and Contemporary Practice," *Virginia Journal of International Law* 42, no. 1 (2001): 81–156.

37. For details and discussion, see Menno T. Kamminga, "Lessons Learned from the Exercise of Universal Jurisdiction in Respect of Gross Human Rights Offenses," *Human Rights Quarterly* 23, no. 4 (2001): 940–974.

38. See Jürgen Bröhmer, *State Immunity and the Violation of Human Rights* (The Hague: Martinus Nijhoff, 1997), and Hazel Fox, *The Law of State Immunity* (Oxford: Oxford University Press, 2002).

39. See Lakshman Marasinghe, "The Modern Law of Sovereign Immunity," *Modern Law Review* 54, no. 5 (September 1991): 664–684.

40. Magdalini Karagiannakis, "State Immunity and Fundamental Human Rights," *Leiden Journal of International Law* 11 (1998): 9–43, 12, and Michael Singer, "Abandoning Restrictive Sovereign Immunity: An Analysis in Terms of Jurisdiction to Prescribe," *Harvard International Law Journal* 26, no. 1 (Winter 1985): 1–61.

41. Magdalini Karagiannakis, "State Immunity and Fundamental Human Rights," *Leiden Journal of International Law* 11 (1998): 9–43, 12.

42. Ibid.

43. "United Kingdom House of Lords: *Regina v. Bartle and the Commissioner of Police for the Metropolis and Others Ex Parte Pinochet* [March 24, 1999]," 38 International Legal Materials (ILM) 581 (1999).

44. Jürgen Bröhmer, "Immunity of a Former Head of State General Pinochet and the House of Lords: Part Three," *Leiden Journal of International Law* 13 (2000): 207–216, 236. See also Andrea Bianchi, "Immunity Versus Human Rights: The Pinochet Case," *European Journal of International Law* 10, no. 2 (1999): 237–277; C. H. Powell and A. Pillay, "Revisiting Pinochet: The Development of Customary International Criminal Law," *South African Journal on Human Rights* 17, no. 4 (2001): 477–502; Rosanne Van-Alebeek, "The Pinochet Case: International Human Rights Law on Trial," *British Yearbook of International Law* 71 (2000): 29–70; and Diana Woodhouse, ed., *The Pinochet Case: A Legal and Constitutional Analysis* (Oxford: Hart, 2000).

45. *Case Concerning the Arrest Warrant of 11 April 2000* (*Democratic Republic of the Congo v. Belgium)*, Order of February 14, 2002, 41 ILM 536 (2002).

46. "Application Instituting Proceedings Filed in the Registry of the Court on 17 October 2000," in ibid., p. 5.

47. Ibid., para. 60. See Campbell McLachlan, "*Pinochet* Revisited," *ICLQ* 51, no. 4 (October 2002): 959–966.

48. "Except in the case of (a) a real action relating to private immovable property situated in the territory of the receiving State, unless he holds it on behalf of the sending State for the purposes of the mission; (b) an action relating to succession in which the diplomatic agent is involved as executor, administrator, heir, or legatee as a private person and not on behalf of the sending

State; (c) an action relating to any professional or commercial activity exercised by the diplomatic agent in the receiving State outside his official functions." Vienna Convention on Diplomatic Relations, article 31.

49. Vienna Convention on Diplomatic Relations, article 41(1).

50. Vienna Convention on Diplomatic Relations, article 29.

3

Intergovernmental Organizations in International Law

A n intergovernmental organization is an international organization made up of states. IGOs play an important role in world politics and international law, although political scientists have long debated the extent to which IGOs have an independent influence on world politics as opposed to functioning as a conduit for the foreign policy of powerful states. The United Nations is the best-known IGO (actually it is a family of IGOs), but it is by no means the most typical. The typical IGO is regional and deals with a single issue. The Northwest Atlantic Fisheries Organization, for example, aims for the optimum utilization, rational management, and conservation of fishery resources in the northwest Atlantic; the Intergovernmental Authority on Development aims to achieve economic integration and sustainable development in East Africa. The UN, by contrast, is a multi-issue global IGO. It is made up of six principal organs: the Security Council, the General Assembly, the Economic and Social Council (ECOSOC), the Trusteeship Council, the Secretariat, and the International Court of Justice. It also includes many other bodies in a complex institutional network. Major regional multi-issue IGOs include the League of Arab States (Arab League), the Organization of American States, and the African Union. The European Union (EU), which was established by the Maastricht Treaty on European Union and Economic and Monetary Union of February 7, 1992,[1] is the most advanced example of regional economic and political integration.

International law is important to IGOs as political actors, most fundamentally because an IGO is established by a multilateral treaty setting out the goals, structure, and methods of operation.[2] The Northwest Atlantic Fisheries Organization was established by the Convention on

Future Multilateral Cooperation in the Northwest Atlantic Fisheries; the United Nations was established by the UN Charter. IGOs have the capacity to enter into treaty relations. International organizations have mostly entered into bilateral treaty relationships, often of an institutional purpose. There are, for example, numerous treaties between international organizations and states setting out details of headquarters arrangements. Other bilateral treaties concluded between states and IGOs are of a functional purpose intended, for example, to give aid to developing countries. The rules for such treaties can be found in the 1986 Vienna Convention on the Law of Treaties Between States and International Organizations or Between International Organizations.[3] Although this has not yet entered into force, it is widely considered to reflect customary international law on the subject. International organizations cannot be a party to contentious proceedings before the ICJ, but the General Assembly, the Security Council, and certain other UN organs and agencies can request advisory opinions from the ICJ.

IGOs play a major role in the system of international law. This is true of the creation of international law, since IGOs sponsor new multilateral treaties and contribute to the development of customary international law through institutional practices. It is also true of the enforcement of international law. IGOs across a whole range of subject areas devise ways to enforce relevant treaties and monitor the effectiveness of the treaties with which they are associated.

The United Nations is ultimately inseparable from the contemporary system of international law. Although virtually all IGOs are created by international treaty and may enter into treaty relationships, the influence on the system of international law of the United Nations is far more than that of other IGOs. The UN is so integral to the current system of international law that we would not recognize international law if we extricated the United Nations from it. There are several reasons for this. First, we have the broad reach of the United Nations and the breadth of the subjects it addresses. The United Nations has almost universal membership, and the UN Charter addresses some of the most basic issues in world politics, such as the use of force. Second, article 103 of the UN Charter states that "in the event of a conflict between the obligations of the Members of the United Nations under the present Charter and their obligations under any other international agreement, their obligations under the present Charter shall prevail." The UN Charter thus "trumps" other treaties. Third, hundreds of treaties have been concluded by UN organs or by diplomatic conferences convened by the UN. These treaties relate not only to a wide range of substantive issue areas but also to the operation of the system of international law itself, such as the laws relating to the negotiation of treaties. And fourth, the UN plays a key role not only in the creation of international law but in its enforcement and in the judicial settlement of disputes at a global level and in a multi-issue capacity.

This chapter will focus on the United Nations because of its enormous importance to the current system of international law. We will look at the principal organs, specialized agencies, and other UN bodies that are of most significance to the system of international law because of the roles they play in creating, implementing, enforcing, and/or undertaking judicial decisionmaking on the basis of the rules, principles, and concepts of international law. Some, such as the General Assembly, deal with a broad range of subject matter; others, as we shall see, specialize in one field. We turn first to the principal organs and to the other United Nations programs and organs whose governing bodies report directly to the principal organs.

The Security Council

The United Nations took its name from the wartime coalition of Allies that was formed to defeat the Axis in World War II. There were fifty founding members.[4] Membership of the United Nations is now virtually universal. Although states obviously value UN membership, any member of the UN accepts a major limitation on its sovereign independence. By article 25 of the UN Charter member states agree to carry out the decisions of the Security Council; this means that the Security Council has legal power over states. Article 24(1) of the Charter confers on the Security Council primary responsibility for the maintenance of international peace and security. The key function in world politics of the Security Council is thus a political one, but it is one closely related to international law. Although it is not a judicial body, the Security Council does have authority to make some quasijudicial determinations, for example to determine an aggressor state, and it is has on a number of occasions made determinations regarding particular points of law. These have generally been uncontroversial, such as stating that genocide is a flagrant violation of international law, but they have not always been so clear-cut.[5] The Security Council also has a role to play in backing up the International Court of Justice. By article 94(2) of the UN Charter, the Security Council may "make recommendations or decide upon measures to be taken to give effect to an ICJ judgment." It has not to date taken such action or even been asked to do so.

Chapter VI of the UN Charter is entitled "Pacific Settlement of Disputes." According to article 33(1):

> The parties to any dispute, the continuance of which is likely to endanger the maintenance of international peace and security, shall, first of all, seek a solution by negotiation, enquiry, mediation, conciliation, arbitration, judicial settlement, resort to regional agencies or arrangements, or other peaceful means of their own choice.

The Security Council may, at any stage, recommend appropriate procedures or methods of adjustment in a dispute. Should the parties to a dispute not have settled it by one of the above means, they are to refer it to the Security Council.[6]

Chapter VII of the UN Charter provides for the Security Council to respond to threats to the peace, breaches of the peace, and acts of aggression. Article 39 is crucial here. It provides the legal, or jurisdictional, basis for the Security Council to take action not dependent on the will of the states impacted by the decision:

> The Security Council shall determine the existence of any threat to the peace, breach of the peace, or act of aggression and shall make recommendations, or decide what measures shall be taken in accordance with Articles 41 and 42, to maintain or restore international peace and security.

The key phrase in this article is that of "any threat to the peace, breach of the peace, or act of aggression." The Security Council must make an affirmative finding of such a threat before it may go forward to exercise its powers under Chapter VII. Hence the significance, for example, of the Security Council adopting Resolution 1368 on September 12, 2001, the day after the terrorist attacks on New York and Washington, condemning the acts "as a threat to international peace and security."

Having recognized a threat to the peace, breach of the peace, or act of aggression, the Security Council may first of all call upon the parties concerned to comply "with such provisional measures as it deems necessary or desirable." The Security Council may, according to article 41, call upon member states to apply nonmilitary means of restoring peace. Such means are listed in article 41 as the complete or partial "interruption of economic relations and of all rail, sea, air, postal, telegraphic, radio, and other means of communication, and the severance of diplomatic relations." They are what are commonly referred to as *sanctions*, although the specific term "sanctions" does not appear in the Charter.[7] The Security Council used sanctions only twice during the Cold War. The first sanctions imposed by the Security Council were on Rhodesia in 1966, and then South Africa in 1977. Sanctions were used much more frequently in the first post–Cold War decade; indeed, the 1990s has been referred to as the "sanctions decade,"[8] with sanctions having been authorized against a number of states, including Iraq, Haiti, Libya, the former Yugoslavia, and Rwanda.

If measures taken under article 41 are deemed to have been inadequate, or if the Security Council considers that they will be inadequate, it may under article 42 "take such action by air, sea, or land forces as may be necessary to maintain or restore international peace and security." Article 43(1) provides for states to enter into "special agreements" with the UN to make available "armed forces, assistance, and facilities . . . necessary for the purpose of maintaining peace and security." The Military Staff Committee was to be established (article 47) to advise the Security Council on its military requirements for maintaining peace and security. The Military Staff Committee was, in fact, established, but the agreements envisaged in article 43 never became a reality in the Cold War environment. The Security Council has nevertheless recommended or requested the use of military action on the part of states. By Resolution 83 (1950) the Security Council determined that an "armed attack upon the Republic of Korea by forces from North Korea constitutes a breach of the peace" and by Resolution 84 (1950) recommended "that all Members providing military forces and other assistance . . . make such forces available to a unified command under the United States of America." By Resolution 678 of November 29, 1990, the Security Council authorized member states to "use all necessary means . . . to restore international peace and security in the area" if Iraq failed to meet a deadline for the fulfillment of previous resolutions.[9]

Since the end of the Cold War the Security Council has on the basis of its Chapter VII powers taken a number of types of actions other than imposing economic sanctions or authorizing the use of force. Following the bombing of a Pan Am airliner over Lockerbie, Scotland, for example, the Security Council ordered Libya to extradite to the United States or the United Kingdom the Libyans allegedly responsible for the bombing.[10] In May 1993 the Security Council established the International Criminal Tribunal for the Former Yugoslavia (ICTY), and in May 1994 it established the International Criminal Tribunal for Rwanda (ICTR), in both cases mandating the cooperation of all states with the tribunal.[11] Other subsidiary bodies created by the Security Council have included the UN Compensation Commission for the payment of damages arising out of Iraq's invasion of Kuwait, and the United Nations Monitoring, Verification, and Inspection Commission. There has been debate as to whether, in taking such actions, the Security Council may have acted *ultra vires*, that is, beyond the mandate provided by article 39. Indeed, debate has broadened to ask what limits, if any, exist on the powers of the Security Council.[12]

The Security Council adopted 646 resolutions during the first forty-five years of its existence and more than 400 resolutions in the six years following that.[13] There were thirteen peacekeeping operations undertaken between 1948 and 1987, compared to twenty-nine operations created between 1988 and 1996 (see Figure 3.1). These different rates of activity have been due largely to the veto power held by the five permanent members of the Council (China, France, the Russian Federation, the United Kingdom, and the United States). The other ten members are elected by the General Assembly for two-year terms. The Security Council makes some decisions of a procedural nature; these require an affirmative vote of any nine members. In the case of all other decisions, there must be an affirmative vote of nine members, which includes the concurring votes (or abstentions) of the permanent members. If there is doubt as to whether an issue is substantive or procedural, there is a procedural vote to decide the matter. Article 27(3) requires that a state that is a party to a dispute must abstain. Council members have treated the word "dispute" quite literally and not abstained in matters that might, for example, lead to a dispute. The Security Council operates continuously.

Given the sweeping powers of the Security Council, it is not surprising that there are periodic calls for the Council to be more democratic and to contain broader geographic representation.[14] It is difficult to envisage how such change will come about given that, by article 108, the UN Charter can be amended only with the consent of all the permanent members of the Security Council. Although it is true that world politics have moved on since the Security Council was first structured, there would be little point in reforming the Council in a manner unrelated to the realities of world power. If the Security Council were to consist of a small group of weak states and it authorized action against the world superpower, it is unlikely that the action would be successful. Here we see the law-politics interplay at its most stark.

The General Assembly

The General Assembly is also essentially a political organ of the United Nations, although by article 13(1)(a) one of its functions is "encourag-

Figure 3.1   United Nations Peace Operations

None of the terms "peacekeeping," "peace enforcement," or "peace-building" are found in the UN Charter. The primary types of peace operations that have nevertheless been conducted by the United Nations are:

Peace Enforcement Operations
These are authorized under Chapter VII of the UN Charter. These are designed to restore international peace and security. The UN inevitably becomes a party to conflict, and these actions may involve massive use of force.

Peacekeeping Operations
Dag Hammarskjöld, former UN Secretary-General, referred to peace-keeping as belonging to Chapter "Six and a half," meaning that it fits somewhere between traditional methods of peaceful dispute resolution and the more forceful actions provided for in Chapter VII. Although there are debates as to the exact constitutional basis of peacekeeping, its constitutionality has not really been in doubt since the decision of the ICJ in the *Expenses* case in the early 1960s.[i] In the case of peacekeeping, the international presence is there with the consent of the state in whose territory it is operating, in a situation in which peace has already been established. Peacekeeping may involve UN military and/or police personnel and may include civilians. The UN presence may implement or monitor the implementation of arrangements relating to the control of conflicts (cease-fires, separation of forces, etc.) and their resolution or undertake a variety of other tasks, such as ensuring the safe delivery of humanitarian relief. Troops are authorized to use force in self-defense only. The UN Truce Supervision Organization (UNTSO), established in 1948 to report on Arab-Israeli cease-fire and armistice violations, is often regarded as having been the first peacekeeping operation. The first UN mission explicitly referred to as a "peacekeeping" operation was the first UN Emergency Force (UNEF I) deployed in response to the 1956 Suez Crisis; this was actually authorized by the General Assembly on the basis of the Uniting for Peace Resolution and article 22 of the Charter. There has been an evolution in peacekeeping since then. More recent examples include those deployed to Somalia in 1992–1993

(continues)

Figure 3.1   continued

(UNOSOM I), 1993–1995 (UNOSOM II); and East Timor since May 2002 (UNMISET).[ii] From 1948 to June 2002 the UN spent an estimated U.S.$26.1 billion on peacekeeping operations, but funding UN peacekeeping has been problematic since the 1960s.

Chapter VII and Peacekeeping
Although there is a clear conceptual difference between peacekeeping and peace enforcement, in practice the difference has become difficult to discern. The use of peacekeeping forces to enforce provisional measures (cease-fires, withdrawals) began with the Congo in 1960.[iii] The first UN operation in Somalia (UNOSOM I) was established in April 1992 to monitor the cease-fire in Mogadishu and escort deliveries of humanitarian supplies.[iv] Resolution 775 (1992) authorized an increase in the strength of UNOSOM. When the situation deteriorated further, the Security Council established the Unified Task Force (UNITAF) to secure a safe environment for the delivery of humanitarian aid. By Resolution 794 of December 3, 1992, the Security Council, "acting under Chapter VII of the Charter of the United Nations, [authorized] the Secretary-General and Member States . . . to use all necessary means to establish as soon as possible a secure environment for humanitarian relief operations in Somalia." UNITAF was replaced by UNOSOM II, which was to complete the task begun by UNITAF for the restoration of peace, stability, and law and order. The size and mandate of the UN Operation was further expanded by Resolution 814 (1993).[v]

Multidimensional Peacekeeping Operations
These are the operations, more common since the end of the Cold War, that are designed to carry out a range of tasks, including peacemaking, peacebuilding, and/or preventive diplomacy (see below). The first multifunctional operation established at the end of the Cold War was the UN Transitional Assistance Group (UNTAG) deployed to Namibia in February 1989.

Preventive diplomacy
Diplomatic activity designed to prevent or limit potential or actual conflict. This action is carried out under Chapter VI and may involve the preventive deployment of military forces to deter violence.

(continues)

Figure 3.1   continued

Peacemaking
In his 1999 annual report on the work of the UN, Secretary-General Kofi Annan defined "peacemaking" as the "use of diplomatic means to persuade parties in a conflict to cease hostilities and to negotiate a peaceful settlement of their dispute." These are actions under Chapter VI of the UN Charter, which may include any of the methods listed in article 33(1)—in particular negotiation or mediation.

Peacebuilding
Operations carried out under Chapter VII in postconflict situations. This action involves the identification and support of measures and structures that will promote peace and build trust and interactions among former enemies in an endeavor to prevent a return to conflict. It often involves strengthening and rebuilding civil infrastructure and institutions to help solidify peace. The practice of peacebuilding predates the term. Examples include El Salvador, Nicaragua, Haiti, Cambodia, Namibia, Haiti, Cambodia, Namibia, Mozambique, Angola, Liberia, Guinea-Bissau, and the Central African Republic.

The Brahimi Report
On March 7, 2000, UN Secretary-General Kofi Annan announced that the Panel on UN Peace Operations chaired by Ambassador Lakhdar Brahimi would undertake a study on improving peacekeeping and related activities. The resulting *Report of the Panel on UN Peace Operations* is known as the Brahimi Report.[vi] It made a number of practical recommendations designed to facilitate the United Nations dealing with complex operations such as those to East Timor and Sierra Leone.[vii]

Notes

i.   Hilaire McCoubrey and Nigel D. White, *The Blue Helmets: Legal Regulation of United Nations Military Operations* (Aldershot: Dartmouth, 1996), p. 39.
ii.   Information on individual peacekeeping missions can be found on the UN Peacekeeping website at www.un.org/Depts/dpko/dpko/home.shtml.
iii. See McCoubrey and White, *Blue Helmets*, pp. 51ff.

(continues)

Figure 3.1   continued

iv.   See, inter alia, E. Clemons, "No Peace to Keep: Six and Three Quarters
        Peacekeepers," *New York University Journal of International Law and
        Politics* 26 (1993): 107-141, 134ff; and Samuel M. Makinda, "Somalia:
        Lessons from the United Nations Experience," in Tom Woodhouse,
        Robert Bruce, and Malcolm Dando, eds., *Peacekeeping and
        Peacemaking: Towards Effective Intervention in Post–Cold War
        Conflicts* (London: Macmillan, 1998), pp. 166-178.

v.   The authorization resolutions of all peacekeeping operations up to the
        time of publication can be found in Michael Bothe and Thomas
        Dörschel, eds., *UN Peacekeeping: A Documentary Introduction* (The
        Hague/London/Boston: Kluwer Law International, 1999).

vi.   The report can be found at http://www.un.org/peace/reports/peace_
        operations/.

vii. For discussion and commentary, see, inter alia, Manuel Fröhlich,
        "Keeping Track of UN Peace-keeping—Suez, Srebrenica, Rwanda, and
        the Brahimi Report," *Max Planck Yearbook of United Nations Law* 5
        (2001): 1; Christine Gray, "Peacekeeping After the 'Brahimi Report': Is
        There a Crisis of Credibility for the UN?" *Journal of Conflict and
        Security Law* 6, no. 2 (December 2001): 267-288; and Nigel D. White,
        "Commentary on the Report of the Panel on United Nations Peace
        Operations (the Brahimi Report)," *Journal of Conflict and Security Law*
        6, no. 1 (June 2001): 127-146.

ing the progressive development of international law and its codification." The General Assembly makes several types of decisions. A
General Assembly resolution is a document recommending a particular
course of action to member states. It is a political document, although it
may contribute to the emergence of new customary international law.[15]
Having greater influence on international law than a General Assembly
resolution, though still not legally binding, is the General Assembly
declaration, such as the Universal Declaration of Human Rights and the
Declaration on Principles of International Law Concerning Friendly
Relations and Cooperation Among States.[16] A declaration may contain a
codification of customary law or of general principles of law.[17] The
General Assembly may use a resolution to adopt a convention or treaty
that has been drafted elsewhere and to recommend that states sign and
ratify the treaty. Treaties adopted in this way include the Genocide
Convention, the ICCPR, the ICESCR, the Convention on the Rights of
the Child, the Treaty on Principles Governing the Activities of States in
the Exploration and Use of Outer Space, and the Treaty on the Non-

Proliferation of Nuclear Weapons (NPT). The General Assembly also on occasion convenes an international conference to which is submitted a draft treaty prepared by, for example, the International Law Commission (ILC). Examples of treaties concluded at such international conferences include the Vienna Convention on Diplomatic Relations and the Vienna Convention on the Law of Treaties.

Unless it is specially convened, the General Assembly meets once a year, from September to December. Time constraints mean that only the most politically explosive issues are explored thoroughly by the General Assembly when meeting in plenary session. Agenda items are usually considered first in committee. Of the six main committees, those most important to international law are the Third Committee, the Social, Humanitarian, and Cultural Committee; and the Sixth, the Legal Committee. The Sixth Committee offers comments on draft treaties, including those prepared by the International Law Commission. Human rights treaties, including the Genocide Convention and the International Covenants, have usually been concluded within the Third Committee or the Commission on Human Rights, with input from the Sixth Committee.[18]

International Law Commission

The International Law Commission was set up by the General Assembly in 1947.[19] It is made up of thirty-four international lawyers, each of whom is elected for a five-year term by the General Assembly to serve in their personal capacity rather than as government representatives. The "progressive development" of international law refers to "the preparation of draft conventions on subjects which have not yet been sufficiently developed in the practice of States";[20] whereas "codification" refers to "the more precise formulation and systematization of rules of international law in fields where there already has been extensive State practice, precedent and doctrine."[21] Codification and progressive development are interrelated. The first session of the ILC was held in 1949, at which time custom was still the primary source of international law. The ILC usually appoints one member as special rapporteur, who will provide reports on a particular issue area. The ILC uses those reports to prepare a first provisional draft of its articles on a particular topic. This is submitted to the General Assembly, which deals with the matter through its Sixth (Legal) Committee. The draft articles may be submitted to member states for comments. When the ILC has completed its final set of draft articles, they are submitted to states for a decision as to what is to be done with them. Although a treaty need not be the end product of the ILC's work it is common for the General Assembly to convene an international conference at which the draft articles are incorporated into a convention. The ILC prepared, for example, a draft of the 1961 Vienna Convention on Diplomatic Relations and the 1963 Vienna Convention on Consular Relations, as well as the 1969 Vienna Convention on the Law of Treaties and the 1997 Convention on the Non-Navigable Uses of International Watercourses. It also prepared a draft statute for an international criminal court. The ILC has in recent years been working on the subject of state responsibility.[22] Information on the work of the ILC can be found in the ILC's *Yearbooks*.

Committee on the Peaceful Uses of Outer Space

The Committee on the Peaceful Uses of Outer Space (COPUOS) was set up by General Assembly Resolution 1472 (XIV) in 1959. It has played a major role in the development of international space law.[23] Treaties drafted by COPUOS include the 1967 Treaty on Principles Governing the Activities of States in the Exploration and Use of Outer Space, Including the Moon and Other Celestial Bodies; and the Agreement Governing the Activities of States on the Moon and Other Celestial Bodies of 1979. Typically, the treaty has been drafted in a working group or in the Legal Sub-Committee of COPUOS before being considered by COPUOS as a whole and passed on to a main committee of the General Assembly; finally the General Assembly adopts a resolution containing the agreed text and recommends it for the approval of states.[24] COPUOS has adopted most of the various conventions by consensus, the idea being that, although this may slow down the work of the committee, the resulting agreements will have the full support of all states

United Nations Environment Programme

The United Nations Environment Programme was established following the 1972 United Nations Conference on the Human Environment in Stockholm. Its headquarters are in Nairobi, Kenya. UNEP's Governing Council reports to the General Assembly through ECOSOC. A number of the major global environmental treaties have been negotiated under its auspices, including the Vienna Convention for the Protection of the Ozone Layer; the Montreal Protocol on Substances That Deplete the Ozone Layer; the Basel Convention on the Control of Transboundary Movements of Hazardous Wastes and Their Disposal; and the Convention on Biological Diversity.

UNEP serves as the secretariat for a number of environmental agreements and has also been active in the development of nonbinding instruments such as the London Guidelines for the Exchange of Information on Chemicals in International Trade. Through its regional offices for Asia and the Pacific, Europe, Latin America and the Caribbean, and West Asia, UNEP also provides, at the request of states, legal and technical assistance to enhance their environmental legislation and institutions, including those involved in implementing international environmental conventions.[25] There have been proposals for replacing UNEP, or linking UNEP to a world environment organization, which would be institutionally independent and better funded than UNEP. One of the tasks generally proposed for such an organization would be that of initiating and preparing new treaties.[26]

Conference on Disarmament

The Conference on Disarmament (CD) was established by the UN General Assembly's first special session on disarmament in 1978 as a forum for the negotiation of multilateral disarmament treaties. It is the successor to other Geneva-based negotiating fora: the Ten-Nation Committee on Disarmament (1960), the Eighteen-Nation Committee on Disarmament (1968), and the Conference of the Committee on Disarmament (1969–1978). The Conference on Disarmament has a special relationship with the United Nations. It adopts its own rules of procedure by which it conducts work by consensus and decides its own agenda. It does, however, take into account the recommendations made by the General Assembly and reports to the General Assembly annually or more frequently. Treaties negotiated by the CD and its predecessors include the Treaty on the Non-Proliferation of Nuclear Weapons (NPT); the Convention on the Prohibition of Military or Any Other Hostile Use of Environmental Modification Techniques; the Convention on the Prohibition of the Development, Production and Stockpiling of Bacteriological (Biological) and Toxin Weapons and on Their Destruction (the Biological Weapons Convention, or BWC); the Convention on the Prohibition of the Development, Production, Stockpiling, and Use of Chemical Weapons and on Their Destruction (the Chemical Weapons Convention, or CWC); and the Comprehensive Nuclear Test-Ban Treaty (CTBT). In the years following its 1996 completion of the CTBT, the CD was unable to agree on which issues to negotiate next. With the conclusion of the Ottawa Convention on landmines outside of the CD, some commentators warned of a loss of status if disarmament negotiations shifted elsewhere.[27]

Economic and Social Council

The UN Economic and Social Council was established by Chapter X of the UN Charter as the principal organ to coordinate the economic and social work of the United Nations and its specialized agencies and institutions. ECOSOC does, however, work "under the authority" of the General Assembly (article 60), and in practice its status hardly differs from that of the subsidiary and special organs created by the General Assembly under article 22.[28] ECOSOC makes recommendations on human rights, convenes international human rights conferences, and prepares draft conventions for submission to the General Assembly on matters falling within its competence. Article 68 of the Charter provides that ECOSOC may create commissions as required; much of the work of ECOSOC is carried out in one of its subsidiary and related bodies.

Several of the multilateral treaties initiated by ECOSOC provide for the establishment of committees to receive reports from states on the implementation of the treaty in question and, in some, to deal with individual petitions or communications. The principal committees are shown in Figure 3.2. These committees have played a significant part in the ongoing development and implementation of international human rights law.

The Commission on Human Rights was set up by ECOSOC in 1946. The role of the commission, in the context of human rights, is

Figure 3.2   The Principal UN Human Rights Treaty Bodies

Monitoring Body	International Human Rights Instrument
Committee on the Elimination of Racial Discrimination	International Convention on the Elimination of All Forms of Racial Discrimination (CERD)
Committee on Economic, Social, and Cultural Rights	International Covenant on Economic, Social, and Cultural Rights (ICESCR)
The Human Rights Committee	International Covenant on Civil and Political Rights (ICCPR)
Committee on the Elimination of Discrimination Against Women	Convention on the Elimination of All Forms of Discrimination Against Women (CEDAW)
Committee Against Torture	Convention Against Torture and Other Cruel, Inhuman, or Degrading Treatment or Punishment (CAT)
Committee on the Rights of the Child	Convention on the Rights of the Child (CROC)

more significant compared to either the General Assembly or ECOSOC.[29] The Commission on Human Rights is responsible for submitting proposals, recommendations, and investigative reports on human rights issues through ECOSOC to the General Assembly. The Human Rights Commission undertook the initial drafting of the Universal Declaration of Human Rights in 1948 and drafted the ICCPR and ICESCR as well as the Convention on the Elimination of Racial Discrimination and the Convention on the Rights of the Child. The Human Rights Commission has, since the 1970s, actively collected information regarding violations of human rights.[30] The Office of the UN High Commissioner for Human Rights was created in 1993. The high commissioner is tasked with supervising the implementation of all human rights.[31]

The Sub-Commission on the Prevention of Discrimination and the Protection of Minorities was set up in 1946 to assist the Human Rights Commission by making recommendations and conducting investigations on issues dealing with the prevention of discrimination and the protection of ethnic, religious, racial, and linguistic minorities. It was renamed the Sub-Commission on the Promotion and Protection of Human Rights in 1999. The Working Group on Indigenous Populations was established under the subcommission in 1982;[32] in 2000 ECOSOC created the Permanent Forum on Indigenous Issues.[33]

The Commission on the Status of Women was established by ECOSOC in 1946 as a subcommission but by ECOSOC Resolution 11(II) of June 21, 1946, was changed into an independent commission. The commission has undertaken the preparatory work for a number of treaties on women's rights. Early efforts included the 1953 Convention on the Political Rights of Women[34] and the 1957 Convention on the Nationality of Married Women.[35] In 1975 the General Assembly called on the commission to prepare a draft for the Convention on the Elimination of All Forms of Discrimination Against Women (CEDAW). The commission began with fifteen members but now consists of forty-five members elected by ECOSOC for four years.

The International Court of Justice (ICJ)

The International Court of Justice, one of the principal organs of the UN, plays three important roles in the system of international law. First, and perhaps most obvious, it makes decisions among disputing parties on the basis of the rules, principles, and concepts of international law. Article 2(3) of the UN Charter imposes a basic obligation on states to settle their disputes by peaceful means. There is a range of ways by which states can do so; a judicial decision by the ICJ is the most formal. Second, the ICJ offers advisory opinions—that is, opinions clarifying specific points of law. And third, the ICJ contributes to the ongoing creation and clarification of the rules, principles, and concepts of international law. This is an indirect process because it may relate to a point of law other than that most obviously the subject of a request for an advisory opinion or judgment in a contentious case. Much of the detail regarding customary international law, for example, has been developed by the ICJ (see Figure 3.3).

During the nineteenth century there was no world court, but there was a considerable amount of international arbitration by ad hoc tribunals. Public international arbitration in its modern form dates from the Jay Treaty of 1794. This agreement between Britain and the United States to address the many disputes still existing after Britain's formal acknowledgment of U.S. independence in 1783,[36] generated 536 arbitral awards between 1799 and 1804. More than 200 other international arbitral tribunals were established between 1795 and 1914.[37]

The 1899 Convention for the Pacific Settlement of International Disputes established the Permanent Court of Arbitration, which was somewhat modified by the second Hague Conference in 1907. States could designate specific arbitrators to sit on ad hoc tribunals that would hear cases voluntarily submitted and give legally binding awards.[38] The Permanent Court of Arbitration still exists, but it is now used only rarely. Hopes that arbitration would become the normal way of dealing with interstate disputes died with World War I and were largely replaced by hopes for international judicial proceedings. The Permanent Court of International Justice was established in 1922 based on article 14 of the Covenant of the League of Nations. Although the Permanent Court of International Justice (PCIJ) was used quite frequently in the 1920s, and operated until 1940, it was dissolved in April 1946, when the ICJ was established to replace it.

Contentious Cases

The International Court of Justice is the prime judicial body in the UN system, although it does not have the power to review decisions of the Security Council in the same way that the highest court is, in some countries, vested with appellate jurisdiction. The ICJ is best known for its work to settle disputes among states (see Figure 3.4). The Court has jurisdiction over a case only if the states involved have given consent to the jurisdiction of the Court, although this can be more com-

**Figure 3.3   Customary International Law
and the International Court of Justice**

Article 38 of the Statute of the International Court of Justice defines custom as "evidence of a general practice accepted as law." Although this definition is provided in the context of the sources of law to be applied by the ICJ, it is widely accepted as a general definition of custom. The definition indicates the two essential elements of custom: state practice, and *opinio juris*. *State practice* is what states do as well as what they do not do. How far from the coast, for example, does a state enforce its customs laws? *Opinio juris* is the "psychological" component of the act: the belief that the state was acting out of due regard for the law on the subject in question. The necessity to customary international law of those two factors was confirmed by the ICJ in its 1996 Advisory Opinion on the Legality of the Threat or Use of Nuclear Weapons.[i]

A definition of "custom" does not, though, go far in helping an international lawyer—or judge—determine whether or not a particular rule of international custom exists. There needs to be more detailed rules and principles regarding the nature and extent of the necessary state practice. A lot of this detail has been provided in judgments of the ICJ. Publicists have also contributed to the ongoing process of its refinement. Bin Cheng, for example, proposed in 1965 that United Nations resolutions on outer space constituted "instant" international customary law, thereby suggesting that only *opinio juris* is essential to the formation of custom.[ii] This was a quite extreme view that has not been generally accepted. Let's take some of the other questions that might be asked in determining whether or not a particular rule of customary international law has yet crystallized and see what the ICJ has said as regards each.

How Will We Know Opinio Juris When We See It?
In the *North Sea Continental Shelf Cases* of 1969 the ICJ stated:

> Not only must the acts concerned amount to a settled practice, but they must also be such, or be carried out in such a way, as to be evidence of a belief that this practice is rendered obligatory by the existence of a rule of law requiring it. . . . The States concerned must therefore feel that they are conforming to what amounts to a legal obligation. The frequency, or even habitual character of the acts is not in itself enough. There are many international acts, e.g. in the field of ceremonial and protocol, which are performed almost invariably, but which are motivated only by considerations of courtesy, convenience or tradition, and not by any sense of legal duty.[iii]

(continues)

Figure 3.3   continued

How Much State Practice Is Required for the Formation of Customary International Law?

It is possible for only two states to create a bilateral custom, but the bulk of customary international law is "general." A rule of general customary law binds all states other than "persistent objectors," even those states that had not participated in the formation of that rule.[iv] In its 1950 Asylum judgment, the ICJ said that a customary rule must be "in accordance with constant and uniform usage."[v] The ICJ has stated that general customary international law requires there to have been "extensive" state practice involving those states that are "specially affected":

> Although the passage of only a short period of time is not necessarily, or of itself, a bar to the formation of a new rule of customary international law on the basis of what was originally a purely conventional rule, an indispensable requirement would be that within the period in question, short though it might be, State practice, including that of States whose interests are specially affected, should have been both extensive and virtually uniform in the sense of the provision invoked.[vi]

What Degree of Uniformity Must There Be in State Practice?

In its 1986 Nicaragua judgment the Court stated:

> The Court does not consider that, for a rule to be established as customary, the corresponding practice must be in absolutely rigorous conformity with the rule. In order to deduce the existence of customary rules, the Court deems it sufficient that the conduct of States should, in general, be consistent with such rules, and that instances of State conduct inconsistent with a given rule should generally have been treated as breaches of that rule, not as indications of the recognition of a new rule.[vii]

With What Implications for Those Not Engaging in the Practice?

By the "persistent objector principle," a state that is aware of a practice with which it does not agree and protests consistently against the emergence of a rule from the very beginning will not be bound by the rule, although the objecting state cannot necessarily prevent the creation of that rule. There have not been many examples of the application of the principle. It is very difficult for a state to establish that it has been a persistent objector. The process by which custom evolves

(continues)

Figure 3.3 continued

is often clear only in retrospect, and a state will tend to deny that a custom has emerged at all rather than to acknowledge the custom but claim to be a persistent objector.[viii] There has been considerable debate as to whether it is really possible for a state—particularly a relatively weak one—to remain indefinitely outside of law recognized by the vast majority of states.[ix] The ICJ nevertheless appeared to recognize the persistent objector principle in the 1951 *Fisheries* case (*United Kingdom v. Norway*) when it stated that the rule in question "would appear to be inapplicable as against Norway, inasmuch as [Norway] has always opposed any attempt to apply it to the Norwegian coast."[x]

Notes

i. *Legality of the Threat or Use of Nuclear Weapons, Advisory Opinion, I.C.J. Reports* 1996, p. 226, 253, para. 64.
ii. Bin Cheng, "United Nations Resolutions on Outer Space: 'Instant' International Customary Law?," *Indian Journal of International Law* 5 (1965): 23–48.
iii. *North Sea Continental Shelf, Judgment, I.C.J. Reports 1969*, pp. 3, 45, para. 77.
iv. See, generally, M. H. Mendelson, "The Formation of Customary International Law," *Recueil des Courses 1998* (The Hague: Martinus Nijhoff, 1999), pp. 214ff.
v. *Asylum, Judgment, I.C.J. Reports* 1950, pp. 266, 276.
vi. *North Sea Continental Shelf, Judgment, I.C.J. Reports* 1969, pp. 3, 43, para. 74.
vii. *Military and Paramilitary Activities in and Against Nicaragua (Nicaragua v. United States of America), Merits, Judgment, I.C.J. Reports* 1986, pp. 14, 98, para. 186.
viii. Maurizio Ragazzi, *The Concept of International Obligations Erga Omnes* (Oxford: Clarendon, 1997), p. 65.
ix. See, inter alia, Jonathan Charney, "The Persistent Objector Rule and the Development of Customary International Law," *British Yearbook of International Law* 56 (1985): 1–24; T. L. Stein, "The Approach of the Different Drummer: The Principle of the Persistent Objector in International Law," *Harvard International Law Journal* 26 (1985) 457–482; and Stephen J. Toope, "Powerful but Unpersuasive? The Role of the United States of America in the Evolution of Customary International Law," in M. Byers and G. Nolte, eds., *United States Hegemony and the Foundations of International Law* (Cambridge: Cambridge University Press, 2003), 287–316.
x. *Fisheries, Judgment, I.C.J. Reports 1951*, pp. 116, 131.

Figure 3.4 Some ICJ Judgments in Contentious Cases

1948 Corfu Channel Case (Preliminary Objection)
1949 Corfu Channel Case (Merits)
1949 Corfu Channel Case (Assessment of Amount of Compensation)
1950 Asylum Case
1950 Request for Interpretation of the Judgment of November 20, 1950, in the Asylum Case
1951 Haya de la Torre Case
1951 Fisheries Case
1952 Ambatielos Case (Preliminary Objection)
1952 Anglo-Iranian Oil Co. Case (Preliminary Objection)
1952 Case Concerning Rights of Nationals of the United States of America in Morocco
1953 Ambatielos Case (Merits)
1953 Minquiers and Ecrehos Case
1953 Nottebohm Case (Preliminary Objection)
1954 Case of the Monetary Gold Removed from Rome in 1943
1955 Nottebohm Case (Second Phase)
1957 Case of Certain Norwegian Loans
1957 Case Concerning Right of Passage over Indian Territory (Preliminary Objections)
1958 Case Concerning the Application of the Convention of 1902 Governing the Guardianship of Infants
1959 Interhandel Case (Preliminary Objections)
1959 Case Concerning the Aerial Incident of July 27, 1955 (*Israel v. Bulgaria*) (Preliminary Objections)
1959 Case Concerning Sovereignty over Certain Frontier Land
1960 Case Concerning Right of Passage over Indian Territory (Merits)
1960 Case Concerning the Arbitral Award Made by the King of Spain on December 23, 1906
1961 Case Concerning the Temple of Preah Vihear (Preliminary Objections)
1962 Case Concerning the Temple of Preah Vihear (Merits)
1962 South-West Africa Cases (Preliminary Objections)
1963 Case Concerning the Northern Cameroons
1964 Case Concerning the Barcelona Traction, Light and Power Company, Limited (Preliminary Objections)
1966 South-West Africa Cases (Second Phase)
1969 North Sea Continental Shelf Cases
1970 Case Concerning the Barcelona Traction, Light and Power Company, Limited (Second Phase)
1972 Case Concerning the Appeal Relating to the Jurisdiction of the ICAO Council
1973 Fisheries Jurisdiction Case (*United Kingdom v. Iceland*) (Jurisdiction of the Court)
1973 Fisheries Jurisdiction Case (*Federal Republic of Germany v. Iceland*) (Jurisdiction of the Court)
1974 Fisheries Jurisdiction Case (*United Kingdom v. Iceland*) (Merits)

continues

Figure 3.4   continued

1974 Fisheries Jurisdiction Case (*Federal Republic of Germany v. Iceland*) (Merits)
1974 Nuclear Tests Case (*Australia v. France*)
1974 Nuclear Tests Case (*New Zealand v. France*)
1978 Aegean Sea Continental Shelf Case (Jurisdiction of the Court)
1980 Case Concerning United States Diplomatic and Consular Staff in Tehran
1981 Case Concerning the Continental Shelf (Tunisia/Libyan Arab Jamahiriya) (Application for Permission to Intervene)
1982 Case Concerning the Continental Shelf (Tunisia/Libyan Arab Jamahiriya)
1984 Case Concerning the Continental Shelf (Libyan Arab Jamahiriya/Malta) (Application for Permission to Intervene)
1984 Case Concerning Delimitation of the Maritime Boundary in the Gulf of Maine Area
1984 Case Concerning Military and Paramilitary Activities in and Against Nicaragua (*Nicaragua v. United States of America*) (Jurisdiction and Admissibility)
1985 Case Concerning the Continental Shelf (Libyan Arab Jamahiriya/Malta)
1985 Application for Revision and Interpretation of the Judgment of February 24, 1982, in the Case Concerning the Continental Shelf (Tunisia/Libyan Arab Jamahiriya)
1986 Case Concerning the Military and Paramilitary Activities in and Against Nicaragua (*Nicaragua v. United States of America*) (Merits)
1986 Case Concerning the Frontier Dispute (Burkina Faso/Republic of Mali)
1988 Case Concerning Border and Transborder Armed Actions (*Nicaragua v. Honduras*) (Jurisdiction and Admissibility)
1989 Case Concerning the Elettronica Sicula S.P.A. (ELSI)
1990 Case Concerning the Land, Island, and Maritime Frontier Dispute (El Salvador/Honduras) (Application for Permission to Intervene)
1991 Case Concerning the Arbitral Award of July 31, 1989 (*Guinea-Bissau v. Senegal*)
1992 Case Concerning Certain Phosphate Lands in Nauru (*Nauru v. Australia*) (Preliminary Objections)
1992 Case Concerning Land, Island, and Maritime Frontier Dispute (El Salvador/Honduras: Nicaragua Intervening)
1993 Case Concerning Maritime Delimitation in the Area Between Greenland and Jan Mayen (*Denmark v. Norway*)
1994 Case Concerning the Territorial Dispute (Libyan Arab Jamahiriya/Chad)
1994 Case Concerning Maritime Delimitation and Territorial Questions Between Qatar and Bahrain (*Qatar v. Bahrain*) (Jurisdiction and Admissibility)
1995 Case Concerning Maritime Delimitation and Territorial Questions between Qatar and Bahrain) (*Qatar v. Bahrain*) (Jurisdiction and Admissibility)
1995 Case Concerning East Timor (*Portugal v. Australia*)
1996 Case Concerning Application of the Convention on the Prevention and Punishment of the Crime of Genocide (*Bosnia and Herzegovina v. Yugoslavia*) (Preliminary Objections)

plex than it might seem at first glance. Jurisdiction is addressed in Chapter 5.

Procedure in contentious cases begins with the institution of proceedings and appointment of agents, then moves to written proceedings, followed by oral proceedings, deliberations, and judgment. If there is no judge of the nationality of a party, that party may choose a person to sit as a judge ad hoc for that case. The written proceedings involve the parties filing pleadings—usually a memorial and a countermemorial—within the time limits fixed by the Court. If the Court thinks it appropriate, there may also be a reply and a rejoinder. A state making an application to have a case heard by the ICJ may request that the Court issue "provisional measures" to protect the interests of the parties pending judgment on the merits (see Figure 3.5). A request for provisional measures is treated by the Court as a matter of urgency, and the Court's decision is given as an order of the Court. Article 41 of the Statute refers to the Court as having the power to "indicate" provisional measures. Until 2001 there was some debate as to whether this meant that it was compulsory to comply with provisional measures. In its LaGrand judgment of June 27, 2001, the Court removed the uncertainty[39] by clarifying that "orders on provisional measures . . . have binding effect."[40]

Preliminary objections must be filed within the time limit set for the filing of the countermemorial. They may involve a respondent state

---

Figure 3.5 Some ICJ Orders Indicating Provisional Measures

1979 Case Concerning United States Diplomatic and Consular Staff in Tehran (Provisional Measures)

1984 Case Concerning Military and Paramilitary Activities in and Against Nicaragua (*Nicaragua v. United States of America*) (Provisional Measures)

1986 Case Concerning the Frontier Dispute (Burkina Faso/Republic of Mali) (Provisional Measures)

1992 Questions of Interpretation and Application of the 1971 Montreal Convention Arising from the Aerial Incident at Lockerbie (*Libyan Arab Jamahiriya v. United Kingdom*) (Provisional Measures)

1992 Questions of Interpretation and Application of the 1971 Montreal Convention Arising from the Aerial Incident at Lockerbie (*Libyan Arab Jamahiriya v. United States of America*) (Provisional Measures)

1993 Case Concerning Application of the Convention on the Prevention and Punishment of the Crime of Genocide (*Bosnia and Herzegovina v. Yugoslavia*) (Serbia and Montenegro) (Provisional Measures)

1996 Case Concerning the Land and Maritime Boundary Between Cameroon and Nigeria (*Cameroon v. Nigeria*) (Provisional Measures)

---

arguing that the Court does not have jurisdiction to hear the case, or that the case is inadmissible. In seeking to argue against admissibility it may be claimed, for example, that essential provisions of the ICJ Statute have not been complied with or that the dispute no longer exists. Where preliminary objections are raised it is usual for the Court to suspend the proceedings on the merits. The opposing party may make a written sub-mission, followed by oral proceedings. The Court will provide a judg-ment on the preliminary objections, or if they are found not to be of an exclusively preliminary character, the preliminary objections may be considered at the same time as the merits. This was done, for example, in the East Timor case. A third-party state, if it considers that it has a legal interest that may be affected by a decision, may request permis-sion to intervene, and it is then up to the Court to decide on the request. Intergovernmental organizations may also provide the Court with infor-mation relevant to the cases before it and will be asked by the Court to do so if its constituent instrument or "an international convention adopt-ed thereunder" is being examined by the Court.

The ICJ does not operate according to the rule of stare decisis (that it must follow the precedent of previous decisions), but primarily for the sake of consistency and predictability, the Court takes its past deci-sions carefully into account in each new judgment it delivers. The judg-ment of the Court is compulsory for states party to the case in question but has no binding force except among the parties and with respect to that particular case. There is no right of appeal, although article 60 of the ICJ Statute states that the Court can provide an interpretation of a judgment at the request of any party. By article 61 of the statute, an application for revision of a judgment can be made only if the applica-tion is based upon the "discovery" of a "fact" of a decisive nature that was unknown to the Court and to the party claiming revision when the judgment was given. Ignorance of the fact cannot have been due to neg-ligence, and the application for revision must be made within six months of the discovery of the new fact and within ten years of the judgment. On February 3, 2003, the ICJ found that an application by the Federal Republic of Yugoslavia for revision of the 1996 judgment in the *Genocide* case (Preliminary Objections) inadmissible because not all of the above conditions had been met. Proceedings had been instituted by Bosnia and Herzegovina on March 20, 1993, against Yugoslavia (Serbia and Montenegro) concerning a series of alleged violations of the 1948 Genocide Convention. Yugoslavia had unsuccessfully challenged the jurisdiction of the Court and the admissibility of the case and in 2001 had requested a revision of the judgment.

Advisory Opinions

The ICJ is authorized to answer any "legal question" asked it by the General Assembly or the Security Council.[41] The General Assembly may authorize other UN organs and specialized agencies to request advisory opinions of the Court on "legal questions arising within the scope of their activities."[42] Those international organizations currently so nominated include the Economic and Social Council, International Labour Organization (ILO), World Health Organization, World Bank, International Monetary Fund, International Maritime Organization, and International Atomic Energy Agency. The UN Secretary-General does not currently enjoy that power, although there have been suggestions that this be changed as well as that IGOs be able to take part in contentious proceedings[43] and that national courts be able to request advisory opinions.[44]

As with contentious cases, written proceedings are usually followed by oral proceedings. The registrar will give notice of the request to all states entitled to appear before the Court. Article 66 of the ICJ Statute provides that, once the Court has received a request for an advisory opinion, it will give states and international organizations considered likely to be able to provide information on the question at hand an opportunity to submit views in writing or orally. Time limits are given within which the Court will receive written statements or hear oral statements relating to the question. In the course of presenting its opinion, the Court may make reference to various of the arguments that were put to it in these statements. Advisory opinions are not legally binding on the requesting party but have generally been accepted—at least in a formal sense.

Although the International Court of Justice does not have a strongly developed role as an organ of judicial review—that is, examining whether UN bodies have operated within their powers—several advisory opinions have responded to "constitutional" questions pertaining to the operation of the United Nations. One such issue was the financing of UN operations. By article 17(2) of the UN Charter, the General Assembly approves the budget of the United Nations and apportions the expenses among UN members. The unwillingness of states to contribute in full and on time has been a perennial issue for the world body. States that have refused to pay have rarely done so because they were unable to but rather out of political opposition to the use to which the finances were to be put.[45]

The ICJ's 1962 advisory opinion on UN expenses[46] addressed the financing of UN peacekeeping operations. The General Assembly had decided that the United Nations Emergency Force in the Middle East (UNEF I) and the UN Operations in the Congo (ONUC) constituted expenses of the UN Organization and that this money could therefore be apportioned in accordance with the power granted to the General Assembly by article 17(2) of the UN Charter.[47] But France, Eastern European states, and the Soviet Union were not happy with the operations and refused to contribute to their financing.[48] On December 20, 1961, the General Assembly adopted Resolution 1731 (XVI), requesting an advisory opinion on the question of whether such peacekeeping expenses "constitute 'expenses of the [UN] Organization' within the meaning of Article 17, paragraph 2, of the Charter of the United Nations."

The opinion of the Court, handed down on July 20, 1962, was that peacekeeping costs should be considered "expenses" of the UN Organization to be borne by all member states, as provided in article 17. The Soviet Union had adopted the position that the financial obligations of UN member states concerning actions for upholding universal peace and security could be determined only on the basis of agreements between the Security Council and member states.[49] The Charter confers "primary" responsibility for the maintenance of international peace and security on the Security Council; the Court pointed out that primary responsibility is not exclusive responsibility.[50] The Charter is clear that the General Assembly is also to be concerned with international peace and security.[51]

Although by Resolution 1854 (XVII) of December 18, 1962, the General Assembly accepted the Court's opinion, France and the Soviet Union still refused to pay their contributions. By article 19 of the UN Charter, a member state that is behind in payments to the equivalent of two years' contributions cannot vote in the General Assembly unless the General Assembly is satisfied "that the failure to pay is due to conditions beyond the control" of the member. During the nineteenth session of the General Assembly, when there were in fact sixty-two member states in arrears on one or both of the special peacekeeping accounts,[52] the issue was avoided by conducting all business without a vote being taken; decisions were either postponed or taken by acclamation. After that, the General Assembly reverted to its normal procedures, but without applying article 19 to the states in question. It was decided that peacekeeping operations would be paid from voluntary contributions to a special fund, which meant that no member state was in arrears in the payment of its contributions under article 19. The United States, which had been adamant that article 19 be applied, acquiesced but made it clear that it "reserved the same option to make exceptions if, in its view, there were strong and compelling reasons to do so."[53]

The question put to the Court for an advisory opinion must be a legal one, but there is likely to be a clear political motive behind it. Since international organizations are made up of states, questions that prompt a request for an advisory opinion are likely to relate to matters of contention among states. Underlying the differences of opinion in regard to the financing of peacekeeping were political differences over the role being played by what were essentially Western peacekeeping operations. The financing of peacekeeping operations has continued to be a problem for the United Nations, many members not paying in full and on time.[54]

The 1975 Western Sahara advisory opinion arose from a dispute as to the status of what was to become Western Sahara after its decolonization by Spain. Western Sahara is a desert area located between Morocco and Mauritania with rich fishing grounds and phosphate resources. It had been colonized by Spain in the nineteenth century. Upon gaining independence in 1956, Morocco claimed territorial rights over Western Sahara, as did Mauritania when it gained independence in 1960. Morocco and Mauritania each sought to strengthen its claim by asserting that it had had legal ties with Western Sahara that predated European colonization.[55] Resolutions of the General Assembly in 1965 and 1966 requested Spain to consent to a referendum to implement the principle of self-determination in the territory. In 1974 Spain agreed that a referendum be held in 1975, hoping to maintain close ties with an independent Western Sahara.

Morocco challenged Spain to submit the dispute to the International Court of Justice. When Spain declined, Morocco and Mauritania proposed to the General Assembly that the issue be the subject of a request for an advisory ruling. By General Assembly Resolution 3292 (XXIX) of December 13, 1974, the Court was asked to provide an advisory opinion on two questions:

> I. Was Western Sahara (Rio de Oro and Sakiet El Hamra) at the time of colonization by Spain a territory belonging to no-one? (*terra nullius*)?
> If the answer to the first question is in the negative,

II. What were the legal ties between this territory and the Kingdom of Morocco and the Mauritanian entity?[56]

The Court avoided the obvious political agenda of both states—to be able to integrate the territory without a referendum of the indigenous inhabitants—to find that, in terms of state practice of the day, the Western Sahara had not been *terra nullius*. Although legal ties with the sultan of Morocco and the Mauritanian entity had existed, they had not been such as to affect the contemporary application to the territory of the principle of self-determination.[57]

Shortly after the decision, Morocco invaded Western Sahara and declared it annexed without conducting a plebiscite.[58] In 1979 Mauritania renounced all claims to Western Sahara, leaving Morocco to annex the rest of the territory. The legal status of the territory remains unresolved.

Morocco had attempted to use the ICJ as a political lever to obtain its objectives. The Western Sahara case thus demonstrates that the difference between contentious proceedings and advisory opinions may not be so great as it appears at first. It may in certain circumstances be easier for states to achieve judicial pronouncements in advisory opinions than to initiate contentious proceedings.[59]

This is particularly the case where the issue at hand is not a dispute between specific states so much as a source of general tension between large groups of states. On May 14, 1993, the World Health Organization (WHO) requested an advisory opinion from the ICJ on the following question:

In view of the health and environmental effects, would the use of nuclear weapons by a State in war or other armed conflict be a breach of its obligations under international law including the WHO Constitution?[60]

Subsequently, on December 15, 1994, the UN General Assembly adopted a resolution asking the ICJ for an "urgent" advisory opinion on the question: "Is the threat or use of nuclear weapons in any circumstances permitted under international law?"[61]

The questions asked of the Court were legal questions, of relevance to the laws of armed conflict, environmental law, human rights law, the UN Charter, and the WHO constitution.[62] At the same time, there could be few questions more political than those pertaining to one of the major determinants of global power relations for more than half a century. Permanent members of the Security Council perceived the question posed to the ICJ by the General Assembly as threatening their privileged status.[63]

The Court decided to consolidate the two requests relating to the legality of nuclear weapons and, in accordance with article 66 of the ICJ Statute, invited states to submit written statements. Public hearings on the two questions were held from October 30 to November 14, 1995. During the proceedings the United Kingdom and France argued that, because certain NGOs had been instrumental in bringing the question to the Court, it was not appropriate for the Court to answer it. The Court rejected this argument, although it also rejected an application by the International Physicians for the Prevention of Nuclear War to file a brief in the case.[64]

As might be expected, nuclear and nonnuclear states tended to have polar views on the question at hand. The nuclear powers argued that there was no existing prohibition on the use or threat of use of nuclear weapons in international law, that the NPT legitimated the possession and thus implicitly the use (by them) of such weapons. Those opposed to nuclear weapons argued that the NPT at most acknowledged the fact of possession by nuclear states; that it was neutral as to their use; and that existing international law pointed in the direction of the illegality of the use or threat of use of nuclear weapons.[65]

On July 8, 1996, the Court delivered two opinions. The Court concluded that the WHO was not competent to ask its question because it was only entitled to request advisory opinions "on legal questions arising within the scope of [its] activities." In response to the question of the General Assembly, the majority view was that

> the threat or use of nuclear weapons would generally be contrary to the rules of international law applicable in armed conflict, and in particular the principles and rules of humanitarian law;
> However, in view of the current state of international law, and the elements of fact at its disposal, the Court cannot conclude definitively whether the threat or use of nuclear weapons would be lawful or unlawful in an extreme circumstance of self-defence, in which the very survival of a State would be at stake.[66]

The Court was of the unanimous opinion that "there exists an obligation to pursue in good faith and bring to a conclusion negotiations leading to nuclear disarmament in all its aspects under strict and effective international control."

This opinion was such that it could be acclaimed by nuclear

weapons states as well as those campaigning for the elimination of nuclear weapons. If the Court had exercised its discretion not to answer the questions it would likely have been accused of failing to apply the rule of law in international relations, but in exercising its power to answer the questions the Court ran the risk of being accused of entering the political domain.[67] If, having accepted the challenge, the Court had gone on to find in favor of the legality of the threat or use of nuclear weapons, it could easily have been accused of backing the agenda of the most powerful states. Were it to have found against the legality of the threat or use of nuclear weapons, the Court risked its findings being ignored and hence detracting from the credibility of international law. In a sense the Court had no option but to "tackle the fate of the earth" while at the same time giving a response that cannot but be regarded as at least "somewhat ambiguous."[68]

It may be considered to have been a little naive of those lobbying to have the question asked of the ICJ to think that, even if they were successful in having the question asked of the Court and even if they had got all they could have hoped for and the Court had opined against the legality of nuclear weapons, the world would then miraculously be rid of these weapons. But the key individuals were more realistic; the hoped-for decision against the legality of nuclear weapons was seen as part of a broader process of "delegitimizing" nuclear weapons and weakening the resistance of the nuclear weapons powers to nuclear disarmament. The Lawyers' Committee on Nuclear Policy reasoned that even a completely negative opinion in relation to nuclear weapons could "shock the public and officials into increased action against nuclear weapons, and thus still assist the process of disarmament."[69]

The ensuing advisory opinion may have been ambiguous, but the considerable debate that it has generated[70] has brought into greater prominence issues regarding the legality—and the morality—of nuclear weapons. The immediate outcome of the opinion may not have been great, but its political significance may at some future date appear greater when viewed in historical context.

Specialized Agencies and Other Autonomous Organizations in the UN system

International Labour Organization
The International Labour Organization (ILO) was founded in 1919 and became the first specialized agency of the UN in 1946. It formulates international labor standards in the form of recommendations or guide-

lines for national action, and conventions, which are open to ratification as treaties; it was the first permanent organization to draft treaties on a regular basis.[71] The ILO has adopted more than 180 conventions and 185 recommendations, of which eight conventions are considered fundamental to the rights of human beings at work.[72] The ILO has a tripartite structure unique in the UN system, by which workers and employers participate as equal partners with governments in the work of its governing organs. A system of supervision provides for regular reporting on measures taken to give effect to the provisions of an instrument. There is a complaint procedure by which a ratifying member state, an International Labour Conference Delegate, or the Governing Body can bring a complaint against another member state believed to be not satisfactorily implementing an ILO convention it has ratified.[73]

International Maritime Organization

The International Maritime Organization (IMO) is a specialized agency of the UN. It was founded by the 1948 Convention on the Inter-Governmental Maritime Consultative Organization (IMCO). This treaty did not enter into force until 1958, and the IMCO met for the first time in 1959. The name was changed to the International Maritime Organization in 1982. By article 3 of the 1948 convention, the IMO was "to provide for the drafting of conventions, agreements, or other suitable instruments, and to recommend these to Governments and to intergovernmental organizations, and to convene such conferences as may be necessary." The IMO has been responsible for a number of important treaties relating to safety at sea as well as marine pollution, including a new version of the International Convention for the Safety of Life at Sea (SOLAS),[74] the International Convention for the Prevention of Pollution from Ships, as Modified by the Protocol of 1978 Relating Thereto (MARPOL 73/78), and more recently the International Convention on Liability and Compensation for Bunker Oil Pollution Damage.

International Atomic Energy Agency

The IAEA is an autonomous agency that plays an essential role in the implementation of several disarmament and nonproliferation treaties, including the NPT. The IAEA was established in 1957 to "accelerate and enlarge the contribution of atomic energy to peace, health and prosperity throughout the world"[75] while ensuring, as far as it is able, that assistance provided by the IAEA, at its request or under its supervision or control, would not be used in such a way as to further any military purpose. In 1961 the IAEA established an international safeguards system to ensure that material was not diverted from peaceful uses to build nuclear weapons or nuclear explosive devices. Under article 3 of the NPT, each non-nuclear-weapon state party to the treaty undertakes to accept safeguards, as set forth in an agreement to be negotiated with the IAEA, to verify the fulfillment of obligations assumed under the treaty and to prevent diversion of nuclear energy from peaceful uses to nuclear weapons or other nuclear explosive devices.

The UN and Other IGOs

The United Nations is integrally related to the contemporary global system of international law to an extent not true of any other IGO. It is in the ICJ Statute, annexed to the UN Charter, that we find the most widely accepted statement of the sources of international law; and the UN Charter contains rules, principles, and concepts fundamental to the contemporary system of international law, including the sovereign equality of states and the peaceful settlement of disputes. Indeed, the UN Charter plays a role akin to the constitution of the international community.[76] Many treaties, on a range of subject matter, have come about via the work of the United Nations, and UN bodies play a key role in monitoring the implementation of many of those treaties. The International Court of Justice, the most important of the international courts and tribunals, is a UN organ.

Although this chapter has focused on the UN as the IGO most important to the system of international law, virtually all IGOs have been founded by a multilateral treaty. We will consider a number of those other IGOs in the context of treaty regimes.

Notes

1. The European Union replaced the European Community, which had been created by the Merger Treaty of 1967, out of the European Economic Community, the European Atomic Energy Community, and the European Coal and Steel Community.

2. Exceptions include the Inter-American Defense Board and the International Wool Study Group. Henry G. Schermers and Niels M. Blokker, *International Institutional Law: Unity Within Diversity*. 3rd rev. ed. (The Hague: Martinus Nijhoff, 1995), p. 23.

3. International Legal Materials (ILM) 543 (1986).

4. These were Argentina, Australia, Belarus, Belgium, Bolivia, Brazil, Canada, Chile, China, Colombia, Costa Rica, Cuba, Denmark, Dominican

Republic, Ecuador, Egypt, El Salvador, Ethiopia, France, Greece, Guatemala, Haiti, Honduras, India, Iran, Iraq, Lebanon, Liberia, Luxembourg, Mexico, Netherlands, New Zealand, Nicaragua, Norway, Panama, Peru, Philippines, Poland, Russian Federation, Saudi Arabia, South Africa, Syria, Turkey, Ukraine, United Kingdom, United States, Uruguay, Venezuela, and Yugoslavia. Lawrence Ziring, Robert Riggs, and Jack Plano, *The United Nations: International Organization and World Politics,* 3rd ed. (Fort Worth, TX: Harcourt College, 2000), p. 68.

5. See discussion in Frederic L. Kirgis Jr. "The Security Council's First Fifty Years," *American Journal of International Law (AJIL)* 89 (1995): 527–532.

6. Charter of the United Nations, article 37(1).

7. See, inter alia, Lori Buck et al., "Sanctions as a Gendered Instrument of Statecraft: The Case of Iraq," *Review of International Studies* 24 (1998): 69–84; Paul Conlon, *United Nations Sanctions Management: A Case Study of the Iraq Sanctions Committee, 1990–1994* (New York: Transnational, 2000); Christopher C. Joyner, "Collective Sanctions as Peaceful Coercion: Lessons from the United Nations Experience," *Australian Yearbook of International Law* 16 (1995): 241–270; Peggy Kozal, "Is the Continued Use of Sanctions as Implemented Against Iraq a Violation of International Human Rights?" *Denver Journal of International Law and Policy* 28, no. 4 (Fall 2000): 383–400; John Mueller and Karl Muller, "Sanctions of Mass Destruction," *Foreign Affairs* 78, no. 3 (May/June 1999): 43–53; Chantal de Jonge Oudraat, "Making Economic Sanctions Work," *Survival* 42, no. 3 (Autumn 2000): 105–127; and Thomas G. Weiss, David Cortright, George A. Lopez, and Larry Minear, *Political Gain and Civilian Pain: Humanitarian Impacts of Economic Sanctions* (Lanham, MD: Rowman & Littlefield, 1997).

8. David Cortright and George A. Lopez, eds., *The Sanctions Decade: Assessing UN Strategies in the 1990s* (Boulder: Lynne Rienner, 2000).

9. Security Council Resolution 678, UN SCOR, 45th Sess., 2963rd mtg., UN Doc S/RES/678 (1990). Some have interpreted the legal basis for the use of force in the Gulf War as being Security Council–sanctioned collective self-defense rather than authorization by the Security Council per se. For discussion of this point, see Christopher Greenwood, "New World Order or Old? The Invasion of Kuwait and the Rule of Law," *Modern Law Review* 55, no. 2 (March 1992): 153–186; Alissa Pyrich, "United Nations: Authorizations of Use of Force," *Harvard International Law Journal* 32 (1991): 265–274; Oscar Schachter, "United Nations Law in the Gulf Conflict," *AJIL* 85 (1991): 452–473; and Yoram Dinstein, *War, Aggression and Self-Defence,* 3rd ed. (Cambridge: Cambridge University Press, 2001), pp. 242–245.

10. Security Council Resolution 748, UN SCOR 47th Sess., 3063rd mtg, p. 3, UN Doc S/RES/748 (1992); Security Council Resolution 731, UN SCOR, 47th Sess., 303rd mtg. at 1, UN Doc. S/RES/731 (1992). See, inter alia, F. Beveridge, "The Lockerbie Affair," *International and Comparative Law Quarterly (ICLQ)* 41 (1992): 907–920; Vera Gowlland-Debbas, "The Relationship Between the International Court of Justice and the Security Council in the Light of the Lockerbie Case," *AJIL* 88, no. 4 (October 1994): 643–677; and W. Michael Reisman, "The Constitutional Crisis in the United Nations," *AJIL* 87, no. 1 (January 1993): 83–100.

11. Security Council Resolution 827, para. 4, and Security Council Resolution 955, para 2.

12. See, for example, Judge Richard J. Goldstone, "The International Tribunal for the Former Yugoslavia: A Case Study in Security Council Action," *Duke Journal of Comparative & International Law* 6 (1995): 5–10; Faiza Patel King, "Sensible Scrutiny: The Yugoslavia Tribunal's Development of Limits on the Security Council's Powers Under Chapter VII of the Charter," *Emory International Law Review* 10 (1996): 509–591; Tara Sapru, "Into the Heart of Darkness: The Case Against the Foray of the Security Council Tribunal into the Rwandan Crisis," *Texas International Law Journal* 32 (1997): 329–354; Danesh Sarooshi, *The United Nations and the Development of Collective Security: The Delegation by the UN Security Council of Its Chapter VII Powers* (Oxford: Clarendon, 1999); and David Schweigman, *The Authority of the Security Council Under Chapter VII of the UN Charter: Legal Limits and the Role of the International Court of Justice* (The Hague: Kluwer Law International, 2001).

13. Faiza Patel King, "Sensible Scrutiny: The Yugoslavia Tribunal's Development of Limits on the Security Council's Powers Under Chapter VII of the Charter," *Emory International Law Review* 10 (1996): 509–591, 509.

14. On the reform of the Security Council see, inter alia, Bardo Fassbinder, *UN Security Council Reform and the Right of Veto: A Constitutional Perspective* (The Hague: Kluwer Law International, 1998); Mary Ellen O'Connell, "The UN, NATO, and International Law After Kosovo," *Human Rights Quarterly* 22, no. 1 (2000): 57–89; Princeton N. Lyman, "Saving the UN Security Council: A Challenge for the United States," *Max Planck Yearbook of United Nations Law* 4 (2000): 127–146; and Ingo Winkelmann, "Bringing the Security Council into a New Era: Recent Developments in the Discussion on the Reform of the Security Council," *Max Planck Yearbook of United Nations Law* 1 (1997): 35–90.

15. For consideration of the question as to whether unanimously adopted resolutions of the General Assembly may create "instant" customary international law, see Bin Cheng, "United Nations Resolutions on Outer Space: 'Instant' International Customary Law?" *Indian Journal of International Law* 5 (1965): 23–48. See also R. A. Falk, "On the Quasi-legislative Competence of the General Assembly," *AJIL* 60 (1966): 782–791; N. G. Onuf, "Professor Falk on the Quasi-legislative Competence of the General Assembly," *AJIL* 64 (1970): 349–355; and Blaine Sloan, *UN General Assembly Resolutions in Our Changing World* (Ardsley-on-Hudson, NY: Transnational, 1991).

16. General Assembly Resolution 2625 (XXV).

17. Henry G. Schermers and Niels M. Blokker, *International Institutional Law: Unity Within Diversity*, 3rd rev. ed. (The Hague: Martinus Nijhoff, 1995), pp. 772–773. See also O. Y. Asamoah, *The Legal Significance of the Declarations of the General Assembly of the United Nations* (The Hague: Martinus Nijhoff, 1966).

18. See Mohammed Ahsen Chaudhri, "Origin, Composition, and Functions of the Sixth Committee," *Revue Egyptienne de droit international* 29 (1973): 211–232.

19. General Assembly Resolution 174 (II), November 21, 1947.

20. Statute of the International Law Commission, article 15.

21. Ibid.

22. On the ILC and its work, see, inter alia, M. R. Anderson, A. E. Boyle, A. V. Lowe, and C. Wickremasinghe, eds., *The International Law Commission and the Future of International Law* (London: British Institute of International and Comparative Law, 1998); Jeffrey S. Morton, *The International Law Commission of the United Nations* (Columbia: University of South Carolina Press, 2000); I. Sinclair, *The International Law Commission* (Cambridge: Grotius, 1987); and Sir Arthur Watts, *The International Law Commission 1949–1998*, 3 vols. (Oxford: Oxford University Press, 1999). On state responsibility, see James Crawford, *The International Law Commission's Articles on State Responsibility: Introduction, Text and Commentaries* (Cambridge: Cambridge University Press, 2002).

23. See, inter alia, N. Jasentuliyana, "Treaty Law and Outer Space: Can the United Nations Play an Effective Role?" *Annals of Air and Space Law* 11 (1986): 219–226; and N. Hosenball, "The United Nations Committee on the Peaceful Uses of Outer Space: Past Accomplishments and Future Challenges," *Journal of Space Law* 7 (1979): 95–113.

24. Ralph G. Steinhardt, "Outer Space," in Christopher C. Joyner, ed. *The United Nations and International Law* (Washington, DC: American Society of International Law; Cambridge: Cambridge University Press, 1997), 336–361, 339–340.

25. For further information, see www.unep.org/SEC/env4.htm.

26. Frank Biermann, "The Case for a World Environment Organization," *Environment* 42, no. 9: 23–31; for a dissenting opinion on the establishment of a world environment organization, see the commentary on page 44 of the same issue.

27. See, inter alia, Wade Boese, "CD Negotiating Session Concludes Without Progress," *Arms Control Today* (October 2001), available at the website www.armscontrol.org.

28. Christian Tomuschat, "General Assembly," in Christiane Philipp and Rüdiger Wolfrum, eds., *United Nations: Law, Policies and Practice*, vol. 1 (Dordrecht: Martinus Nijhoff, 1995), 548–557, 555.

29. Henry J. Steiner and Philip Alston, *International Human Rights in Context: Law, Politics, Morals,* 2nd ed. (Oxford: Oxford University Press, 2000), p. 600.

30. Schermers and Blokker, *International Institutional Law,* p. 876.

31. See, inter alia, Bhaswati Mukherjee, "United Nations High Commissioner for Human Rights: Challenges and Opportunities," in Gudmundur Alfredsson, Jonas Grimheden, Bertram G. Ramcharan, and Alfred de Zayas, eds., *International Human Rights Monitoring Mechanisms: Essays in Honour of Jakob Th. Möller* (The Hague: Martinus Nijhoff, 2001), 403–414.

32. See, inter alia, Russel Lawrence Barsh, "Indigenous Peoples: An Emerging Object of International Law," *AJIL* 80 (1986): 369–385; Douglas Sanders, "The UN Working Group on Indigenous Populations," *Human Rights Quarterly* 11 (1990): 406–433; and Sarah Pritchard, "Working Group on Indigenous Populations: Mandate, Standard-Setting Activities, and Future Perspectives," in Sarah Pritchard, ed., *Indigenous Peoples, the United Nations, and Human Rights* (London: Zed Books, 1998), 40–64.

33. Its Internet address is www.unhchr.ch/indigenous/ind_pfii.htm.

34. 193 United Nations Treaty Series (UNTS) 2613.

35. 309 UNTS 65.

36. Mark Janis, "The International Court," in Mark W. Janis, ed., *International Courts for the Twenty-First Century* (The Hague: Kluwer, 1992), p. 14.

37. Ibid.

38. Ibid.

39. See, e.g., discussion in Bernard H. Oxman, "Jurisdiction and the Power to Indicate Provisional Measures," in Lori F. Damrosch, ed., *The International Court of Justice at a Crossroads* (Dobbs Ferry, NY: Transnational, 1987), pp. 332–333; and Peter J. Goldsworthy, "Interim Measures of Protection in the International Court of Justice," *AJIL* 68 (1974): 258–277, 273–274.

40. *LaGrand (Germany v. United States of America)*, June 27, 2001, at para. 109, at www.icj-cij.org/icjwww/idocket/igus/igusframe.htm.

41. Charter of the United Nations, article 96(1).

42. Charter of the United Nations, article 96(2).

43. See, e.g., Roberto Ago, "'Binding' Advisory Opinions of the International Court of Justice," *AJIL* 85 (1991): 439–451.

44. Taslim O. Elias, "How the International Court of Justice Deals with Requests for Advisory Opinions," in Makarczyk, *Essays in International Law in Honour of Judge Manfred Lachs*, p. 357, n. 4. See also Hersch Lauterpacht, "Decisions of Municipal Courts as a Source of International Law," *British Yearbook of International Law* 10 (1929): 65–95; and Stephen M. Schwebel, "Preliminary Rulings by the International Court of Justice at the Instance of National Courts," *Virginia Journal of International Law* 28 (1988): 495–496.

45. See Robert F. Gorman, *Great Debates at the United Nations: An Encyclopedia of Fifty Key Issues 1945–2000* (Westport, CT: Greenwood, 2001), 162–168.

46. *Certain Expenses of the United Nations (Article 17, paragraph 2, of the Charter), Advisory Opinion, ICJ Reports 1962*, p. 151.

47. Ibid., p. 178.

48. For a detailed account of the politics behind the *Certain Expenses Advisory Opinion*, see David Wilkinson, "The Article 17 Crisis: The Dispute over Financing the United Nations," in Lawrence Scheinman and David Wilkinson, *International Law and Political Crisis: An Analytic Casebook* (Boston: Little, Brown, 1968), pp. 211–249; and Stanley Hoffmann, "A World Divided and a World Court Confused: The World Court's Advisory Opinion on UN Financing," in Scheinman and Wilkinson, *International Law and Political Crisis*, pp. 251–273.

49. The views of the Soviet Union were presented to the ICJ in "Memorandum of the USSR Government on the Procedure of Financing the Operations of the United Nations Emergency Force in the Middle East and the United Nations Operations in the Congo," *ICJ Pleadings, Certain Expenses of the United Nations (Article 17, paragraph 2, of the Charter)*, pp. 270–274.

50. *Certain Expenses Advisory Opinion*, p. 163.

51. Ibid.

52. Norman J. Padelford, "Financing Peacekeeping: Politics and Crisis," *International Organization* 19 (1963): 444–462, 445.

53. UN General Assembly, Official Record, 19th Sess., Annexes, Annex no. 21, A/5916/Add.1, pp. 86–87, cited in Marjorie M. Whiteman, *Digest of International Law* 13 (1968): 331–332. See also Wilfried Koschorreck, "Financial Crisis," in Christiane Philipp and Rüdiger Wolfrum, eds., *United Nations: Law, Policies, and Practice*, vol. 1 (Dordrecht: Martinus Nijhoff, 1995), 523–531.

54. Andrzej Abraszewski, "Financing of the Peace-keeping Operations of the United Nations," *International Geneva Yearbook* 7 (1993): 79–95, 84–85. On UN financing, see Jose E. Alvarez, "Financial Responsibility," in O. Schachter and C. C. Joyner, eds., *United Nations Legal Order*, vol. 2 (Cambridge: Cambridge University Press and American Society of International Law, 1995), 1091–1119; M. J. Peterson, *The General Assembly in World Politics* (Boston: Allen & Unwin, 1986), pp. 123–135; Anthony McDermott, *The New Politics of Financing the UN* (New York: St. Martin's, 1999); and Schermers and Blokker, *International Institutional Law*, pp. 598–599.

55. See M. Shaw, "The Western Sahara Case" *British Yearbook of International Law* 49 (1978): 121ff.

56. *Western Sahara Advisory Opinion, I.C.J. Reports 1975*, pp. 12, 14.

57. *Western Sahara Advisory Opinion*, p. 68. See also Mark W. Janis, "The International Court of Justice: Advisory Opinion on the Western Sahara," *Harvard International Law Journal* 17 (1976): 609–621; and B. O. Okere, "The Western Sahara Case," *ICLQ* 28 (April 1979): 296–312.

58. See Abigail Byman, "The March on the Spanish Sahara: A Test of International Law," *Journal of International Law and Policy* 6 (1976): 95–121.

59. See discussion in D. W. Greig, "The Advisory Jurisdiction of the International Court and the Settlement of Disputes Between States," *ICLQ* 15 (1966): 325–368.

60. Health and Environmental Effects of Nuclear Weapons, World Health Assembly Res. 46.40, adopted May 14, 1993. Cited in *Legality of the Use by a State of Nuclear Weapons in Armed Conflict, Advisory Opinion, ICJ Reports 1996*, p. 66, at para. 1.

61. Request for an Advisory Opinion from the International Court of Justice on the Legality of the Threat or Use of Nuclear Weapons. General Assembly Resolution 75, 49th Sess., 90th mtg., pp. 15–16, UN Doc A/Res/49/75 (1994).

62. These were the bodies of law primarily drawn on in the written observations and oral hearings of the two cases. Roger S. Clark, "International Court of Justice: Advisory Proceedings on the Legality of the Threat or Use of Nuclear Weapons (Question Posed by the General Assembly): The Laws of Armed Conflict and the Use or Threat of Use of Nuclear Weapons," *Criminal Law Forum* 7 (1996): 265–298, 271.

63. Kate Dewes and Commander (ret.) Robert Green, "The World Court Project: How a Citizen Network Can Influence the United Nations," *Pacifica Review* 7, no. 2 (1995): 17–37, 28.

64. Peter Weiss, "The World Court Tackles the Fate of the Earth: An Introduction to the ICJ Advisory Opinion on the Legality of the Threat and Use of Nuclear Weapons," *Transnational Law & Contemporary Problems* 7 (Fall 1997): 314–332, 320–321.

65. Clark, "International Court of Justice," p. 265.

66. Para. 105(2)(E).

67. Laurence Boisson de Chazournes and Philippe Sands, "Introduction," in Laurence Boisson de Chazournes and Philippe Sands, eds., *International Law, the International Court of Justice and Nuclear Weapons* (Cambridge: Cambridge University Press, 1999), p. 21.

68. Richard A. Falk, "Nuclear Weapons, International Law, and the World Court: A Historic Encounter," *AJIL* 91 (1997): 64–75, 64.

69. Williams Epstein, Alyn Ware, and Peter Weiss, *World Court Project: How Might the Court Rule? What Effect Will That Have?* Lawyers' Committee on Nuclear Policy, September 1993, p. 10, cited in Ved P. Nanda and David Krieger, *Nuclear Weapons and the World Court* (Ardsley, NY: Transnational, 1998), p. 82.

70. For academic literature in response, see, inter alia, Dapo Akande, "Nuclear Weapons, Unclear Law? Deciphering the Nuclear Weapons Advisory Opinion of the International Court," *British Yearbook of International Law* 68 (Annual 1997): 165–217; Falk, "Nuclear Weapons, International Law, and the World Court," p. 64; Michael J. Matheson, "The Opinions of the International Court of Justice on the Threat or Use of Nuclear Weapons," *AJIL* 91 (1997): 417–435; Nicholar Grief, "Legality of the Threat or Use of Nuclear Weapons," *ICLQ* 46 (1997): 681–688; Kazuomi Ouchi, "The Threat or Use of Nuclear Weapons: Discernible Legal Policies of the Judges of the International Court of Justice," *Connecticut Journal of International Law* 13 (1998): 107–118; Antonio F. Perez, "The Passive Virtues and the World Court: Pro-Dialogic Abstention by the International Court of Justice," *Michigan Journal of International Law* 18 (1997): 399, 426–443; Christyne J. Vachon, "Sovereignty Versus Globalization: The International Court of Justice's Advisory Opinion on the Threat or Use of Nuclear Weapons," *Denver Journal of International Law and Policy* 26 (1998): 691–724; and Prosper Weil, "'The Court Cannot Conclude Definitively....' Non Liquet Revisited," *Columbia Journal of Transnational Law* 36 (1997): 109–119.

71. Steve Charnovitz, "The International Labour Organization in its Second Century," *Max Planck Yearbook of United Nations Law* 4 (2000): 147–184, 148. See also Héctor Bartolomei de la Cruz, Geraldo von Potobsky, and Lee Swepston, *The International Labor Organization: The International Standards System and Basic Human Rights* (Boulder: Westview, 1996).

72. These are the Freedom of Association and Protection of the Right to Organize Convention of 1948; the Right to Organize and Collective Bargaining Convention of 1949; the Forced Labour Convention of 1930; the Abolition of Forced Labour Convntion of 1957; the Discrimination (Employment and Occupation) Convention of 1958; the Equal Remuneration Convention of 1951; the Minimum Age Convention of 1973; and the Worst Forms of Child Labour Convention of 1999.

73. Steve Charnovitz, "The International Labour Organization," p. 171.

For further information, see http://www.ilo.org/public/english/standards/norm/ enforced/index.htm.

74. The first version of SOLAS was adopted in 1914, the second in 1929, the third in 1948, and the fourth in 1960. The 1960 convention was the first major task of the IMO. A completely new version was adopted in 1974, which made it easier to amend the treaty rather than to have to replace it.

75. The Statute of the International Atomic Energy Agency was approved on October 23, 1956, and entered into force on July 29, 1957. The text is available at the website of the IAEA at www.iaea.org/worldatom/Documents/ statute.html. See B. G. Bechoefer, "Negotiating the Statute of the International Atomic Energy Agency," *International Organization* 13, no. 1 (Winter 1959): 38–59; and Lawrence Scheinman, *The International Atomic Energy Agency and World Nuclear Order* (Washington, DC: Resources for the Future, 1987).

76. Cf. Pierre-Marie Dupuy, "The Constitutional Dimension of the Charter of the United Nations Revisited," *Max Planck Yearbook of United Nations Law* 1 (1997): 1–33; B. Fassbender, "The United Nations Charter as Constitution of the International Community," *Columbia Journal of Transnational Law* 36 (1998): 529–619; and R. Macdonald, "The Charter of the United Nations in Constitutional Perspective," *Australian Year Book of International Law* 20 (1999): 205–231.

4

Nonstate Actors
in International Law

S tates and intergovernmental organizations of states may be the dominant actors in international law, but they are not the only actors. In this chapter we consider the role of nonstate actors in international law: these include multinational corporations, public interest NGOs, and individuals. Nonstate actors have not been given a very large formal role in making, implementing, and/or enforcing international law, or in making judicial decisions on the basis of international law. In this chapter we will examine the ways in which nonstate actors nevertheless exert considerable influence on the rules, principles, and concepts of international law.

Nongovernmental Organizations

Strictly speaking, the acronym "NGO" encompasses all nongovernmental organizations, including public interest organizations, the vast majority of which are nonprofit organizations, and multinational corporations (MNCs), or multinational enterprises (MNEs), as they are now often termed. Examples of MNEs include large oil companies such as ExxonMobil and Shell, which wield political power primarily through sheer economic muscle. There are now a number of MNEs with greater economic weight than virtually all states; of the world's twenty largest economic entities approximately thirteen are states and seven, MNCs.[1] Examples of public interest NGOs include humanitarian NGOs such as CARE and Community Aid Abroad; human rights organizations such as Amnesty International; and environmental organizations such as Greenpeace. The International Chamber of Commerce is an NGO, as is the International Olympic Committee. Like intergovernmental organizations, the International Olympic Committee has a general assembly consisting of its members, a more limited governing body, and a permanent secretariat. However, its membership is not made up of representatives of states, or of the national Olympic committees, but of leading personalities from national and international sports.[2]

Just as there are enormous differences among states and among IGOs, so is there a huge variety of public interest NGOs. Public interest NGOs differ, for example, in the distribution of their membership, the way they operate, the ratio of paid staff to volunteers, and in whether or not they receive funding from governments. NGOs in the developed North tend to be wealthier and to have greater access to information than NGOs in the underdeveloped South.[3] International NGOs (INGOs) are sometimes distinguished from national NGOs; some believe that the acronym "NGO" should be reserved exclusively for those with members in at least three countries.[4] In recognition of the fundamental differences between MNCs and other types of NGOs, and of the widespread usage of the acronym "NGO" to refer only to public interest NGOs, the acronym "NGO" will be used here to refer only to nonprofit organizations.

Public interest NGOs can to some extent be perceived as the political counterweight to giant corporations. Although both are generally single-issue actors in contrast to states, which must deal with a multitude of issues, the ultimate objectives of each are in contrast. Corporations must necessarily focus on profits; public interest NGOs work for their perception of the common good. And though public interest NGOs are generally comparatively rich in legitimacy but capital-poor, profit-oriented organizations are generally capital-rich but lack legitimacy.[5]

There is a considerable discrepancy between the political influence wielded by MNEs and public interest NGOs and their formal roles in the system of public international law. We have seen that treaties are negotiated by states and by IGOs; the rights and obligations specified in multilateral treaties fall overwhelmingly on states; and the existence or not of a rule of customary international law is determined on the basis of state practice. Neither a public interest NGO nor an MNC can request an advisory opinion of the International Court of Justice or be a party to contentious proceedings before the ICJ, although a state may take up the claim of a corporation that has been created and is regulated by its laws. The ICJ has on one occasion permitted an NGO to file an amicus curiae brief in an advisory case, although the NGO in question failed to file on time.[6] At this stage it appears that the Court's rules would need to be amended to permit it to accept amicus filings in contentious cases.[7] Some other international courts and tribunals are more open to the involvement of MNCs and NGOs. NGOs have been permitted to appear before the International Criminal Tribunal for the Former Yugoslavia and have appeared before the European Court of Justice, the European Court of Human Rights, and the Inter-American Court of Human Rights.

Despite their small formal role in international law, NGOs and MNCs influence international law, often combining with other like-minded NGOs and MNCs working on the same issue to maximize that influence. The 1996 Advisory Opinion on the Legality of the Threat of Use of Nuclear Weapons, for example, received its impetus from the work of NGOs. Its origins were in the work of a small group of international jurists, who in March 1987 had written an open letter to the prime ministers of New Zealand and Australia.[8] The document "Case for the World Court" had then been circulated to all UN members having accredited representatives in New Zealand and Australia.[9] The World Court Project, an umbrella grouping of NGOs, was launched in May 1992, sponsored by the International Association of Lawyers Against Nuclear Arms, the International Peace Bureau, and International Physicians for the Prevention of Nuclear War.[10] Intensive lobbying by a network of antinuclear activists and NGOs and support from the Non-Aligned Movement[11] resulted in requests for an advisory opinion being produced by both the World Health Organization and the UN General Assembly.[12]

Transnational networking of NGOs has been greatly facilitated by the Internet. One thousand or so NGOs worked under an umbrella organization, the International Campaign to Ban Landmines, to bring about a multilateral treaty on landmines.[13] The Global Climate Coalition, to take an industry example, is a group of multinationals, which has sought a "voice for business in the global warming debate." The influence of NGOs and MNCs on multilateral treaty-making is often indirect. Knowledge is a source of power for many NGOs; some environmental NGOs, for example, possess greater scientific, technical, and statistical expertise than many governments. The vigorous opposition of Exxon to scientific evidence of human-induced climate change and to the Kyoto Protocol on global warming based on that evidence is likely to have influenced the decision of the U.S. government not to ratify the Kyoto Protocol; the Republican administration of George W. Bush was elected with the help of U.S.$1.2 million from ExxonMobil, and key officials within the administration formerly worked in the oil industry.[14] NGOs are sometimes accredited as observers at intergovernmental meetings at which treaties are negotiated. A notable example was the 1992 UN Conference on Environment and Development (UNCED), at which some 1,500 NGOs were formally recognized.[15]

Although the influence of NGOs and MNCs is usually thought of as indirect, in practice they may both exert a direct influence on treaty negotiations. NGO and corporate interests sometimes fund a delegation to, say, an international environmental conference; they may even write speeches and contribute directly to the formulation of national policy.[16] Of course, there may be more than one corporate interest on any specific issue. At the climate change negotiations, oil and gas interests were pitted against the insurance industry.[17]

Public interest NGOs play an important role in helping to implement, and monitor compliance with, international law, particularly in the fields of the environment and human rights. The bodies of the UN human rights treaties could not operate effectively without NGO participation.[18] NGOs channel independent information to the committees, promote knowledge and understanding of the committees' work, and monitor the implementation by governments of the recommendations of the treaty bodies.[19] Under article 8 of the Convention on Wetlands of International Importance, the International Union for the Conservation of Nature and Natural Resources was given the function of performing the secretariat's duties until the appointment of another organization or government.[20] Under article 8(3) of the Convention Concerning the Protection of the World Cultural and Natural Heritage, NGOs can attend, in an advisory capacity, the meetings of the UNESCO Intergovernmental Committee for the Protection of the Cultural and Natural Heritage.[21]

Public interest NGOs work closely with the United Nations. In the relief and refugee sector, for example, member governments may provide financial support and aid packages, but much of the work on the ground is subcontracted to NGOs.[22] The UN Charter, however, makes only one reference to NGOs. Article 71 provides that ECOSOC may make "suitable arrangements for consultation with non-governmental organizations which are concerned with matters within its competence." Arrangements were made in the late 1940s to bring article 71 into effect, and these have been reviewed in 1950, 1968, and 1996. There are three categories of NGO status at the United Nations. *General consultative status* is for large, international NGOs whose area of work covers most of the issues on the Council's agenda. *Special consultative status* is for NGOs that have special competence in a few fields of the Council's activity. *Inclusion on the roster* is for NGOs whose competence enables them to make occasional and useful contributions to the work of the United Nations and that are available for consultation upon request. NGOs with general status have the right to place items on the provisional agenda of the Council, and NGOs of general and special status may submit brief written statements that can be published as UN documents and circulated to members of the Council or subsidiary bodies.[23] As of 1996, NGOs that are based in a single country, known as national NGOs, have been encouraged to apply for consultative status.[24] NGOs have been particularly active in the work of some subsidiary bodies. The Working Group on Indigenous Populations is attended by nearly 1,000 NGOs annually and accepts statements from NGOs, mainly indigenous ones, even those that do not have consultative status.[25]

Two NGOs that have had a particular impact on the body of rules, principles, and concepts that constitute international law are the International Commission of Jurists and the International Committee of the Red Cross (ICRC). We will look at each in turn.

The International Commission of Jurists[26] is an international NGO whose global goal is to support and advance the international rule of law. The International Commission of Jurists achieves its mission through a variety of activities, including the promotion and monitoring of human rights mechanisms and the preparation of amicus curiae and legal opinions to build and strengthen human rights jurisprudence and influence policymakers. The International Commission of Jurists was, for example, influential in ensuring the timely entry into force of the African Charter of Human and Peoples' Rights. Members of the International Commission of Jurists engaged in a series of visits to the heads of state of African countries to help overcome doubts and fears regarding this charter.[27]

The International Committee of the Red Cross has played a major role in the development and implementation of international humanitarian law, having a more direct impact on both than any other NGO. ICRC fact-finding has paved the way for new treaty initiatives in the field of international humanitarian law. At the diplomatic conference at which a treaty text is to be finalized, the ICRC has been granted official access to plenary sessions and working groups as well as permission to speak directly to delegations, to issue official statements at meetings, and to submit draft articles; indeed it has on occasion functioned as a legal expert and unofficial cohost of conferences.[28] The ICRC concludes agreements with states concerning, for example, the visitation of

political detainees or the exchange of prisoners of war. The role of the
ICRC in the implementation of that law is explicitly provided for in
several of the treaties of international humanitarian law, including the
Geneva Conventions.

The ICRC was founded on the initiative of a Genevese merchant,
Henri Dunant, who in 1859 witnessed the Battle of Solferino in the
Italian War of Unification. He was shocked at the lack of systematic
care for the wounded, who were simply left to die on the battlefields,
often robbed and murdered by locals. Dunant organized volunteers to
care for the wounded and in 1862 published *A Memory of Solferino*.[29]
The next year a small group of Genevese established a committee to
propagate Dunant's ideal of an impartial corps of civilian volunteers to
care for the wounded in wartime, and this was the beginning of the
International Committee of the Red Cross.[30] The International Red
Cross movement consists of three interrelated components: the set of
National Red Cross Societies, the League of Red Cross Societies, and
the ICRC.

Although the ICRC has been included here among NGOs that have
been important to international law, it is unlike any other NGO; aspects
of its functioning are more akin to those of an IGO. The ICRC budget is
covered mostly by contributions from states; it has signed headquarters
agreements with more than fifty states; and ICRC delegates enjoy a status similar to that of officials from IGOs. But the ICRC is definitely not
an IGO; it is established under Swiss private law, and no government
has control over its composition or activity.[31]

The Individual as an Actor in International Law

Even though the state is by far the most important actor in international
law, individuals have some measure of what international lawyers refer
to as "legal personality," that is, being capable of exercising certain
rights and being subject to certain duties on their own account.[32] One
field of international law in which this has for centuries been the case is
that relating to diplomats. The field remained largely part of customary
international law for many years, until the 1961 Vienna Convention on
Diplomatic Relations provided a "comprehensive formulation of the
rules of modern diplomatic law."[33] The oldest established rule of diplomatic law is that the person of a diplomatic agent is inviolable.[34] This
was codified in article 29 as having two components. First, the individual is not liable to any form of arrest or detention; and second, the individual is to be treated with respect by the receiving state. The receiving

state is to "take all appropriate steps to prevent any attack on his person, freedom or dignity." Article 31 provides that a diplomatic agent has immunity from the criminal jurisdiction of the receiving state and its civil and administrative jurisdiction. It is intended to ensure that diplomats can play the role accorded to them. But diplomatic staff and other persons enjoying privileges and immunities do have some corresponding obligations toward the receiving state. Article 41 specifies the duty to respect laws and regulations of the receiving state, not to interfere in the internal affairs of the receiving state, to communicate with the government of the receiving state through the ministry of foreign affairs, and not to use the mission premises in any manner incompatible with the functions of the mission.

There is always a danger that the privileges and immunities may be abused. But the receiving state does have some comeback. By article 32 of the Vienna Convention, the sending state may expressly waive the immunity of a diplomatic agent. It is also open to the receiving state under article 9 at any time to declare a member of the diplomatic staff of a mission persona non grata, or that any other member of the staff of the mission is not acceptable. One celebrated case involved the shooting of a London police officer from the Libyan diplomatic mission in 1984. All the occupants of the Libyan People's Bureau were declared persona non grata and ordered to leave the country.[35] Concerned with the high level of illegal parking of diplomatic vehicles and the failure to pay resultant fines, the United Kingdom decided in the mid-1980s that continued failure to respect parking regulations or to pay fines would result in individuals being declared persona non grata. Although the decision of the UK government was without precedent, the number of parking tickets cancelled on grounds of diplomatic immunity fell from 108,845 in 1984 to 2,328 in 1993.[36]

In international law as a whole, it is the fields of international human rights and international humanitarian law that deal most with individuals.[37] The Nuremberg Tribunal following World War II established unequivocally that individuals receive obligations under international law and that international law must be enforced against individuals. Article 4 of the 1948 Convention on the Prevention and Punishment of the Crime of Genocide stipulates that "persons committing genocide . . . shall be punished, whether they are constitutionally responsible rulers, public officials or private individuals." Crimes against humanity and war crimes also incur individual criminal responsibility under international law.

Article 25 of the Rome Statute of the International Criminal Court

gives the Court jurisdiction over not only those individuals who have,
individually or jointly, committed a crime but also over those who have
ordered or induced such a crime; who have facilitated or contributed to
the commission of a crime or attempted to commit a crime (unless the
person gave up the criminal purpose without the crime having been
committed); or who have directly and publicly incited others to commit
genocide.[38] Well established in international law is the principle of
command responsibility, by which a superior—whether military or
civilian—is criminally responsible for the acts committed by subordinates if he or she knew or had reason to know that the subordinate was
about to commit such acts or had done so and the superior failed to take
the necessary and reasonable measures to prevent such acts or to punish
the perpetrators thereof.[39]

Although international human rights law does concern individuals,
the obligations of states toward individuals under international human
rights law is, strictly speaking, vis-à-vis other parties to the treaty in
question, rather than vis-à-vis its citizens. Individuals gain their rights
when the states concerned implement the relevant legal instrument
through legislation and acts of execution at the national level. A number
of human rights instruments provide for individuals to petition human
rights monitoring bodies, but this is generally the case only if the state
in question has accepted the treaty provision. An exception to this is the
Eleventh Protocol to the European Convention on Human Rights, which
entered into force on November 1, 1998, and by which citizens of states
that became parties to the convention can automatically take a case to
the European Court of Human Rights. And even though several human
rights treaties provide for one state to act against another accused of
committing human rights violations, in practice states have been very
reluctant to do so.

Individuals are in their own right important to the creation of international law since the writings of publicists are a secondary source of
international law. The first "comprehensive and systematic" treatise in
modern international law is considered to be *De Jure Belli ac Pacis,*
written by Hugo Grotius in 1625. Individuals serve on some international bodies, such as the International Law Commission and the Sub-
Commission on the Promotion and Protection of Human Rights, in their
own private capacity on the basis of their individual expertise rather
than as representatives of states. Judges on the International Court of
Justice are "independent"; article 2 of the ICJ Statute provides that the
judges be elected "regardless of their nationality from among persons of
high moral character, who possess the qualifications required in their

respective countries for appointment to the highest judicial offices, or are jurisconsults of recognized competence in international law."

Individuals are not able to be a party to a case before the ICJ or to ask an advisory opinion of the Court, but a state can bring a claim on behalf of one of its nationals. The *Ambatielos* case of 1953,[40] for example, involved the government of Greece taking up the claim of one of its nationals against the UK government. The involvement of individuals in international adjudication has more typically taken the form of special arbitration schemes to deal with claims from private parties against a specific country arising out of a specific event.[41] The U.S.-Iran Claims Tribunal was established following the Tehran hostage crisis and the restructuring of the Iranian economy. Although nationals of either party were entitled to access to the tribunal, there is no doubt that the tribunal was primarily established for the settlement of the claims of U.S. nationals against Iran.[42]

It is worth remembering that states, even though they retain a much more important formal role in the creation and operation of international law than individuals, are inanimate entities; it is in each case elites who make decisions on behalf of the state.

The Significance of a State-Centric
System of International Law in a Globalized World

Political scientists have for many decades debated whether the state is "withering away" at the hands of other international actors, in particular the MNC.[43] Despite the apparent increase in political and legal importance of other international actors vis-à-vis states, the formal workings of the system of international law retains a preeminent role for states. As we have seen, states play a leading role as the primary creators and subjects of international law. Other actors—such as the media—may often be influential in world politics without having a legal "personality" in international law. It is important to note, however, that while most writing on NGOs asserts their increasing political significance,[44] some writers have pointed out that the political influence of public interest NGOs is often assumed rather than established by empirical evidence.[45] It is clear that the role of nonstate actors in international law, and in world politics more generally, is a subject deserving of further research and debate.[46]

The discrepancy between the real-world influence of some nonstate actors and the formal supremacy of states is a challenge to the effectiveness of international law. Most wars, for example, are now civil wars rather than interstate wars. How, then, can state-based international humanitarian law, which addresses human rights during times of conflict, hope to regulate effectively the actions of players that are in many cases at war with the state?[47] A comparable challenge is faced by nonstate actors who are seeking to influence the evolution of international law. An NGO—or even the UN Secretary-General—who wants to ask an advisory opinion of the ICJ must at this stage work indirectly through an IGO.

Perhaps the most obvious implication of the dominance of states in international law is that all issues to be addressed by international law have to be transformed into issues between states, whether or not states are the key political player in the issue area under consideration. International law has thus responded to the acts of nonstate terrorist groups in terms of the legality of forceful responses by states to terrorist acts and the responsibility of a state to arrest and prosecute or extradite those who commit terrorist acts. Similarly, in the case of marine pollution, corporations are the main polluters of the world's oceans, but the current regulatory regime, negotiated by states, relies primarily on states taking measures to reduce and monitor oil pollution.[48]

In Chapter 5 we will explore in more detail how international law functions to address issues that arise in relationships among states and, to a lesser extent, the relationships among states and other international actors in world politics.

Notes

1. A list produced in 2002 showed General Electric as the twelfth largest economic entity; Microsoft was placed at position 13, ExxonMobil at 15, Wal-Mart at 16, Pfizer at 17, Citigroup Inc. at 18, and Intel at 20. All are U.S. corporations. The United States was the world's largest economic entity. *Sydney Morning Herald,* January 26–27, 2002, p. 26.

2. Christoph Vedder, "The International Olympic Committee: An Advanced Non-Governmental Organization and the International Law," *German Yearbook of International Law* 27 (1984): 233–258.

3. A. Doherty, "The Role of Nongovernmental Organizations in UNCED," in B. I. Spector, G. Sjöstedt, and I. W. Zartman, eds., *Negotiating International Regimes: Lessons Learned from the United Nations Conference on Environment and Development (UNCED)* (London: Graham & Trotman, 1994), pp. 199–218, 211–212.

4. Martin A. Olz, "Non-Governmental Organizations in Regional Human Rights Systems," *Columbia Human Rights Law Review* 28 (1997): 307–374, 314, n. 16.

5. Russel Lawrence Barsh and Nadia Khattak, "Non-Governmental Organisations in Global Governance: Great Expectations, Inconclusive

Results," in G. Alfredsson and M. Stravropoulou, eds., *Justice Pending: Indigenous Peoples and Other Good Causes* (The Hague: Martinus Nijhoff, 2002), pp. 15–31, 30.

6. "Amicus curiae" means literally "friend of the court." An amicus curiae brief is one filed to a court by a person or organization who is not a party to the case but who has an interest in the outcome.

7. Ruth Wedgwood, "Legal Personality and the Role of Non-Governmental Organizations and Non-State Political Entities in the United Nations System," in Rainer Hofmann, ed., *Non-State Actors as New Subjects of International Law. International Law: From the Traditional State Order Towards the Law of the Global Community*, proceedings of an International Symposium of the Kiel Walther-Schücking Institute of International Law, March 25–28, 1998 (Berlin: Ducker & Humblot, 1999), pp. 21–36, 25. See also Dinah Shelton, "The Participation of Non-Governmental Organizations in International Judicial Proceedings," *American Journal of International Law* 88 (1994): 611–642.

8. The origins of the process by which the ICJ came to address the question of the legality of nuclear weapons, between 1945 and 1987, are traced in Kate Dewes and Commander (ret.) Robert Green, "The World Court Project: How a Citizen Network Can Influence the United Nations," *Pacifica Review* 7, no. 2 (1995): 17–37, 18–20.

9. H. J. Evans, "The World Court Project on Nuclear Weapons and International Law," *New Zealand Law Journal* (July 1993): 249–252.

10. Ibid. For the story of how the questions came to be asked of the Court, see also Ved P. Nanda and David Krieger, *Nuclear Weapons and the World Court* (Ardsley, NY: Transnational, 1998), pp. 69–86.

11. Edda Kristjansdottir, "The Legality of the Threat or Use of Nuclear Weapons Under Current International Law: The Arguments Behind the World Court's Advisory Opinion," *International Law and Politics* 30 (1997–98): 291–368, 298–299.

12. Ibid., 291.

13. Gay Alcorn, "Canberra's Kyoto Stand Gives Comfort to US," *Sydney Morning Herald,* April 21–22, 2001, p. 17.

14. Julian Borger and Terry Macalister, "The Good Oil for Exxon Is Having a Buddy in the White House," *Sydney Morning Herald,* April 18, 2001, p. 10.

15. Dianne Otto, "Nongovernmental Organizations in the United Nations System: The Emerging Role of International Civil Society," *Human Rights Quarterly* 18 (1996): 107–141, 118.

16. Comments of Philippe Sands, in a panel session titled "The Challenge of Non-State Actors," chaired by Anne-Marie Slaughter, 92 *American Society of International Law Proceedings (ASIL Proc.)* 29 (1998).

17. Ibid.

18. See Anne F. Bayefsky, ed., *The UN Human Rights Treaty System in the 21st Century* (The Hague: Kluwer Law International, 2000), chaps. 13–17.

19. See Michael O'Flaherty, *Human Rights and the UN: Practice Before the Treaty Bodies* (London: Sweet and Maxwell, 1996), pp. 1–15. NGOs also

play an important role in regional human rights systems. See Olz, "Non-Governmental Organizations in Regional Human Rights Systems."

20. Convention on Wetlands of International Importance, October 12, 1972, 11 International Legal Materials (ILM) 963 (1972).

21. UNESCO Convention Concerning the Protection of the World Cultural and Natural Heritage, November 16, 1972, 11 ILM 1358 (1972).

22. Wedgwood, "Legal Personality," p. 23.

23. UN Secretary-General, "Arrangements and Practices for the Interaction of Non-Governmental Organizations in All Activities of the United Nations System," Report of the Secretary-General, UN Doc. A/53/170, July 10, 1998.

24. Peter Willetts, "From 'Consultative Arrangements' to 'Partnership': The Changing Status of NGOs in Diplomacy at the UN," *Global Governance* 6 (2000): 191–212, 192.

25. UN Secretary-General, "Arrangements and Practices."

26. See Howard B. Tolley Jr., *The International Commission of Jurists: Global Advocates for Human Rights* (Philadelphia: University of Pennsylvania Press, 1994).

27. C. Tomuschat, "General Course on Public International Law," *Recueil des Cours* 281 (1999): 312.

28. Louise Doswald-Beck, "Non-Governmental Entities in Treaty-Making," in V. Gowlland-Debbas, ed., *Multilateral Treaty-Making* (The Hague: Kluwer, 2000), pp. 41–44, 43; and David P. Forsythe, *Humanitarian Politics: The International Committee of the Red Cross* (Baltimore: Johns Hopkins University Press, 1977), p. 30.

29. H. Dunant, *A Memory of Solferino*, English ed. (Washington, DC: American Red Cross, 1959).

30. See Michael Ignatieff, "Unarmed Warriors," *The New Yorker,* March 24, 1997, pp. 54–71.

31. For discussion of the legal status of the ICRC, see Anton Schlögel, "IRC: International Red Cross," in Rüdiger Wolfrum and Christiane Philipp, eds., *United Nations: Law, Policies, and Practice*, vol. 2. (Doredrecht: Martinus Nijhoff, 1995), pp. 814–819.

32. P. K. Menon, "The International Personality of Individuals in International Law: A Broadening of the Traditional Doctrine," *Journal of Transnational Law & Policy* 1 (1992): 151–182, 152.

33. Eileen Denza, *Diplomatic Law: A Commentary on the Vienna Convention on Diplomatic Relations,* 2nd ed. (Oxford: Clarendon, 1998), p. 2.

34. Ibid., p. 210.

35. See J. Craig Barker, *The Abuse of Diplomatic Privileges and Immunities: A Necessary Evil?* (Aldershot, UK: Dartmouth, 1996).

36. Denza, *Diplomatic Law*, pp. 70–71.

37. See, inter alia, Thomas Graditzky, "Individual Criminal Responsibility for Violations of International Humanitarian Law Committed in Non-International Armed Conflicts," *International Review of the Red Cross* 322 (1998): 29–56; Edoardo Greppi, "The Evolution of Individual Criminal Responsibility Under International Law," *International Review of the Red Cross* 81 (1999): 531–552; Steven R. Ratner and Jason S. Abrams,

Accountability for Human Rights Atrocities in International Law, 2nd ed. (Oxford: Oxford University Press, 2001); and Louis B. Sohn, "The New International Law: Protection of the Rights of Individuals Rather Than States," *American University Law Review* 32 (1982): 1–64.

38. For discussion, see K. Kittichaisaree, *International Criminal Law* (Oxford: Oxford University Press, 2001), pp. 233–250.

39. Ibid., p. 251. This is found in article 28 of the ICC Statute.

40. *Ambatielos Case (Merits), Judgment, ICJ Reports 1953*, p. 10.

41. Neville March Hunnings, *The European Courts* (London: Cartermill, 1996), p. 6.

42. Wayne Mapp, *The Iran-United States Claims Tribunal: The First Ten Years 1981–1991: An Assessment of the Tribunal's Jurisprudence and Its Contribution to International Arbitration* (Manchester: Manchester University Press, 1993), p. 21.

43. See, inter alia, J. A. Camilleri and J. Falk, *The End of Sovereignty? The Politics of a Shrinking and Fragmented World* (Aldershot, UK: Edward Elgar, 1992); Goldblatt et al., "Economic Globalization and the Nation-State: Shifting Balances of Power," *Alternatives* 22 (1997): 269–285; S. Hobe, "Global Challenges to Statehood: The Increasingly Important Role of Nongovernmental Organizations," *Global Legal Studies Journal* 5 (1997): 191–209; M. Lind, "The Catalytic State," *National Interest* (Spring 1992): 3–12; S. Strange, "The Defective State," *Daedalus* 24 (Spring 1995): 55–74; L. Weiss, "Globalization and National Governance: Antimony or Interdependence?" *Review of International Studies* 25, no. 5 (1999): 59–88; David Held, "Globalization and the Liberal Democratic State," *Government and Opposition* 28, no. 2 (1993): 261–288; James Fulcher, "Globalisation, the Nation-State, and Global Society," *Sociological Review* 48, no. 4 (November 2000): 522–543; and Martin Wolf, "Will the Nation-State Survive Globalization?" *Foreign Affairs* 80 (January–February 2001): 178–190.

44. See, for example, Kal Raustiala, "States, NGOs, and International Environmental Institutions," *International Studies Quarterly* 41 (1997): 719–740.

45. Russel Lawrence Barsh and Nadia Khattak, "Non-Governmental Organisations in Global Governance: Great Expectations, Inconclusive Results," in Alfredsson and Stravropoulou, *Justice Pending,* pp. 15–31.

46. The journal *Non-State Actors and International Law* has been established to further understanding of nonstate actors in international law.

47. See Lindsay Moir, *The Law of Internal Armed Conflict* (Cambridge: Cambridge University Press, 2002).

48. See, inter alia, David S. Ardia, "Does the Emperor Have No Clothes? Enforcement of International Laws Protecting the Marine Environment," *Michigan Journal of International Law* 19 (Winter 1998): 497–567; and Emeka Duruigbo, "Reforming the International Law and Policy on Marine Oil Pollution," *Journal of Maritime Law and Commerce* 31, no. 1 (January 2000): 65–87, 85.

5

The Logical Structure
of International Law

Although it is important to note the extent to which international law can be understood only in relation to the political context within which it operates, it is just as vital to recognize the degree to which international law is a discrete entity distinguishable, even if with somewhat blurred boundaries, from the political milieu in which it operates. International law may be entwined with world politics, but it is not enmeshed. International law has considerable autonomy as a system of interrelated rules, principles, and concepts. The rules, principles, and concepts of international law can be found within the sources of international law that we considered in Chapter 1. They function as a medium of communication and interaction in world politics.

The constituent rules, principles, and concepts of international law can be divided into three groups on the basis of the subject matter they address. Since there is a logical interrelatedness between the ideas at the three levels, they can be depicted in a pyramid shape (see Figure 5.1). At the base is a theory or philosophy of international law that justifies and unifies the system of international law. Level 2 consists of a body of principles and rules that relates to the operation of the system of international law itself. And at Level 3 is the mass of rules, principles, and concepts concerning all the substantive issues that arise in relations among states (and, to a lesser extent, other international actors).

The wider bottom represents the foundational role played by the underlying philosophy of international law and the way in which each level builds logically on that below it. But in terms of quantity, the pyramid would be more accurate if drawn upside down, since the bulk of the content of the rules, principles, and concepts of international law pertains to world politics, as depicted at Level 3. The interrelationship

**Figure 5.1   International Law as a System of
                Interrelated Rules, Principles, and Concepts**

LEVEL THREE
Rules, principles,
and concepts per-
taining to the operation of
the system of world politics
(e.g., law relating to the use of
force; international aviation law)

LEVEL TWO
Rules, principles, and concepts
pertaining to the operation of the system
of international law (e.g., sources of international
law; law relating to the operation of the ICJ)

LEVEL ONE
The underlying philosophy/theory
of the system of international law (e.g., natural law; positivism)

of the ideas at the three levels of the system lends the system strength and cohesion and facilitates distinguishing ideas that are part of the pyramid from those that belong to other realms.

This chapter aims to introduce some of the substantive content of international law by looking at examples in these three levels and at the interrelationship between the three levels. Chapter 6 will show how elements from all three levels are combined in the construction of a legal argument.

Level 1: The Underlying Philosophy/
Theory of the System of International Law

If international law is to have cohesion as a set of interrelated ideas, there must be an underlying theory or philosophy of the system that answers such fundamental questions as where international law comes from and why a state should comply with a rule of international law. International lawyers have come up with two main answers to such questions: natural law and legal positivism. Positivism is currently the dominant philosophy, but elements of natural law thinking remain detectable in the system.

Natural Law

Advocates of a naturalist theory of law believe that there are principles of natural law that exist independently of people; the task for people is to find what the law is. Aristotle and the ancient Greeks are generally regarded as having first developed the concept of natural law, although it gained far greater prominence under the Romans.[1] The heyday of a naturalist theory of law was the sixteenth and seventeenth centuries. The Spaniards Vitoria (1486–1546) and Suarez (1548–1617) expounded a theological version of natural law by which law was merged with theology and God was the source of legal authority. But the best known of the naturalist writers was the Dutchman Hugo Grotius (1583–1645), often regarded as the founder of modern international law. Grotius enunciated a secular theory of natural law in his work *De Jure Belli ac Pacis* (1625), by which "the source of all law is mankind's native sense of justice, which corresponds with the needs of society since without a bond of mutual trust no association of any kind can exist."[2] According to Grotius:

> This maintenance of the social order . . . is the source of law properly so-called. To this sphere of law belong the abstaining from that which is another's, the restoration to another of anything of his which we may have, together with any gain which we may have received from it; the obligation to fulfil promises, the making good of a loss incurred through our fault, and the inflicting of penalties upon men according to their deserts.[3]

Customary international law is subordinate to natural law; "the binding force even of that part of [international law] that originates in consent is based on the law of nature as expressive of the social nature of man."[4] As for God:

> Natural law is the rule of right reason which teaches us that an act is just in so far as it conforms to natural reason, and morally just or unjust and consequently forbidden or commended by God himself as the Author of nature. This natural law does not change. God Himself cannot change the scheme of things so that two and two do not make four.[5]

Despite his emphasis on natural law, Grotius also drew on the "voluntary" law of nations, as evidenced in the practice of states, when it came to the detail of matters such as diplomatic immunities or the law of war. "The significance of the law of nature in [*De Jure Belli ac Pacis*] is that it is the ever-present source for supplementing the voluntary law of nations, for judging its adequacy in the light of ethics and reason, and for making the reader aware of the fact that the will of states cannot be the exclusive or even, in the last resort, the decisive source of the law of nations."[6]

Samuel Pufendorf (1632–1694), in contrast, denied that any international law could arise from custom or from treaties; the only international law that could exist was part of natural law.[7] In expounding his purely natural law conception of the law of nations, Pufendorf did not go into as much detail as Grotius as to just what the content of international law should be.[8] Indeed, it may well have been difficult to do so within a purely natural law framework. A naturalist philosophy of law works well to justify some legal rules but has a harder time with others. An adherent of a naturalist philosophy of law would likely claim, for example, that there is a universal prohibition on murder. But a prohibition on murder is one of the least contentious of all rules. And even here, it is difficult to determine if there should be any exceptions to the basic rule, and what, if any, they should be.[9] As a theory that might be called on to justify one interpretation of the law over another or to settle a fine point of law, a naturalist theory of law is inadequate. It could not, for example, readily settle a dispute as to whether a fishing zone extends five or seven kilometers from the shore. By 1700 the natural law theory of international law was beginning to lose favor. Several late-eighteenth-century jurists such as Moser and Martens attempted to reconcile natural law with the emergent positivism, but by the late nineteenth century key jurists such as Westlake and Hall were exclusively positivist.[10]

Positivism

Positivism is the belief that law is made by people. Positivists claim that people, rather than deduce the law that derives from some higher source, make rules. In a domestic situation the rules are likely to be made by either a legislative authority or a sovereign. In the international legal system states make the law. "International law is a law between states, which concerns states only and exclusively," wrote Lasso Oppenheim in 1908.[11] Positivists believe that because states make the law, law derives from the will of states; it is the fact that states have consented to international law that makes it obligatory. The importance to the modern system of international law of consent was explained by the Permanent Court of International Justice in the 1927 *Lotus* case: "International law governs relations between independent States. The rules of law binding upon States therefore emanate from their own free will as expressed in conventions or by usages generally accepted as expressing principles of law."[12]

In the early twentieth century U.S. international lawyers set out to develop a "science of international law," to be contrasted to natural law.[13] Writing in the second volume of the *American Journal of International Law*, Oppenheim sought to distinguish positivism from the natural law of Grotius:

> The fact that Grotius and many of his followers did start from the law of nature can not be authoritative for the method to be applied now-a-days when there are enough customary and conventional rules in existence for the construction of a fairly complete system of international law, and when we know that any rule of the so-called law of nature lacks all legal force and authority.
>
> Now, how are the existing recognized rules of international law to be ascertained?
>
> In so far as conventional rules are concerned, it is to a certain extent easy to find them. They are written rules. . . . However great the authority of a writer may be who asserts the existence of a rule, and be it Grotius himself, the science of international law has no right to lay down the rule concerned as really existent and universally or generally recognized unless it can be ascertained that the members of the family of nations have customarily or by a law-making treaty accepted the rule.[14]

Although positivists have sought to distance themselves from natural theory, and the two are often contrasted, in practice the two traditions have not been diametrically opposed. Although closely associated with the natural law tradition, Grotius has, for example, been subject to a wide variety of interpretations, not all of which portray his views as diametrically contrastable with positivism.[15] Despite the prominence today of positivism, there has been something of a scholarly revival of natural law thinking under the banner of *new natural law theory*.[16]

Positivism arguably provides a better philosophical basis for a sophisticated system of international law as we have it today because it is much easier to identify what the law is: the law is what states have constructed the law to be. But there is an obvious problem in practice, and it is the perennial problem for lawyers during the era of positivism. The positivist challenge has been how to distinguish international law from policy. If international law is what states construct international law to be, presumably because those involved perceive it to be in their interests, then how is it possible to make international law something more than a mere excuse for state behavior? Legal positivism must constantly work to establish a clear divide between what is in the realm of international law and what is politics if it is to be able to justify why states should comply with international law.

In their efforts to develop a system of international law that can be identified and justified as such, international lawyers have sought to exclude all nonlegal considerations. The set of interrelated ideas that we call "international law" is kept distinct from moral and religious ideas or ideas of natural justice. The key questions asked about a political action by a legal positivist are: Is the action in question legal? and Is this state or intergovernmental organization in compliance with international law? The answers provided are reasoned on the basis of the rules, principles, and concepts found within the sources of international law. In Chapter 1 these sources were identified as treaties, custom, general principles of law, judicial decisions, and the teachings of the most highly qualified publicists.

Refer to Figure 5.2 as an example of positivism in practice. Its subject is a sanctuary for whales in the Southern Ocean. The International Whaling Commission (IWC) was established by the 1946 International Convention for the Regulation of Whaling. In 1982 the IWC instituted what was effectively a moratorium on commercial whaling. In a further move to protect depleting whale stocks, the IWC established the Southern Ocean Whale Sanctuary in 1994 to protect Antarctic whale stocks from exploitation.[17] Although welcomed by many as a step forward in the protection of whales, the creation of the sanctuary was firmly opposed by Japan.

Japan claimed that the establishment of the sanctuary was illegal. In support of its position Japan drew on a legal analysis prepared by William Burke of the University of Washington (see Figure 5.2). As you read the analysis by Burke, try to view it solely as an example of a legal argument premised on positivism. First, note that it is providing an answer as to whether a certain action—in this case the designation of the Southern Ocean Whale Sanctuary—is or is not legal, and whether a particular actor—in this case the IWC—is or is not in compliance with the treaty by which it was founded. Underpinning this piece of writing is an assumption that action in world politics is capable of being categorized as either legal or illegal; the IWC is or is not in compliance with the treaty by which it established. Second, consider the way in which the writing develops an answer to the question of legality: it does so by drawing on the rules, principles, and concepts found within the

**Figure 5.2   Memorandum of Opinion on
the Legality of the Designation of the Southern
Ocean Sanctuary by the International Whaling Commission**

*by Professor William T. Burke,
School of Law, University of Washington*

This is a memorandum of opinion on the legality of the action taken
by the International Whaling Commission (IWC) in adoption [of] the
Southern Ocean Sanctuary. The specific legal issue is whether the
IWC complied with its basic charter, the International Convention for
the Regulation of Whaling (ICRW). The conclusion is that it did not,
considering the actions of the IWC and subsidiary bodies and the
requirements spelled out in Articles I and V. . . .

Applicable Law in the Light of the ICRW
The IWC has clear authority under its basic charter to establish a
sanctuary area. Article V(1) provides for adoption of amendments to
the Schedule "fixing (c) open and closed areas, including the designation of marine sanctuaries." Under Article 1, the Schedule is agreed to
be a part of the Convention which the Commission is authorized to
amend from time to time "in accordance with the provisions of Article
V." This provision of Article I raises the fundamental question
involved in the sanctuary, whether the Commission acted "in accordance with Article V."

    To comply with Article V(2), amendments to the Schedule (desig-
nation of a Sanctuary for present purposes) shall (a) "be such as are
necessary to carry out the objectives and purposes of the Convention
and to provide for the conservation, development and optimum utilization of the whale resources"; (b) "be based on scientific findings";
and (d) "take into consideration the interests of the consumers of
whale products and the whaling industry." In the actual text, the term
"shall" is appended to each one of these requirements, suggesting that
each is to be met when an amendment is adopted. It is apparent, however, that the third listed requirement is not a significant condition;
"shall take into consideration" is a formula that serves mainly as a
reminder of relevant interests rather than mandating satisfaction of
such interests. . . .

Notes
    Source: Presented to the 1995 annual meeting of the International Whaling
Commission by Japan as paper IWC/47/38 under agenda item 13. The memo-
randum is available on the Internet at www.highnorth.no/Library/
Management_Regimes/IWC/me-of-op.htm. It was published in *Ocean
Development and International Law* 27 (1996): 315–326.

sources of international law. In this extract the legal instrument in question is the International Convention for the Regulation of Whaling.

We will look at a longer example of positivism in practice once we have examined some of the content of the other two levels of the pyramid of ideas that constitute international law.

Level 2: International Law Pertaining to the Operation of the System of International Law

Any system of law must include rules about the operation of the legal system itself. International law must, for example, include rules regarding who can participate in the negotiation of a treaty, who can initiate proceedings before the International Court of Justice, how long a treaty will last, and so on. The answers given to such questions must be commensurate with the underlying philosophy of international law. Thus, for example, since positivism assumes states to be the principal actors in international law, it is likely to be states that are accorded the most important role in the formulation of a treaty's text. Questions pertaining to the sources of international law are themselves answered on the basis of the rules, principles, and concepts found in the sources of international law. Details of the international law on custom, for example, have been clarified in judgments of the International Court of Justice, as was shown in Figure 3.3. We will look at the law on ICJ jurisdiction as an example of the content of Level 2.

Jurisdiction of the ICJ

Because positivism is the philosophy underpinning the contemporary system of international law, the assumptions of positivism underpin law relating to the operation of the International Court of Justice. Positivism regards states as sovereign, and the related principle of consent stipulates that international law exists only because states have agreed to it. Applied to the jurisdiction of the ICJ, this means that the Court has jurisdiction only if states have given consent. A state's consent, however, is not always clear-cut. When considering whether or not to bring a case before the Court, states may be in disagreement not only over the substance of the dispute itself but over the question of whether or not the Court has jurisdiction to hear the case. Article 36(6) of the ICJ Statute provides that, in the event of a dispute as to whether the Court has jurisdiction, the matter is settled by a decision of the Court. A state against which proceedings have been initiated may well raise preliminary objections to the admissibility of the claim (whether the Court should reject the claim on some grounds other than its merits) and/or to the jurisdiction of the Court (whether the Court has the authority to hear the case in question). Although the possibility of raising preliminary objections is a necessary safeguard in the process, it also offers a useful tactic for a state that does not want the issue heard by the Court at all, or that hopes to slow down the process. About half the cases brought before the Court never reach the merits stage, at which is addressed the substance of the dispute.

Let us therefore go on to look at the rules, principles, and concepts pertaining to the jurisdiction of the ICJ. The two key documents relating to the operation of the ICJ are the ICJ Statute and the Rules of Court.[18] The ICJ Statute, an annex to the UN Charter, provides the broad framework within which the Court is to operate, whereas the Rules of Court detail its procedure. Article 30 of the UN Charter provides that "the Court shall frame rules for carrying out its functions. In particular, it shall lay down rules of procedure." The Rules of Court currently in force were adopted in 1978 and have subsequently been amended.

Under article 93(1) of the UN Charter all members of the UN are automatically parties to the Statute of the ICJ. The ICJ does not have jurisdiction over a state that is not a party to the ICJ Statute. A state that is not a member of the UN may become a party to the ICJ Statute on conditions to be determined in each case by the General Assembly upon the recommendation of the Security Council, or become a party to the ICJ Statute without being a member of the UN by accepting the conditions set out in article 93(2). Nauru and Switzerland became parties to the ICJ Statute without becoming members of the United Nations.[19]

Being a party to the ICJ Statute alone is not enough to give the Court jurisdiction over a case. A state must also have given its consent to the jurisdiction of the Court. A state may give the Court an "open slate" to decide any case brought against it, give its consent to decide only the particular case in question, or adopt a position somewhere between. There are four ways in which a state party to the ICJ Statute may indicate its consent to the jurisdiction of the ICJ.

Special agreement, or "compromis." States in a dispute with each other may agree to take that dispute to the ICJ. They will then negotiate a treaty containing the wording of the dispute as it is to be presented to the Court for a decision. This is a minimalist, case-by-case approach to consenting to the jurisdiction of the Court because consent relates only to the immediate dispute. The issues brought to the ICJ by this means tend not to have been the most highly charged politically[20] but also tend to be ones regarding which the Court's decision is respected, leading to the peaceful resolution of the dispute.[21] Cases initiated by agreement between the parties are indicated in the title of a case by a slash (/). They include the *Asylum* case (Colombia/Peru), the *Minquiers and Ecrehos* case (France/UK), and the *Continental Shelf* case (Tunisia/Libyan Arab Jamahiriya).

However, states do not always want a particular issue heard by the ICJ. This means that it is not always possible to negotiate a *compromis*. Instead, one state may elect to bring a case before the Court unilaterally. In its application instituting proceedings it must then demonstrate to the Court that the other party or parties have given their consent to its jurisdiction elsewhere. These cases are indicated by use of the abbreviations of the word "versus" in the title (e.g., *Cambodia v. Thailand*). There are three ways other than special agreement by which a state might be found to have consented to the jurisdiction of the Court. The first is by being a party to a treaty containing a compromissory clause.

Compromissory clause. More than 270 bilateral and multilateral treaties contain a clause providing that in the event of a dispute concerning the interpretation or operation of that treaty, the parties will take the matter to the ICJ. Such a clause is called a *compromissory clause*. Treaties containing a compromissory clause include the Convention Relating to the Status of Refugees (1951); the Treaty of Peace with Japan (1951); the Convention on the Elimination of All Forms of Racial Discrimination (CERD, 1966); and the United Nations Framework Convention on Climate Change (1992).[22] The UN Charter does not contain such a clause.

A good example of a compromissory clause in a multilateral treaty is found in article 9 of the Genocide Convention:

> Disputes between the Contracting Parties relating to the interpretation, application or fulfilment of the present Convention, including those relating to the responsibility of a State for genocide or any of the other acts enumerated in Article 3, shall be submitted to the International Court of Justice at the request of any of the parties to the dispute.

Sometimes when a state agrees to be bound by a treaty, it enters a reservation to the compromissory clause, which means that the clause is an exception to which the state has not consented. This makes it possible for a state to be a party to a treaty with a compromissory clause without consenting to the jurisdiction of the Court to decide matters arising from the implementation of that treaty.

Article 36(2) of the ICJ Statute. Article 36(2) is the so-called optional clause and constitutes the second basis on which the Court might find that a state has consented to jurisdiction other than through a special agreement. When the ICJ was being planned, some wanted it to have compulsory jurisdiction and some did not. Article 36(2) was the agreed compromise by which a state can choose to give its consent to ICJ jurisdiction ahead of any dispute.[23]

Article 36(2) of the ICJ Statute states:

> The States parties to the present Statute may at any time declare that they recognise as compulsory *ipso facto* and without special agreement, in relation to any other States accepting the same obligation, the jurisdiction of the Court in all legal disputes concerning:
> a.   the interpretation of a treaty;
> b.   any question of international law;
> c.   the existence of any facts which, if established, would constitute a breach of an international obligation;
> d.   the nature or extent of the reparation to be made for the breach of an international obligation.

Declarations of the acceptance of the compulsory jurisdiction of the Court under article 36(2) are published in the *Yearbook of the International Court of Justice*. In 1995 the minister of foreign affairs of the Republic of Georgia, Alexander Chikvaidze, made the following declaration:

> I have the honour on behalf of the Republic of Georgia to declare that, in accordance with paragraph 2 of Article 36 of the Statute of the International Court of Justice, the Republic of Georgia recognizes as compulsory *ipso facto* and without special agreement, in relation to any other State accepting the same obligation, the jurisdiction of the Court in all legal disputes referred to in paragraph 2 of Article 36 of the Statute of the International Court of Justice.[24]

It is rare for a state not to include in its declaration some limits on the sorts of cases it is prepared to have the Court hear. Specified exceptions are referred to as "reservations." Some of the most common types of reservations that states have included in their declarations under article 36(2) are:

- Temporal. If a state does not place some time limits on its acceptance of the Court's jurisdiction, that acceptance will apply to all cases, whether or not the dispute began before the declaration was made. A state may stipulate, for example, that its declaration will not enter into force immediately; or that the declaration may cover only a limited time—say, the next five years.

Alternatively, the declaration may only include disputes arising after a certain date or those in which the "situations or facts giving rise to a dispute" are subsequent to a particular date.

- Subject matter. A declaration sometimes includes a reservation to particular topics about which the state does not want the Court to hear a dispute, or occasionally it will refer only to topics on which the state is prepared to have the Court hear a case. Reservations as to subject matter often relate to territorial issues. Egypt's 1957 declaration accepts the jurisdiction of the ICJ only should a dispute arise involving the Egyptian control and management of the Suez Canal.

- Multilateral treaty reservation (the Vandenburg reservation). This was first used by the United States in 1946. It excludes disputes arising under a multilateral treaty unless: all parties to the treaty affected by the decision are also parties to the case before the Court; or the United States specifically agrees to jurisdiction.

- Regarding particular states. A state may include a reservation to disputes with particular states. The UK declaration has included a reservation to disputes with the government of any other country that is a member of the British Commonwealth.[25]

- Domestic jurisdiction reservation. This was first used in the UK's 1929 declaration of jurisdiction of the PCIJ, which excluded "disputes with regard to questions which by international law fall exclusively within the jurisdiction of the UK." Many regard this reservation as redundant. It is a general principle of international law that an international court has no jurisdiction over domestic issues.

- Another type of domestic jurisdiction reservation is the "self-judging" (or Connally) reservation. This was first used by the United States, which in 1946 exempted from the Court's compulsory jurisdiction "disputes with regard to matters [that] are essentially within the domestic jurisdiction of the [United States] as determined by the [United States]." There has been widespread debate regarding the validity of this type of domestic jurisdiction reservation. Many agree with Sir Hersch Lauterpacht in his minority opinion in the *Norwegian Loans* case that it is contrary to article 36(6) of the statute; in the event of a dispute regarding jurisdiction the Court will determine the issue. In the 1986 *Nicaragua* case, Judge Stephen M. Schwebel said that, while continuing to see "great force" in the position of

Lauterpacht, he appreciated the argument that "since declarations incorporating self-judging provisions apparently have been treated as valid, certainly by the declarants, for many years, the passage of time may have rendered Judge Lauterpacht's analysis less compelling today than when it was made."[26]

- On condition of reciprocity. Many states include a condition of reciprocity in their declaration. Article 36(3) allows a state a choice as to whether its declaration is to be on condition of reciprocity, although some international lawyers consider this reservation unnecessary because article 36(2) provides that the optional clause applies only "in relation to any other state accepting the same obligation."[27]

In the *Norwegian Loans* case (1957) the ICJ allowed Norway to draw on the reservations in the declaration of France and hence deny the jurisdiction of the Court. The case arose from a dispute regarding a French loan to Norway. It had been agreed that France could ask to be repaid in gold; later, concerned with its gold supplies, Norway passed legislation withdrawing the convertibility of the krone; France wanted the matter settled by the ICJ, whereas Norway argued that it could be settled by municipal courts. The French declaration included a reservation to "all matters within its domestic jurisdiction as it understood that phrase." Norway was able to rely on the French declaration to avoid the jurisdiction of the Court. In the *Interhandel* case (1959) the Court explicitly recognized that a state may invoke a reservation contained in the declaration of the other party to the dispute.[28]

There has been an increase in the number of states accepting the compulsory jurisdiction of the ICJ, from twenty-three in 1945 to forty-five in 1975, to sixty-three in 2002, although this is not an increase as a proportion of the total number of states. States that had accepted the optional clause (with or without reservations) as of 1999 are Australia, Austria, Barbados, Belgium, Botswana, Bulgaria, Cambodia, Cameroon, Canada, Costa Rica, Cyprus, Democratic Republic of the Congo, Denmark, Dominican Republic, Egypt, Estonia, Finland, Gambia, Georgia, Greece, Guinea, Guinea-Bissau, Haiti, Honduras, Hungary, India, Ivory Coast, Japan, Kenya, Lesotho, Liberia, Liechtenstein, Luxembourg, Madagascar, Malawi, Malta, Mauritius, Mexico, Nauru, Netherlands, New Zealand, Nicaragua, Nigeria,

Norway, Pakistan, Panama, Paraguay, Philippines, Poland, Portugal, Senegal, Somalia, Spain, Sudan, Suriname, Swaziland, Sweden, Switzerland, Togo, Uganda, United Kingdom of Great Britain and Northern Ireland, Uruguay, and Yugoslavia.

Why would a state choose to agree ahead of time to have a case against it heard by the Court? Perhaps because a state cannot take another state to Court on the basis of article 36(2) unless it has itself accepted the clause. In addition, states are sometimes keen to demonstrate their faith in the system and preparedness to have their own actions held up to judicial scrutiny.

States have sometimes withdrawn their acceptance but, within a short space of time, replaced it with a new one, usually with an additional or modified reservation. Canada used such a tactic in relation to its concerns regarding marine pollution in waters off the Canadian Arctic coast. Canada's 1970 Arctic Waters Pollution Prevention Act gave the Canadian government wide powers to regulate shipping up to 100 nautical miles off its Arctic coast. No doubt concerned that another state would claim that this was not consistent with existing international law, Canada added a reservation to its declaration under article 36(2) so as to exclude from the Court's compulsory jurisdiction "disputes arising out of or concerning jurisdiction or rights claimed or exercised by Canada in respect of the conservation, management or exploitation of the living resources of the sea, or in respect of the prevention or control of pollution or contamination of the marine environment in marine areas adjacent to the coast of Canada." Prime Minister Pierre Trudeau explained that there was a "very grave risk that the World Court would find itself obliged to find that coastal States cannot take steps to prevent pollution. Such a legalistic decision would set back immeasurably the development of law in this critical area."[29] Canada's unilateral move appears to have been an important factor in changing customary international law with respect to the rights of coastal states to introduce and enforce pollution prevention measures beyond the territorial sea.[30] In 1994 Canada again amended its declaration when it amended the Coastal Fisheries Protection Act.[31]

Since 1951 a number of declarations have expired, been withdrawn, or been terminated without being replaced. These have included the declarations of Bolivia, Brazil, China, El Salvador, France, Guatemala, Iran, Israel, South Africa, Thailand, Turkey, and the United States. The withdrawal of the United States from the compulsory jurisdiction of the Court came in 1985, a U.S. reaction to the 1984 decision of the Court in the *Nicaragua* case (jurisdiction and admissibility).[32] This case concerned a dispute that arose from military and paramilitary activities in Nicaragua and in the waters off its coasts, responsibility for which was attributed by Nicaragua to the United States. In its application instituting proceedings, Nicaragua relied on article 36 of the ICJ Statute and the declarations accepting the compulsory jurisdiction of the Court of itself and the United States to establish that the Court had jurisdiction to hear the case. The United States argued against the Court having jurisdiction, but much to the anger of the United States, the ICJ found that it did indeed have jurisdiction. The United States did not participate further in the proceedings and in 1985 terminated its optional clause declaration.

The U.S. secretary of state, George Shultz, in a letter to the UN Secretary-General, stated:

> I have the honor on behalf of the Government of the United States of America to refer to the declaration of my Government of 26 August 1984, concerning the acceptance by the United States of America of the compulsory jurisdiction of the International Court of Justice, and to State that the aforesaid declaration is hereby terminated, with effect six months from the date hereof.[33]

This left the UK as the only remaining permanent member of the Security Council to have accepted the optional clause.

Forum prorogatum. The third means by which a state might indicate its consent to ICJ jurisdiction is under the doctrine of *forum prorogatum,* whereby the parties consent by separate acts expressly or impliedly accepting jurisdiction, one of those acts being the making of a unilateral application under article 40(1) of the ICJ Statute.[34] This means that a state may submit a dispute to the Court under article 40(1) of the ICJ Statute on the basis of forum prorogatum even if the other state has not yet validly recognized jurisdiction. The other state may then give its consent implicitly by, for example, making a submission to the Court on the merits of the case.

An example of an attempt to bring a case to the ICJ on the basis of forum prorogatum is the *Antarctica* cases of 1956.[35] After World War II, the United Kingdom, Chile, and Argentina claimed title to overlapping pieces of territory in Antarctica. Attempts to resolve the dispute by diplomatic means having been unsuccessful, the UK proposed on a number of occasions that the ICJ be asked to rule on the matter. On May

4, 1955, the United Kingdom instituted proceedings before the Court against Argentina and Chile, although in its application to the Court the UK recognized that, as far as it was aware, Argentina and Chile had not yet accepted the Court's jurisdiction. Neither Argentina nor Chile was prepared to have the matter heard by the Court; they did not regard the question as one amenable to compromise. In a note of August 1, 1955, Argentina informed the Court of its refusal to accept the Court's jurisdiction to deal with the case. In these circumstances, the Court found that neither Chile nor Argentina had accepted its jurisdiction to deal with the cases. The Court removed the cases from its list on March 16, 1956. The issue of overlapping asserted sovereignties in the area of Antarctica opposite South America remains unresolved to this day, the 1959 Antarctic Treaty providing for the parties to agree to disagree on the question of Antarctic sovereignty.

The Rules of Court now provide in article 38(5) that an application based on forum prorogatum will be transmitted to the state against which the application is made, but not entered onto the general list of the Court, or any action be taken in the proceedings, unless and until the state against which such an application is made consents to the jurisdiction of the Court for the purposes of the case.

Level 3: International Law Pertaining to Substantive Issues in World Politics

Level 3 of the system of rules, principles, and concepts that constitute international law pertains to substantive issues in relations among states and, to a lesser extent, other international actors. There is thus international law dealing with postal services, telecommunications, regulation of air travel, international trade, and so on. Perhaps the central substantive issue addressed by contemporary international law is the use of force. The prevention of the use of force by aggressor states is a goal shared by international law and the United Nations. Both seek to do a lot more than prevent the use of force—the UN deals with education, poverty alleviation, and other pressing issues, and international law covers technical fields such as postal arrangements and virtually every issue in relations between states. But international law and the United Nations are commonly judged to a very considerable extent on their capacity to keep world peace. Philip Alston has referred to a right to peace as the raison d'être of modern international law;[36] J. L. Brierly referred to establishing and maintaining a distinction between the legal and the illegal use of force as the "primary task of all legal systems."[37] The UN Charter aimed "to save succeeding generations from the scourge of war" and provided rules as to when force is and is not permissible.

International law has not always opposed the initiation of war. In fact, rules outlawing the use of war as a means of settling disputes are relatively new in the evolution of international law. Naturalist lawyers such as Aquinas and Augustine argued for a distinction between just and unjust wars, maintaining that, in the natural sphere of things, it was sometimes moral to go to war. But this distinction never became a part of modern, positivist international law.[38] In the years after the peace of Westphalia, war was accepted as part of the political reality; indeed, the right to resort to arms was considered an important attribute of state sovereignty.[39] During the era of colonization from the seventeenth to the nineteenth centuries, for example, international law regulated the acquisition of territory by European states. Where the Europeans encountered a political unit interacting with other political units in a manner to which the European state could relate—in the East Indies, for example—international law required that the unit be respected as a like form of legal entity. Relations were conducted with it on the basis that it was an international political-legal unit in its own right. But international law did not forbid war. It was acceptable, where necessary, to utilize force against foreign political units, as long as that war was conducted in accordance with contemporary legal standards. Older than the international law pertaining to whether or not force can be used (*jus ad bellum*) was thus a body of law imposing limitations on the conduct of hostilities (*jus in bello*).[40]

The horrors of World War I led to attempts to limit the instances in which states could resort to the use of force. By article 12(1) of the Covenant of the League of Nations members agreed that "if there should arise between them any dispute likely to lead to a rupture, they will submit the matter either to arbitration or to inquiry by the Council, and they agree in no case to resort to war until three months after the award by the arbitrators or the report by the Council." By article 13(4) members agreed to "not resort to war against a Member of the League which complies" with the award rendered. The fact that states were required to submit to certain procedures of peaceful dispute settlement did not, however, displace the assumption that war was a right of a sovereign state.[41] The trouble with the phrase "resort to war" was that, in the conflict between China and Japan between 1937 and 1941, for example, all involved were able to maintain the fiction that, despite the hostilities, the fact that there had been no declaration of war[42] meant that actual war did not exist.[43]

The General Treaty for the Renunciation of War,[44] also known as the Kellogg-Briand Pact and Pact of Paris (1928), marked another major milestone in the evolution of *jus ad bellum*.[45] This was the first time that states recognized a comprehensive prohibition of war as an instrument of national policy. Article I of the General Treaty for the Renunciation of War stated:

> The High Contracting Parties solemnly declare in the names of their respective peoples that they condemn recourse to war for the solution of international controversies, and renounce it as an instrument of national policy in their relations with one another.

This meant that states could still distinguish between use of force and an actual declaration of war; it was not clear as to whether the treaty prohibited armed force short of war.[46] Sixty-three states, virtually the entire international community at that time, were parties to the treaty when World War II started in 1939.[47]

Following World War II, international law took another major step in the direction of forbidding armed conflict. This time it was not war, but the use of force, that was outlawed. Article 2(4) of the UN Charter stated:

> All members shall refrain in their international relations from the threat or use of force against the territorial integrity or political independence of any State, or in any other manner inconsistent with the Purposes of the United Nations.

This remains the general rule, to which there are two exceptions. The first is self-defense. The right to defend oneself if attacked is a part of customary international law and could be said to be a part of natural law. Article 51 of the UN Charter states:

> Nothing in the present Charter shall impair the inherent right of individual or collective self-defence if an armed attack occurs against a Member of the United Nations, until the Security Council has taken measures necessary to maintain international peace and security. Measures taken by Members in the exercise of this right of self-defence shall be immediately reported to the Security Council and shall not in any way affect the authority and responsibility of the Security Council under the present Charter to take at any time such

actions as it deems necessary in order to maintain or restore international peace and security.

Customary international law fills in much of the detail regarding the law of self-defense, in particular that the key requirements of an act of self-defense are *necessity* and *proportionality*. These were part of pre-Charter customary international law and date from correspondence between Great Britain and the United States in 1841–1842, in what is known as the *Caroline* case. Webster of the United States wrote to Fox: "It will be for . . . [Her Majesty's] Government to show a necessity of self-defence, instant, overwhelming, leaving no choice of means, and no moment for deliberation." The UK acquiesced in that test for the legality of an act of self-defense.[48] The customary law requirements of necessity and proportionality were confirmed by the ICJ in the 1986 *Nicaragua* case.[49] The *Nicaragua* case also confirmed that the right to collective self-defense, which allows a nonattacked state to lend assistance to an attacked state,[50] must involve the state in question believing that it is the victim of an armed attack and requesting such assistance.[51]

Although there is universal acceptance of the right to self-defense, the question of the timing of actions taken in self-defense is not so clear-cut. Article 51 expresses it in terms of "if an armed attack occurs," but some believe that self-defense can be "anticipatory"—that is, one can take action in anticipation of a likely future attack rather than wait for the attack to begin. It is of course difficult to "prove" that there will be an attack before it has happened. The 2002 *National Security Strategy of the United States of America* appeared to make reference to a right of anticipatory self-defense when it referred to pre-emption:

> The United States has long maintained the option of preemptive actions to counter a sufficient threat to our national security. The greater the threat, the greater is the risk of inaction—and the more compelling the case for taking anticipatory action to defend ourselves, even if uncertainty remains as to the time and place of the enemy's attack. To forestall or prevent such hostile acts by our adversaries, the United States will, if necessary, act preemptively.
>
> The United States will not use force in all cases to preempt emerging threats, nor should nations use preemption as a pretext for aggression. Yet in an age where the enemies of civilization openly and actively seek the world's most destructive technologies, the United States cannot remain idle while dangers gather.[52]

Although it is possible to argue that anticipatory self-defense is legal as long as it meets the *Caroline* standards of necessity and proportionality, the mainstream view is strongly against a right of anticipatory self-defense.[53] It is perhaps largely because of strong opposition to anticipatory self-defense that the United States, the United Kingdom, and Australia did not present their use of force against Iraq beginning on March 20, 2003, as an act of self-defense. They instead justified it in terms of UN Security Council Resolutions 678, 687, and 1441,[54] prompting considerable debate as to its legality.[55]

Security Council authorization for the use of force constitutes the second exception to the prohibition on the use of force in the UN Charter.[56] Article 42 states:

> Should the Security Council consider that measures provided for in Article 41 [complete or partial interruption of economic relations and of rail, sea, air, postal, telegraphic, radio, and other means of communication, and the severance of diplomatic relations] would be inadequate or have proved to be inadequate, it may take such action by air, sea, or land forces as may be necessary to maintain or restore international peace and security. Such action may include demonstrations, blockade, and other operations by air, sea, or land forces of Members of the United Nations.

There is some discussion among international lawyers regarding whether there is a customary rule permitting the use of force without a Security Council resolution in the event of gross violations of human rights. The appropriateness of there being a right of "humanitarian intervention"[57] finds support in scholarly writings from as early as the seventeenth century, when Hugo Grotius wrote that "where [tyrants] provoke their people to despair and resistance by unheard of cruelties, having themselves abandoned all the laws of nature, they lose the rights of independent sovereigns, and can no longer claim the privilege of the law of nations."[58] In terms of positivist international law, the crystallization of a customary law of humanitarian intervention would require sufficient instances of states intervening in areas of humanitarian crisis, interventions that had been accompanied by the necessary *opinio juris*. Some international lawyers believe that customary international law predating the Charter permitted humanitarian intervention;[59] but others consider that pre-Charter state practice illustrates a paucity of evidence of a general right of humanitarian intervention in customary international law. The three main examples of allegedly humanitarian intervention in the nineteenth century are: the joint intervention of Great Britain, France, and Russia in aid of Greek insurgents in 1827; the French occupation of Syria in 1860–1861; and the U.S. intervention in Cuba during the Spanish-American War of 1898.[60]

The majority of international lawyers do not consider that the right, if it existed, survived the Charter's general prohibition on the use of force.[61] Article 2(4) makes no explicit reference to humanitarian intervention. The two most discussed cases of humanitarian intervention between the UN Charter of 1945 and the NATO intervention during the Kosovo crisis are those of the Indian intervention in East Pakistan leading to the secession of East from West Pakistan in 1971, and Tanzania's intervention in Uganda in 1979 to overthrow Idi Amin's regime. It is unlikely that the requisite *opinio juris* was present in either case; indeed, both India and Tanzania quoted the right to self-defense under article 51 rather than a right or obligation of humanitarian intervention.[62] Examples of humanitarian intervention by the United Nations since the end of the Cold War—Bosnia-Herzegovina, Somalia, and Rwanda—were UN actions authorized by the Security Council. Also countering the idea of an existing customary international law of humanitarian intervention is the fact that there have been numerous examples of human rights atrocities since World War II that did not meet with an international response.[63]

The Autonomy of International Law Versus Its Entwining with World Politics

In this chapter we have stepped inside the pyramid of rules, principles, and concepts that constitute international law to look at some of the content in the three levels. We have seen that legal positivism has as its most basic premise that law is made by people and that positivism, as the underlying philosophy of the system, assumes that international law derives from the will of sovereign states. In seeking to exclude all "nonlegal" factors from legal analysis, positivism assumes that any answer to the legality of an action or the compliance of a state (if at Level 3), or to the operation of an aspect of the system of international law (if at Level 2), can be answered on the basis of the rules, principles, and concepts found within the sources of international law. As an example of international law at the third of these levels, we have looked at international law on the use of force.

The exclusion of nonlegal factors from positivist legal argument lends considerable autonomy to the system of interrelated ideas that constitutes international law. Although they may not think of their task in these terms, international lawyers work hard to retain the relative autonomy and cohesion of the system of ideas that constitutes international law. In recent years, for example, there have been efforts to develop a clear-cut definition of "indigenous persons" in international law.[64] This is a very difficult endeavor, but as a system international law requires such efforts because of the need of legal positivism to distinguish the legal from the political, anthropological, and everyday uses of the word.[65] A similar endeavor has been going on for a number of years in relation to the legal definition of "terrorism";[66] the truism bears out that one person's terrorist is another's freedom fighter. Instead of one comprehensive convention, a patchwork of treaties has appeared over the years, most of which address specific types of terrorist actions (see Figure 5.3); following the 1988 bombing of Pan Am flight 103, for example, states negotiated the Convention on the Marking of Plastic Explosives for the Purpose of Identification. In the aftermath of September 11, 2001, UN Secretary-General Kofi Annan expressed the hope that renewed efforts to conclude a comprehensive convention on terrorism would shortly produce success. But hopes for an immediate breakthrough were dashed, primarily because of the long-standing problem of definition.[67]

Aspects of international law where the boundary is not clear-cut come under criticism and elicit proposals for change. Customary international law, for example, is sometimes criticized for not being sufficiently distinguishable from policy.[68] The lack of precision in the international law on humanitarian intervention, as highlighted by events during the Kosovo crisis, prompted debate regarding the merits of codifying the law of humanitarian intervention and what the suitable criteria for its legality might look like.[69]

Although there is an ongoing process by which the boundary between the rules, principles, and concepts of international law are distinguished from those of politics, there may be some blurring of that boundary. The term "soft law" is sometimes used to designate an ambiguous zone at the boundary of international law and politics. It is used to refer to political norms that may nevertheless appear to function as "quasilaw," or law-in-the-making, as well as to the contents of a treaty or other clearly legal source where those provisions are vague or weak.[70] "Nonlegal soft law"[71] is found primarily in the economic and environmental branches of international law and includes industry

Figure 5.3   Global Multilateral Treaties on Terrorism

1963 Convention on Offences and Certain Other Acts Committed on Board Aircraft
1970 Convention for the Suppression of Unlawful Seizure of Aircraft
1971 Convention for the Suppression of Unlawful Acts Against the Safety of Civil Aviation
1973 Convention on the Prevention and Punishment of Crimes Against Internationally Protected Persons, Including Diplomatic Agents
1979 International Convention Against the Taking of Hostages
1980 Convention on the Physical Protection of Nuclear Material
1988 Protocol for the Suppression of Unlawful Acts of Violence at Airports Serving International Civil Aviation, Supplementary to the Convention for the Suppression of Unlawful Acts Against the Safety of Civil Aviation
1988 Convention for the Suppression of Unlawful Acts Against the Safety of Maritime Navigation
1988 Protocol for the Suppression of Unlawful Acts Against the Safety of Fixed Platforms Located on the Continental Shelf
1991 Convention on the Marking of Plastic Explosives for the Purpose of Identification
1997 International Convention for the Suppression of Terrorist Bombings
1999 International Convention for the Suppression of the Financing of Terrorism

codes of conduct, "declarations," resolutions of international organizations, and non–legally binding agreements between states.[72] The final act of the 1975 Conference on Security and Cooperation in Europe (the Helsinki Final Act),[73] for example, declared the determination of the parties to "act in accordance with the provisions contained in the above texts" but also stipulated that the document "is not eligible for registration under Article 102 of the Charter of the United Nations" as it would if it had been a treaty. Of course from a positivist perspective "it remains essential to maintain the distinction between the law *de lege lata* and the law *de lege ferenda*, between the codification of existing law and the progressive development of law, between legal norms and non-legal norms as regards their binding effect, and ultimately between the legal system and the political system."[74]

The relative autonomy of the system of international law depends not only on the retention of a sharp delineation between "law" and "politics" or "morality" but also on the continued cohesiveness of the contents of the system of international law. This cohesion derives from the logical interrelationship between ideas at the three levels of international law. One of the key concepts in legal positivism is consent. Its influence on law at other levels can most readily be seen in debates relating to the operation of the system of international law (i.e., at Level 2). A fundamental principle of the law of treaties, for example, is that treaties are binding only on those states that are parties to that treaty. This could not be otherwise if the law of treaties is to be consistent with the principle of consent, which is integral to legal positivism.

The interrelatedness of the ideas at all three levels of international law means that international law cannot change fundamentally on any one level without implications for international law at other levels. We have seen how the principle of consent pervades not only the law of treaties but also that of the International Court of Justice. Proposals to improve international law commonly contain the proposition that the ICJ should have compulsory jurisdiction, that states accused of breaching international law be compelled to appear before the Court. In this chapter we have demonstrated that unless the system is to be left with internal inconsistencies, which would likely weaken its normative force,[75] such a change could not be implemented without it forcing some corresponding change in the philosophy underpinning the system of international law as a whole.

Notes

1. Robert J. Beck, Anthony Clark Arend, and Robert D. Vander Lugt, eds., *International Rules: Approaches from International Law and International Relations* (New York and Oxford: Oxford University Press, 1996), p. 34.

2. C. G. Roelofsen, "Grotius and International Law: An Introduction to Some Themes in the Field of the Grotian Studies," in L. E. Van Holk and C. G. Roelofsen, eds., *Grotius Reader: A Reader for Students of International Law and Legal History* (The Hague: T. M. C. Asser Institut, 1983), p. 17.

3. Cited in James Brown Scott, "Introduction," in Hugo Grotius, *The Law of War and Peace,* translated by Francis W. Kelsey (Indianapolis: Bobbs-Merrill, 1925), p. xxxv.

4. H. Lauterpacht, "The Grotian Tradition in International Law," *British Year Book of International Law 1946*: 1–53, 21.

5. Scott, "Introduction," p. xxxiii.

6. Lauterpacht, "The Grotian Tradition," pp. 21–22.

7. Hans Wehberg, "Introduction," in Samuel Pufendorf, *Elementorum Jurisprudentiae Universalis Libri Duo,* vol. 2, translated by William Abbott Oldfather (Buffalo: William S. Hein, 1995), p. xv.

8. Ibid., pp. xiv–xv.

9. Cf. the discussion in P. Malanczuk, *Akehurst's Modern Introduction to International Law*, 7th rev. ed. (London: Routledge, 1997), p. 16.

10. Antony Anghie, "Finding the Peripheries: Sovereignty and

Colonialism in Nineteenth-Century International Law," *Harvard International Law Journal* 40, no. 1 (Winter 1999): 1–80, 12–13.

11. Lassa Oppenheim, "The Science of International Law: Its Task and Method," *American Journal of International Law (AJIL)* 2 (1908): 313–356, 340.

12. Permanent Court of International Justice, series A, no. 10, 18.

13. Francis Boyle, *World Politics and International Law* (Durham: Duke University Press, 1985), pp. 17–27.

14. Lassa Oppenheim, "The Science of International Law: Its Task and Method," *AJIL* 2 (1908): 313–356, 333–334.

15. See discussions by Benedict Kingsbury and Adam Roberts, "Introduction: Grotian Thought in International Relations," in Hedley Bull, Benedict Kingsbury, and Adam Roberts, eds., *Hugo Grotius and International Relations* (Oxford: Clarendon, 1992), pp. 1–64, 30–38; and Roelofsen, "Grotius and International Law," pp. 16–17.

16. See, for example, John Finnis, *Natural Law and Natural Rights* (Oxford: Clarendon; and New York: Oxford University Press, 1980); and Robert P. George, *In Defense of Natural Law* (Oxford: Clarendon; New York: Oxford University Press, 1999).

17. See, inter alia, Maria Clara Maffei, "The International Convention for the Regulation of Whaling," *International Journal of Marine and Coastal Law* 12, no. 3 (1997): 287–305.

18. The Court has adopted "practice directions" in addition to the Rules of Court. The Statute, Rules of Court, and Practice Directions can be found on the ICJ website, www.icj-cij.org/icjwww/icj002.htm.

19. In March 2002 a Swiss referendum supported Switzerland joining the United Nations.

20. Mark W. Janis, *An Introduction to International Law*, 3rd ed. (Gaithersburg, MD: Aspen, 1999), pp. 128–129.

21. Ibid., p. 128.

22. A chronological list of treaties containing compromissory clauses can be found on the website of the ICJ, at http://www.icj-cij.org/icjwww/ibasicdocuments/ibasictext/ibasictreatiesandotherdocs.htm.

23. Malanczuk, *Akehurst's Modern Introduction to International Law*, p. 284.

24. Republic of Georgia Declaration Recognizing as Compulsory the Jurisdiction of the Court, reprinted in International Court of Justice, *Yearbook 1998–1999,* pp. 99–100.

25. United Kingdom Declaration Recognizing as Compulsory the Jurisdiction of the Court, reprinted in International Court of Justice, *Yearbook 1998–1999,* pp. 129–130.

26. *Military and Paramilitary Activities in and Against Nicaragua (Nicaragua v. United States of America), Jurisdiction and Admissibility, Judgment, ICJ Reports 1984,* p. 392, 601–602.

27. See discussion in Stanimir A. Alexandrov, *Reservations in Unilateral Declarations Accepting the Compulsory Jurisdiction of the International Court of Justice* (Dordrecht: Martinus Nijhoff, 1995), pp. 17–32.

28. *Interhandel Case, Judgment of March 21st, 1959: ICJ Reports 1959,*

p. 6, 23.

29. Cited in Michael Byers, *Custom, Power, and the Power of Rules: International Relations and Customary International Law* (Cambridge: Cambridge University Press, 1999), p. 93.

30. Ibid., p. 94.

31. See discussion in ibid., pp. 97–98.

32. *Military and Paramilitary Activities in and Against Nicaragua (Nicaragua v. United States of America), Jurisdiction and Admissibility, Judgment, ICJ Reports 1984*, p. 392.

33. U.S. Department of State, Letter from George P. Shultz to UN Secretary-General Javier Perez de Cuellar, Concerning Termination of Acceptance of ICJ Compulsory Jurisdiction, October 7, 1985, 24 International Legal Materials (ILM) 1743 (1985).

34. D. J. Harris, *Cases and Materials on International Law*, 5th ed. (London: Sweet & Maxwell, 1998), p. 999.

35. *Antarctica (United Kingdom v. Argentina), Order of March 16, 1956, ICJ Reports 1956*, p. 12, and *Antarctica (United Kingdom v. Chile), Order of March 16, 1956, ICJ Reports 1956*, p. 15.

36. P. Alston, "Peace as a Human Right," *Bulletin of Peace Proposals* 11 (1980): 319.

37. J. L. Brierly, "International Law and Resort to Armed Force," *Cambridge Law Journal* 4 (1932): 308–319, 308.

38. Christian Wolff was the first to recognize that the question of the justice of wars falls outside the pale of positive law. Joachim von Elbe, "The Evolution of the Concept of the Just War in International Law," *AJIL* 33 (1939): 665–688, 682. In the contemporary world, Michael Waltzer has attempted to "recapture the just war for political and moral theory." Michael Waltzer, *Just and Unjust Wars: A Moral Argument with Historical Illustrations* (New York: Basic, 1977).

39. Rein Müllerson, "The Use of Force Between Its Past and Future," *International Peacekeeping* 5, no. 4–5 (July-October 1999): 115–128, 115.

40. For discussion on the relationship between the two, see Christopher Greenwood, "The Relationship Between *Ius Ad Bellum* and *Ius In Bello*," *Review of International Studies* 9 (1983): 221–234.

41. Ian Brownlie, *International Law and the Use of Force by States* (Oxford: Clarendon, 1963), p. 66.

42. H. Lauterpacht, "'Resort to War' and the Interpretation of the Covenant During the Manchurian Dispute," *AJIL* (1934): 43–60, 44.

43. Brownlie, *International Law and the Use of Force by States*, p. 60.

44. 94 League of Nations Treaty Series (LNTS) 57.

45. For an historical account of the political origins of the treaty, see Robert H. Ferrell, *Peace in Their Time: The Origins of the Kellogg-Briand Pact* (New Haven: Yale University Press, 1952).

46. Harris, *Cases and Materials on International Law*, p. 861, n. 2.

47. Ibid., p. 861, n. 1.

48. Ibid., p. 895.

49. Ibid., p. 896.

50. Albrecht Randelzhofer, "Article 51," in Bruno Simma, ed., *The Charter of the United Nations: A Commentary* (Oxford: Oxford University Press, 1994), p. 675.

51. *Military and Paramilitary Activities in and Against Nicaragua (Nicaragua v. United States of America), Merits, Judgment, ICJ Reports 1986,* pp. 14, 554, paras. 227–238.

52. The *2002 National Security Strategy* is available through the White House website, www.whitehouse.gov/nsc/nss.html.

53. See, inter alia, Louis René Beres, "Preserving the Third Temple: Israel's Right of Anticipatory Self-Defense Under International Law" *Vanderbilt Journal of Transnational Law* 26 (1993–1994): 111–148; Thomas M. Franck, *Recourse to Force: State Action Against Threats and Armed Attacks* (New York: Cambridge University Press, 2002), chap. 7; and George K. Walker, "Anticipatory Collective Self-Defense in the Charter Era: What the Treaties Have Said," *Cornell International Law Journal* 31 (1998) 321–376.

54. Letter dated March 20, 2003, from the Permanent Representative of the United states of America to the United Nations Addressed to the President of the Security Council, UN Doc. S/2003/351 (March 21, 2003). The United Kingdom and Australia sent similar letters.

55. See, inter alia, Anthony Clark Arend, "International Law and the Preemptive Use of Military Force," *Washington Quarterly* 26, no. 2 (Spring 2003): 89–103; Sam Blay and Ryszard Piotrowicz, "The Use of Force and the Force of Law in Iraq," *Australian Law Journal* 77 (2003): 283–289; Ivo H. Daalder, "The Use of Force: US and European Perspectives," *Leiden Journal of International Law* 16 (2003): 171–180; and Adam Roberts, "Law and the Use of Force After Iraq," *Survival* 45, no. 2 (Summer 2003): 31–56.

56. For a useful listing of Security Council authorizations to use force, see Simon Chesterman, *Just War or Just Peace? Humanitarian Intervention and International Law.* (Oxford: Oxford University Press, 2001), pp. 241–259.

57. There is no general consensus on the definition of humanitarian intervention. Ved P. Nanda, "Tragedies in Northern Iraq, Liberia, Yugoslavia, and Haiti: Revisiting the Validity of Humanitarian Intervention Under International Law, Part 1," *Denver Journal of International Law and Policy* 20, no. 2 (1992): 305–334, 311. Franck and Rodley have referred to humanitarian intervention as recognition of "the right of one State to exercise an international control *by military force* over the acts of another in regard to its internal sovereignty when contrary to the laws of humanity." Thomas M. Franck and Nigel S. Rodley, "After Bangladesh: The Law of Humanitarian Intervention by Military Force," *AJIL* 67 (1973): 275–305, 277, n. 12.

58. Hugo Grotius, *The Rights of War and Peace: Including the Law of Nature and of Nations*, translated by A. C. Campbell with an introduction by David J. Hill (Westport, CT: Hyperion, 1979), p. 288.

59. David J. Scheffer, "Toward a Modern Doctrine of Humanitarian Intervention," *University of Toledo Law Review* 23 (1992): 253–293, 258–59.

60. Chesterman, *Just War or Just Peace?* pp. 24–25.

61. Brownlie, *International Law and the Use of Force by States*, p. 342.

62. Harris, *Cases and Materials on International Law*, p. 918. India

apparently initially defended its action on grounds of humanitarian need. Barry Benjamin, "Unilateral Humanitarian Intervention: Legalizing the Use of Force to Prevent Human Rights Atrocities," *Fordham International Law Journal* 16, no. 1 (1992): 120–158, 141.

63. For recent literature on a possible right of humanitarian intervention, see, inter alia, Stephen A. Garrett, *Doing Good and Doing Well: An Examination of Humanitarian Intervention* (Westport, CT: Praeger, 1999); Brian D. Lepard, *Rethinking Humanitarian Intervention: A Fresh Legal Approach Based on Fundamental Ethical Printiplcs in International Law and World Religions* (University Park: Pennsylvania State University Press, 2002); Jules Lobel, "Benign Hegemony? Kosovo and Article 2(4) of the UN Charter," *Chicago Journal of International Law* 1, no. 1 (Spring 2000): 19–36; John J. Merriam, "Kosovo and the Law of Humanitarian Intervention," *Case Western Reserve Journal of International Law* 33, no. 1 (Winter 2001): 111–154; Mary Ellen O'Connell, "The UN, NATO, and International Law After Kosovo," *Human Rights Quarterly* 22, no. 1 (2000): 57–89; *The Responsibility to Protect: Report of the International Commission on Intervention and State Sovereignty* (Ottawa: International Development Research Centre, 2001), available at http://www.iedrc.ca; J. L. Holzgrefe and Robert O. Keohane, *Humanitarian Intervention: Ethical, Legal, and Political Dilemmas* (Cambridge: Cambridge University Press, 2003); and Nicholas Tsagourias, "Humanitarian Intervention After Kosovo and Legal Discourse: Self-Deception or Self-Consciousness?" *Leiden Journal of International Law* 13 (2000): 11–32.

64. See Maria Stavropoulou, "Indigenous Peoples Displaced from Their Environment: Is There Adequate Protection?" *Colorado Journal of International Environmental Law and Policy* 5 (1994: 105–126, 105–106.

65. B. Kingsbury, "'Indigenous Peoples' in International Law: A Constructivist Approach to the Asian Controversy," 92 *AJIL* (1998): 414–457.

66. See, inter alia, Geoffrey M. Levitt, "Is Terrorism Worth Defining?" *Ohio Western University Law Review* 13, no. 1 (Winter 1986): 97–115; and A. Obote-Odora, "Defining International Terrorism," *Murdoch University Electronic Journal of Law* 6, no. 1 (March 1999), at www.murdoch.edu.au/elaw/issues/v6n1/obote-odora61_text.html.

67. "Annan Hopes UN Will OK Terror Treaty," *Associated Press*, January 24, 2002, at www.globalpolicy.org/wtc/un/2002/0124hope.htm, accessed June 14, 2002; and Michael Jordan, "Terrorism's Slippery Definition Eludes UN Diplomats," *Christian Science Monitor,* February 3, 2002, available at www.globalpolicy.org/wtc/un/2002/0203definition.htm.

68. On this theme and related challenges of customary international law more generally, see Hilary Charlesworth, "The Unbearable Lightness of Customary International Law," *Proceedings of the Ninety-Second Annual Meeting of the American Society of International Law: The Challenge of Non-State Actors* 92 (1998): 44–47; Major Ian G. Corey, "The Fine Line Between Policy and Custom: *Prosecutor v. Tadic* and the Customary International Law of Internal Armed Conflict," *Military Law Review* 166 (2000): 145–157; and M. Koskenniemi, "The Normative Force of Habit: International Custom and Social Theory," *Finnish Yearbook of International Law 1990* 1 (1990): 77–89.

69. See, inter alia, Peter Hilpold, "Humanitarian Intervention: Is There a Need for a Legal Reappraisal?" *European Journal of International Law (EJIL)* 12, no. 3 (2001): 437–467; Nicholas J. Wheeler, "Legitimating Humanitarian Intervention: Principles and Procedures," *Melbourne Journal of International Law* 2, no. 2 (2001): 550–567; and the UK House of Commons, Foreign Affairs Committee Fourth Report, Session 1999–2000, available at www.parliament.the-stationery-office.co.uk/pa/cm199900/cmselect/ cmfaff/28/2802.htm.

70. See Tadeusz Gruchalla-Wesierski, "A Framework for Understanding Soft Law," *McGill Law Journal* 30 (1984): 37–88, 44.

71. C. M. Chinkin, "The Challenge of Soft Law: Development and Change in International Law," *International and Comparative Law Quarterly (ICLQ)* 38 (October 1989): 850–866.

72. See, inter alia, R. R. Baxter, "International Law in 'Her Infinite Variety,'" *ICLQ* 29 (1980): 549–566; A. E. Boyle, "Some Reflections on the Relationship of Treaties and Soft Law," *ICLQ* 48, no. 4 (October 1999): 901–913; Chinkin, "The Challenge of Soft Law"; Ulrich Fastenrath, "Relative Normativity in International Law," *EJIL* 4 (1993): 305–340; and Prosper Weil, "Towards Relative Normativity in International Law?" *AJIL* 77 (1983): 413–442.

73. 14 ILM 1293 (1975). See Oscar Schachter, "The Twilight Existence of Nonbinding International Agreements," *AJIL* 71 (1977): 296–304, 296.

74. Malanczuk, *Akehurst's Modern Introduction to International Law*, p. 54.

75. See, generally, Thomas M. Franck, *The Power of Legitimacy Among Nations* (New York and Oxford: Oxford University Press, 1990), pp. 150ff.

6

Legal Argument as Political Maneuvering

W e have seen that legal positivism provides a philosophical underpinning to what can be thought of in terms of a three-tiered system of principles, rules, and concepts. Legal positivism requires that an
analysis of a specific point of law be done on the basis of the components of law found within the sources of international law, thereby
shunning argument based on other grounds such as morality, economics, or politics. This contributes to an image of international legal argument as objective and apolitical and means that it is often difficult for a
newcomer to international law to appreciate the distinction between the
image of international law conveyed in such international legal analysis
and reality. As will be explored in this chapter, it is precisely because
legal analysis appears apolitical that it can be brought into service in the
pursuit of political objectives.

The Legality of Bombing the Federal
Republic of Yugoslavia During the Kosovo Crisis
In Chapter 5 we looked at some examples of the components of international law at each of the three levels. We also looked at one very brief
example of legal argument premised on the foundation of legal positivism. We are now going to consider a more substantial example of
how a legal positivist might combine elements from all three of the levels of principles, concepts, and rules to construct a legal argument and
use that as a medium through which to interact with other actors in
world politics. The example we are going to use is that of the use of
force by NATO against the Federal Republic of Yugoslavia in March
1999. As we might expect from what we have already learned about

legal positivism, the principal question is whether the bombing was or was not legal.[1]

The Kosovo crisis and the NATO bombing campaign gave rise to outrage against those committing atrocities, as well as those inflicting suffering by their bombing. Analysis within the framework of legal positivism requires us to put aside all emotional responses to focus on the rules, principles, and concepts found within the sources of international law. We will, naturally, be most interested in the law relating to the use of force, as found in Level 3 of the pyramid of international law (see Chapter 5). But we will need to treat the rules, principles, and concepts relating to the use of force in accordance with the law relating to the sources of international law as found at Level 2 of the pyramid.

For the majority of international lawyers the case is clear that the NATO bombing was illegal. The source most important to reaching that conclusion is the UN Charter. Article 103 provides that:

> In the event of a conflict between the obligations of the Members of the UN under the present Charter and their obligations under any other international agreement, their obligations under the present Charter shall prevail.

This means that the Charter trumps other treaties. Consistent with article 103 of the UN Charter, article 7 of the 1949 North Atlantic Treaty reads:

> The Treaty does not affect, and shall not be interpreted as affecting, in any way the rights and obligations under the Charter of the Parties which are Members of the United Nations, or the primary responsibility of the Security Council for the maintenance of international peace and security.[2]

Article 2(4) of the UN Charter categorically prohibits the use of force. The collective self-defense exception is not applicable in this case because article 51 refers to attacks against members of the United Nations; it has to be a state claiming a right of self-defense. Kosovo was part of a sovereign state; Yugoslavia was not attacking another state. The second exception to the prohibition on the use of force is on the authorization of the Security Council. Although there were three relevant Security Council resolutions,[3] none explicitly authorized the use of force. Under article 53(1) authorization can be given to a regional organization, but a regional organization must not take action without that authorization.

Just as there does not appear to be a basis in treaty law for the NATO bombing, most international lawyers consider there not to have crystallized a customary international rule of humanitarian intervention. Even if there were such a rule, the nature of the NATO use of force disqualified it as an example of humanitarian intervention. Bombing from a height of 15,000 feet inevitably endangers civilians and would not seem to be compatible with the concept of humanitarian intervention.

Many international lawyers have, on a personal level, found it difficult to reach the conclusion that the NATO bombing was contrary to international law because it appeared to have been the morally correct action. This has led to considerable debate regarding the relationship between international law and morality and between *de lege lata* (international law as it currently stands) and *de lege ferenda* (law as it should be). Bruno Simma concluded that only a thin red line separated NATO's action from international legality but that NATO's use of force without Security Council authorization should remain an exception lest NATO undermine the universal system of collective security.[4] Other writers, including Michael Glennon,[5] have concluded that the discrepancy between international law and morality in this scenario meant that the law should be changed and brought into line with contemporary standards of morality and justice. The UK Select Committee on Foreign Affairs found that the intervention had been of dubious legality and supported moves to establish in the United Nations new principles governing humanitarian intervention.[6]

The UK submitted to the Secretary-General a framework for intervention based on six principles: that there should be more concentration on conflict prevention; that the use of armed force should only be a last resort; that responsibility in the first place lies with the state where severe violations are taking place; that when a government has shown that it is unwilling or unable to cope with a humanitarian catastrophe, the international community has a duty to intervene; that any use of force should be proportionate to achieving the humanitarian purposes of the mission and carried out in accordance with international law; and that the use of force must be collective and only in exceptional circumstances should it be undertaken without the express authority of the UN Security Council.[7] Debate in the General Assembly during 1999 did not reflect a consensus view that a right to humanitarian intervention should be codified.

Some consider, however, that the morality of the bombing campaign was even more dubious than its legality. Key considerations raised here are, first, that from relatively few refugees prior to the air strikes, up to 800,000 fled their homes after the strikes had begun;[8] and second, that if NATO's motivation was really humanitarian, why did it conduct a high-altitude bombing campaign in which civilians were bound to suffer casualties?

Although a mainstream legal analysis would most readily lead to the conclusion that the use of force by NATO states during the Kosovo crisis was not legal, there have been some who have constructed legal arguments for its having been legal. One way in which this can be done is by considering the detail of the phrases in article 2(4) of the UN Charter. The argument is sometimes made that article 2(4) does not rule out a "lawful" use of force and that a lawful humanitarian intervention will not undermine the "territorial integrity or political independence of any State 'or be' inconsistent with the purposes of the UN."[9] Julie Mertus has argued, for example, that a close reading of the UN Charter supports humanitarian intervention in Kosovo-like situations—that is, in cases in which an outside alliance acts unilaterally to redress human rights violations committed by the regime of a third state.[10] By article 51 of the Charter, the UN is to promote, inter alia, "universal respect for, and observance of, human rights and fundamental freedoms for all without distinction as to race, sex, language, or religion." By article 56, members "pledge themselves to take joint and separate action in co-operation with the Organisation for the achievement of the purposes set forth in Article 55." Some lawyers maintain that these provisions temper what would most readily be interpreted as a total prohibition on the use of force in article 2(4). This is not, however, the predominant interpretation of article 2(4), nor would it appear to have been the intention of those crafting the Charter text.[11]

A second way of arguing within a legal positivist framework that the bombing was legal is to justify it in terms of customary international law as a case of humanitarian intervention. Both lines of argument are made more difficult by the fact that NATO did not argue them; indeed NATO provided no single, coherent legal justification for its actions but emphasized their legitimacy as a response to the humanitarian catastrophe in Kosovo.[12] In the joint hearings before the ICJ on Yugoslavia's requests for interim measures during the NATO bombing campaign only Belgium justified its actions on the basis of a right to humanitarian intervention.[13]

Is there any other action that the NATO states could have taken to make their campaign legal? One other possibility, although it may not have been successful, is by way of the Uniting for Peace Resolution. In 1950 the Security Council had been able to take action in relation to North Korea only because the Soviet Union was boycotting the Council in protest over the membership of Taiwan. Once the Soviet representative returned to the Council it became very hard to pass subsequent resolutions on Korea. The United States then introduced a discussion paper into the General Assembly, which became the basis for the Uniting for Peace Resolution. The resolution provided, inter alia, that

> if the Security Council, because of lack of unanimity of the permanent members, fails to exercise its primary responsibility for the maintenance of international peace and security in any case where there appears to be a threat to the peace, breach of the peace, or act of aggression, the General Assembly shall consider the matter immediately with a view to making appropriate recommendations to members for collective measures, including in the case of breach of the peace or act of aggression the use of armed force when necessary, to maintain or restore international peace and security.[14]

The resolution also provided that an emergency special session of the General Assembly may be convened outside of the session period if there is a breach of or a threat to peace or an act of aggression. The session may be summoned either by the Security Council—the veto power does not apply on a procedural resolution—or by a simple majority of members of the General Assembly.

The Uniting for Peace Resolution was of particular value to the United States and the West during the years of their domination of the General Assembly but became less relevant as the North-South dynamic grew in importance. It was used on a number of occasions (in relation to Hungary in 1956; the Middle East in 1956, 1958, 1967, and 1980; the Congo in 1960; Bangladesh in 1971; Afghanistan in 1980; and Namibia in 1981) to bring about emergency special sessions though not as a basis for recommending collective military measures.

The Indeterminacy of International Law and the "Rule-Book" Image of International Law

Analysis of the legality of the NATO bombing campaign has showed that, even in relation to a subject area in international law that is relatively straightforward, such as the use of force, it is possible to arrive at differing assessments as to the legality of a specific action. It was not that both conclusions could be arrived at with equal ease—in this case it was found to be much easier to argue for illegality than for legality—but both conclusions were possible. It has, similarly, been possible for NATO and its critics to differ as to the legality of the manner in which the campaign was waged.[15] In any particular scenario it is usually possible to make a case both for and against the legality of a specific action; this is referred to as the *indeterminacy* of international law. The extent to which international law is indeterminate varies across issue areas and among sources; customary international law, for example, is generally less determinate than treaty law.[16]

Recognition of the indeterminacy of international law comes as a surprise to many observers of world politics because this is not the image of law conveyed by international law rhetoric or even by most references to international law in political rhetoric. Legal argument is expressed so as to give the impression that the decision arrived at—whether for or against legality—is the only one possible. A state in dispute with another state will, for example, usually present an argument of international law that contrasts the legality of its own actions/policy position with those of other states. Take, for example, the following extract from the account provided by Chinese foreign ministry spokesman Zhu Bangzao of the midair collision between U.S. and Chinese military planes on April 1, 2001. It would have been extraordinary if the representative of China had said that China's actions had been illegal, or if he hinted that international law was indeterminate. Rather, the assessment of the legality of Chinese, and illegality of the U.S., actions is presented as if such actions are the only ones possible given the content of the existing sources of international law:

> The US plane suddenly veered at a wide angle towards the Chinese planes, which were closer to baseline of the Chinese side. The US plane's nose and left wing rammed the tail of one of the Chinese planes, causing it to lose control and plunge into the sea. . . .
>   It should be pointed out that it was proper and in accordance with international law for Chinese military fighters to follow and monitor the US military surveillance plane within airspace over China's exclusive economic waters. . . .
>   The surveillance flight conducted by the US aircraft overran the scope of "free over-flight" according to international law. The move also violated the United Nations Convention on the Law of the Sea, which stipulates that any flight in airspace above another nation's exclusive zone should respect the rights of the country concerned.[17]

As might be expected, this statement draws a clear contrast between the purported legality of China's actions and what is presented as the clear illegality of U.S. actions.

Let us take another example: U.S. actions during the Cuban Missile Crisis of 1962. The United States wanted to ensure that the Soviet Union remove missiles it had already installed in Cuba and not send any others. It wanted to use international law to facilitate this. But in constructing an argument contrasting the legality of U.S. actions with the illegality of Soviet actions it ran into a basic problem: what the Soviets were doing was not obviously illegal, but any actions that the United States might take to meet its goals were likely to be illegal.[18] Great effort was put into constructing a legal argument that would support the United States acting to achieve its foreign policy goals. The missiles were characterized as "offensive" rather than defensive and an immediate meeting of the Organ of Consultation of the Organization of American States was called; it passed a resolution recommending, under articles 6 and 8 of the Rio Treaty, all measures, including the use of force, to prevent Cuba from receiving materials from the Soviet Union that threatened the peace and security of the hemisphere. The United States coined the term "quarantine" to describe what might have otherwise been regarded as an illegal blockade and worked hard diplomatically to ensure that a Soviet-proposed resolution condemning the action not be pressed to a vote in the Security Council.[19] Although there was no explicit Security Council authorization for the U.S. actions as might be anticipated under article 53 of the UN Charter, at least there was no explicit vote condemning the U.S. actions. Abram Chayes, who was the State Department legal counsel during John F. Kennedy's administration and was instrumental in crafting the legal justification for the quarantine, reflected many years later that the legal position had been very important in the diplomatic resolution of the crisis. "Having to consider the legal position carefully contributed, I think, to the wisdom of our choices."[20]

Recognizing the indeterminacy of international law is essential to gaining some appreciation of the role that international legal argument can play in world politics, because the indeterminacy of international law permits it to be used as a medium of political maneuvering between states and in their relations with other international actors. Dialogues regarding questions of legality can be a mechanism by which political positions are mediated. In Chapter 5 we looked at a legal analysis drawn on by Japan in support of its opposition to the creation of a sanctuary for whales in the Southern Ocean. But another eminent international lawyer, Patricia Birnie of the United Kingdom, also undertook a legal analysis of the sanctuary and declared it legal under the Charter of the IWC.[21] Naturally enough, it was the opinion of Patricia Birnie that was drawn on by many antiwhaling nations.[22]

The indeterminacy of international law means that it is possible for an international lawyer to construct a legal argument to support either side in a dispute, as opposed to working from the rules, principles, and concepts of international law to arrive ineluctably at a particular conclusion as international legal rhetoric suggests is possible. A practical example of this difference relates to providing legal advice to foreign policy decisionmakers. Most states have attorneys within government agencies who appraise and sort out the international legal implications of foreign policy. In Canada it is the Bureau of Legal Affairs in the Department of Foreign Affairs and Trade; in the United Kingdom it is the Legal Adviser's Department of the Foreign and Commonwealth Office; in Australia it is the Legal Adviser's Branch in the Department of Foreign Affairs and Trade; and in the United States it is the Office of the Legal Adviser in the Department of State.[23] The legal adviser generally operates as an objective expounder of law before a foreign policy action is taken or a policy course selected. Once the executive branch has taken action, that adviser must transform into a subjective advocate of the government position, presenting the best legal case possible in its defense even if the executive has chosen a course contrary to that which the adviser previously advocated.[24] When told by the British foreign secretary that the lawyers were having difficulty justifying the planned 1999 intervention in Yugoslavia, the response of the U.S. secretary of state was, reportedly, to "get new lawyers."[25]

Beyond determinacy, there are other mismatches between reality and the image of international law conveyed both in positivist rhetoric and in references to international law in political documents. Here are some other assumptions about international law that are implicit in positivist analyses:[26]

- International law is ultimately distinguishable from, and even superior to, politics.
- International law is politically neutral or universal in the sense that it treats all states equally.
- It is possible to distinguish objectively between legal and illegal action.
- It is compulsory for a state to comply with international law.
- International law is (virtually) timeless—at least in the sense that it predates policy.
- International law is (virtually) self-contained.
- It is possible to apply the rules of law objectively to settle a dispute between states.
- International law is (virtually) comprehensive—it can deal with any issue that arises among states.

This set of assumptions adds up to what can be described as the "rule book" image of international law. If a nonlawyer were presented with a large, heavy, and well-worn volume and told that it contained all the rules of international law, he or she might well believe it. According to the rule-book image of international law, decisionmakers faced with a decision as to how to act call in the legal adviser. The legal adviser then consults the relevant page in this large volume, reads what it says must be done, and advises the decisionmakers accordingly. The decisionmakers should, of course, do as the advisers say, and if they do, the state will have "complied" with international law. As far as an international judiciary is concerned, the rule-book image assumes that when dealing with a dispute between two parties, judges would, similarly, open their rule book to the appropriate page, ascertain how each party should act in the given circumstances, and thereby settle impartially the differences between those parties. The rule-book image of international law considers that "law is 'rules'; that these rules are politically neutral; that the judiciary is 'objective'; and that its prime task is to 'apply,' rather than to 'make,' the rules."[27] International law is widely perceived as a "body of timeless absolutes, good for all seasons and all places, and postulated *a priori* in advance of actual problem situations."[28] International law is seen as a unified system with international cohesion.[29] In "international relations, most every event, including large areas of administrative activity, is considered to be classifiable as lawful or unlawful."[30]

There is some truth in this image of international law. Foreign policy decisionmakers do often consult their legal advisers, who prepare a statement of the relevant law to be taken into consideration during the policymaking process. Judges of the International Court of Justice do, of course, consult the various sources of international law and endeavor to apply what they find therein to settle a dispute. International law is not as "political" as pure politics, and international law does tend to be more stable than the dynamics of political relations. The indeterminacy of international law is by no means absolute; a lawyer cannot get away with justifying as legal just any action whatsoever. And though there is some truth in the rule-book image of international law, there is an important mismatch between this image and reality. It is not that the assumptions of legal positivism do not contain an element of truth but that in their absolute sense they are not true.

Just as the notion that a strict legal/illegal division of behavior does not correspond exactly to reality, so do these other assumptions not correspond exactly to reality. States are assumed to have sovereign equality, but they may not, for example, have equivalent opportunity to contribute to the negotiation of a new treaty (see Chapter 1); for example, there may often be parallel sessions at an international conference at which a treaty is being negotiated, and small delegations may not have the resources to cover all meetings.[31] There has been considerable concern since the end of the Cold War over the degree to which the United States, as the world's only remaining superpower, is able to influence the content and the operation of international law.[32] International law is not static but rather evolves in tandem with political events. It was not until the terrorist attacks of September 11, 2001, and the U.S. response to them, that the international community accepted that a state may invoke self-defense to respond with force to the actions of terrorists.[33]

There is a clear dynamic between policymaking and international law. Whereas the rule-book image of international law assumes that international law always precedes policy, there are many instances in which it has not done so. International law did not, for example, precede and "effortlessly resolve the problem" of Spanish-native relations when Spain first arrived in North America. Rather, the discovery posed special problems for international jurists such as Vitoria, who reconceptualized prevailing international legal doctrines or invented new ones.[34]

The notion that international law can settle any dispute that arises among states is also manifestly untrue. International law has not always been sufficiently developed to deal with an issue in question, or a particular solution may be so important to a country that it is not prepared to accept any compromise, whether or not mandated by international law. Territorial disputes tend to fall into this category. It is widely assumed, by those who have heard of its existence, that a world court can and would make an impartial determination as to the legality of the actions of two or more states in a dispute and that this should then settle the dispute, presumably in favor of the state or states in the legal right. Again, it is not that there is no truth in this image, but it certainly does not tell the whole story. Even if a case reaches the International Court of Justice and proceeds to a judgment on the merits, this may not be the end of the political story. The Iranian hostage crisis lasted for 444 days, between November 1979 and January 1981. During this period the United States initiated proceedings in the ICJ, and the Court issued provisional measures and went on to rule on the merits. But from Iran's point of view the issue at stake was much broader than that addressed by the majority decision; it involved a history of U.S. interference in Iran's internal affairs. The judgment had little effect on the course of the dispute, which, once the internal instability in Iran had subsided, was finally resolved through mediation by Algeria.[35]

The rhetoric of international law proceeds as if the principles were true, but as a system of interrelated rules, principles, and concepts, it also provides for the fact that they do not wholly match reality. *Non liquet*, for example, is a term of international law that refers to a gap in the law. The possibility that a particular issue is not accounted for stands in contrast to the image of international law as complete and as providing for any eventuality. Another example of the rules and principles of international law providing for the discrepancy between the image and reality of international law is that judges of the International Court of Justice are "independent" and elected regardless of their nationality, and yet if the Court includes upon its bench a judge of the nationality of one of the parties to a case, any other party may choose a person to sit as judge, and if the Court includes upon the bench no judge of the nationality of the parties to a case, each of those parties may choose a judge.[36]

Another example is the international law of territorial acquisition, which in many respects is out of date. Unlike during the seventeenth to the nineteenth centuries, it is no longer acceptable for a state to "acquire" territory in a colonial grab. International morality and international law have moved on.[37] Contrary to its image, international law is not timeless; it is very much a product of the political interactions of the time; or to express it differently, there is historical relativity in international law. The system of international law thus needs to cater to this discrepancy between the image and reality of international law in relation to territorial acquisition, and it does so by way of the *intertemporal principle*, which stipulates that title must be valid in accordance with the law in force at the time at which it is claimed to have been established, rather than in contemporary terms. Thus, when the International Court of Justice was asked to decide whether the territory to be known as Western Sahara had been *terra nullius* at the time of its colonization by Spain, the Court premised its response by saying that the question would have to be interpreted "by reference to the law in force at that period."[38]

The pervasive image of international law does not match reality. Nevertheless, if it were not assumed to be at least largely true, there would be no basis on which to draw on international law in political maneuvering. And it is unlikely that it would continue to be assumed true if there were no element of truth in it. It is the cohesion of international law as a set of interrelated principles, rules, and concepts that lends international law its considerable degree of autonomy and that, at the same time, permits it to be used as a vehicle of political interaction.

An Example of International Legal Discourse: The Cases Yugoslavia Brought Against the Member States of NATO in Relation to the Bombing Campaign in Kosovo

Sometimes a state, if in dispute with another state, will seek to have the alleged legal/illegal contrast between its behavior and that of the other state confirmed by a third party such as a judicial body. This is, not surprisingly, most likely when the state concerned believes that there is a high probability that the Court will decide in favor of the legality of its actions. We will now move on to another example of legal positivism in practice. This time we will look at a set of cases brought by Yugoslavia before the International Court of Justice. This example, an attempt to have the Court confirm the illegality of the other states' actions, will help us to consider further the limitations of a rule-book image of law as well as to show in more detail the operation of legal positivism as a mechanism for political interaction and maneuvering.

No doubt encouraged by the seemingly clear illegality of NATO actions, Yugoslavia on April 29, 1999, instituted proceedings (separate cases) before the ICJ against the United States, United Kingdom, France, Germany, Italy, the Netherlands, Belgium, Canada, Portugal, and Spain. Yugoslavia maintained that each of these ten states had committed acts that violated a number of legal obligations, the first being the obligation not to use force against another state. Yugoslavia likely saw this as an opportunity, at a minimum, to influence world opinion and delegitimize NATO's actions. Yugoslavia also filed, in each case, a request for interim measures of protection, asking the Court to order the states involved to "cease immediately [their] acts of use of force" and to "refrain from any act of threat or use of force against the Federal Republic of Yugoslavia."

The International Court of Justice can issue interim measures designed to ensure that no permanent damage is done to one of the parties pending the conclusion of the case. The Court is understandably wary of doing so if it has not yet even determined whether it has jurisdiction over the case. The Court thus begins by looking to see whether it would appear that it does have jurisdiction and indicates provisional measures only if it has determined that it does have prima facie jurisdiction. In June 1999 the Court found that it did not have prima facie jurisdiction in any of the cases brought against the NATO states by Yugoslavia and on that basis declined to indicate provisional measures. In relation to the proceedings brought against the United States and Spain the ICJ found that it "manifestly lacked jurisdiction" and so dismissed the cases. As regards the other cases, the Court said, in effect, that it did not have an obvious basis for jurisdiction; that issue could be determined later, but at this stage it was not sufficiently clear for the Court to indicate provisional measures on that basis.

ICJ Jurisdiction over the Cases Brought by
Yugoslavia Regarding the Legality of the Use of Force

In Chapter 5 we looked at the international law relating to the jurisdiction of the ICJ. Let us now put this into practice so as to understand better the process that led to the decision of the Court as regards jurisdiction and provisional measures in the *Legality of Use of Force* cases. There was no *compromis* involved. Yugoslavia made a written application to the Court. By article 38(2) of the Rules of Court an application instituting proceedings is required to specify as far as possible the legal grounds upon which the jurisdiction of the Court is said to be based and to specify the precise nature of the claim, as well as to provide a succinct statement of the facts and grounds on which the claim is based. Yugoslavia drew on all three bases of jurisdiction other than special agreement, although it did not draw on all of them in relation to every state.

The first basis given by Yugoslavia was the compromissory clause contained in the 1948 Convention on the Prevention and Punishment of the Crime of Genocide. Yugoslavia asserted that this gave the Court a basis of jurisdiction regarding all ten states. The ICJ did not accept this argument in relation to Spain and the United States, both of which had entered reservations against article 9 of the Genocide Convention. As regards the other states, the Court said in essence that the bombing was not obviously a case of attempted genocide and that it would need to investigate further.

Second, in relation to France, Germany, Italy, and the United States, Yugoslavia tried to establish jurisdiction on the basis of article 38(5) of the Rules of Court. None of the states gave its consent. The United States made its position clear: "The United States has not consented to jurisdiction under Article 38, paragraph 5, and will not do so."[39]

Third, Yugoslavia drew on the optional clause in attempting to establish the jurisdiction of the ICJ in the cases brought against

Belgium, Canada, the Netherlands, Portugal, Spain, and the United Kingdom. Yugoslavia had filed its acceptance of the compulsory jurisdiction of the ICJ on April 26, 1999, three days before instituting the ICJ proceedings. Vladislav Jovanovic, chargé d'affaires of the permanent mission of Yugoslavia to the United Nations, stated in a letter:

> I hereby declare that the Government of the Federal Republic of Yugoslavia recognizes, in accordance with Article 36, paragraph 2, of the Statute of the International Court of Justice, as compulsory *ipso facto* and without special agreement, in relation to any other State accepting the same obligation, that is on condition of reciprocity, the jurisdiction of the said Court in all disputes arising or which may arise after the signature of the present Declaration, with regard to the situations or facts subsequent to this signature, except in cases where the parties have agreed or shall agree to have recourse to another procedure or to another method of pacific settlement. The present Declaration does not apply to disputes relating to questions which, under international law, fall exclusively within the jurisdiction of the Federal Republic of Yugoslavia, as well as to territorial disputes.
>
> The aforesaid obligation is accepted until such time as notice may be given to terminate the acceptance.
>
> New York, 25 April 1999.
> *Vladislav Jovanovic,*
> Chargé d'affaires a.i. of
> The Permanent Mission of Yugoslavia
> to the United Nations.[40]

The Court found that article 36(2) definitely did not establish a basis for its jurisdiction in the cases brought against Spain and the United States, both of which had made a reservation in their acceptance of the Court's jurisdiction with respect to "disputes to which the other party or parties have accepted the compulsory jurisdiction of the Court less than 12 months prior to the filing of the application bringing the dispute before the Court." As regards the others, the Court found that the legal dispute had arisen before the date specified in Yugoslavia's acceptance of article 36(2), which, because of the principle of reciprocity, applied also to the other states.

Although the Court had definitely not found a basis of jurisdiction for Spain or the United States, there was still a possibility of its finding jurisdiction in relation to the other states.

Because it did not establish prima facie jurisdiction in any of the cases, the Court declined to issue provisional measures. In the cases brought against Spain and the United States the Court found that it "manifestly lacked jurisdiction" and so dismissed the cases.

The next step was for written submissions from each side, beginning with the applicant. The Court said that Yugoslavia should submit its memorial (written pleadings) by January 5, 2000, and the remaining respondents submit their countermemorials (responses) by July 5, 2000. However, on July 5, 2000, the NATO countries for which the Court might still find jurisdiction (all but Spain and the United States) each filed preliminary objections to jurisdiction and admissibility. By orders dated September 8, 2000, the Court then fixed April 5, 2001, as the time limit within which Yugoslavia should present a written statement of its observations and submissions on the preliminary objections raised by the NATO countries. On January 18, 2001, Yugoslavia requested an extension and by orders of February 21, 2001, the ICJ extended the time limit for Yugoslavia to April 5, 2002. By letter dated February 8, 2002, Yugoslavia requested the Court "for a stay of proceedings or . . . for an extension by twelve months of the time period for the submission of observations on the preliminary objections raised by . . . [the respondent state]" in each case. The respondent states indicated that they were not opposed to a stay of proceedings or to an extension of the time limit for the filing of the observations and submissions of Yugoslavia on their preliminary objections. By orders of March 20, 2002, the Court fixed April 7, 2003, as the new time limit.

In this example, we see how what may appear to be dry rules and procedures pertaining to the jurisdiction of the International Court of Justice became the mechanism by which a state attempted to draw on international law in pursuance of its political objectives. The relevant law may more readily support the objectives of one party than another. There was no easy way by which Yugoslavia could force the NATO states to participate in proceedings before the International Court of Justice even though the question as to the legality of their actions appeared to be relatively clear-cut. But we can also see that there is considerable skill involved in legal maneuvering. There was no way that Yugoslavia would have been able to demonstrate that the Court had jurisdiction over Spain and the United States on the basis of the Genocide Convention when they had both clearly made reservations to the compromissory clause in that treaty. The extent of the knowledge, skill, and experience of the international lawyers at the disposal of the government of a state is an important aspect of its capacity to achieve its objectives on the international stage. When issues are to be settled other than by military means, legal skill is an important form of national power.

Efforts to Characterize International Law as Something Other than a "Rule Book"

This chapter has referred to the "rule-book" image of international law as that conveyed by international legal discourse and in most references to international law in political rhetoric. It is in recognition of the fact that international law does not match its pervasive image of being generally static, politically neutral, clear-cut, universal, self-contained, and comprehensive that a number of theorists have in recent years attempted to characterize international law as something other, or at least more, than "mere" rules. Members of the so-called New Haven school (or Yale school) of international law,[41] for example, have played down law as rules in favor of international law as a "comprehensive process of authoritative decisions." The New Haven approach emphasizes the dynamic nature of international law and takes into account not only rules but also the explicit discussion of values, interests, goals, and conditioning factors, prompting the criticism that international law, viewed from a New Haven perspective, becomes indistinguishable from politics or social science.[42] Others expand a conceptualization of international law to encompass not only rules but also "legal procedures, methodologies, institutions, and processes generating legitimacy."[43]

What can broadly be referred to as "critical legal theorists"[44] or the "newstream"[45] have emphasized the discrepancy between particular principles found within what has been referred to as the rule-book image of international law and reality although they may have used different language to do so. A. Carty, for example, denied that there is a universal system of international law;[46] Martti Koskenniemi, that international law provides a nonpolitical way of dealing with disputes.[47] Koskenniemi has defined the newstream as "a critical sensibility that examines international law from a wide range of intellectual strands: philosophy, political theory, sociology, anthropology, cultural and women's studies and so on in order to reassess its meaning, contemporary relevance and future role."[48] Not only do critical theorists recognize that international law does not match the rule-book image of international law; they claim that it is not capable of doing so. This has given rise to considerable introspection on the part of many of the individuals writing in the newstream genre, and not surprisingly a sense of futility has pervaded much of their output.[49]

Work done by non-Western international law specialists in the first decades after the collapse of the colonial order virtually all relied on Western approaches in a relatively uncritical manner.[50] More recently, Third World Approaches to International Law (TWAIL) has been referred to as an "emergent discipline" highlighting the role that international law has played in the subordination of third world peoples; this discipline also seeks, through scholarship, policy, and politics, to eradicate the conditions of underdevelopment in the third world.[51] Critical third world scholars oppose a number of aspects of current international law that "[attempt] to confer universality on norms and practices that are European in origin, thought, and experience" such as human rights and the protection of intellectual property through the treaty on Trade Related Aspects of Intellectual Property Rights (TRIPS).[52] Third world criticism has taken as its starting point the fact that international law was "complicit in the subjugation of non-European people."[53] "[International law] is a predatory system that legitimizes, reproduces and sustains the plunder and subordination of the Third World by the West."[54] The process began through the international law of territorial acquisition that, from the seventeenth to the late nineteenth century, offered the legal means by which a European state could "acquire" overseas territory.

Feminist writers on international law have also stressed the fact that international law, in contrast to the image of law portrayed in positivist discourse, is not universal; nor does it treat everyone equally.[55] There are a number of schools of feminist writing in international law, which have been categorized variously as liberal feminism, cultural feminism, radical feminism, postmodern feminism, and third world feminism.[56] Feminist writers emphasize the fact that women have been almost completely excluded from international law–making arenas; the rules of international law have developed in response to the experiences of a male elite. "Feminist analysis must thus explore the unspoken commitments of apparently neutral principles of international law and the ways that male perspectives are institutionalised in it."[57] Discussions as to when the use of force is allowed, for example, tend to focus on ostensibly neutral rules contained in the UN Charter, without taking into account the impacts of the use of force on the lives of women. The expulsion of Iraq from Kuwait may appear to have been brought about by a successful, Security Council–authorized military operation, but it may nevertheless have had deleterious impacts on women. Kuwaiti women suffered significant violations of their rights after the "liberation" of Kuwait, including worse levels of rape, the detention of large numbers of domestic workers, and a continued denial of democratic rights to suffrage.[58]

What critical theorists, third world critics, feminists, and indigenous writers on international law have in common is an appreciation of the historical—and political—relativity of international law. S. James Anaya has stressed, for example, that from the time that the Treaty of Westphalia confirmed the state as the principal international actor, the very idea of the nation-state has made it difficult for non-European aboriginal peoples to qualify as such:

> The concept of the nation-State in the post-Westphalian sense is based on European models of political and social organisation whose dominant defining characteristics are exclusivity of territorial domain and hierarchical, centralized authority. By contrast, indigenous peoples . . . at least prior to European contact, typically have been organized primarily by tribal or kinship ties, have had decentralized political structures often linked in confederations, and have enjoyed shared or overlapping spheres of territorial control.[59]

International law is a medium of interaction among states and, to a lesser extent, other international actors. It is ineluctably embedded in a particular spatial, historical, and political context, and yet the rhetoric of international law generally conveys an image of international law as separate from politics and as ahistorical, existing ahead of any specific political scenario. Although entwined with the political context in which it operates, international law has a considerable degree of autonomy as a set of interrelated principles, rules, and concepts. This body of intangible ideas gains cohesion from the logical interrelatedness of its component elements, and the process of dialogue in international law can be understood as an ongoing attempt to clarify the point at which the components of the system of international law are distinguishable from their counterparts in other fields of thought. Although many terms of international law—such as "sovereignty" and "statehood"—may be used in world politics, the process of dialogue in international law can be understood as an ongoing effort to define them in a very precise manner and to maintain the boundary between their "absolute" meaning for the purposes of international law and what may well be their more fluid usages in world politics. We are now going to consider multilateral treaties in more detail to better understand their place as a source of international law in the framework of legal positivism and as living documents integral to particular historical and political trajectories.

Notes

1. For the background to the crisis, see, inter alia, R. Caplan, "International Diplomacy and the Crisis in Kosovo," *International Affairs* 74,

no. 4 (1998): 745–761; and M. Weller, "The Rambouillet Conference on Kosovo," *International Affairs* 75, no. 2 (1999): 211–251.

2. 34 United Nations Treaty Series (UNTS) 243.

3. Resolutions 1160, 1199, and 1203.

4. Bruno Simma, "NATO, the UN, and the Use of Force: Legal Aspects" *European Journal of International Law (EJIL)* 10 (1999): 1–22.

5. Michael J. Glennon, "The New Interventionism: The Search for a Just International Law," *Foreign Affairs* (May/June 1999): 2–7.

6. House of Commons, Select Committee on Foreign Affairs, Fourth Report, para. 144, at http://www.parliament.the-stationery-office.co.uk/pa/cm199900/cmselect/cmfaff/28/2813.htm, accessed June 30, 2000.

7. Article by the Foreign Secretary, Robin Cook, and Liberal Democrat Foreign Affairs Spokesman, Menzies Campbell, in the *Financial Times*, September 4, 2000, at http://www.fco.gov.uk/news/newstext.asp?4108, accessed January 14, 2001.

8. Simon Chesterman, *Just War or Just Peace? Humanitarian Intervention and International Law* (Oxford: Oxford University Press, 2001), p. 224.

9. John J. Merriam, "Kosovo and the Law of Humanitarian Intervention," *Case Western Reserve Journal of International Law* 33, no. 1 (2001): 111–154, 122.

10. Julie Mertus, "Reconsidering the Legality of Humanitarian Intervention: Lessons from Kosovo," *William and Mary Law Review* 41 (2000): 1743–1787.

11. In his commentary on article 2(4), Randelzhofer maintains, however, that the inclusion of the phrases relating to territorial integrity and political independence did not reflect any intention to restrict the general and comprehensive prohibition of force. Albrecht Randelzhofer, "Article 2(4)," in Bruno Simma, ed., *The Charter of the United Nations: A Commentary* (Oxford: Oxford University Press, 1994), p. 118.

12. On the justifications advanced by NATO states, see Abraham D. Sofaer, "International Law and Kosovo," *Stanford Journal of International Law* 1 (2000): 1–21.

13. See the verbatim record of the hearings by the ICJ on Yugoslavia's request for the indication of provisional measures in the case concerning the Legality of Use of Force. Available at http://www.icj-cij.org/icjwww/idocket/iyall/iyallcr/iyallicr9914199990510.html.

14. United Nations General Assembly, Res. 377(v). *United Nations Yearbook 1950*, pp. 193–195.

15. Nicholas J. Wheeler, "Legitimating Humanitarian Intervention: Principles and Procedures," *Melbourne Journal of International Law* 2 (2001): 550–567, 557–557.

16. Michael Byers, *Custom, Power, and the Power of Rules: International Relations and Customary International Law* (Cambridge: Cambridge University Press, 1999), p. 37.

17. "Spokesman Zhu Bangzao Gives Full Account of the Collision Between US and Chinese Military Planes," Embassy of the People's Republic of China in the United States of America, www.china-embassy.org/eng/9585.html, accessed April 5, 2001.

18. James G. Blight and David A. Welch, *On the Brink: Americans and Soviets Reexamine the Cuban Missile Crisis,* 2nd ed. (New York: Noonday, 1990), p. 40.

19. See, inter alia, Abram Chayes, "Law and the Quarantine of Cuba," *Foreign Affairs* 41 (1963): 550–557; and Leonard C. Meeker, "Defensive Quarantine and the Law," *American Journal of International Law (AJIL)* 57 (1963): 515–524.

20. Blight and Welch, *On the Brink*, p. 53.

21. Patricia Birnie, "Opinion on the Legality of the Designation of the Southern Ocean Whale Sanctuary by the International Whaling Commission," available at http://www.highnorth.no/Library/Management_Regimes/IWC/op-on-th.htm.

22. Nicole Garbin, "Effectiveness and Legitimacy of the International Whaling Commission," Research Report no. 20 (Hobart: Cooperative Research Centre for the Antarctic and Southern Ocean Environment, 2000), p. 18.

23. C. C. Joyner, "International Law and the Conduct of Foreign Policy," in S. V. Scott and A. Bergin, eds., *International Law and Australian Security*. (Canberra: Australian Defence Studies Centre, 1997), pp. 5–22, 12.

24. Antonio Cassese, "The Role of Legal Advisers in Ensuring that Foreign Policy Conforms to International Legal Standards," *Michigan Journal of International Law* 14 (Fall 1992): 139–170. On the role of the legal adviser, see, inter alia, Richard B. Bilder, "The Office of the Legal Adviser: The State Department Lawyer and Foreign Affairs," *AJIL* 56 (1962): 633–684; *Collection of Essays by Legal Advisers of States, Legal Advisers of International Organization, and Practitioners in the Field of International Law* (New York: United Nations, 1999); Ashley Deeks, "Inside 'L': Some Thoughts on the Office of the Legal Adviser," *Chicago Journal of International Law* 2, no. 2 (Fall 2001): 503–510; R. St. J. MacDonald, "The Role of Legal Adviser of Ministries of Foreign Affairs," *Recueil des Cours* 1977(III): 377–482; Stephen M. Schwebel, "Remarks on the Role of the Legal Advisor of the US State Department," *EJIL* 2, no. 1 (1991): 132–135; and Edwin D. Williamson, "International Law and the Role of the Legal Adviser in the Persian Gulf Crisis," *New York University Journal of International Law and Politics* 23, no. 2 (Winter 1991): 361–371.

25. Cited in Edward McWhinney, "President Bush and the New US National Security Strategy: The Continuing Relevance of the Legal Adviser and International Law," *Chinese Journal of International Law* (2002): 420–435, 422.

26. See Shirley Scott, "Beyond 'Compliance': Reconceiving the International Law-Foreign Policy Dynamic," *Australian Year Book of International Law* 19 (1998): 35–48, 44–45.

27. R. Higgins, "The Identity of International Law," in B. Cheng, ed., *International Law: Teaching and Practice* (London: Stevens & Sons, 1982), p. 58.

28. E. McWhinney, *United Nations Law Making: Cultural and Ideological Relativism and International Law Making for an Era of Transition* (New York: Holmes & Meier, 1984), pp. 27–44, 23.

29. O. Schachter, "International Law in Theory and Practice: General Course in Public International Law," *Recueil des Cours* 178 (1982/V): 22.

30. Ian Brownlie, *The Rule of Law in International Affairs: International Law at the Fiftieth Anniversary of the United Nations* (The Hague: Martinus Nijhoff, 1998), p. 16.

31. This complaint was made of the Rome diplomatic conference for an international criminal court. Fanny Benedetti and John L. Washburn, "Drafting the International Criminal Court Treaty: Two Years to Rome and an Afterword on the Rome Diplomatic Conference," *Global Governance* 5, no. 1 (January–March 1999): 1–37, 29.

32. See generally Michael Byers and Georg Nolte, eds., *United States Hegemony and the Foundations of International Law* (Cambridge: Cambridge University Press, 2003).

33. See Jack M. Breard, "America's New War on Terror: The Case for Self-defense Under International Law," *Harvard Journal of Law and Public Policy* (Spring 2002): 559–590. Michael Byers has sought to explain the legal justification offered by the United States for its use of force in Afghanistan in terms of legal strategy. Michael Byers, "Terrorism, the Use of Force, and International Law After 11 September," *International and Comparative Law Quarterly* 51 (April 2002): 401–414.

34. A. Anghie, "Francisco de Vitoria and the Colonial Origins of International Law," *Social and Legal Studies* 5 (1996): 321–336.

35. Randa M. Slim, "Small-State Mediation in International Relations: The Algerian Mediation of the Iranian Hostage Crisis," in Jacob Bercovitch and Jeffrey Z. Rubin, eds., *Mediation in International Relations: Multiple Approaches to Conflict Management* (New York: St. Martin's Press in association with the Society for the Psychological Study of Social Issues, 1992), pp. 206–231.

36. Statute of the International Court of Justice, article 31(2) and (3).

37. See Joshua Castellino and Steve Allen, *Title to Territory in International Law: A Temporal Analysis* (Aldershot, UK: Ashgate, 2003).

38. *Western Sahara, Advisory Opinion, ICJ Reports 1975*, pp. 12, 38–39.

39. *Legality of Use of Force (Yugoslavia v. United Kingdom), Provisional Measures, Order of 2 June 1999, ICJ Reports 1999*, p. 925.

40. Yugoslav Declaration Recognizing as Compulsory the Jurisdiction of the Court, reprinted in International Court of Justice, *Yearbook 1998–1999*, p. 131.

41. The New Haven school grew out of the work of scholars at the Yale Law School in New Haven, Connecticut. See, inter alia, M. S. McDougal, *Studies in World Public Order* (New Haven: Yale University Press, 1960); Myres S. McDougal, "Some Basic Theoretical Concepts About International Law: A Policy-Oriented Framework of Inquiry," *Journal of Conflict Resolution* 4 (1960): 337–354; and M. S. McDougal, H. D. Lasswell, and W. M. Reisman, "Theories About International Law: Prologue to a Configurative Jurisprudence," *Virginia Journal of International Law* 8, no. 2 (1968): 188–299. Judge Rosalyn Higgins is an exponent of this approach; see her *Problems and Process: International Law and How We Use It* (Oxford: Clarendon, 1994).

42. Robert J. Beck, Anthony Clark Arend, and Robert D. Vander Lught, eds., *International Rules: Approaches from International Law and*

International Relations (New York and Oxford: Oxford University Press, 1996), p. 111.

43. Martha Finnemore and Stephen J. Toope, "Alternatives to 'Legalization': Richer Views of Law and Politics," *International Organization* 55, no. 3 (Summer 2000): 743–758, 744. See also Jutta Brunée and Stephen J. Toope, "International Law and Constructivism: Elements of an Interactional Theory of International Law," *Columbia Journal of Transnational Law* 39 (2000): 19–74.

44. The two most important works have been D. Kennedy, *International Legal Structures* (Baden-Baden: Nomos Verlagsgese Ilschaft, 1987), and M. Koskenniemi, *From Apology to Utopia* (Helsinki: Lakimiesliiton Kustannus, 1989). See also D. Cass, "Navigating the Newstream: Recent Critical Scholarship in International Law," *Nordic Journal of International Law* 65 (1996): 341–383, 341; and N. Purvis "Critical Legal Studies in Public International Law," *Harvard International Law Journal* 32 (1991): 81–127.

45. This is David Kennedy's term, first used in "A New Stream of International Law Scholarship," *Wisconsin International Law Journal* 7 (1988): 1–49.

46. A. Carty, "Critical International Law: Recent Trends in the Theory of International Law," 2 *EJIL* (1991): 66–96.

47. Koskenniemi, *From Apology to Utopia*, p. 50.

48. Martti Koskenniemi, "Introduction," *Nordic Journal of International Law* 65 (1996): 337–340, 340.

49. A good example is the contribution by Pal Wrange to the special issue of the *Nordic Journal of International Law* devoted to the subject. In the space of only a few pages, the reader finds out that Wrange's father is dead and we learn much about his personal journey to find meaning in his work as a teacher of international law and indeed in his life as a whole. "An Open Letter to My Students," *Nordic Journal of International Law* 65 (1996): 569–595.

50. Richard Falk, "Foreword," in B. S. Chimni, *International Law and World Order: A Critique of Contemporary Approaches* (New Delhi: Sage, 1993), p. 9.

51. Makau Mutua, "What Is TWAIL?" *American Society of International Law: Proceedings of the 94th Annual Meeting*. Washington, DC, 2000, pp. 31–38. See also Karin Mickelson, "Rhetoric and Rage: Third World Voices in International Legal Discourse," *Wisconsin International Law Journal* 16, no. 2 (Summer 1998): 353–419, and the special issue of the *Harvard International Law Journal* 41 (2000) devoted to research and scholarship on developing countries and their contribution to international legal theory.

52 Mutua, "What Is TWAIL?" pp. 31–38.

53. J. T. Gathii, "Review Essay: International Law and Eurocentricity: 1 Anti-Colonial Reconstructions of International Legal History," *EJIL* 9, no. 1 (1998): 184–211.

54. Mutua, "What Is TWAIL?" pp. 31–38.

55. Feminist writing came relatively late to international law. A landmark was H. Charlesworth, C. Chinkin, and S. Wright, "Feminist Approaches to International Law," *AJIL* 85 (1991): 613–645.

56. Hilary Charlesworth and Christine Chinkin, *The Boundaries of*

International Law: A Feminist Analysis (Manchester: Manchester University Press, 2000), pp. 38–48. See also D. Dallmeyer, ed. *Reconceiving Reality: Women and International Law* (Washington, DC: American Society of International Law, 1993); Aaron Xavier Fellmeth, "Feminism and International Law: Theory, Methodology, and Substantive Reform," *Human Rights Quarterly* 22 (2000): 658–733.

57. Charlesworth and Chinkin, *The Boundaries of International Law,* p. 50.

58. Ibid., pp. 260–262.

59. S. James Anaya, *Indigenous Peoples in International Law* (New York: Oxford University Press, 1996), p. 15.

7

Reading a Multilateral Treaty

A treaty is an agreement legally binding under international law. In the era since World War II treaties have taken over from custom as the most important source of international law. Treaty law addresses a wide range of issue areas, including trade, the environment, human rights, and arms control. Much of the law relating to treaties is itself found in treaties: the Vienna Convention on the Law of Treaties (1969)[1] and the Vienna Convention on the Law of Treaties Between States and International Organizations or Between International Organizations.[2] The Vienna Convention on the Law of Treaties entered into force on January 27, 1980. Although this convention is the starting point for a discussion of the law of treaties, and much of it was a codification of customary international law, it applies only to those treaties made after its entry into force[3] and only to written treaties.[4] The other convention, on the law of treaties between states and international organizations or between international organizations, has not yet entered into force.

This chapter will focus on multilateral, as distinct from bilateral, treaties. Multilateral treaties may be entered into by a small group of states, they may be regional, or they may aim for universal participation. Some multilateral treaties establish an international organization to implement the provisions; indeed the sole purpose of some treaties is to create an international organization. The North Atlantic Treaty Organization, for example, was established by the North Atlantic Treaty (the so-called Washington Treaty) of April 4, 1949.[5] In these cases, the treaty functions like a constitution for the relevant IGO.

Figure 7.1 lists some of the most common subject groupings of treaties. It is convenient to categorize treaties under subject headings — the environment, human rights, and so on — but it is important to

Figure 7.1   Examples of Multilateral Treaties at a Regional and Global Level

Selected Subject Areas	Examples at a Regional Level	Examples at a Global Level
Human rights	African Charter on Human and Peoples' Rights	Convention Against Torture and Other Cruel, Inhuman, or Degrading Treatment or Punishment
Laws of war (international humanitarian law)	Havana Convention on Maritime Neutrality	Geneva Convention VI Concerning the Treatmentof Prisoners of War
Arms control	Treaty for the Prohibition of Nuclear Weapons in Latin America and the Caribbean (Treaty of Tlatelolco)	Treaty on the Non-Proliferation of Nuclear Weapons
Trade and commercial relations	North American Free Trade Agreement	UN Convention on Contracts for the International Sale of Goods
International criminal law	European Convention on the Suppression of Terrorism	UN Convention Against Illicit Traffic in Narcotic Drugs and Psychotropic Substances
Environment	Oslo Convention on Marine Dumping	The Vienna Convention on Substances That Deplete the Ozone Layer

remember that a treaty often falls under more than one heading. The Comprehensive Nuclear Test-Ban Treaty, for example, can be regarded as a treaty pertaining to military security and to the environment. The 1982 Law of the Sea Treaty could perhaps be classified as a "political" treaty because it functions like a constitution for the oceans, but it also has much to say about the marine environment and is integral to the maritime security interests of a number of states.

Reading a Multilateral Treaty

It is easy for newcomers to international law, particularly those without a legal background, to avoid reading the texts of treaties, relying instead on secondary accounts of treaty contents. This may be for convenience or out of deference to international law experts. But it is a dangerous habit; the precise wording of a legal document matters. Treaties are not difficult to comprehend, and it is usually much easier in the long run to go straight to the treaty text, using commentaries on the treaty as a supplementary source of information. In the following chapters, references are provided to the location of treaties in the United Nations Treaty Series (UNTS) and in International Legal Materials (ILM). There are also good collections of documents in book form and on the Internet. Such collections can be of great assistance, particularly for researching the key treaties on a specific subject. If the treaty's title is known, then often the quickest way to locate its text is to conduct an Internet search for the treaty title. Glossaries of standard treaty terms can be found on websites of several national departments of foreign affairs or external relations.[6]

When reading a treaty it is useful to divide it into five main sections: the title, the preamble, the substantive clauses, the final clauses, and the testimonium. Let's look at each in turn. Examples will be given from the Antarctic Treaty. It is recommended that readers use one of the search engines available to locate the complete text of this treaty, as well as the Vienna Convention on the Law of Treaties.

The Title

The title of a treaty often expresses the aims of the treaty or at least its subject matter. The title may contain the term "convention," "protocol," "statute," "covenant," "charter," "act," "declaration," "exchange of notes," "agreed minute," "memorandum of agreement," or "modus vivendi" rather than "treaty" without affecting the legal status of the instrument. Although there are no set rules as to when these terms are to be used, each term tends to be used in slightly different situations, as set out in Figure 7.2.

The Preamble

At the beginning of a treaty there is usually a preamble, a list of phrases, often couched in flowery language, that serves as an introduction. If there is later disagreement as to the interpretation of the treaty, the preamble may be looked at to help determine the "object and purpose" of the treaty. The preambular paragraphs are written in either the past tense, as in "convinced" or "assured" or in the continuous present tense, as in "hoping" or "aiming." The length of the preamble varies considerably, but recent treaties tend to have much longer preambles than older

Figure 7.2   The Meaning of Various Terms That Commonly Appear in the Title to Multilateral Treaties

Agreement
A treaty of less high political significance and involving fewer states and a narrower range of subject matter than a convention. An agreement might, for example, deal with technical issues. The term "agreement" is commonly used in international economic law to indicate a broad multilateral agreement.

Charter or *Statute*
Reserved for treaties establishing an international institution, such as the UN Charter or Statute of the International Court of Justice. Such treaties play a role equivalent to that of a constitution. The term "charter" is occasionally used in reference to a non–legally binding MOU (defined below).

Convention
A formal multilateral treaty. The term is used to refer to treaties created by the organs of international institutions.

Covenant
More or less synonymous with "convention," though not as common. An example is the UN Covenant on Civil and Political Rights.

Declaration, *General Act*
A formal treaty or a less formal statement of agreement.

Exchange of Notes or of Letters
The means by which states notify each other that they agree to act in a certain manner. They may constitute either a treaty or a non–legally binding MOU.

Final Act
The document that records the results of a conference convened to create an international treaty. The final act may contain the treaty or points of agreement not incorporated in the treaty.

(continues)

Figure 7.2 continued

Memorandum of Understanding (MOU)
A treaty may have "Memorandum of Understanding" in its title, but the term "MOU" usually refers to an instrument concluded between states that is not legally binding. Non–legally binding MOUs may be preferred when the parties desire confidentiality. Unlike a treaty, there is no international requirement to publish an MOU. An MOU can usually be brought into operation more quickly than a treaty because most come into effect on signature (see Anthony Aust, cited below, pp. 26–46).

Modus Vivendi
An informal agreement of a temporary or provisional nature intended to be replaced with a more detailed and formal treaty.

Procès Verbale
An information agreement containing a record of certain understandings.

Protocol
A treaty that is less formal than a convention. The term is often used to refer to an agreement concluded subsequent to a treaty, to deal with issues that arise during its operation. In several human rights treaties, an optional protocol to the treaty has been adopted on the same day to establish additional obligations to which not all negotiating states could agree.

Treaty
Use of the term "treaty" in the title usually indicates that the subject matter of the treaty was regarded as of some gravity.

Notes

Source: From I. A. Shearer, *Starke's International Law,* 11th ed. (London: Butterworths, 1994), pp. 401–404; Anthony Aust, *Modern Treaty Law and Practice* (Cambridge: Cambridge University Press, 2000), pp. 20–25; and *United Nations Treaty Collection Treaty Reference Guide* (1999).

ones; the preamble to the 1948 Genocide Convention was only four paragraphs long. The Antarctic Treaty begins:

> The Governments of Argentina, Australia, Belgium, Chile, the French Republic, Japan, New Zealand, Norway, the Union of South Africa, the Union of Soviet Socialist Republics, the United Kingdom of Great Britain and Northern Ireland, and the United States of America,
>   *Recognizing* that it is in the interest of all mankind that Antarctica shall continue for ever to be used exclusively for peaceful purposes and shall not become the scene or object of international discord;
>   *Acknowledging* the substantial contributions to scientific knowledge resulting from international cooperation in scientific investigation in Antarctica;
>   *Convinced* that the establishment of a firm foundation for the continuation and development of such cooperation on the basis of freedom of scientific investigation in Antarctica as applied during the International Geophysical Year accords with the interests of science and the progress of all mankind;
>   *Convinced* also that a treaty ensuring the use of Antarctica for peaceful purposes only and the continuance of international harmony in Antarctica will further the purposes and principles embodied in the Charter of the United Nations

The preamble usually finishes with words similar to "have agreed as follows," leading into the main treaty text.

The main treaty text may be one or two pages in length, or it may be the size of a small book. It is divided into articles. In a long treaty the articles may be grouped into chapters, sections, and parts and may include annexes. The 1982 Law of the Sea Convention consists of 320 articles divided into seventeen parts.

Substantive Articles

The substantive articles contain the obligations that the parties are assuming through the treaty. It is now common for the first article to contain key definitions, although definitions may be given elsewhere in the treaty text. Multilateral treaties now often include provisions specifying how the treaty in question is to relate to others addressing the same subject matter. A treaty may specify that the parties shall not enter into later inconsistent treaties; that an existing treaty shall not be affected; that for parties the treaty prevails over earlier treaties; or that compatible supplementary treaties are permitted. Disagreement over mineral resources of the seabed and ocean floor prevented a final consensus document at the Third Law of the Sea Conference. Four years of informal consultations conducted by the UN Secretary-General on several issues relating to the deep seabed mining provisions of the convention culminated on July 28, 1994, with the General Assembly adopting an agreement relating to the implementation of part XI of the 1982 UN Convention on the Law of the Sea.[7] By article 2(I) the provisions of the agreement and part XI of the Law of the Sea Convention are to be interpreted and applied together as a single instrument: "In the event of any inconsistency between this Agreement and Part XI, the provisions of the Agreement are to prevail." Where a treaty says nothing about its relationship to other treaties addressing the same subject matter, customary international law as codified by article 30 of the Vienna Convention on the Law of Treaties applies. This specifies, inter alia, that where all the parties to the earlier treaty are parties also to the later treaty but the earlier treaty is not terminated or suspended in operation, the earlier treaty applies only to the extent that its provisions are compatible with those of the later treaty.

Final Clauses

This section of a treaty deals with the mechanics of how the treaty will function, that is, with the operation of the treaty itself as opposed to the issue being addressed by the treaty. Recent treaties contain much more in the way of formal or final clauses than earlier treaties.

The final clauses will usually include information on the following:

How long the treaty will be open for signature. It is now common for a treaty aiming at global membership to be left open for signature for a specified time after its conclusion or adoption—up to about nine months—in order to increase the number of signatories. The treaty may specify which other states—other members of the United Nations, for example—are to be allowed to sign the treaty during that time. Once the specified period is up, any nonsignatory wanting to become a party has to accede rather than sign and ratify (see below).

How signatories are to express their consent to be bound by the provisions of the treaty. This usually involves signature and ratification. Ratification involves two steps. The first is that by which a state makes the internal decision to be bound by the treaty and the executive executes an instrument of ratification. The second step in the ratification process is the external one, which in the case of a multilateral treaty involves lodging the instrument of ratification with the depositary of the treaty. A state or international organization usually acts as a depositary for written instruments of ratification. Although it is usual for a state that has signed a treaty to proceed to ratification, it is not legally obliged to do so. The United States made clear its intention not to proceed to ratification of the Rome Statute of the International Criminal Court. Not all states that had signed the Environmental Protocol to the Antarctic Treaty proceeded to ratification, in that case blocking its entry into force. In the case of a protocol, there is usually a requirement that a state wishing to sign the treaty also be a party to the initial treaty.

Reservations.   A multilateral treaty may specify whether it is possible for a state to accept part but not all of its provisions. The Vienna Convention defines a reservation as a "unilateral statement, however phrased or named, made by a State, when signing, ratifying, accepting, approving or acceding to a treaty, whereby it purports to exclude or to modify the legal effect of certain provisions of the treaty in their application to that State." Some treaties, such as the Convention for the Protection of the Ozone Layer and the Third UN Convention on the Law of the Sea, do not permit of reservations. If the treaty says nothing about reservations, a state may nevertheless make a reservation as long as it is not "incompatible with the object and purpose of the treaty."[8] When signing or ratifying a treaty a state may also make a declaration. This is a statement that, in legal terms, does not lessen the state's obligations under that treaty in the way that a reservation would, but, for example, clarifies how that state is to interpret a particular clause.[9]

How and when the treaty is to enter into force.   Multilateral treaties usually stipulate the conditions to be met in order for the treaty to take effect as law. This might be the receipt by the depositary of a certain number of instruments of ratification, or a date, or some other requirement. In some cases the negotiating states may have agreed that the treaty will enter into force only if specific states proceed to ratification. Article XIV of the CTBT provides that a specified group of forty-four states listed in annex 2 (those with nuclear reactors on their territories) must ratify the treaty in order for it to enter into force. Although the provision was controversial, it was reasoned that the treaty must capture a certain minimum set of nuclear weapon–capable states to be effective in promoting nonproliferation objectives.[10] The Antarctic Treaty came into force on June 23, 1961, in accordance with article XIII(5) of the treaty, upon deposit of the instruments of ratification of all the signatory states. The Antarctic Treaty provided that the treaty would enter into force when the twelve signatories had all deposited their instruments of ratification. Where a treaty is silent about its entry into force, this happens as soon as all negotiating states have indicated their consent to be bound by the treaty.[11]

If and how other states that have not signed the treaty may nevertheless become parties to it. This is known as accession. Acceding to a treaty has the same legal effect as signing and ratifying it, although in the case of the Antarctic Treaty, the text provides that the implications of each will differ. States that are original signatories to the Antarctic Treaty are automatically "consultative parties" (those with the key decisionmaking responsibilities), whereas acceding states remain such only "during such times as that Contracting Party demonstrates its interest in Antarctica by conducting substantial research activity there."[12]

Withdrawal, duration, and termination of the treaty. A treaty may be terminated at any time, or a state can withdraw from it, by the consent of all the parties.[13] Most multilateral treaties specify how an individual state can withdraw if it chooses to do so, and for how long the treaty will last. Article X of the NPT provides that:

> 1. Each State Party shall, in exercising its national sovereignty, have the right to withdraw from this Convention if it decides that extraordinary events, related to the subject-matter of this Convention, have jeopardized the supreme interests of its country. It shall give notice of such withdrawal 90 days in advance to all other States Parties, the Executive Council, the Depositary and the United Nations Security Council. Such notice shall include a statement of the extraordinary events it regards as having jeopardized its supreme interests.
> 2. Twenty-five years after the entry into force of the Treaty, a conference shall be convened to decide whether the Treaty shall continue in force indefinitely, or shall be extended for an additional fixed period or periods. This decision shall be taken by a majority of the Parties to the Treaty.

If the treaty does not include provisions on withdrawal, but it can be established that the parties intended it to be possible to do so, a state may in certain circumstances be able to invoke a material breach of a treaty by another state, the impossibility of performing a treaty, or a fundamental change of circumstances (*rebus sic stantibus*), as grounds for withdrawing from, or terminating, a treaty.[14] Otherwise a treaty is perpetual, and the unilateral denunciation of it by one state is a breach.

How and when the treaty may be modified or amended.   The treaty may specify how it can be modified, which means changed only as between some parties, whereas in their relations with the other parties the original treaty provisions still apply. If the treaty says nothing about modification, article 41 of the Vienna Convention stipulates that modifications are allowed only if they do not affect the rights or obligations of the other parties to the treaty and do not contravene the object and the purpose of the treaty. "Amendment" refers to a change to the treaty that will apply to all parties. If the treaty says nothing about amendment, article 40 of the Vienna Convention applies, by which an amendment requires the consent of all the parties.

Provisions on dispute resolution.   Dispute resolution provisions in a multilateral agreement set out how treaty parties are to deal with matters of contention that arise during the life of the multilateral treaty. Methods of dispute resolution may be either voluntary or compulsory, as may be any decision by a third party. Article 2(3) of the UN Charter places a basic obligation on all member states to "settle their international disputes by peaceful means in such a manner that international peace and security, and justice, are not endangered." Article 33(1) offers them a range of ways by which they might go about doing so: negotiation, enquiry, mediation, conciliation, arbitration, judicial settlement, resort to regional agencies or arrangements, or other peaceful means of their own choice. *Negotiation* is the least formal of these alternatives; it involves direct talks between the parties to the dispute. No third party is involved. This is the most common means by which states resolve their differences. One step more formal is an *inquiry*; here a third party is charged not with resolving the dispute but with ascertaining the answers to certain questions of fact, which can then be used as a basis of negotiation. *Mediation* involves a neutral third party approved by both sides to help broker a compromise. Reference of the dispute to a third party such as a commission or committee to recommend proposals for settlement is known as *conciliation*. The proposals of the conciliator are advisory only. Although hundreds of treaties providing for conciliation have been concluded, there have been only about twenty actual conciliations.[15] Moving one step more formal is *arbitration*, by which each state nominates judges and agrees to accept the decision of those judges. The most formal method of dispute resolution in international law is *judicial settlement*.

The settlement of a dispute through negotiation, inquiry, mediation, or conciliation may involve political and/or legal compromise. If a dispute is submitted to arbitration or judicial settlement the dispute must be settled only on the basis of the applicable law. Here is article XI of the Antarctic Treaty, which addresses dispute resolution in the treaty regime:

> 1. If any dispute arises between two or more of the Contracting Parties concerning the interpretation or application of the present Treaty, those Contracting Parties shall consult among themselves with a view to having the dispute resolved by negotiation, inquiry, mediation; conciliation, arbitration, judicial, settlement or other peaceful means of their own choice.
> 2. Any dispute of this character not so resolved shall, with the consent, in each case, of all parties to the dispute, be referred to the International Court of Justice for settlement; but failure to reach agreement on reference to the International Court shall not absolve parties to the dispute from the responsibility of continuing to seek to resolve it by any of the various peaceful means referred to in paragraph 1 of this Article.

Several of the more recent major multilateral treaties establish their own dispute resolution mechanisms and bodies. These are typically less formal and costly than the International Court of Justice and aim for greater participation and a quicker outcome. The phenomenon has nevertheless come under debate as a perhaps unnecessary proliferation, which may weaken the unity of the international legal system as a whole and favor some fields of international law over others. This is particularly so since there is no hierarchy within the group of judicial bodies as there is in most national court systems.

One of the most important differences between the World Trade Organization, established in 1995, and the General Agreement on Tariffs and Trade, which it incorporated and went beyond, was its more far-reaching provisions on dispute settlement. GATT operated on a "positive consensus" principle: Consensus was required before the dispute resolution mechanism would go into operation; the procedure for dispute resolution operates much more automatically under the WTO

Dispute Settlement Understanding. By article 6(1), a panel is established automatically once a complaining party so requests, unless the Dispute Settlement Body (DSB) decides by consensus not to establish a panel.[16] The report of the panel is later adopted by the DSB unless a party to the dispute formally notifies the DSB of its decision to appeal, or the DSB decides by consensus not to adopt the report.[17] Members are to "comply promptly" with recommendations or rulings of the DSB.[18]

The Third Law of the Sea Convention offers a wide choice of methods for dispute settlement. When a dispute relating to the treaty arises, states are to "proceed expeditiously" to agree on a method of dispute settlement. Annex V sets out conciliation procedures that may be used if both agree on the conciliation procedure. If a party does not agree to conciliation, or if conciliation fails to bring about a settlement, the dispute can be submitted, at the request of any party to the dispute, to the court or tribunal having jurisdiction under section 2 of part XV.[19] Section 2 of part XV provides that parties to the convention may make a declaration regarding their choice of dispute settlement procedures: the International Tribunal for the Law of the Sea, the International Court of Justice, an arbitral tribunal established under annex VII, or a special technical arbitral tribunal established under annex VIII. If the parties to a dispute have not accepted the same procedure, a dispute is to be submitted to arbitration in accordance with annex VII unless the parties agree otherwise.[20]

The Law of the Sea Tribunal (ITLOS), whose statute appears as annex VI to the Convention, was inaugurated in October 1996. There have been some critics of what is seen as an unnecessary addition to the range of dispute resolution bodies, but supporters maintain that the tribunal has some distinctive features of particular value to the peaceful resolution of disputes. One is its capacity to deliver judgments in a relatively short time. Special chambers, including one on the marine environment, are designed in part for this purpose. Each has seven judges selected for their specialist expertise in the area. A state may still have a case heard by the full tribunal if it so wishes.[21] The tribunal enjoys special competence to deal with requests for provisional measures. At the request of a party to a dispute, the tribunal may, as long as a prima facie case for jurisdiction can be made, prescribe, modify, or revoke provisional measures necessary to preserve the respective rights of the parties to a dispute or to prevent harm to the marine environment.[22]

The Testimonium

The final clauses are followed by the testimonium, the part below which the representatives sign, as well as by signature block and any annexes. Here is a standard testimonium:

> In witness whereof the undersigned, being duly authorised [by their respective Governments], have signed this [Agreement].
>   Done at [place], this [   ] day of [   ], two thousand and [   ]
>   For [the Government of . . .]: [signature]
>   For [the Government of . . .]: [signature]
>   [Etc.][23]

Beyond the Treaty Text:
The Antarctic Treaty and Political Process

A treaty does not come into existence as an isolated phenomenon but as part of a political process that begins well before, and continues well after, the finalization of the treaty text; the conclusion of the treaty is just one stage in a longer political process by which a group of states addresses an issue of mutual concern. Every treaty has a political and historical story to tell and can only be understood as a political as well as a legal document if viewed in a longer time frame and broader context. This section will illustrate the political and historical embedment of a multilateral treaty by reference to the Antarctic Treaty. In Chapter 8, we will consider the politics of this process in more depth.

Treaty Origins: Background of the Antarctic Treaty

As we saw in Chapter 1, sovereignty is one of the most fundamental concepts in the international states system and in the system of international law. In the case of Antarctica there has been little agreement as to who has sovereignty over what territory. The unresolved nature of the sovereignty issue has underpinned most political questions relating to the continent. Prior to 1959 there were three groups of states with "interests" in Antarctica. The first group could be referred to as the "South American claimants." Chile and Argentina each asserted territorial rights over that portion of the Antarctic continent nearest to their mainland territory. Both states recognized the right of the other to a portion of South American Antarctica. These rights were believed to derive from a papal bull of 1493 by which Alexander VI gave, granted, and assigned forever to Spain and its successors all territory from the North Pole to the South Pole west of a meridian 370 leagues west of the Cape Verde Islands. As successor states to Spain in South America, Argentina and Chile believed that they had inherited rights to a portion of Antarctica. From their perspectives all that remained to be done was to negotiate their mutual boundary.[24]

The second group of states with interests in Antarctica prior to 1959 consisted of the United Kingdom, France, Norway, New Zealand, and Australia. The United Kingdom originally had ambitions to acquire the entire continent. But between the two world wars it negotiated a division of the continent with the other states in this group. It was unable to settle the issue with the South American claimants, however, both of whose territorial claims overlapped that of the United Kingdom.

The third set of states with interests in Antarctica consisted of those that had not made a formal territorial claim but that either asserted their right to do so at a later date or had at least displayed an active interest in the continent. This group consisted of the United States, the Soviet Union, Japan, South Africa, and Belgium.

The issue of disputed Antarctic sovereignty was most serious in relation to the Antarctic Peninsula, where the claims of Chile, Argentina, and the United Kingdom overlapped. A series of incidents in the early post–World War II years brought the UK and Argentina close to conflict.[25] In 1947 the United Kingdom proposed that the case be submitted to the International Court of Justice. The suggestion was repeated on a number of occasions, but the issue never came before the Court. In 1948 the United States, which had made no territorial claim, proposed a draft agreement by which Argentina, Australia, Chile, France, Norway, New Zealand, the United Kingdom, and the United States would be designated the administering authority of the trust territory of Antarctica.[26] The United Kingdom proposed an eight-power condominium arrangement.[27] During discussions in Santiago in 1948, a Chilean law professor, Julio Escudero Buzman, suggested that existing legal rights and interests in Antarctica be frozen for a period of five or ten years during which activities in Antarctica would have no legal effect.[28] This idea was effectively trialed during the International Geophysical Year of 1958, for which the participating governments "reached a sort of gentleman's agreement not to engage in legal or political argumentation during that period, in order that the scientific program might proceed without impediment."[29] The arrangement appeared to work well and was formalized in the Antarctic Treaty of 1959. The treaty was proposed by the United States, which provided a draft text and a venue for the negotiations.

The Finalization of the Antarctic Treaty

The Antarctic Treaty was signed in Washington on December 1, 1959, and entered into force on June 23, 1961, after ratification by all signatory states. The treaty addresses a number of issues: scientific cooperation, the denuclearization of Antarctica, and the "freezing" of claims to territorial sovereignty in Antarctica. The treaty is sometimes listed as a scientific treaty,[30] and it is true that the treaty was an important contribution to the management of the continent so as to facilitate scientific endeavor. The treaty is also sometimes listed as an arms control treaty, notable as being the first arms control agreement to be negotiated after World War II. Article I of the treaty prohibits "any measure of a military nature, such as the establishment of military bases and fortifications, the carrying out of military manoeuvres, as well as the testing of any type of weapon," and article V prohibits "any nuclear explosions in Antarctica and the disposal there of radioactive waste material." From a political point of view, however, the treaty is most significant for its treatment of the question of sovereignty in Antarctica. By article IV of the treaty:

1. Nothing contained in the present Treaty shall be interpreted as:
   a. a renunciation by any Contracting Party of previously asserted rights of or claims to territorial sovereignty in Antarctica;
   b. a renunciation or diminution by any Contracting Party of any basis of claim to territorial sovereignty in Antarctica which it may have whether as a result of its activities or those of its nationals in Antarctica, or otherwise;
   c. prejudicing the position of any Contracting Party as regards its recognition or non-recognition of any other State's rights of or claim or basis of claim to territorial sovereignty in Antarctica.
2. No acts or activities taking place while the present Treaty is in force shall constitute a basis for asserting, supporting or denying a claim to territorial sovereignty in Antarctica or create any rights of sovereignty in Antarctica. No new claim, or enlargement of an existing claim, to territorial sovereignty in Antarctica shall be asserted while the present Treaty is in force.

Article IV has functioned as the cornerstone of the Antarctic Treaty and the set of political relationships founded thereon.

The Antarctic Treaty System

With the conclusion of the treaty, what is known as the Antarctic Treaty System (ATS) came into operation. During the early years of the treaty the question of the management of Antarctica's living resources was addressed in three new treaties: the 1964 Agreed Measures for the Conservation of Antarctic Fauna and Flora, the 1972 Convention for the Conservation of Antarctic Seals, and the 1980 Convention on the Conservation of Antarctic Marine Living Resources. From 1982 to 1988 consultative parties to the Antarctic Treaty negotiated a treaty dealing with a nonliving resource: minerals. The issue of who could mine Antarctica and where confronted the sovereignty issue head-on because it is usually up to the territorial sovereign to determine that.

The mineral negotiations focused considerable international attention on Antarctica and prompted certain members of the third world, led by Malaysia, to claim that the ATS was not the best or the fairest way to manage Antarctica. Particularly in the General Assembly of the United Nations, third world critics of the ATS argued that Antarctica should be the "common heritage of mankind." This was a concept that had first been used in 1967 in relation to the law of the sea. The third world referred to the ATS as an "exclusive club." Some believed that Antarctica should be managed by the UN; others argued that the ATS be retained but all states be able to join and all given equal decisionmaking status. Members of the ATS responded with the argument that Antarctica was already being managed in the interests of all—Antarctica was dedicated to science and all would benefit from the scientific knowledge obtained there. The ATS did, however, allow all contracting parties to attend the minerals meetings, and several third world states, notably India and China, were granted consultative party status by the mid-1980s. There was an annual debate on the question of Antarctica in the General Assembly until 1994, but the ATS withstood this external challenge.

Meanwhile, on June 2, 1988, the Convention for the Regulation of Antarctic Mineral Resources (CRAMRA) was concluded. When Australia announced that it would not ratify this convention, however, political relations became strained because the treaty could not enter into force without Australian ratification. CRAMRA was effectively replaced by the 1992 Environmental Protocol, which, by article 7, prohibits any activity relating to mineral resources other than scientific research. The protocol entered into force in January 1998. Since the conclusion of the Environmental Protocol, members of the ATS have devoted a lot of attention to negotiating a liability annex to the Environmental Protocol. ATS members decided in 2001 that a secretariat would be established in Buenos Aires.

Tracing the background to, and subsequent political activity centered on, the Antarctic Treaty has sought to illustrate the fact that a multilateral treaty is the culmination of what may have been a long process of negotiation and of attempts to address an issue of concern to members of the international community. Once in place, a treaty provides a basis on which states can cooperate to manage the issue it was designed to address. We have looked briefly at the political dynamics that gave rise to the Antarctic Treaty and that have continued since. We will now look at the generic process in detail before examining a range of multilateral treaties.

Notes

1. International Legal Materials (ILM) 679 (1969). The negotiating history of the Vienna Convention can be found in S. Rosenne, *The Law of Treaties* (Leyden: A. W. Sijthoff; Dobbs Ferry, NY: Oceana, 1970). David Anderson gives his personal impressions of the negotiations in David H. Anderson, "Law-Making Processes in the UN System: Some Impressions," *Max Planck Yearbook of United Nations Law* 2 (1998): 23–50.

2. 25 ILM 543 (1986)

3. Vienna Convention on the Law of Treaties, article 4.

4. Vienna Convention on the Law of Treaties, article 2(1)(a).

5. Found at www.nato.int/docu/basictxt/treaty.htm.

6. See, for example, that available from the UK Foreign and Commonwealth Office at www.fco.gov.uk/directory/treaty.asp or www.access.gpo.gov/congress/cong006.html.

7. UN Doc. A/RES/48/263 (August 17, 1994), Annex, reproduced in 33 ILM 1309 (1994). See, inter alia, D. Anderson, "Efforts to Ensure Universal Participation in the United Nations Convention on the Law of the Sea," *International and Comparative Law Quarterly (ICLQ)* 42 (1993): 654–664; D. Anderson, "Further Efforts to Ensure Universal Participation in the United Nations Convention on the Law of the Sea," *ICLQ* 43 (1994): 886–893; Moritaka Hayashi, "The 1994 Agreement for the Universalization of the Law of the Sea Convention," *Ocean Development & International Law* 27 (1996): 31–39; L. D. M. Nelsen, "The New Deep Seabed Mining Regime," *International Journal of Marine and Coastal Law* 10 (1995): 189–203.

8. Vienna Convention on the Law of Treaties, article 19 (c).

9. For detailed discussion of the law of reservations, see Anthony Aust,

Modern Treaty Law and Practice (Cambridge: Cambridge University Press, 2000), pp. 100ff.

10. E. Arnett, "The Comprehensive Nuclear Test-Ban Treaty," *SIPRI Yearbook 1997: Armaments, Disarmament, and International Security* (Oxford: Oxford University Press, 1997), pp. 403–413, 405.

11. Vienna Convention on the Law of Treaties, article 24(2).

12. The Antarctic Treaty, article IX (2).

13. Vienna Convention on the Law of Treaties, article 54 (b).

14. Vienna Convention on the Law of Treaties, part V, section 3.

15. J. G. Merrills, *International Dispute Settlement*, 3rd ed. (Cambridge: Cambridge University Press, 1998), p. 84.

16. Understanding on Rules and Procedures Governing the Settlement of Disputes, Article 6(1).

17. Understanding on Rules and Procedures Governing the Settlement of Disputes, Article 16(4).

18. Understanding on Rules and Procedures Governing the Settlement of Disputes, Article 21(1).

19. United Nations Convention on the Law of the Sea (1982), article 286, 21 ILM 1261 (1982).

20. United Nations Convention on the Law of the Sea, article 287(5).

21. On the tribunal specifically, and on the question of the proliferation of courts and tribunals, see, inter alia, A. E. Boyle, "Dispute Settlement and the Law of the Sea Convention: Problems of Fragmentation and Jurisdiction," *ICLQ* 46 (January 1997): 37–54; Carl-August Fleischhauer, "The Relationship Between the International Court of Justice and the Newly Created International Tribunal for the Law of the Sea in Hamburg," *Max Planck Yearbook of United Nations Law* 1 (1997): 327–333; Benedict Kingsbury, "Foreword: Is the Proliferation of International Courts and Tribunals a Systemic Problem?" *International Law and Politics* 31 (1999): 679–696; J. E. Noyes, "The International Tribunal for the Law of the Sea," *Cornell International Law Journal* 32 (1998): 109–182; and Cesar P. R. Romano, "The Proliferation of International Judicial Bodies: The Pieces of the Puzzle," *International Law and Politics* 31, no. 709 (1999): 709–751.

22. United Nations Convention on the Law of the Sea, article 290(1).

23. Information taken from Aust, *Modern Treaty Law and Practice,* p. 352.

24. See Shirley V. Scott, "Universalism and Title to Territory in Antarctica," *Nordic Journal of International Law* 66 (1997): 33–53.

25. This paragraph draws on Peter Beck, *The International Politics of Antarctica* (London: Croom Helm, 1986).

26. "United States Draft Agreement Placing Antarctica Under a United Nations Trusteeship," June 1948, in W. M. Bush, *Antarctica and International Law: A Collection of Inter-state and National Documents*, vol. 3 (London: Oceana, 1988), p. 462.

27. "Editorial Note," in *Foreign Relations of the United States (FRUS)* (1948/I), p. 992.

28. "The Ambassador in Chile (Bowers) to the Secretary of State," July 19, 1948, in *FRUS* (1948/I), p. 995. The proposal was repeated, in conversation, in August 1948. "Memorandum of Conversation, by the Under Secretary of State (Lovett)," August 16, 1948, in *FRUS* (1948/I), p. 1002.

29. Paul C. Daniels, "The Antarctic Treaty," in R. S. Lewis and P. M. Smith, eds., *Frozen Future: A Prophetic Report from Antarctica* (New York: Quadrangle Books, 1973), pp. 31–45, 35.

30. N. J. Rengger, *Treaties and Alliances of the World*, 5th ed. (Harlow, Essex: Longman, 1990), p. 96.

8

The Evolution of a
Multilateral Treaty Regime

I n the final section of Chapter 7 we looked briefly at the political process by which the Antarctic Treaty came about and at the life of the treaty after its conclusion. In this chapter we will detail the political process of which a multilateral treaty is a part. Figure 8.1 depicts the "typical" political process centered on a multilateral treaty in terms of four principal phases: pretreaty, finalization of the multilateral treaty, operation of the treaty regime, and the supplantation or supplementation of the treaty regime.

A multilateral treaty is the culmination of what may have been a long political process. But it is, in another sense, only the beginning. Once the treaty document is in place it provides the central focus for the continuation of that political process that, together with the treaty itself, can now be referred to as a "regime." The term "regime" can lead to some confusion because it is used in several ways. Lawyers use the term to refer to "all the law on a particular subject." Instead of talking about "all the law on human rights" a lawyer might refer to the "human rights regime"; instead of talking about the international law pertaining to arms control, reference is made to the "arms control regime," and so on. In the mid-1970s international relations theorists adopted another meaning of "regime," referring to a process of international cooperation. Until then international cooperation had mainly been studied by analysts of international organizations. Intergovernmental organizations and international cooperation were considered more or less synonymous. But much international cooperation takes place other than through a formal organizational structure. International relations scholars began using the term "regime" to refer to a process of international cooperation, particularly in the field of economics, whether or not it

**Figure 8.1   The Typical Process of International Cooperation
Centered on a Multilateral Treaty**

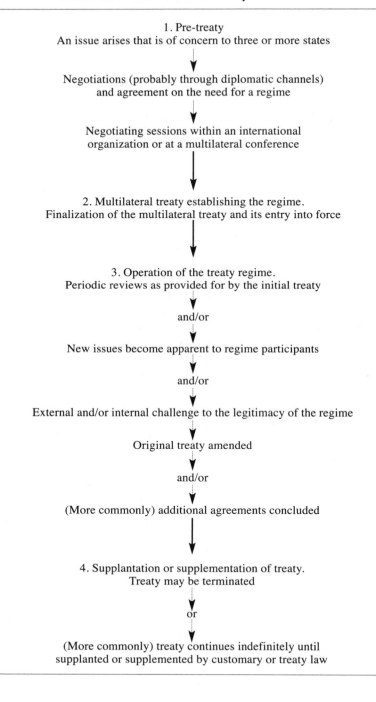

1. Pre-treaty
An issue arises that is of concern to three or more states

Negotiations (probably through diplomatic channels)
and agreement on the need for a regime

Negotiating sessions within an international
organization or at a multilateral conference

2. Multilateral treaty establishing the regime.
Finalization of the multilateral treaty and its entry into force

3. Operation of the treaty regime.
Periodic reviews as provided for by the initial treaty

and/or

New issues become apparent to regime participants

and/or

External and/or internal challenge to the legitimacy of the regime

Original treaty amended

and/or

(More commonly) additional agreements concluded

4. Supplantation or supplementation of treaty.
Treaty may be terminated

or

(More commonly) treaty continues indefinitely until
supplanted or supplemented by customary or treaty law

involves a formal organizational structure. The General Agreement on Tariffs and Trade, for example, was a treaty negotiated in 1947, on the basis of which several additional "negotiating rounds" were held. But there was no GATT organization with staff and a building. GATT appeared to operate as an international organization but was not one. The "regime" concept began to be used to refer to a pattern of cooperation whether or not it had a formal organizational structure. GATT was a regime; so is the UN.

In the classic book on international regimes, the editor, Stephen Krasner, defined a "regime" as "principles, norms, rules and decision-making processes around which actor expectations converge in a given issue area."[1] The early writing on international regimes by political scientists did not say much about international law.[2] It was not clearly defined as to how the rules, principles, and norms of the international political regime related to those of international law. The tendency to skirt around the subject of international law on the part of regime theorists has no doubt been, in part, a legacy of a general dismissal of the importance of international law by post–World War II political realists. Some leading regime theorists have sought to maintain a distinction between international law and international regimes, maintaining that formalization is not a necessary condition for the effective operation of international regimes.[3] The exact nature of the relationship between a "legal" regime and a "political" regime cannot be precisely defined, most basically because of the lack of universality in the treatment of the term by political scientists. But it is true to say that the vast majority of entities and processes that political scientists consider to be regimes — formal international organizations as well as patterns of cooperation short of a formal organizational structure — have in common their foundation in a multilateral treaty. Even though a number of scholars have pointed to the possibilities of fruitful interdisciplinary interaction in the study of regimes,[4] it remains more common for disciplinary boundaries to remain, with complementary meanings attributed to the term "regime." Thus, when political scientists refer to a "regime," they are emphasizing the normative aspect of rules and norms as well as decisionmaking processes, social practices, and institutional structure, whereas when international lawyers refer to a "regime" they are focusing on the contents of one or more legal sources on a particular subject.[5]

In this book the phrase "treaty regime" is used to emphasize the fact that we are looking at the law contained in one or more multilateral treaties in the context of the political process of which the law is a part.

An Issue Arises That Is of
Concern to Three or More States

A multilateral treaty results from a perceived need to manage an issue of mutual concern, whether that be climate change or genocide. The title of the treaty will often give a good indication of the regime issue. What is of interest politically is how the issue came to be recognized as one deserving of international cooperation. Who defined it as an issue? Of course, a treaty may be a long document, and a treaty often appears to address a number of issues. But even if a multilateral treaty does address more than one issue, it is usually possible, particularly if one investigates the historical record, to identify the central issue that prompted the parties to act. An understanding of the perception of the issue in the years immediately preceding the conclusion of the treaty can do much to help understand the evolution of that regime in later years.

Negotiations and
Agreement on the Need for a Regime

Whereas the outsider could be excused for thinking that the primary negotiating phase is that of the international conference at which the text of the multilateral treaty is finalized, the most important negotiations have usually occurred in the months or years before that. The process of getting to the table has been referred to as "prenegotiations"[6] to emphasize their role prior to the more formal and publicized negotiations. During prenegotiations the participants usually reach agreement as to who is to be at the table and the boundaries within which the topic is to be discussed.[7] This was acknowledged by the Australian representative at the opening session of the Antarctic conference when he recalled that it had only been "when it became clear that there was fairly general agreement [that the best solution would be to include provisions in the treaty that would preserve the status quo as regards territorial claims] that we believed that the calling of a Conference was justified."[8]

Much of the prenegotiations may take place at a bilateral level. Governments may be sounded out through normal diplomatic channels well ahead of the formal announcement of a multilateral conference. In this way, positions can be negotiated in an "invisible" way that does not require any party to back down publicly on its policy position. In the case of some environmental negotiations there have also been informal workshops, which participants—scientists, academics, industry representatives, and so on—attend in their personal capacities. An example of this was the Intergovernmental Panel on Climate Change. Public support for a particular course of action may also be garnered through use of the media. The negotiations may be quite rapid or take a number of sessions, spanning a number of years. The negotiation of the third UN Convention on the Law of the Sea took nine years of negotiations, which followed six years of preparatory work by the UN Sea-Bed Committee.

Let us now consider the role in the negotiating phase leading up to a multilateral treaty of the hegemon, of middle powers, of the South, and of nonstate actors. As will be seen, the respective influence of the various types of international actors depends to some extent on the issue at hand.

The Hegemon

The theory of hegemonic stability suggests, most basically, that a regime emerges when a hegemon, a state with preponderant power, regards such a regime as being in its best interests.[9] Since the United States has been a world hegemon at least since World War II, this theory suggests that a regime has emerged where the United States has estimated that the anticipated gains would exceed the costs of supplying the regime.[10] The theory of hegemonic stability was developed primarily in relation to trade, explaining the emergence of GATT as a multilateral trade regime in terms of U.S. interests. The hegemonic influence of the United States would appear to have been most notable in relation to trade and arms control regimes; some have argued that there is no hegemonic power for environmental issues.[11]

There have been two schools of thought regarding how the most powerful state uses its preponderant resources to create the regimes it prefers. Charles Kindleberger advanced the notion of a "benign hegemon" that exercises positive leadership in enticing others to accept its preferences; the benign hegemon is willing to bear an undue part of the short-term costs because it will pay off in the long term in terms of prestige.[12] In the case of the 1987 ozone negotiations, U.S. negotiations involved extensive bilateral consultations in order to find the "real interests" behind states' positions; when the Soviet Union refused to accept the 1986 reference year for controlled output levels, the head of the U.S. delegation discovered that Soviet opposition stemmed from the domestic legal constraints of a Five Year Plan, ending in 1990, that provided for a modest increase in chlorofluorocarbons (CFCs). U.S. officials were able to design a clause that would effectively apply only to the former Soviet Union and would meet this concern but with only a minimal potential impact on CFC emissions.[13] The United States also gained leadership credibility by legislating controls at a national level before suggesting that they be incorporated into an international treaty.

Those who believe in a coercive hegemon believe that it imposes its will whatever the preferences of others; others tolerate it because they have no choice.[14] In the negotiations for the International Criminal Court the U.S. secretary of defense, William Cohen, apparently indicated to several allies that if they did not support the U.S. proposal for limiting the jurisdiction of the ICC, the United States might withdraw forces from bases in their territory.[15] There may, of course, be a fine line between being a benign and a coercive hegemon. In the case of the Antarctic Treaty, the United States did not necessarily "bully" the other states into signing. But the United States certainly had the greatest influence over the text of the treaty and stood to gain by conclusion of the treaty. The United States had made no territorial claim, but the terms of the treaty gave it access to the whole continent.[16] In some treaty negotiations—such as those leading to the 1951 Refugee Convention— the United States has influenced significantly the treaty negotiations but not signed the resultant treaty. Although there are plenty of examples of regimes in which the United States has played a leadership role, hegemonic stability theory has not been without its critics.[17] And it can quite readily be seen that other actors have influenced significantly the course of treaty negotiations.

Middle Powers

The term "middle power" is used to refer to those states between the most powerful and the weakest in world politics. Middle powers such as Canada, Australia, and the Scandinavian states have been active in the creation and operation of treaty regimes in the post-1945 period. Canada is regarded as primarily responsible for the Ottawa Convention on landmines.[18] Middle-power leadership has not involved domination so much as acting as a peer of other group members. Middle-power leadership in international institutions has characteristically involved fulfilling three functions: as catalysts, offering the intellectual and political energy to trigger an initiative and to take the lead in dealing with that issue; as facilitators, planning, convening, and hosting formative meetings, setting agendas and priorities, and so on; and as managers, finding practical solutions to stumbling blocks in the creation or operation of a regime.[19] Great powers also do these things, but because middle powers have fewer issues to tackle they are able to concentrate resources on a small number of issues of particular importance to them. Middle powers may have the greatest freedom in policy choices because mistakes by superpowers may have global impacts, whereas smaller powers often feel they have no room to maneuver.[20]

Australia's role in providing an impetus for the final negotiations that produced the Chemical Weapons Convention is an example of the role of middle powers in treaty negotiation. In 1991 the UN General Assembly passed a resolution calling for the draft convention to be concluded in 1992. But progress within the negotiations made such an outcome appear improbable at best. Under the dedicated interest of Gareth Evans, Australian officials produced a model convention, which included compromise solutions to the outstanding areas of disagreement. Convinced that a breakthrough in the negotiations was possible, Australian officials discussed the text with officials in many state capitals, and on March 19, 1992, Evans presented to the Conference on Disarmament what he referred to as an "accelerated refinement" of the rolling text. The chairman of the negotiating committee took up the Australian initiative to produce his own chairman's text, which provided the basis for the final rounds of intense negotiations. On September 3, 1992, the annual report adopted by the CD contained the draft Convention on the Prohibition of the Development, Production, Stockpiling and Use of Chemical Weapons and their Destruction. The text was unanimously endorsed by the UN General Assembly in November 1992 and was opened for signature on January 13, 1993.

The South

States of the South, also referred to as developing states or less-developed countries, are a diverse group, but most are former colonies (with the exception of Ethiopia and Thailand), and most are poor (with the exception of the oil-producing states in the Middle East).[21] The developing world does not always have a common negotiating position but is most likely to do so if economic issues are at stake. This has included environmental negotiations, which virtually always have an economic dimension. Developing states have sometimes viewed the environmental concerns of the North as a new form of colonialism, a way by which developed states can "pull up the development ladder behind them."[22] President George H. W. Bush proposed an initiative on forests at the Group of Seven summit in July 1990.[23] The statement by Prime Minister Mathahir Mohamad of Malaysia appeared to encapsulate the South's response to the North's demand for a forests convention:

Obviously the North wants to have a direct say in the management of forests in the poor South at next to no cost to themselves. The pittance they offer is much less than the loss of earnings by the poor countries and yet it is made out as a generous concession. . . .

The poor are not asking for charity. When the rich chopped down their own forests, built their poison-belching factories and scoured the world for cheap resources, the poor said nothing. Indeed they paid for the development of the rich. Now the rich claim a right to regulate the development of the poor countries. And yet any suggestion that the rich compensate the poor adequately is regarded as outrageous. As colonies we were exploited. Now as independent nations we are to be equally exploited.[24]

Developing states have been successful in negotiating the inclusion of environment funds to facilitate their contributing to the implementation of environmental treaties. The 1990 Amendments to the Montreal Protocol, for example, included a mechanism to enable developing countries' compliance with the control measures established under the protocol. Part XII of the Third UN Convention on the Law of the Sea similarly provides some measures specially designed to assist developing states. In taking all measures consistent with the convention to prevent, reduce, and control pollution of the environment from any sources, states are to use "the best practicable means at their disposal and in accordance with their capabilities."[25] Special mention is made of differentiation in relation to establishing global and regional rules regarding land-based sources of pollution; states are to take into account, inter alia, "the economic capacity of developing States and their need for economic development."[26] Developing states are also to be given assistance to protect and preserve the marine environment. States, directly or through competent international organizations, are to assist developing states by training scientific and technical personnel; facilitating participation in relevant international programs; supplying necessary equipment and facilities; enhancing capacity to manufacture such equipment; providing advice and developing facilities for research, monitoring, educational, and other programs; and assisting with the minimization of the effects of major accidents that may cause serious pollution of the marine environment and with the preparation of environmental assessments.[27] International organizations are to give preferential treatment for developing states in the allocation of appropriate funds and technical assistance and in the utilization of specialized services.[28]

Even on environmental matters there may not always be a single voting position among developing states. In the case of the 1991 climate change negotiations, positions ranged from those of the oil producers, led by Saudi Arabia and Venezuela, which opposed possible international restraints on their major asset; to that of the Association of Small Island States, made up of twenty-five countries of the Pacific and Caribbean, whose very existence was threatened by rising sea levels.[29]

Nonstate Actors

Nonstate actors are a third category that may be influential in treaty negotiations. Subject-matter experts often play an essential role in defining the issue, bringing the issue to the attention of governments, and suggesting solutions. The literature on treaty regimes now widely uses the phrase "epistemic community" to refer to a "network of professionals with recognized expertise and competence in a particular domain and an authoritative claim to policy-relevant knowledge within that domain or issue-area."[30] The study of epistemic communities shifted attention away from the role of states in multilateral treaty negotiations to that of scientists or other professional groups who constitute a community based on shared knowledge and who may also play an important part in the creation of a regime. Of course, there may well be a degree of overlap among states and an epistemic community if, as in the case of the scientific community, much of its work is made possible by government funding.

Public interest NGOs are a second type of nonstate actor influential in treaty negotiations; sometimes they are referred to more generally as "civil society."[31] Public interest NGOs are particularly apparent in the process of creating human rights, humanitarian, and environmental regimes. Without the determined efforts of NGOs, the UN Charter would have contained, at most, a "passing reference" to human rights.[32] In the campaign against landmines, to take another example, the NGO community is credited with accelerating the process and successfully seeking the transfer of negotiations from the UN Conference on Disarmament in Geneva to the convocation of "like-minded" states in Ottawa.[33] NGOs often form a coalition to work toward a specific treaty. In the case of the negotiations for the UN Framework Convention on Climate Change, for example, an umbrella NGO called the Climate Action Network coordinated the work of a number of NGOs, including the World Wildlife Fund, Greenpeace, the Environmental Defense Fund, the Sierra Club, Ozone Action, and the Worldwatch Institute.[34] Industry NGOs that became involved included the Climate Council, the Global Climate Coalition, the American Petroleum Institute, the World Business Council for Sustainable Development, the U.S. Council for

International Business, and the International Chamber of Commerce.[35] Oil companies also made millions of dollars of donations to individual U.S. senators.[36] NGOs that worked for the conclusion of a treaty to establish an international criminal court include Amnesty International, Human Rights Watch, and the Lawyers' Committee for Human Rights. At the preparatory committee stage most NGOs organized their activities through the NGO Coalition for an International Criminal Court (CICC), which grew from thirty to some 800 NGOs.[37]

Although the influence of NGOs on international negotiations appears to have increased in recent years, it should be borne in mind that just as there is not necessarily a clear dividing line between the views of the state and an epistemic community, so do NGOs often work in conjunction with governments.[38] As the CICC grew in strength it sought to assist its efforts for a strong international criminal court by, for example, preparing researched commentaries on each issue discussed and making them available to government delegations.[39]

Negotiating Sessions Within an International Organization or Multilateral Conference

The text of most modern multilateral treaties has been finalized either by a UN body such as the Conference on Disarmament or the Commission on Human Rights; or else at a multilateral conference specially convened for that purpose, often by a resolution of the UN General Assembly.[40] The venue and nature of the forum are not of legal significance as long as the conclusion of the treaty has not been procured by the threat or use of force;[41] a state is under no legal obligation if its representative was coerced into giving consent to be bound by a treaty.[42] Some treaty negotiations may extend over years, with representatives meeting for several weeks each year. The third Law of the Sea conference held sessions between 1973 and 1982. Negotiations for the Chemical Weapons Convention took place during more than ten years.

If a conference is to be specially convened, the decision as to location can in itself be political. Although the host state does not formally have any impact on the conference and its outcome, it may gain stature from that role. A treaty is often known by a colloquial name that includes the city that was most important to its creation. The Convention on International Civil Aviation[43] is usually referred to as the "Chicago Convention" after the city in which it was adopted. The Convention on the Prohibition of the Use, Stockpiling, Production, and Transfer of Anti-Personnel Mines and Their Destruction is often referred to as the "Ottawa Convention," where it was conceived and opened for signature, although it was adopted in Oslo.[44] In the case of conferences not convened by the UN, the host country usually supplies the presiding officer, although this may also become a question of political debate.[45] Once the chair has been selected, he or she is expected to be neutral. If a subject arises with which the chair has some close personal involvement, he or she may choose to have someone else in the chair while that subject is being addressed.

Delegations attending a conference are obliged to be equipped with a document, known as "credentials," authorizing them to represent a state. An individual who is to sign a treaty requires another document, known as "full powers," as evidence of authority to do so. The permanent representative of a state to the United Nations or other organization at which treaties are signed may be issued with general full powers. The practice of credentials dates from the time when communications were slower and when it would have been difficult to check if the person who appeared to be representing a government had the authority to do so. It is now usual to send a faxed copy of credentials prior to the opening of a conference, but the original must still be submitted. At the conference, a credentials committee is appointed to examine the credentials and report back. This is usually a straightforward technical exercise, although it can occasionally become a political exercise. A practice has evolved in which the credentials committee does not report back to plenary until toward the end of the proceedings, by which time any approval has lost most of its significance.[46]

The conference often begins work with a "basic text," which may have been prepared, for example, by a preparatory committee, UNEP, the ICRC, or the International Law Commission. In the case of the Antarctic Treaty, the United States had prepared the preliminary draft. But the degree to which there is already a negotiating text that is largely acceptable to the participants when the formal negotiations begin varies enormously. One extreme example of a relative lack of agreement at the opening of a diplomatic conference was the 1998 Rome conference at which the statute of the International Criminal Court was adopted. Despite the earlier drafting work of the Preparatory Committee (PrepCom), the conference began with a draft statute that still contained some 1,400 square brackets, indicating points of disagreement.[47] The third Law of the Sea conference began without any basic text.

The original draft treaty and other documents from the negotiating process are together referred to as the *travaux préparatoires*. They may become of legal significance during the life of the treaty regime. Article

32 of the Vienna Convention on the Law of Treaties provides that if a literal reading of a treaty makes interpretation of the treaty difficult, reference may be made to the preparatory work of the treaty as well as to the circumstances of its conclusion as supplementary means of interpretation.

The work of getting from the basic text to the treaty is usually undertaken by a series of committees, each of which is allocated a portion of the text. Reports are then submitted to the plenary. In the nineteenth and early twentieth centuries, French was the official language of diplomacy. The United Nations began with five "official" languages, of which English and French were the only "working" languages, into which all documents were translated. The UN and most multilateral conferences now have six official languages, all of which are working languages: Arabic, Chinese, English, French, Russian, and Spanish. It can, of course, be of considerable advantage to a state if its negotiators are able to work in their preferred language.

An international conference, unless convened by an IGO, is an independent body. One of the first tasks at an international conference is therefore to adopt the rules of procedure; this is usually done by acclamation.[48] If specific rules are to be amended, this will usually be done by simple majority vote. The first conferences with detailed rules of procedure were those of the League of Nations. These were the direct predecessors of the UN General Assembly, and other international conferences have, in turn, taken the General Assembly as their model. Just as we distinguished rules pertaining to the operation of the system of international law from those dealing with all other issues of relations among states (see Chapter 5), so is it necessary, when dealing with a multilateral conference giving rise to a multilateral treaty, to distinguish between questions of procedure and those of substance. The rules of procedure may sound dry and unexciting, but sometimes if a delegation does not think it will be able to command support for a particular issue of substance, it attempts to achieve the same result via the rules of procedure. Rules of procedure may therefore be an important tactical device. This is all the more so because procedural decisions are taken by simple majority, whereas in treaty-making conferences issues of substance are usually decided by a two-thirds majority.[49]

Although the aim of many global treaties is universal membership, negotiating states often have to reconcile this goal with differences in the negotiating positions of the various states. Treaties often suffer from the so-called lowest-common-denominator factor—treaties reflecting only that change which is acceptable to every state participating in the negotiations. In the case of the Basel Convention on the Control of Transboundary Movements of Hazardous Wastes and Their Disposal, environmental NGOS wanted the international trade in hazardous wastes made illegal but could get agreement on no more than regulation of the trade. Particularly in the case of human rights regimes, the lowest-common-denominator factor manifests itself in debate as to whether or not to permit reservations to the treaty; negotiators must decide whether to maximize "the universal application of the instrument" or to "protect its integrity."[50] No reservations are permitted to the Rome Statute of the International Criminal Court or to the Montreal Protocol, but the negotiators of the Convention on the Elimination of All Forms of Discrimination Against Women decided to permit of reservations other than those incompatible with the object and purpose of CEDAW.[51] Some states have nevertheless entered reservations to what the committee has considered to be key components of the treaty, whereas other reservations are drawn so widely that their effect cannot be limited to specific provisions in the convention.[52]

Treaty Adoption and Entry into Force

Once the negotiations are complete the negotiating states need to express their agreement to the finalized treaty text. This is referred to as "adopting" the text. At an international conference, adoption of the treaty text takes place by a vote of two-thirds of the states present and voting, unless by the same majority it is decided to apply a different rule.[53] If it is not an international conference, then adoption of the text takes place by the consent of all negotiating states. Voting by consensus is a fairly recent innovation. The best-known example of consensus voting is the third Law of the Sea conference. It had been agreed that negotiations should proceed by way of consensus in order to adopt a convention that would enjoy the widest possible support, as well as to protect the interests and views of minorities at the conference.[54] The conference proceeded by consensus until 1982 when the final text was adopted by vote, with opposition from the United States, Israel, Turkey, and Venezuela; seventeen other states, mainly European, abstained.[55] The 1995 UN Agreement on Straddling Fish Stocks and Highly Migratory Fish Stocks was adopted without a vote. The use of consensus decision-making by the UN Committee on the Peaceful Uses of Outer Space has been deemed a success in terms of the treaties concluded and their wide ratification.[56]

Conferences establishing a regime usually complete their work by adopting a document known as the "final act," which includes the text of the treaty drafted, texts of resolutions adopted, and organizational details of the conference. A treaty negotiated by the main committees of the General Assembly is usually recommended to the General Assembly for adoption, which is done by annexing the treaty to a resolution. The treaty must next be authenticated, indicating that the text, often translated into several languages, is correct. Authentication may be by signature, or by initialing the text of the final act.

States that have consented to be bound by a treaty are referred to as "contracting states." In the period between a state having expressed its consent to be bound by the treaty and entry into force of that treaty, or between a state having signed a treaty and making clear its intention not to become a party to that treaty, a state is obliged to "refrain from acts which would defeat the object and purpose" of the treaty, provided that entry into force is not "unduly delayed."[57] There is often a significant period of time between the conclusion of negotiations for a multilateral treaty and its entry into force. In the case of the Antarctic Treaty there was a two-year gap, but in some instances the time lapse may be much greater. The Geneva Conventions of 1949, for example, came into force in 1954; the 1969 Vienna Convention on the Law of Treaties did not enter into force until 1980; and the Third Law of the Sea Convention was concluded in 1982 but did not enter into force until November 1994.

Article 102 of the UN Charter provides that "every treaty and every international agreement entered into by any Member State of the United Nations after the present Charter comes into force shall as soon as possible be registered with the Secretariat and published by it." An equivalent provision in article 18 of the Covenant of the League of Nations derived from one of Woodrow Wilson's Fourteen Points and was intended to prevent a proliferation of secret treaties that had been blamed, at least in part, for the outbreak of World War I.[58] All treaties and international agreements registered or filed and recorded with the Secretariat since 1946 are published in the United Nations Treaty Series. An annual UN publication entitled *Multilateral Treaties Deposited with the Secretary-General* is a guide to the status of the treaties for which the UN Secretary-General is the depositary. It includes information on signatures, ratifications, accessions, reservations, objections by other states to those reservations, declarations, entry into force, and so on. It is available over the Internet. Status lists for other treaties are now also usually available on the Internet.

Aspects of Regime Life

The treaty provides the basis for a process of cooperation via that the regime members manage the issue that gave rise to the treaty. In some regimes, particularly those in the environmental and nonproliferation fields, this is done by what is termed the *conference of the states parties*, a body consisting of all states that are party to the treaty. In some regimes, an international organization comes into operation on entry into force of the treaty. The Chemical Weapons Convention, for example, provided for the establishment of the Organization for the Prohibition of Chemical Weapons. Particularly when a treaty establishes an international organization it may be useful for a preparatory commission (the PrepCom) to prepare for entry into force of the treaty by drafting rules of procedure, engaging staff, finding premises, and/or settling financial arrangements.[59] In the case of the Comprehensive Nuclear Test-Ban Treaty, a PrepCom was established on November 19, 1996, to set up the global verification regime and to prepare for entry into force of the treaty. Following the first conference of the states parties to the CTBT, the PrepCom will cease to exist and the Comprehensive Nuclear Test-Ban Treaty Organization will be established.

During the course of regime life the original issue will likely remain of central concern, but other matters may also need to be addressed. In some circumstances this may involve amending the original agreement but rather than reopen aspects of the negotiations it is more typical to leave the original treaty in place and negotiate subsequent agreements or "protocols" to address subissues that arise or increase in importance during the life of the regime. The International Whaling Convention detailed industry regulations in an annex that could be revised without amending the original treaty.

As the regime operates, it may come under challenge from states either internal or external to the regime. In Chapter 7 we noted how the Antarctic regime withstood the external challenge from members of the third world as well as an internal challenge by Australia and France when they decided not to proceed with ratification of the Minerals Convention. In the case of the NPT, the 1998 tests of India and Pakistan were widely perceived as threatening the integrity of the regime, which had been designed to accommodate only five nuclear weapon states;[60] the tests have been referred to as "the most significant challenge to the NPT to date."[61]

Regime effectiveness.   There has in recent years been enhanced scholarly interest in analyzing what makes for an effective treaty regime. This has been in part a reaction to the post–World War II proliferation of treaties:

> In 1988 . . . we had horrible films of Iraq using poison gas against Iranian soldiers, which was a clear violation of the Geneva Protocol against chemical weapons. There was a big conference on chemical weapons in Paris shortly thereafter, and they didn't even mention Iraq in their report. Rather, their response was to create a new treaty, which became the Chemical Weapons Convention. And if there was use of chemical weapons today, I would expect their reaction to be holding another meeting in Paris and writing another treaty.[62]

Similar comments have been made about most fields of international law. In relation to the International Labor Organization, for example, Steve Charnovitz has called for a "de-emphasis on writing new conventions" to "enable the ILO to devote more time to communicating information to member countries on how to conduct more effective labor and employment programs."[63] In the field of human rights, Gudmundur Alfredsson has noted that politicians often find it easier to draft a whole new instrument than a protocol or amendments to an existing one. "In light of continuing violations, the main focus should now be on national implementation and international monitoring."[64]

The relationship between a multilateral treaty regime and the distribution of political power among those states with an interest in the subject matter may well make a significant contribution toward determining the effectiveness of the regime. The question has thus been raised as to whether the Ottawa Convention and the International Criminal Court can be effective without U.S. involvement.[65] The U.S. ambassador-at-large for war crimes issues, David Scheffer, commented that he considered U.S. participation in a permanent international criminal court to be essential to its effectiveness. "History has shown that when new international institutions are started without full United States participation—like the League of Nations—they can fail. When they start with United States leadership—like the United Nations, the war crimes tribunals for the former Yugoslavia and Rwanda, the new Organization for the Prohibition of Chemical Weapons—they can succeed."[66] A similar concern has been expressed in relation to NGOs having a disproportionate influence over the negotiating process if it means that the resultant treaty does not reflect the "real political forces necessary to its successful implementation."[67]

The issues of compliance, transparency, verification, and dispute resolution are all relevant to the effectiveness of multilateral treaty regimes. Let's consider each in turn.

Compliance. Those seeking to enhance the effectiveness of international law understandably assume that compliance is a key determinant of regime effectiveness. In accordance with the concept of consent, treaties are binding only on those states that have become parties to the agreement; the treaty provisions are not applicable to a third state unless they are also part of customary international law.[68] Some writers recognize the existence of "objective regimes," which means that a treaty—relating, for example, to a particular territory or waterway—even though created by a few states, establishes general obligations for all states.[69] The Vienna Convention on the Law of Treaties does not acknowledge the existence of objective regimes, and the concept remains controversial.[70] The fact that a treaty creates obligations and rights only for states parties to the treaty poses fundamental problems for regime design because nonparties may render a treaty ineffective. The Antarctic Treaty System has faced this dilemma in relation to unregulated fishing in the Southern Ocean by so-called flag-of-convenience vessels registered in states not party to the Convention on the Conservation of Antarctic Marine Living Resources.[71]

One of the most influential books on compliance has been that by Antonio and Abram Chayes, titled *The New Sovereignty: Compliance with International Regulatory Agreements*. They argued that it is not so much the actual enforcement of legal obligations that matters most; states in regimes will be predisposed to attempt to make the regime work. In place of the standard "enforcement model" of compliance, the authors proposed a "managerial mode," suggesting that compliance can be facilitated by managerial stratagems including the enhancement of transparency and verification and the continuous review of treaty performance and compliance.

There would seem to be good reasons for states complying with their obligations, not least of which is the efficiency of policy continuity. Chayes and Chayes have pointed out that states do not constantly review whether or not to comply with a treaty but set up the procedures to comply and then simply keep going.[72] Particularly for those states that contributed to the negotiation of a treaty, it is likely that their perceived interests and their commitments coincide.[73] When a powerful state makes a policy decision to comply, that decision can usually be attributed largely to the concern of even powerful states that if they flout a particular provision of international law, other states will treat them likewise on another occasion. On June 24, 1993, Angel Francisco

Breard was convicted of the attempted rape and murder of Ruth Dickie in Virginia. Breard was a Paraguayan, but the Paraguayan consular authorities did not learn about the arrest and trial of Breard until 1996. This was contrary to article 36(1)(b) of the Vienna Convention on Consular Relations of 1963,[74] which states that the "authorities shall inform the person concerned without delay" of his rights to have the consular post advised of his arrest or committal to prison or custody pending trial or other form of detention. The U.S. State Department recognized the lapse on July 7, 1997, and apologized. In 1998 the State Department released a booklet for law enforcement and other U.S. officials that set out the procedures required to comply with the Vienna Convention on Consular Relations; the forward to the booklet stated that it aimed to "help ensure that the United States can insist upon rigorous compliance by foreign governments with respect to United States citizens abroad."[75]

By article 27 of the Vienna Convention on the Law of Treaties, a party may not invoke the provisions of its internal law as justification for its failure to perform a treaty obligation. But it is possible for a state to be in breach of international law even if not acting illegally within municipal law. This is because the domestic legal system of states determines the status of international law within that system. Constitutional law varies among states. The basic division, at least in theory, is between those states that have adopted a *monist* conceptualization of the relationship between international law and municipal (i.e., domestic) law—that is, they regard international law and municipal law as part of one system of law—and those that have adopted a *dualist* approach, regarding the two systems as separate. Monism and dualism are, however, "ideal types"; in practice, most systems contain elements of both. A state adopting a pure monist interpretation of the relationship between international law and its municipal legal system would consider treaties to be part of national law; those adopting a dualist interpretation of the relationship would assume the need for treaty terms to be somehow made into domestic law before they would carry any weight in the domestic legal system. In fact three main categories of states can be discerned.[76]

In Belgium, Chile, Ethiopia, France, Switzerland, the Netherlands, and the United States, some form of legislative approval is required for at least some categories of treaties. Once a treaty has been approved by the state and it has entered into force, it automatically becomes part of municipal law without any separate act of "incorporation" or "transformation" being required. In France and Switzerland, for example, a treaty that has been ratified and has entered into force is binding and can suspend any inconsistent national statutes. In Chile, a treaty that has been approved by its congress preempts domestic law. Similarly, under article 9.4 of the Ethiopian constitution, all treaties ratified by Ethiopia are part of the laws of the country. In the United States, the U.S. Constitution provides that a treaty must have the "advice and consent" of a two-thirds vote of the Senate before it can be ratified by the president. The president is also able, however, to enter into "executive agreements" that in U.S. law are distinguishable from treaties and so do not require Senate approval. Indeed, what is termed a "treaty" in international law may come under one of five categories in U.S. domestic law: a treaty (requiring two-thirds Senate consent for ratification), a congressionally authorized executive agreement (approved previously or subsequently), a presidential executive agreement, and a treaty-authorized executive agreement. This makes the law regarding the application of treaties in the United States very complex.[77]

In the case of the second group of states, including Germany and Italy, a treaty itself has no effect in the internal legal system and requires transformation by a legislative act in order to give it municipal effect. Once legislative approval has been given, the situation is similar to that in the first category of states. In the third category of states, which includes the United Kingdom, Australia, and India, a treaty has no domestic effect. The terms of a treaty must be implemented or incorporated through national law, whose terms therefore may not be precisely the same as those of the treaty. Sometimes the treaty is simply appended to legislation, but usually the act of parliament will embody the treaty provisions in different terms, not necessarily even revealing their treaty source.

The main difference among these three groups of states is thus whether the treaty itself or the incorporating legislation is applied by courts. National courts can be vital to the effective implementation of international treaties.[78] But national legal systems have varied in their degree of permeability to international law. Where crimes against humanity have been prosecuted at the municipal level, it has usually been by foreign courts; the Canadian High Court of Justice, for example, convicted a Hungarian national for deporting Jews during World War II.[79] As with the question of the relationship between treaties and municipal law, the situation is not as straightforward as the monist-dualist distinction might suggest. It is not necessarily the case that judges in predominantly monist systems take treaties into account more than their counterparts in predominantly dualist systems. The U.S. system has been one of the least permeable of national systems.[80]

The principle of *complementarity* embodied in the Rome Statute of the International Criminal Court assumes that municipal courts are the first option in judging and punishing the crimes covered by the statute. There is said to be universal jurisdiction for crimes against humanity: any state can exercise its jurisdiction over an individual, no matter where the crime was committed. A number of terrorism treaties, including the 1973 Convention on the Prevention and Punishment of Crimes Against Internationally Protected Persons, Including Diplomatic Agents,[81] and the 1998 International Convention on the Suppression of Terrorist Bombings,[82] oblige a state either to prosecute or to extradite individuals who have committed certain offences of universal concern. Article VI of the Genocide Convention requires the state in whose territory the acts of genocide took place to try the responsible persons.

Transparency and verification. It is now recognized that a badly designed regime cannot necessarily solve the problem it was established to address, even if all states comply perfectly with all treaty obligations.[83] It is now accepted wisdom that transparency—the availability of regime-relevant information—is a key to the regime's effectiveness. States are more likely to comply if the way they behave is monitored and publicized and they can see evidence that others are also adhering to their regime obligations. Promoting transparency involves fostering the acquisition, analysis, and dissemination of regular, prompt, and accurate regime-relevant information.[84] Regimes vary considerably in their degree of transparency. Most regime information systems rely on self-reporting, although in some cases governments serve as conduits for information from substate actors, as in, for example, industry reports on CFC production under the Montreal Protocol.[85] In the Antarctic Treaty System all parties have an obligation to give notice in advance of all expeditions to and within Antarctica, on the part of its ships or nationals, and all expeditions to Antarctica organized in or proceeding from its territory; all stations in the Antarctica occupied by its nationals; and any military personnel or equipment intended to be introduced by it into Antarctica for scientific research or for any other peaceful purpose.[86]

 Transparency is particularly important in promoting compliance with human rights regimes; reciprocity and systems that provide for interstate complaints are not so effective when states do not perceive their own interests as threatened by the noncompliance of another state.[87] Reporting systems have been the mainstay of the enforcement mechanisms in human rights treaties. Although the treaty bodies have experienced considerable success in attracting the participation of states, the inadequacy of committee resources has contributed to delays in processing reports.[88] Problems of delay and a lack of follow-up mechanisms have also characterized the process of individual petitioning that is available in some human rights regimes. Enhanced interest in improving the effectiveness of human rights regimes has led to debate regarding how to improve the procedure and institutions established to promote the accountability of states parties to the treaties.[89]

Verification refers to the process of checking whether a state is complying with its legal obligations. It is a politically sensitive issue because the very idea of verification clashes with the notion of sovereignty by which a state has control over its territory and what goes on there. In the arms control field the focus is on verification because the stakes seem highest, and acceptable verification procedures have often been the key to getting the treaty negotiated in the first place. The early years of the Cold War — up to the early 1960s — saw notable failures on verification provisions during disarmament negotiations.[90] The Antarctic Treaty, by which consultative parties have the right to designate "observers" with complete freedom of access at any time to all areas of Antarctica, including all stations and all ships and aircraft at points of discharging or embarking cargoes or personnel in Antarctica, was an exception. There was considerable variation in the strength of the verification provisions included in arms control treaties during the remainder of the 1960s and 1970s. The Biological Weapons Convention, for example, had little in the way of verification provisions, but the NPT contained considerable verification procedures to be undertaken by the International Atomic Energy Agency.

There have been important advances since the mid-1980s in developing sophisticated rules for on-site inspections and in combining various means of verification. In the case of the Chemical Weapons Convention, states have thirty days in which to reject any individual on a list of inspectors. The secretariat of the Organization for the Prohibition of Chemical Weapons must approve equipment to be used in inspections. The party in question cannot object to this. At the site inspectors may interview staff, inspect records they deem relevant, take photos, samples, and so on. This is very sensitive because the chemical industry is used for many purposes other than weapons, and there may be information a company does not want its rivals to glean for commercial reasons. Although this system may still not deliver 100 percent verification, it is a much more detailed system than was provided for in the earlier arms control treaties.

Dispute resolution. It is standard for multilateral treaties to stipulate how any dispute "regarding the interpretation or application of the treaty" is to be settled.[91] In practice, states are generally not bickering over the "interpretation or application" of a treaty per se but over a clash in the pursuit of their respective interests; a treaty text may then become the pivot around which one state seeks to change the policy position or actions of the state with which it has come into conflict in the pursuit of its interests. States may engage in considerable negotiations as to the appropriate means by which to attempt to resolve a dispute. For a state to agree to involve a third party — whether a court or an arbiter — in the resolution of a dispute is to indicate a preparedness to be at least partly flexible in its own position. Just as sovereignty is the main stumbling block to getting 100 percent verification of obligations in international law, so can it prevent states wanting to involve, or accept the decision of, a third party. In the case of the overlapping claims to Antarctica of the United Kingdom, Chile, and Argentina, the United Kingdom wanted to take the case to the ICJ, but the other two sides refused. Sovereignty was an issue on which they were not prepared to compromise.

Integral to a dispute and its resolution may be the exact meaning to be given to the wording of the treaty. The Vienna Convention contains provisions regarding the interpretation of a treaty. The general rule is that a "treaty is to be interpreted in good faith in accordance with the ordinary meaning to be given to the terms of the treaty in their context and in the light of its object and purpose."[92] If a treaty has been authenticated in two or more languages, the text is equally authoritative in each language, unless the treaty provides or the parties agree that, in case of divergence, a particular text shall prevail.[93]

Treaty Regimes and the Globalization of Politics

What, then, has been the political outcome of the appearance of so many new multilateral treaties in the years since World War II? We have so far viewed a multilateral treaty as a response to an issue of mutual concern. But have multilateral treaties as a whole solved the problems they were designed to address? The ozone depletion regime has been held up as a model of success. But if the mass of treaties is taken as a whole, the answer would seem to be negative; few treaties have completed their work and gone on to become redundant. Neither have the goals specified in the preambles of the multilateral treaties usually been achieved.

It may, however, be unreasonable to judge a regime by the idealistic-sounding goals written into the preamble of its founding treaty.

According to the preamble of the Chemical Weapons Convention, for example, states parties to the convention are "determined for the sake of all mankind, to exclude completely the possibility of the use of chemical weapons." Was this a realistic aim, particularly given that a treaty is binding only on parties to that treaty? Would it really be possible for multilateral treaties to achieve all their stated objectives? A treaty may result in unintended consequences. International humanitarian law is usually assumed to have developed as a restraint on violence, but critics have argued that the laws of war have merely legitimated the violence and hence promoted it; the Hague Laws, for example, banned only those means and methods of combat that had no military utility while permitting new and destructive technologies, like aerial warfare, to develop unhindered.[94]

This is far from suggesting that multilateral treaties are meaningless or that state representatives are intrinsically cynical. Treaty regimes have not been totally useless, but neither have they achieved the idealistic ambitions of some of their keenest supporters, particularly NGOs. They are perhaps best thought of as management devices—means by which national decisionmakers have chosen to keep under tabs, but not necessarily solve, a broad range of issues of mutual concern. As such they can be viewed as part of the increasing interconnectedness and policy coordination at a global level—that is, globalization. Multilateral treaties have become a common medium through which states coordinate policies in a range of issue areas.

Notes

1. Stephen Krasner, ed., *International Regimes* (Ithaca: Cornell University Press, 1983). The chapters in this book appeared earlier as the articles in a special edition of the journal *International Organization* (Spring 1982).

2. For discussion of the conceptual issues involved in selecting a definition of a regime, see Andreas Hasenclever, Peter Mayer, and Volker Rittberger, *Theories of International Regimes* (Cambridge: Cambridge University Press, 1997), pp. 8–22.

3. Oran Reed Young, *International Cooperation: Building Regimes for Natural Resources and the Environment* (Ithaca: Cornell University Press, 1989), p. 24. But compare the reference to "environmental agreements," hereafter referred to as "regimes," in Jørgen Wettestad, *Designing Effective Environmental Regimes: The Key Conditions* (Cheltenham, UK, and Northampton, MA: Edward Elgar, 1999), p. 1.

4. See Anne-Marie Slaughter, Andrew S. Tulumello, and Stepan Wood, "International Law and International Relations Theory: A New Generation of Interdisciplinary Scholarship," *American Journal of International Law (AJIL)*

92 (1993): 367–397; and Michael Byers, *Custom, Power, and the Power of Rules: International Relations and Customary International Law* (Cambridge: Cambridge University Press, 1999).

5. International relations literature on regime theory other than that in references above includes Bas Arts, "Regimes, Non-State Actors and the State System: A 'Structurational' Regime Model," *European Journal of International Relations* 6, no. 4 (2000): 513–542; Stephen Haggard and Beth Simmons, "Theories of International Regimes," *International Organization* 41, no. 3 (1987): 491–517; Andreas Hansenclever, Peter Mayer, and Volker Rittberger, "Integrating Theories of International Regimes," *Review of International Studies* 26, no. 1 (2000): 3–33; Marc Levy, Oran Young, and Michael Zürn, "The Study of International Regimes," *European Journal of International Relations* 1, no. 3 (1995): 267–330; and Marc W. Zacher and Brent A. Sutton, *Governing Global Networks: International Regimes for Transportation and Communication* (Cambridge: Cambridge University Press, 1995).

6. Janice Gross Stein, ed., *Getting to the Table: The Processes of International Prenegotiation* (Baltimore: John Hopkins University Press, 1989).

7. Ibid.

8. "Statement by Mr. Casey (Australia)," opening plenary session, in *The Conference on Antarctica, Conference Documents: The Antarctic Treaty and Related Papers* (Washington, DC: U.S. Department of State, 1960), p. 26.

9. The term was coined by Robert Keohane. David A. Lake, "Leadership, Hegemony, and the International Economy: Naked Emperor or Tattered Monarch with Potential?" *International Studies Quarterly* 37 (1993): 459–489, 489–490.

10. Robert O. Keohane, "The Demand for International Regimes," in Krasner, *International Regimes*.

11. D. Humphreys, "Regime Theory and Non-governmental Organisations: The Case of Forest Conservation," *Journal of Commonwealth and Comparative Politics* 34, no. 1 (March 1996): 90–115, 91, citing Karen Litfin, "Eco-regimes: Playing Tug of War with the Nation-State," in Ronnie D. Lipschutz and Ken Conca, eds., *The State and Social Power in Global Environmental Politics* (New York: Columbia University Press, 1993).

12. Charles Kindleberger, "Dominance and Leadership in the International Economy," *International Studies Quarterly* 25 (June 1981): 242–254.

13. Richard Elliot Benedick, "Perspectives of a Negotiation Practitioner," in Gunnar Sjöstedt, ed., *International Environmental Negotiation* (Newbury Park: Sage, 1993), p. 234.

14. For a useful review of the hegemonic stability literature, see Michael Webb and Stephen Krasner, "Hegemonic Stability Theory: An Empirical Assessment," *Review of International Studies* 15, no. 2 (1989): 183–198.

15. Michael P. Scharf, "Results of the Rome Conference for an International Criminal Court," *ASIL Insight* (August 1998), at http://www.asil.org/insights/insigh23.htm.

16. Contrast the view, expressed in relation to Antarctica, that the theory of hegemonic stability "does not seem to be of great use in analysing this case study." Cornelis van der Lugt, "An International Environmental Regime for the

Antarctic: Critical Investigations," *Polar Record* 33, no. 186 (1997): 223–238, 227.

17. Webb and Krasner, "Hegemonic Stability Theory: An Empirical Assessment."

18. See "Notes for an Address by the Honourable Lloyd Axworthy, Minister of Foreign Affairs, at the Closing Session of the International Strategy Conference Towards a Global Ban on Anti-Personnel Mines," at http://198. 103.104.118/minpub/Publication.asp?FileSpec=/Min_Pub_Docs/102423.htm, accessed June 27, 2001.

19. Andrew F. Cooper, Richard A. Higgott, and Kim Richard Nossal, *Relocating Middle Powers: Australia and Canada in a Changing World Order* (Vancouver: University of British Columbia Press, 1993), pp. 24–25.

20. Annette Baker Fox, "The Range of Choice for Middle Powers: Australia and Canada Compared," *Australian Journal of Politics and History* 26, no. 2 (1980): 193–203, 193.

21. Daniel S. Papp, *Contemporary International Relations: Frameworks for Understanding*, 6th ed. (New York: Longman, 2002), p. 196.

22. Adil Najam, "The South in International Environmental Negotiations," *International Studies* 31, no. 4 (1994): 427–464.

23. Edith Brown Weiss, "Introductory Note," 31 International Legal Materials (ILM) 814 (1992): 817.

24. UN Conf. Rep. A/CONF.151/26/Rev.1 (vol. 3), p. 233, quoted in Karin Mickelson, "Seeing the Forest, the Trees, and the People: Coming to Terms with Developing Country Perspectives on the Proposed Global Forests Convention," in Canadian Council of International Law, *Global Forests and International Environmental Law* (London: Kluwer), p. 240.

25. United Nations Convention on the Law of the Sea, article 194(1), 21 ILM 1261 (1982).

26. United Nations Convention on the Law of the Sea, article 207(4).

27. United Nations Convention on the Law of the Sea, article 202.

28. United Nations Convention on the Law of the Sea, article 203.

29. Richard Elliot Benedick, "Perspectives of a Negotiation Practitioner," in Sjöstedt, *International Environmental Negotiation,* p. 236.

30. Peter M. Haas, "Introduction: Epistemic Communities and International Policy Coordination," *International Organization* 46, no. 1 (Winter 1992): 3.

31. See, inter alia, Humphreys, "Regime Theory and Non-governmental Organisations," pp. 90–115; Richard Price, "Reversing the Gun Sights: Transnational Civil Society Targets Land Mines," *International Organization* 52, no. 3 (Summer 1998): 613–644; Susan Carr and Roger Mpande, "Does the Definition of the Issue Matter? NGO Influence and the International Convention to Combat Desertification in Africa," *Journal of Commonwealth and Comparative Politics* 34, no. 1 (March 1996): 143–166.

32. John P. Humphrey, "The UN Charter and the Universal Declaration of Human Rights," in Evan Luard, ed., *The International Protection of Human Rights* (New York: Praeger, 1967), pp. 39–58, 39–40.

33. Ruth Wedgwood, "Legal Personality and the Role of Non-Governmental Organizations and Non-State Political Entities in the United

Nations System," in Rainer Hofmann, ed., *Non-State Actors as New Subjects of International Law. International Law: From the Traditional State Order Towards the Law of the Global Community*, proceedings of an international symposium of the Kiel Walther-Schücking Institute of International Law, March 25–28, 1998 (Berlin: Ducker & Humblot, 1999), pp. 21–36, 25.

34. Chiara Giorgetti, "The Role of Nongovernmental Organizations in the Climate Change Negotiations," *Colorado Journal of International Environmental Law and Policy* 9, no. 1 (Winter 1998): 115–137, 127.

35. Ibid., pp. 131–132.

36. Bill Hare, "Undermining the Kyoto Protocol: Environmental Effectiveness Versus Political Expediency?" at www.greenpeace.org/~climate/politics/reports/loopholes.pdf+Undermining+the+Kyoto+Protocol&hl=en&lr=lang_en&ie=UTF-8.

37. Fanny Benedetti and John L. Washburn, "Drafting the International Criminal Court Treaty: Two Years to Rome and an Afterword on the Rome Diplomatic Conference," *Global Governance* 5, no. 1 (January–March 1999): 1–37, 21.

38. D. Humphreys, "Regime Theory and Non-governmental Organisations," pp. 90–115.

39. Benedetti and Washburn, "Drafting the International Criminal Court Treaty," p. 23.

40. For information on the range of techniques and procedures used in the preparation of treaties by various UN organs and agencies, see part 4 of *Review of the Multilateral Treaty-Making Process* (New York: United Nations, 1985).

41. Vienna Convention on the Law of Treaties, article 52, 1155 United Nations Treaty Series (UNTS) 336.

42. Vienna Convention on the Law of Treaties, article 51.

43. 15 UNTS 295.

44. Anthony Aust, *Modern Treaty Law and Practice* (Cambridge: Cambridge University Press, 2000), p. 23.

45. Robbie Sabel, *Procedure at International Conferences: A Study of the Rules of Procedure of Conferences and Assemblies of International Inter-Governmental Organisations* (Cambridge: Cambridge University Press, 1997), p. 53.

46. The information in this paragraph draws on Robbie Sabel, ibid., p. 49.

47. UN Doc.A/CONF.183/2/Add.1 (1998), cited in Philippe Kirsch and John T. Holmes, "The Rome Conference on an International Criminal Court: The Negotiating Process," *AJIL* 93, no. 2 (1999): 2–12, 3.

48. Sabel, *Procedure at International Conferences*, p. 25.

49. Ibid., p. 4.

50. Rebecca J. Cook, "Reservations to the Convention on the Elimination of All Forms of Discrimination against Women," *Virginia Journal of International Law* 30, no. 3 (1990): 643–713, 673. See also C. Redgwell, "Universality or Integrity? Some Reflections on Reservations to General Multilateral Treaties," *British Yearbook of International Law* 64 (1993): 245–282.

51. Article 28(2). This is in accordance with article 19 of the Vienna Convention on the Law of Treaties.

52. See C. Chinkin and J. P. Gardner, *Human Rights as General Norms and a State's Right to Opt Out: Reservations and Objections to Human Rights Conventions* (London: British Institute of International and Comparative Law, 1997); M. Coccia, "Reservations to Multilateral Treaties on Human Rights," *California Western International Law Journal* 15, no. 1 (Winter 1985): 1–15; J. K. Gamble Jr. "Reservations to Multilateral Treaties: A Macroscopic View of State Practice," *AJIL* 74, no. 2 (1980): 372–394; Ryan Goodman, "Human Rights Treaties, Invalid Reservations, and State Consent," *AJIL* 96, no. 3 (July 2002): 531–560; Daniel N. Hytton, "Default Breakdown: The Vienna Convention on the Law of Treaties—Inadequate Framework on Reservations," *Vanderbilt Journal of Transnational Law* 27, no. 2 (May 1994): 419–451; P. H. Imbert, "Reservations and Human Rights Conventions," *Human Rights Review* 6, no. 1 (Spring 1981): 28–60; Catherine J. Redgwell, "Reservations to Treaties and Human Rights Committee General Comment No. 24(52)," *International and Comparative Law Quarterly* 46, no. 2 (April 1997): 390–412; William A. Schiabas, "Reservations to Human Rights Treaties: Time for Innovation and Reform," *Canadian Yearbook of International Law* 32 (Annual 1994): 39–81; and E. F. Shenman, "The US Death Penalty Reservation to the International Covenant on Civil and Political Rights: Exposing the Limitations of the Flexible System Governing Treaty Formation," *Texas International Law Journal* 29, no. 1 (Winter 1994): 69–93.

53. Vienna Convention on the Law of Treaties, article 9(2).

54. T. T. B. Koh, "Negotiating a New World Order for the Sea," in Alan K. Henrikson, ed., *Negotiating World Order: The Artisanship and Architecture of Global Diplomacy* (Wilmington, DE: Scholarly Resources, 1986), p. 41.

55. See Barry Buzan, "Negotiating by Consensus: Developments in Technique at the United Nations Conference on the Law of the Sea," *AJIL* 75, no. 2 (1981): 324–348; and Tommy T. B. Koh and Shanmugam Jayakumar, "The Negotiating Process of the Third United Nations Conference on the Law of the Sea," in Myron H. Nordquist, ed., *United Nations Convention on the Law of the Sea 1982: A Commentary*, vol. 1 (Dordrecht: Martinus Nijhoff, 1985).

56. Eilene Galloway, "Consensus Decisionmaking by the United Nations Committee on the Peaceful Uses of Outer Space," *Journal of Space Law* 7, no. 3 (1979): 3–13.

57. Vienna Convention on the Law of Treaties, article 18(b).

58. Ursula Knapp, "Article 102," in Bruno Simma, ed., *The Charter of the United Nations: A Commentary* (Oxford: Oxford University Press, 1994), p. 1104.

59. Anthony Aust, *Modern Treaty Law and Practice* (Cambridge: Cambridge University Press, 2000), p. 141.

60. T. Graham Jr. and D. B. Shaw, "Nearing a Fork in the Road: Proliferation or Nuclear Reversal?" *Nonproliferation Review* 6, no. 1 (Fall 1998), at http://cns.miis.edu/pubs/npr/graham61.htm.

61. Tariq Rauf, "The Strengthened NPT Review Process: Legal and Diplomatic Considerations," in Carl Ungerer and Marianne Hanson, *The Politics of Nuclear Non-proliferation* (St. Leonards, NSW: Allen & Unwin in association with the Department of International Relations Research School of Pacific and Asian Studies, Australian National University, 2001), pp. 31–53, 32.

62. Cited in James Kitfield, "Is Arms Control Dead?" *National Journal*, July 14, 2001, p. 2224. Cf. comments on compliance with the Biological Weapons Convention in an interview with John R. Bolton, undersecretary of state for arms control and international security, Center for Nonproliferation Studies, Monterey Institute of International Studies, at http://cns.miis.edu/cns/dc/011102.htm, accessed February 18, 2002.

63. Steve Charnovitz, "The International Labour Organization in its Second Century," *Max Planck Yearbook of United Nations Law* 4 (2000): 147–184, 174.

64. Gudmundur Alfredsson, "Concluding Remarks: More Law and Less Politics," in Gudmundur Alfredsson, Jonas Grimheden, Bertram G. Ramcharan, and Alfred de Zayas, eds., *International Human Rights Monitoring Mechanisms: Essays in Honour of Jakob Th. Möller* (The Hague: Martinus Nijhoff, 2001), p. 918.

65. See, for example, Peter Malanczuk, "The International Criminal Court and Landmines: What Are the Consequences of Leaving the US Behind?" *European Journal of International Law (EJIL)* 11, no. 1 (2000): 77–90.

66. David Scheffer, "US Policy and the Proposed Permanent International Criminal Court," address before the Carter Center, Atlanta, Georgia, November 13, 1997, at www.state.gov/www/policy_remarks/971113_scheffer_tribunal.html.

67. Ruth Wedgwood, "Legal Personality," in Hofmann, *Non-State Actors*, pp. 25–26.

68. Vienna Convention on the Law of Treaties, articles 34 and 38.

69. In relation to the Antarctic Treaty see, inter alia, Bruno Simma, "The Antarctic Treaty as a Treaty Providing for an 'Objective Regime,'" *Cornell International Law Journal* 19, no. 2 (1986): 189–209; and A. Watts, *International Law and the Antarctic Treaty System* (Cambridge: Grotius, 1992), pp. 295–298.

70. Maurizio Ragazzi, *The Concept of International Obligations Erga Omnes* (Oxford: Clarendon, 1997), p. 41.

71. The terminology used is "IUU fishing," which stands for "illegal, unreported, or unregulated" fishing. See W. Edeson, "Closing the Gap: The Role of 'Soft' International Instruments to Control Fishing," *Australian Yearbook of International Law* 20 (1999): 83–104.

72. Chayes and Chayes, *The New Sovereignty*, p. 4.

73. Ibid., pp. 4–7.

74. Vienna Convention on Consular Relations, 596 UNTS 261.

75. Department of State Publication 10518, *Consular Notification and Access: Instructions for Federal, State, and Local Law Enforcement and Other Officials Regarding Foreign Nationals in the United States and the Rights of Consular Officials to Assist Them,* January 1998, at www.state.gov/www/global/legal_affairs/ca_notification/ca_prelim.html.

76. These categories are taken from Francis G. Jacobs and Shelley Roberts, eds., *The Effect of Treaties in Domestic Law* (London: Sweet & Maxwell, 1987), p. xxivff.

77. Ibid., p. 141.

78. This role should not be exaggerated. See, inter alia, Eyal Benvenisti, "Judicial Misgivings Regarding the Application of International Law: An Analysis of Attitudes of National Courts," *EJIL* 4 (1993): 159–183; and Karen Knop, "Here and There: International Law in Domestic Courts," *International Law and Politics* 32 (2000): 501–535. For identification and exploration of the rationales offered by national court judges in support of references to international human rights law, see Reem Bahdi, "Globalization or Judgement: Transjudicialism and the Five Faces of International Law in Domestic Courts," *George Washington International Law Review* 34, no. 3 (2002): 555–603.

79. *Regina v. Finta*, Canada, High Court of Justice, July 10, 1989, 93 ILR 424.

80. Thomas M. Franck and Gregory H. Fox, eds., *International Law Decisions in National Courts* (New York: Transnational, 1996), p. 5.

81. 13 ILM 41 (1974).

82. 37 ILM 249 (1998).

83. A preliminary consideration for this work has been the definitional question of just what we mean by "regime effectiveness." See A. Andresen and J. Wettestad, "International Problem-Solving Effectiveness: The Oslo Project Story So Far," *International Environmental Affairs* 7, no. 2 (Spring 1995): 127–150. On regime effectiveness see, inter alia, A. Underdal, "The Concept of Regime 'Effectiveness,'" *Cooperation and Conflict* 27, no. 3 (1992): 227–240; D. G. Victor, K. Raustiala, and E. B. Skolnikoff, eds., *The Implementation and Effectiveness of International Environmental Commitments* (Cambridge: MIT Press, 1998); and Oran R. Young, ed., *The Effectiveness of International Environmental Regimes: Causal Connections and Behavioral Mechanisms* (Cambridge: MIT Press, 1999).

84. Ronald B. Mitchell, "Sources of Transparency: Information Systems in International Regimes," *International Studies Quarterly* 42 (1998): 109–130, 109.

85. Ibid., 116–117.

86. The Antarctic Treaty, article VII (5).

87. A point made by V. Leary, *International Labour Conventions and National Law* (The Hague: Martinus Nijhoff, 1982), p. 17. See also Robert Blackburn and Jørg Polakiewicz, eds., *Fundamental Rights in Europe: The European Convention on Human Rights and Its Member States, 1950–2000* (Oxford: Oxford University Press, 2001), p. 11.

88. James Crawford, "The UN Human Rights Treaty System: A System in Crisis?" in Philip Alston and James Crawford, eds., *The Future of UN Human Rights Treaty Monitoring* (Cambridge: Cambridge University Press, 2000).

89. See Alston and Crawford, *The Future of UN Human Rights Treaty Monitoring;* and Anne F. Bayefsky, ed., *The UN Human Rights Treaty System in the 21st Century* (The Hague: Kluwer Law International, 2000).

90. See Harald Müller, "The Evolution of Verification: Lessons from the Past for the Present," *Arms Control* 14, no. 3 (December 1993): 333–356.

91. See J. G. Merrills, *International Dispute Settlement*, 3rd ed. (Cambridge: Cambridge University Press, 1998).

92. Vienna Convention on the Law of Treaties, article 31(1).
93. Vienna Convention on the Law of Treaties, article 33(1).
94. Chris af Jochnick and Roger Normand, "The Legitimation of Violence: A Critical History of the Laws of War," *Harvard International Law Journal* 35, no. 1 (Winter 1994): 49–95.

9

International Law
and Arms Control

D isarmament is the reduction or elimination, through negotiation of an international agreement, of the means of waging war.[1] The Hague Conferences of 1899 and 1907 had the declared aim of ensuring universal peace and bringing about a reduction of "excessive" armaments,[2] although the disarmament goals of those conferences were not achieved. The Covenant of the League of Nations also "recognise[d] that the maintenance of peace requires the reduction of national armaments to the lowest point consistent with national safety and the enforcement by common action of international obligations." Disarmament efforts under the auspices of the League culminated in the 1932 Disarmament Conference, convened in Geneva and attended by representatives of sixty states. Although it appeared to be moving toward agreement on certain topics, the conference was suspended in 1936 without having formalized a convention text.[3] Once Hitler was known to be rearming Germany in defiance of the Versailles Treaty, disarmament was effectively off the international agenda.

In comparison to the Covenant of the League of Nations, the UN Charter did not make much reference to disarmament. This is because, though many after World War I believed that the war had been caused by the prewar arms race, the dominant belief was that World War II could have been avoided if the great powers had maintained, and been prepared to use, adequate military force.[4] The "regulation of armaments" is nevertheless one of the subjects on which the General Assembly may make recommendations to members or to the Security Council.[5] The Security Council, assisted by the Military Staff Committee, was to formulate plans "to be submitted to the Members of

191

the United Nations for the establishment of a system for the regulation of armaments."[6]

During the Cold War, the phrase "arms control" came into use to refer to rules for limiting competition in armaments between the two superpowers; the phrase is now used more broadly to refer to means of trying to constrain reciprocal threats by regulating the acquisition, testing, numbers, ratios, types, location, deployment, spread, or use of current or prospective armaments; this may, but need not necessarily include, disarmament—the actual reduction or elimination of armaments.[7] Each of the weapons of mass destruction—nuclear, biological, and chemical—has its own global treaty, and in this chapter we will look at each in turn. Arms control treaties play an important role in the international management of security threats, despite the more diffuse nature of post–Cold War security threats and the increased significance of nonstate actors not parties to treaties (see Figure 9.1).

Treaty on the Nonproliferation of Nuclear Weapons, 1968

The NPT has been the centerpiece of multilateral efforts at arms control. Richard Butler has described it as "supplemental to" and "comparable in stature to" the UN Charter.[8] In 1963 John F. Kennedy commented in a well-known statement that

> personally I am haunted by the feeling that by 1970, unless we are successful, there may be ten nuclear powers instead of four, and by 1975, fifteen or twenty. . . . I see the possibility in the 1970s of the President of the United States having to face a world in which fifteen or twenty or twenty-five nations may have these weapons. I regard that as the greatest possible danger and hazard.[9]

The NPT was concluded in June 1968 and entered into force on March 5, 1970.[10] The crux of the nonproliferation obligations are found in articles I and II. By article I, nuclear-weapon states undertook "not to transfer to any recipient whatsoever nuclear weapons or other nuclear explosive devices or control over such weapons or explosive devices directly, or indirectly; and not in any way to assist, encourage, or induce any non-nuclear-weapon State to manufacture or otherwise acquire nuclear weapons or other nuclear explosive devices, or control over such weapons or explosive devices." Conversely, by article II, non-nuclear-weapon states undertook "not to receive the transfer from any transferor whatsoever of nuclear weapons or other nuclear explosive

Figure 9.1   Some Global Treaties on Arms Control

1963 Treaty Banning Nuclear-Weapon Tests in the Atmosphere, in Outer Space and Under Water (PTBT)

1966 Treaty on Principles Governing the Activities of States in the Exploration and Use of Outer Space, Including the Moon and Other Celestial Bodies (Outer Space Treaty)

1968 Treaty on the Non-Proliferation of Nuclear Weapons (NPT)

1971 Treaty on the Prohibition of the Emplacement of Nuclear Weapons and Other Weapons of Mass Destruction on the Sea Bed and Ocean Floor and in the Subsoil Thereof (Seabed Treaty)

1972 Convention on the Prohibition of the Development, Production, and Stockpiling of Bacteriological (Biological) and Toxin Weapons and on Their Destruction (BWC)

1979 Agreement Governing the Activities of States on the Moon and Other Celestial Bodies (Moon Agreement)

1993 Convention on the Prohibition of the Development, Production, Stockpiling, and Use of Chemical Weapons and on Their Destruction (CWC)

1996 Comprehensive Nuclear-Test Ban Treaty (CTBT)

---

devices or of control over such weapons or explosive devices directly, or indirectly; not to manufacture or otherwise acquire nuclear weapons or other nuclear explosive devices; and not to seek or receive any assistance in the manufacture of nuclear weapons or other nuclear explosive devices." A "nuclear-weapon state" was defined in article IX(3) as "one which has manufactured and exploded a nuclear weapon or other nuclear explosive device prior to 1 January 1967." Five states met this definition: the United States, the Soviet Union, the UK, France, and China. France and China did not sign.

The NPT provisions were obviously inequitable. Not only did the non-nuclear-weapon states (NNWS) pledge never to become nuclear powers, but by article III(1) each non-nuclear-weapon state party undertook to accept IAEA safeguards to verify its compliance with the treaty. The treaty did, however, recognize the right of each party to develop nuclear energy for peaceful purposes; indeed, by article V parties undertook to ensure that the potential benefits from peaceful applications of nuclear explosions would be made available to non-nuclear states at a low charge and on a nondiscriminatory basis.

The inequity was mediated by article VI, by which nuclear-weapon states (NWS) were to "undertake . . . to pursue negotiations in good faith on effective measures relating to cessation of the nuclear arms race at an early date and to nuclear disarmament, and on a treaty on general and complete disarmament under strict and effective international control." Article VI was something of a quid pro quo for non-nuclear-weapon states. The alleged failure of the nuclear-weapons states to comply with their obligations under article VI has been a source of ongoing dissatisfaction within the regime.

The trade-off between nuclear-weapon states and non-nuclear-weapon states went a little further. The NPT was accompanied by UN Security Council Resolution 255 of June 19, 1968, which welcomed "the intention expressed by certain States that they will provide or support immediate assistance, in accordance with the Charter, to any non-nuclear-weapon State Party to the Treaty on the Non-Proliferation of Nuclear Weapons that is a victim of an act or an object of a threat of aggression in which nuclear weapons are used." China and France, which were not at that time parties to the NPT, are not bound by this resolution. Declarations that nuclear-weapons states will come to the assistance of a non-nuclear-weapons state threatened with nuclear weapons are known as "positive security assurances." In the years since the conclusion of the NPT, all five nuclear-weapons states parties to the treaty have issued "negative assurances": guarantees that they will refrain from using the nuclear weapons against non-nuclear-weapons states that are parties to the NPT. Security Council Resolution 984 (1995) reinforced the 1968 commitment and took note of the unilateral assurances given by nuclear-weapons states against the use of nuclear weapons.[11]

The post–Cold War years have been a particular challenge for the NPT regime. The regime has come under external challenge from "second generation" or "opaque" states—Israel, India, Pakistan, North Korea, Argentina, Brazil, and South Africa—which developed nuclear weapons subsequent to the conclusion, and in defiance of, the NPT. Incorporating a date into the definition of a nuclear-weapons state in the NPT meant that if and when other states openly conducted tests—as did India and Pakistan in 1998—they were still not eligible to join the treaty regime as nuclear-weapons states. Until the tests by India and Pakistan, not one new state had declared itself to be a nuclear state.[12] Indeed, the 2000 Review and Extension Conference called on India and Pakistan to join the regime as non-nuclear-weapons states. Following the 1998 tests the Indian prime minister declared that India was "now a nuclear weapon State. This is a reality that cannot be denied. It is not a conferment that we seek; nor is it a status for others to grant. It is an endowment to the nation by our scientists and engineers."[13]

Iraq signed the NPT in 1968 and ratified it the following year. As part of the 1991 cease-fire agreement between Iraq and the United

Nations, UN Security Council Resolution 687 of April 3, 1991, required Iraq to "unconditionally accept the destruction, removal or rendering harmless, under international supervision" of all nuclear, chemical, and biological weapons–related assets. It authorized the IAEA, and created the United Nations Special Commission (UNSCOM), to conduct on-site inspections at facilities suspected of being part of an Iraqi nuclear weapons program. The IAEA had regularly inspected Iraq's declared nuclear facilities but had never found diversions of nuclear material from declared sites to illegal nuclear activities.[14] The IAEA discovered a large and advanced Iraqi secret complex for producing nuclear material necessary for manufacturing a nuclear weapon, thereby calling into question the adequacy of its own system of safeguards.[15] After years of strained relations between UNSCOM and the Iraqi regime, the UN arms inspectors were in December 1998 denied access to Iraq. The work of UNSCOM was officially terminated by Resolution 1284 (1999),[16] and UNSCOM was replaced by the United Nations Monitoring, Verification and Inspection Commission (UNMOVIC).

UNMOVIC began inspections in late 2002. Security Council Resolution 1441, adopted on November 8, 2002,[17] stated that Iraq was in material breach of its disarmament obligations under Resolution 687; it directed UNMOVIC and the IAEA to report immediately any interference by Iraq with their inspection duties. Maintaining that Iraqi cooperation with the inspections was inadequate, the United States and United Kingdom in mid-February 2003 embarked on a diplomatic campaign to gain Security Council authorization for the use of force against Iraq. When it became clear that there was little support for such a resolution, the United States offered Saddam Hussein an ultimatum: if he and his sons did not leave Iraq within forty-eight hours there would be military conflict.[18] Saddam Hussein rejected the ultimatum and on March 19 President George W. Bush announced that war had begun. Many lawyers found the argument that Resolution 1441, in conjunction with Resolutions 678 and 687, authorized the use of force against Iraq far-fetched, particularly given that the United States and United Kingdom governments had themselves stated that the resolution contained no "automaticity" with respect to the use of force.[19] The fact that no weapons of mass destruction were found in Iraq in the months following the initiation of hostilities produced a domestic backlash, particularly in the United Kingdom, against the political spin by which the government was able to take the country to war.

In 1993 the Democratic People's Republic of Korea (DPRK, i.e., North Korea) announced its intention to exercise its legal right to withdraw from the NPT and refused to allow international inspections of its nuclear facilities despite mounting evidence of attempts to develop nuclear weapons. In 1994 North Korea signed the so-called Agreed Framework with the United States by which the DPRK was to freeze its nuclear program and remain a party to the NPT.[20] In exchange, the United States, the Democratic Republic of Korea (ROK, i.e., South Korea), and Japan founded the Korean Peninsula Energy Development Organization (KEDO) in March 1995 to build two lightwater reactors for North Korea as well as to finance and supply North Korea with shipments of heavy fuel oil as an interim energy source. In October 2002 North Korea admitted that it had continued a uranium-enrichment program after the 1994 Agreed Framework went into effect. KEDO took steps to pressure North Korea to eliminate its program, including the suspension of oil deliveries.[21] North Korea responded by ousting international inspectors and moving to restart a plutonium facility that had been closed under the Agreed Framework and then, on January 10, 2003, announced that it would withdraw from the NPT.[22]

A review and extension conference for the NPT took place in New York from April 17 to May 12, 1995. Article X of the treaty had provided that a conference would be convened twenty-five years after entry into force of the treaty "to decide whether the Treaty shall continue in force indefinitely, or shall be extended for an additional fixed period or periods." This decision was to be taken by a majority of the parties to the treaty. Non-nuclear-weapon states were reluctant to agree to the indefinite extension of the NPT, fearing that they would then lose their leverage over the nuclear-weapons states. Opposition to indefinite extension on the part of non-nuclear states stemmed from objections regarding the discriminatory nature of the NPT. Indonesia claimed, for example, that

> an indefinite extension would mean the permanent legitimisation of nuclear weapons and the five privileged powers would be permitted to keep their nuclear arsenals while others are barred forever from acquiring them. It will thus lead to a permanent division of the world into nuclear-haves and have-nots, ratify inequality in international relations and relegate the vast majority of non-nuclear nations into a second class status.[23]

In contrast, some observers have not regarded the obvious inequity in the NPT as a problem. "Sincere indignation over the double standard implies a utopian assumption that greater equality of States breeds peace; historical support for this view is, at best, ambiguous."[24] The

NPT was extended indefinitely on May 12, 1995, as the third in a package of three decisions. Decision One related to strengthening the review process for the treaty. As from 1997, for example, ten-day prepcom meetings were to be held in each of the four years preceding quinquennial review conferences. Decision Two involved agreement on a statement of "principles and objectives" for nuclear nonproliferation. This called, inter alia, for a reaffirmed commitment by the nuclear-weapons states to article VI, involving a program of action that included the completion of a comprehensive test-ban treaty no later than 1996, the immediate commencement and early conclusion of negotiations on a convention banning production of fissionable material for nuclear weapons, and the "determined pursuit" by the nuclear-weapons states of "systematic and progressive efforts to reduce nuclear weapons globally, with the ultimate goal of eliminating those weapons."

China supported the 1995 decision to indefinitely extend the NPT. China had originally opposed the treaty as discriminatory. During the 1960s and 1970s China publicly endorsed the spread of nuclear weapons as a way of countering the nuclear superpower duopoly, although it appears to have stood by its declarations that it would not help other states in their efforts to develop nuclear weapons.[25] In the 1980s China gradually moved toward embracing the regime and acceded to the NPT on March 9, 1992. Since then China has declared its commitment to nonproliferation, although during this period China has been a significant nuclear proliferator. Of greatest concern to arms controllers has been its unsafeguarded transfers and exports of highly enriched uranium, heavy water, nuclear reactors, nuclear weapon designs, and ballistic missiles to Pakistan, North Korea, and Iran.[26]

After the indefinite extension of the NPT in 1995, a "new agenda" emerged in nuclear arms control debates. The new agenda takes its name from the eight-nation New Agenda Coalition formed in June 1998, a month after the South Asian tests, by the foreign ministers of Brazil, Egypt, Ireland, Mexico, New Zealand, Slovenia, South Africa, and Sweden to push for the elimination of nuclear weapons. The New Agenda Coalition built to some extent on the efforts of the Canberra Commission, a group of eminent scientists, disarmament experts, military strategists, and statesmen formed by the Australian government in October 1995 to develop "concrete and realistic steps for achieving a nuclear weapons-free world." The 1996 report of the commission had reiterated the theme that nuclear nonproliferation and nuclear disarmament cannot be pursued separately.[27]

The New Agenda Coalition was influential at the 2000 NPT Review

Conference.[28] On, May 1, 2000, China, France, Russia, the UK, and the
United States issued a joint statement in which they formally reiterated
their strong and continuing support for the treaty and their "unequivocal
commitment to the ultimate goals of a complete elimination of nuclear
weapons and a treaty on general and complete disarmament under strict
and effective international control."[29]

In June 2003 the director-general of the IAEA reported that Iran
had failed to meet its obligations under its safeguards agreement with
respect to the reporting of nuclear material, the subsequent processing
and use of that material, and the declaration of facilities where the
material was stored and processed. Iran, which had signed the NPT in
1968 and ratified it in 1970, had been pursuing a civil nuclear power
program aided for more than a decade by Russia. In July 2002 Moscow
approved plans to construct up to six civil nuclear reactors in Iran, in
addition to an earlier agreement to build a nuclear power plant at
Bushehr. Angered by Iranian-Russian nuclear cooperation, the United
States had claimed that, given Iran's vast domestic energy resources, its
only interest in nuclear civil power could be to support a nuclear
weapons program.[30]

Convention on the Prohibition
of the Development, Production, and
Stockpiling of Bacteriological (Biological) and
Toxin Weapons and on Their Destruction, 1972

Biological warfare is "the intentional use of disease-causing micro-
organisms or other entities that can replicate themselves (e.g., viruses,
infectious nucleic acids and prions) against humans, animals or plants
for hostile purposes. It may also involve the use of toxins: poisonous
substances produced by living organisms, including micro-organisms
(e.g., botulinum toxin), plants (e.g., ricin derived from castor beans)
and animals (e.g., snake venom). If they are utilized for warfare purpose, the synthetically manufactured counterparts of these toxins are
biological weapons."[31] Biological weapons can kill at an equivalent rate
to nuclear weapons, although without damaging infrastructure. This is
the subject of the 1972 Biological Weapons Convention.[32]

The 1925 Geneva Protocol for the Prohibition of the Use in War of
Asphyxiating, Poisonous, or Other Gases, and of Bacteriological
Methods of Warfare[33] prohibited the use of biological weapons but did
not outlaw their development, production, or possession. The next
major development in the international management of biological

weapons was the Biological Weapons Convention, negotiated between 1969 and 1971, which was opened for signature in 1972 and entered into force in 1975. Article 1 provides:

> Each State Party to this Convention undertakes never in any circumstance to develop, produce, stockpile or otherwise acquire or retain:
>
> (1) Microbial or other biological agents, or toxins whatever their origin or method of production, of types and in quantities that have no justification for prophylactic, protective or other peaceful purposes;
>
> (2) Weapons, equipment or means of delivery designed to use such agents or toxins for hostile purposes or in armed conflict.

The second paragraph of article I contains a major loophole: the parties to the BWC undertake never to acquire or retain biological weapons "that have no justification for prophylactic, protective or other peaceful purposes"; in practice it is virtually impossible to distinguish programs with purely defensive purposes from those designed with offensive use in mind. By article II, each state party undertakes to destroy, or to convert to peaceful purposes, any existing stockpiles of agents, toxins, weapons, equipment, and means of delivery specified in article I. The BWC specified in article XII that a review conference was to be held within five years after entry into force. The first review conference took place in 1980, the next in 1986, and since then they have been held at five-year intervals.

In contrast to both the NPT that preceded it, and the Chemical Weapons Convention that was to follow, the Biological Weapons Convention contains no verification measures. Article VI provided for enforcement only insofar as any state party finding that another state party is acting in breach of the BWC may lodge a complaint with the Security Council; all states parties are to cooperate with any investigation that the Security Council may initiate as a result of such a complaint. The absence of effective verification measures facilitated conclusion of the BWC, as did the unilateral renouncement of biological weapons by the United States in 1969 and its decision in 1970 to destroy its stockpiles. In 1970 the United States announced that military programs for biological agents and toxins would be limited to research and development for defensive purposes.[34]

Ongoing developments in biotechnology and genetic engineering, which, although with great potential to improve the quality of life, could also be turned into deadly weapons, generated in the post–Cold War years momentum to negotiate a protocol on verification. At the 1986 review conference, parties had decided to take a series of confi-

dence-building measures to compensate, in part at least, for the absence
of meaningful verification provisions.[35] Further impetus came from the
discovery of a major clandestine Soviet biological weapons program
and the information regarding the Iraqi program that emerged following
the Gulf War. The 1991 third review conference created VEREX, an ad
hoc group of governmental experts to identify and examine potential
verification measures from a scientific and technical standpoint.
Between 1995 and 2001 an ad hoc group of states worked further on the
issue of verification and, at the fourth review conference in 1996,
received a mandate to negotiate a legally binding instrument. Formal
talks on a verification protocol began in 1995 by a group of about fifty
states.

The administration of Bill Clinton played a key role in the
post–Cold War push for a verification mechanism within the regime,[36]
but in 2001 the Bush administration formally rejected the draft protocol, stating that it was "forced to conclude that the mechanisms envi-
sioned for the protocol would not achieve their objectives, that no modification of them would allow them to achieve their objectives, and that
trying to do more would simply raise the risk to legitimate United
States activities." This effectively marked the withdrawal of the United
States from the negotiations.[37] The U.S. administration had three basic
objections to the protocol. First, as written and if implemented, it would
compromise U.S. biodefense preparations. Inspectors would be able to
develop countermeasures to frustrate the defenses that the United States
was preparing. Second, inspections would compromise the intellectual
property assets of U.S. pharmaceutical and biotech industries. Third,
there was the undermining of the U.S. system of export controls and the
multilateral framework of export controls known as the Australia Group
to prevent the export of dual-use items and others that could be used in
an offensive biological weapons program.[38] In response to the view that
a flawed protocol was better than no protocol, the U.S. undersecretary
of state for arms control and international security, John Bolton,
responded that it was "even worse than nothing," that "better than nothing" is a formula that could have led to a protocol that would have simply rewarded hypocrisy by permitting countries to sign the protocol and
then to lie about compliance.[39] At the fifth review conference, which
met from November 19 to December 12, 2001, the United States proposed the termination of the existing diplomatic process to strengthen
compliance with the treaty; the conference adjourned without reaching
agreement on a final declaration.[40]

Convention on the Prohibition of the Development, Production, Stockpiling, and Use Of Chemical Weapons and on Their Destruction, 1993

Chemical weapons are the topic of the 1993 Chemical Weapons Convention.[41] Such weapons are nothing new, the Greeks having used sulfur mixtures on the battlefield as long ago as 431 B.C.[42] International attempts to limit or prevent their usage date from a 1675 Franco-German agreement not to use poisoned bullets.[43] The Hague Convention of 1899 prohibited the use of projectiles "the object of which is diffusion of asphyxiating or deleterious gases." The 1925 Geneva Protocol for the Prohibition of the Use in War of Asphyxiating, Poisonous, or Other Gases, and of Bacteriological Methods of Warfare banned the use of chemical weapons in war but not the development, production, or possession of such weapons. It had been anticipated that chemical weapons would be banned simultaneously with biological weapons, but in the lead-up to the 1972 convention several Western countries proposed proceeding with the agreement only for the less militarily useful biological weapons, arguing that they required less rigorous verification provisions.[44]

Formal negotiations for the CCW began in the Conference on Disarmament in 1984. The basis for negotiations was the so-called rolling text, an evolving draft that was updated annually with provisionally agreed elements and those on which disagreement remained. Progress toward a treaty was slow. States disagreed over whether the ban should be total, as well as the nature of verification provisions. If very stringent they appeared as intrusive on national sovereignty; if too lax, the regime would not be deemed effective. Developing countries demanded that all discriminatory export control measures for chemical weapons–related chemicals be abolished. Negotiations gained impetus with the Gulf War and with the submission by Australia of a complete draft convention in 1992.[45] The Conference on Disarmament adopted the final text on September 3, 1992, and it was opened for signature on January 13, 1993. The CWC entered into force on April 29, 1997, 180 days after deposit of the sixty-fifth instrument of ratification.

The CWC was the first multilateral treaty to provide for the elimination of an entire category of weapons of mass destruction. By article I of the CWC, each state party undertakes never to develop, produce, otherwise acquire, stockpile, or retain chemical weapons or transfer, directly or indirectly, chemical weapons to anyone. Each state party also undertakes to destroy chemical weapons it owns or possesses and any chemical weapons production facilities it owns or possesses. By article

IV(6) destruction is to begin not later than two years after entry into force of the CWC and to finish not later than ten years after its entry into force.

Pursuant to article VIII of the CWC, the Organization for the Prohibition of Chemical Weapons (OPCW) was established in The Hague upon entry into force of the CWC in 1997, "to achieve the object and purpose of this Convention, to ensure the implementation of its provisions, including those for international verification of compliance with it, and to provide a forum for consultation and cooperation among State Parties."[46] The OPCW comprises the conference of the states parties, the main body of the organization made up of all states that have ratified the CWC, as well as the executive council, consisting of forty-one elected representatives from states that have ratified the CWC, the Technical Secretariat, and the Scientific Advisory Board. The OPCW has been described as a "quantum leap in the institutional law of arms control."[47]

The CWC is notable for its far-reaching verification provisions. A routine monitoring regime involves submission by states parties to the OPCW of initial and annual declarations, visits, and systematic inspections of declared chemical weapons storage, production, and destruction facilities. But it is the system of *challenge inspections* that is of particular note. Under this system, a state party may request an inspection to be conducted of any facility or location in the territory or under the jurisdiction of any other state party, in order to clarify and resolve questions of possible noncompliance.[48] Within twelve hours of the submission of a request to conduct a challenge inspection, the executive council is to decide whether the request is abusive, frivolous, or inconsistent with the CWC. If the Executive Council decides that the request is valid, the OPCW conducts a challenge inspection of the facility or location in question. The inspected state party has the obligation to provide access for the inspection, although it also has the right to take measures to protect sensitive installations and to prevent disclosure of confidential information and data unrelated to the CWC.[49]

Comprehensive Nuclear Test-Ban Treaty, 1996

A global halt to nuclear weapons test explosions was first proposed by Indian prime minister Jawaharlal Nehru in April 1954[50] after a U.S. thermonuclear test exposed a Japanese fishing trawler and more than 200 Marshall Islanders to radioactive fallout.[51] Following the dangerous stand-off during the 1962 Cuban Missile Crisis, talks began in 1963 for a comprehensive nuclear test ban. Negotiators failed to agree on the number of on-site verification inspections, and a limited test ban treaty was concluded instead. This was the 1963 Treaty Banning Nuclear Weapon Tests in the Atmosphere, in Outer Space, and Under Water, known as the Partial Test-Ban Treaty (PTBT).[52] Nuclear testing could continue underground. The Threshold Test-Ban Treaty of 1974 limited the yield of underground nuclear weapon tests to 150 kilotons. Although little progress was made toward a comprehensive test ban treaty during the Cold War, this objective was far from forgotten, having been raised at every NPT review conference. Many states believed that article VI of the NPT placed the nuclear states under a legal obligation to take positive steps toward the conclusion of a comprehensive test-ban treaty. At the 1975, 1980, 1985, and 1990 review conferences, NNWS made it clear that they expected the disarmament obligations found in article VI to begin through a comprehensive treaty. The idea of a comprehensive treaty remained a central objective of nuclear disarmament and arms control campaigners throughout the 1960s, 1970s, and 1980s. As the CTBT preamble was later to say, it was believed that "by constraining the development and qualitative improvement of nuclear weapons and ending the development of advanced new types of nuclear weapons," a comprehensive test ban constitutes "an effective measure of nuclear disarmament and non-proliferation in all its aspects."[53]

The end of the Cold War appeared to offer new opportunities for progress toward nuclear disarmament. In 1991 parties to the PTBT held an amendment conference to discuss a proposal to convert the PTBT into an instrument banning all nuclear weapons tests. The proposal was not accepted, but the initiative contributed to the pressure for a comprehensive test-ban treaty. Negotiations for the CTBT began in the Conference on Disarmament in January 1994. As the 1995 NPT review and extension conference loomed, the nuclear-weapon states came under increased pressure to show how they had complied with article VI. Lack of a CTBT had come to be seen as indicative of a lack of real effort. At the 1995 review and extension conference the NPT was indefinitely extended as part of a politically binding package of three decisions. The Principles and Objectives of Nuclear Non-Proliferation and Disarmament contained a paragraph calling for a CTBT no later than 1996 (to be followed by the Fissile Material Cut-Off Treaty [FMCT]). The final draft of the CTBT was adopted by the General Assembly on September 10, 1996, and opened for signature on September 24, 1996.

Article I contains the basic obligation on states "not to carry out any nuclear weapon test explosion or any other nuclear explosion, and to prohibit and prevent any such nuclear explosion at any place under its jurisdiction or control"; as well as to "refrain from causing, encouraging, or in any way participating in the carrying out of any nuclear weapon test explosion or any other nuclear explosion." Under article XIV the treaty is to enter into force 180 days after the date of deposit of the instruments of ratification by all states listed in annex 2, "but in no case earlier than two years after its opening for signature." Annex 2 contains the forty-four states members of the Conference on Disarmament operating nuclear reactors.[54]

The role of the Comprehensive Nuclear Test-Ban Treaty Organization, which will come into existence following the first conference of the states parties to the CTBT, is, according to article II of the treaty, "to achieve the object and purpose of [the] Treaty, to ensure the implementation of its provisions, including those for international verification of compliance with it, and to provide a forum for consultation and cooperation among States Parties." Article IV sets out the general verification provisions. The verification regime is to include an international monitoring system, consultation and clarification, on-site inspections, and confidence-building measures. The International Monitoring System, whose purpose is to detect and identify nuclear explosions prohibited under the treaty, is to consist of fifty primary and 120 auxiliary seismological stations to detect seismic activity, as well as eighty radionuclide stations to identify radioactive particles released during a nuclear explosion and sixty infrasound and eleven hydroacoustic stations to pick up the sound of a nuclear explosion in the atmosphere or under water, respectively.[55] Provision is also made for on-site inspections if consultations have not been able to clarify an ambiguous event.

When negotiations for the CTBT began in 1994 India was an enthusiastic supporter. By the conclusion of the negotiations in 1996 India was the fiercest critic. Together with Iran it blocked consensus on a final CTBT text, the Indian representative telling the General Assembly that India would "never sign this unequal Treaty. Not now. Not later."[56] The shift was in part because of concern with the nuclear programs of China and Pakistan, but it also had a lot to do with India's dissatisfaction with the outcome of the 1995 NPT review and extension conference. India took the position that, because the NPT extension conference had not adequately addressed the disarmament issue, the CTBT represented the next, and possibly the only remaining, opportunity to extract a stronger disarmament commitment.[57] It was after India announced that it would not subscribe to the CTBT that the final draft treaty contained the forty-four-state requirement for entry into force. A previous draft had made entry into force contingent on ratification by the thirty-seven states that would host facilities for the CTBT's International Monitoring System. India had withdrawn its monitoring stations from the network and so would no longer have been on the list of states whose signature was required for entry into force. India resented being forced to either join a regime with which it had expressed its profound dissatisfaction, or else shoulder responsibility for the whole treaty not entering into force.

There was some hope that India's attitude toward the CTBT would change after the completion of its 1998 tests. Moderates in the Indian government believed that signing would remove Indian isolation and that India had sufficient data to conduct the subcritical and computer simulation experiments permitted under the treaty. Critics of the CTBT within India maintained that India needed to do more tests; they objected to the U.S. Stockpile Stewardship Program, which they believed would permit the more advanced nuclear-weapons states to introduce modifications into existing weapon designs.[58]

The UK, France, and Russia, as well as all the European and Western bloc countries, strongly support entry into force of the CTBT. India has said that it will not block the treaty's entry into force. North Korea is an obstacle to its entry into force, as is the United States. The CTBT was a key foreign policy objective of the Clinton administration, and the United States was the first state to sign the CTBT. And yet on October 13, 1999, the U.S. Senate voted to reject ratification of the CTBT, thereby blocking—at least temporarily—its entry into force. The U.S. boycotted a conference in November 2001 to encourage support for the CTBT. Nuclear states have nevertheless put unilateral moratoriums on nuclear tests. Russia has not conducted a nuclear test since 1991, the United States since 1992. France began a moratorium in 1992 but ended it in 1995 to begin a series of tests at Mururoa Atoll. It resumed its moratorium in early 1996. China placed a moratorium on its nuclear tests in 1996.

Regional Treaties Establishing Nuclear-Weapons-Free Zones

The Antarctic Treaty (1959), Outer Space Treaty (1967), Moon Agreement (1979), and Seabed Treaty (1971) all denuclearized their respective locations. Several nuclear-weapons-free zones (NWFZs) have also been established by treaty in populated areas. The first was the Treaty of Tlatelolco (Latin America) of 1967, followed by the Treaty of Rarotonga in the South Pacific in 1985, the Treaty of Bangkok in Southeast Asia in 1995, and the Treaty of Pelindaba in Africa in

1996. The five states of Central Asia (Kazakhstan, Kyrgyzstan, Tajikistan, Turkmenistan, and Uzbekistan) have engaged in talks regarding the establishment of a Central Asian NWFZ. NWFZs can be understood as confidence-building measures designed to remove regional pressures to acquire nuclear weapons.[59]

U.S.-Soviet Union Bilateral
Treaties on Nuclear Arms Control

During the Cold War there was a prospect that the world would be destroyed by nuclear war between the superpowers. As well as the multilateral efforts to manage weapons of mass destruction, a series of bilateral arms reduction treaties was concluded between the Soviet Union and the United States.

In 1969 the United States and the Soviet Union initiated bilateral negotiations on restricting their strategic nuclear arsenals (weapons with an intercontinental range). The Strategic Arms Limitation Talks (SALT) resulted in the signing in 1972 of both the U.S.-Soviet Treaty on the Limitation of Anti-Ballistic Missile Systems (the ABM Treaty)[60] and the U.S.-Soviet Interim Agreement. An ABM system is a system to counter strategic ballistic missiles (or their elements) in flight trajectory. The ABM Treaty prohibited the development of an antiballistic missile system to protect the whole of either country or of an individual region, except where expressly permitted. The ABM Treaty became the centerpiece of bilateral strategic arms control because the doctrine of mutually assured destruction relied on each side having strong offensive capabilities while itself remaining vulnerable to attack. The Interim Agreement, designed to last until a more detailed and far-reaching agreement could be negotiated, froze for five years the aggregate number of fixed land-based intercontinental ballistic missile launchers and ballistic missile launchers on submarines, although it did not prevent both sides from pursuing developments—such as multiple-warhead missiles—not covered by the treaty.

The SALT negotiations resumed in 1977. The 1979 U.S.-Soviet Treaty on the Limitation of Strategic Offensive Arms, known as SALT II, capped armaments at a level higher than that existing at the time of their negotiation, thus keeping in check the arms race, although not requiring any actual disarmament. Unlike SALT I, SALT II provided for quantitative parity. Although it was not ratified by the U.S. Senate, both sides complied for several years with the new limits placed on the size of their arsenals. With the assumption to office of President Ronald Reagan in 1981, the SALT negotiations were renamed the Strategic

Arms Reduction Talks (START). After nine years of negotiations, the two sides signed the Treaty on the Reduction and Limitation of Strategic Offensive Arms, which came to be known as the START I Treaty. Unlike SALT, which had limited the future growth of strategic nuclear arms, START required reductions in existing levels of strategic nuclear arms to 1,600 launchers and 6,000 warheads for each side. It entered into force on December 5, 1994. The 1987 Intermediate-Range Nuclear Forces (INF) Treaty[61] provided for the elimination of all nuclear missiles with a range of between 310 and 3,400 miles.[62] The ban on intermediate-range missiles under INF is of unlimited duration.

The end of the Cold War led to new proposals for negotiated arms reductions, even to some unilateral disarmament as tactical and battle-field nuclear weapons became of much less importance to security in Europe. Presidents George H. W. Bush and Boris Yeltsin signed the U.S.-Russian Treaty on Further Reduction and Limitation of Strategic Offensive Arms, or START II, in Moscow on January 3, 1993. Both sides undertook to deploy no more than 3,000–3,500 strategic nuclear warheads on their land-based intercontinental ballistic missiles, submarine-launched ballistic missiles, and heavy bombers. Following the dissolution of the Soviet Union, the START, INF, and ABM Treaties were effectively changed into multilateral agreements with Belarus, Kazakhstan, Russia, and the Ukraine as successor states to the former Soviet Union.[63] In September 1997 representatives of the United States, Russia, Belarus, Kazakhstan, and Ukraine signed a package of agreements, including the START II extension protocol, which extended the deadline for the completion of START II reductions from January 1, 2003, to December 31, 2007. The United States ratified the original START II agreement in January 1996 but has not ratified the 1997 protocol extending the treaty's implementation deadline and other concurrently negotiated treaties. Having postponed a vote on START II ratification several times, the Russian Duma approved ratification of START II and its extension protocol and concurrently negotiated agreements on April 14, 2000, but made the exchange of instruments of ratification contingent on U.S. ratification of the extension protocol and other, concurrently negotiated, agreements.[64]

The United States and Russia agreed in 2000 to begin negotiating START III but agreed subsequently to strategic reductions outside the START framework. On December 13, 2001, President George W. Bush gave the requisite six months' notice of U.S. withdrawal from the ABM Treaty in order to continue development of its controversial missile defense program.[65] And yet on May 24, 2002, Presidents Bush and Vladimir Putin signed the Treaty on Strategic Offensive Reductions, setting out commitments to reduce their deployed strategic warheads to less than 2,200 each by 2012.[66] In announcing the successful conclusion of the six-month negotiations, Bush claimed that the treaty would "liquidate the legacy of the cold war."[67]

As is true with other types of treaties, arms control agreements may not have been 100 percent successful, and verification provisions can never be 100 percent foolproof. But arms control treaties have constituted a very important part of the post–World War II security framework. This is why any perceived indications of a lack of respect for arms control, whether on the part of North Korea when announcing that it would withdraw from the NPT, or on the part of the United States in withdrawing support for a verification protocol in the BWC regime, prompts strong reaction from the international community and arms control experts. Few would deny the importance to the structures of world politics of this group of bilateral and multilateral treaties.

Notes

1. Robert J. Mathews and Timothy L. H. McCormack, "The Relationship Between International Humanitarian Law and Arms Control," in Helen Durham and Timothy L. H. McCormack, eds., *The Changing Face of Conflict and the Efficacy of International Humanitarian Law* (The Hague: Martinus Nijhof, 1999), pp. 65–98, 78.

2. Jozef Goldblat, *Arms Control: A Guide to Negotiations and Agreements* (London: Sage, 1994), p. 11.

3. Ibid., pp. 15–20.

4. Jozef Goldblat, "Contribution of the UN to Arms Control," in Dimitris Bourantonis and Marios Evriviades, eds., *A United Nations for the Twenty-First Century: Peace, Security and Development* (The Hague: Kluwer, 1996), pp. 243–257, 244.

5. Charter of the United Nations, article 11(1).

6. Charter of the United Nations, articles 26 and 47(1).

7. Ramesh Thakur and William Maley, "The Ottawa Convention on Landmines: A Landmark Humanitarian Treaty in Arms Control," *Global Governance* 5 (1999): 273–302, 274.

8. Richard Butler, *Fatal Choice: Nuclear Weapons and the Illusion of Missile Defense* (Crows Nest, NSW: Allen & Unwin, 2001), p. 52.

9. Quoted in Michael Reiss, *Without the Bomb: The Politics of Nuclear Nonproliferation* (New York: Columbia University Press, 1988), p. 16.

10. For the details of the process by which the NPT was negotiated, see United Nations, *Review of the Multilateral Treaty-Making Process* (New York: United Nations, 1985), pp. 220–221.

11. The texts of the negative security assurances can be found in *The United Nations and Nuclear Non-Proliferation* (New York: United Nations,

1995). See also George Bunn, "The Legal Status of US Negative Security Assurances to Non-Nuclear Weapon States," *Nonproliferation Review* (Spring-Summer 1997): 1–17.

12. Benjamin Frankel, ed., *Opaque Nuclear Proliferation: Methodological and Policy Implications* (London: Frank Cass, 1991), p. 18.

13. "Statement to Parliament by Prime Minister Vajpayee, 27 May 1998," at www.acronym.org.uk/spind.htm.

14. Bill Monahan, "Giving the Non-Proliferation Treaty Teeth: Strengthening the Special Inspection Procedures of the International Atomic Energy Agency," *Virginia Journal of International Law* 33, no. 1 (Fall 1992): 161–196.

15. Ibid.

16. See, inter alia, R. Butler, *The Greatest Threat: Iraq, Weapons of Mass Destruction, and the Crisis of Global Security* (New York: PublicAffairs, 2000), and the review of that by David Malone, "Iraq: No Easy Response to 'The Greatest Threat,'" *American Journal of International Law (AJIL)* 95 (2001): 235–245; Chantal de Jonge Oudraat, "UNSCOM: Between Iraq and a Hard Place," *European Journal of International Law* 13, no. 1 (2002): 139–152; Scott Ritter, *Endgame: Solving the Iraq Problem Once and for All* (New York: Simon & Schuster, 1999), and the review of that by Brian Urquhart, "How Not to Fight a Dictator," *New York Review of Books,* May 6, 1999, p. 25; and "The Lessons and Legacy of UNSCOM: An Interview with Ambassador Richard Butler," *Arms Control Today* (June 1999): 3–9.

17. For more detail on the background to the resolution, see Sean D. Murphy, "Contemporary Practice of the United States," *AJIL* 96 (2002): 956–962.

18. See Sean D. Murphy, "Contemporary Practice of the United States," *AJIL* 97 (2003): 419–432.

19. Explanation of Vote by Ambassador John D. Negroponte, United States Permanent Representative to the United Nations, following the vote on the Iraq Resolution, Security Council, November 8, 2002. Press release no. 197(02)(rev.), available at the website of the United States Mission to the United Nations, www.un.int/usa/02_187.htm. See also statement by Ambassador Greenstock to the Security Council, "Explanation of Vote on Security Council Resolution 1441 on Iraq, 8 November 2002," at the website of the UK Mission to the United Nations, at www.ukun.org/xq/asp/SarticleType.17/Article_ID.516/qx/articles_show.htm.

20. Marian Nash (Leigh), "United States–Democratic People's Republic of Korea," *AJIL* 89 (1995): 372–375.

21. Paul Kerr, "KEDO Suspends Oil Shipments to North Korea," *Arms Control Today* (December 2002), at www.armscontrol.org; Stephen Lunn, "Halt N-program or Lose Oil, N Korea Told," *Weekend Australian,* November 16–17, 2002, p. 15.

22. Glen Kessler, "US Plays Down North Korean Move," *Washington Post,* January 11, 2003, at www.washingtonpost.com/wp-dyn/articles/A40691–2003Jan10.htm, accessed January 13, 2003.

23. *Nuclear Proliferation News,* ACRONYM Consortium, issue no. 23, May 3, 1995, at http://csf.colorado.edu/dfax/npn/npn23.htm.

24. R. K. Betts, "Paranoids, Pygmies, Pariahs, and Nonproliferation," *Foreign Policy* 26 (Spring 1977): 157–183, 158. See also Richard Betts, "Paranoids, Pygmies, Pariahs, and Nonproliferation Revisited," *Security Studies* 2 (Spring/Summer 1993): 100–126.

25. Quoted in Mingquan Zhu, "The Evolution of China's Nuclear Nonproliferation Policy," *Nonproliferation Review* 4, no. 2 (Winter 1997): 40–48, 43.

26. Mohan Malik, "Chinese Perspectives on Nuclear Non-proliferation and Asian Security," in Carl Ungerer and Marianne Hanson, eds., *The Politics of Nuclear Non-proliferation* (St. Leonards, NSW: Allen & Unwin in association with the Department of International Relations Research School of Pacific and Asian Studies, Australian National University, 2001), pp. 132–157. See also Steven Dolley, "China's Record of Proliferation Misbehavior," *Issue Brief*, Nuclear Control Institute, Washington, D.C., September 29, 1997, at www.nci.org/ib92997.htm; Ming Zhang, *China's Changing Nuclear Posture: Reactions to the South Asian Nuclear Tests*. (Washington, DC: Carnegie Endowment for International Peace, 1999); and Zhu, "The Evolution of China's Nuclear Nonproliferation Policy."

27. J. Dhanapala, "A Strengthened Review Process for the NPT," *Fordham International Law Journal* 20 (1997): 1532–1542, 1538.

28. Carl Ungerer and Marianne Hanson, "The 2000 NPT Review Conference: A Normative Advance," in Ungerer and Hanson, *The Politics of Nuclear Non-proliferation*, pp. 72–84.

29. See, inter alia, Jayantha Dhanapala, "Eliminating Nuclear Arsenals: The NPT Pledge and What It Means," *Disarmament Diplomacy* 47 (June 2000): 3–6; Tariq Rauf, "An Unequivocal Success? Implications of the NPT Review Conference," *Arms Control Today* 30, no. 6 (2000): 9–16; and Douglas Roche, "An Unequivocal Landmark: The 2000 Review of the Non-Proliferation Treaty," Ploughshares Working Paper no. 00–2, Ploughshares Project, Institute of Peace and Conflict Studies, Ontario, May 27, 2000, at www.ploughsahres. ca/CONTENT/ABOLISH%20NUCS/RocheNPTReportMay27.html.

30. "Anger at Russia-Iran Nuclear Ties," August 1, 2002, CNN.com, at www.cnn.com/2002/WORLDEUROPE/08/01/RUSSIA.IRAN/. See also Michael Eisenstadt, "Russian Arms and Technology Transfers to Iran: Policy Challenges for the United States," Arms Control Association, March 2001, at www.armscontrol.org/act/2001_03/eisenstadt.asp?print.

31. Adam Daniel Rotfeld, "Introduction," in "Biotechnology and the Future of the Biological and Toxin Weapons Convention," *SIPRI Fact Sheet* (November 2001), at http://projects.sipri.se/cbw/research/biotechnologyfact-sheet.pdf.

32. Convention on the Prohibition of the Development, Production, and Stockpiling of Bacteriological (Biological) and Toxin Weapons and on Their Destruction, 11 International Legal Materials (ILM) 309 (1972).

33. *AJIL* 25 (1931), Supp. 94–96.

34. Jozef Goldblat, *Arms Control*, p. 93.

35. Ibid., p. 229.

36. Scott Keefer, "International Control of Biological Weapons," *ILSA Journal of International & Comparative Law* 6 (1999): 107–141, 108.

37. Oliver Meier, "Neither Trust nor Verify, Says U.S.," *Bulletin of the Atomic Scientists* 57, no. 6 (Nov.–Dec. 2001): 19–21, 73.

38. Interview with John R. Bolton, undersecretary of state for arms control and international security, Center for Nonproliferation Studies, Monterey Institute of International Studies, at http://cns.miis.edu/pubs/programs/dc/briefs/011102.htm, accessed October 11, 2003.

39. Ibid.

40. Seth Brugger, "BWC Conference Suspended After Controversial End," *Arms Control Today* (January/February 2002), available at www.armscontrol.org.

41. 32 ILM 804 (1993).

42. Amy E. Smithson, "Chemical Weapons: The End of the Beginning," *Bulletin of the Atomic Scientists* (October 1992): 37–43, 37.

43. Ibid.

44. Jozef Goldblat, *Arms Control*, pp. 93–96.

45. "The Chemical Weapons Convention: A Guided Tour of the Convention on the Prohibition of the Development, Production, Stockpiling, and Use of Chemical Weapons and on Their Destruction," at www.opcw.org/guide.htm, accessed January 1, 2002.

46. The Convention on the Prohibition of the Development, Production, Stockpiling, and Use of Chemical Weapons and on Their Destruction, article VIII (1).

47. Eric P. J. Myjer, "The Organization for the Prohibition of Chemical Weapons: Moving Closer Towards an International Arms Control Organization? A Quantum Leap in the Institutional Law of Arms Control," in Eric P. J. Myjer, ed., *Issues of Arms Control Law and the Chemical Weapons Convention: Obligations Inter Se and Supervisory Mechanisms* (The Hague: Martinus Nijhoff, 2001, pp. 61–139.

48. The Convention on the Prohibition of the Development, Production, Stockpiling, and Use of Chemical Weapons and on Their Destruction, article IX (8).

49. The Convention on the Prohibition of the Development, Production, Stockpiling, and Use of Chemical Weapons and on Their Destruction, article IX (11).

50. Rebecca Johnson and Daryl Kimball, "Who Needs the Nuclear Test Ban?" *Disarmament Diplomacy* 59 (July–August 2001), at www.acronym.org.uk.

51. Dinshaw Mistry, "Domestic-International Linkages: India and the Comprehensive Test Ban Treaty," *Nonproliferation Review* (Fall 1998): 25–38, 26–27.

52. 480 United Nations Treaty Series (UNTS) 43.

53. 35 ILM 1443 (1996).

54. Or, more precisely, the states that formally participated in the 1996 session of the Conference on Disarmament, and that appear in table 1 of the December 1995 edition of "Nuclear Research Reactors in the World," and table 1 of the April 1996 edition of "Nuclear Power Reactors in the World," both compiled by the International Atomic Energy Agency.

55. The details are found in part 1 of the accompanying Protocol to the Comprehensive Nuclear Test-Ban Treaty.

56. Dinshaw Mistry, "Domestic-International Linkages," p. 25.

57. This paragraph draws on ibid.

58. Gaurav Kampani, "In Praise of Indifference toward India's Bomb," *Orbis* (Spring 2001): 241–257, 248.

59. Ramesh Thakur, ed., *Nuclear Weapons-Free Zones* (Houndmills, Basingstoke, Hampshire: Macmillan, 1998), p. 30. See also Jozef Goldblat, "Nuclear-Weapon-Free-Zones: A History and Assessment," *Nonproliferation Review* (Spring–Summer 1997): 18–32.

60. 944 UNTS 13.

61. 27 ILM 84 (1988).

62. The text can be found at www.armscontrol.org/documents/inf.asp.

63. By the 1997 Memorandum of Understanding on Succession to the ABM Treaty, for example, the United States, Russia, Belarus, Kazakhstan, and Ukraine were designated parties to the ABM Treaty.

64. "START II and Its Extension Protocol at a Glance," fact sheet prepared by the Arms Control Association, available at www.armscontrol.org/factsheets/start2.asp; "START II Ratification: A Chronology," compiled by Dr. Scott Parrish, at http://cns.miis.edu/research/summit/s2chrono.htm.

65. See, inter alia, Charles L. Glaser and Steve Fetter, "National Missile Defense and the Future of US Nuclear Weapons Policy," *International Security* 26, no. 1 (Summer 2001): 40–92; David Edward Grogan, "Power Play: Theater Ballistic Missile Defense, National Ballistic Missile Defense, and the ABM Treaty," *Virginia Journal of International Law* 39, no. 4 (Summer 1999): 799–879; and Keith Wilson, "Why Are the Missiles (and Missile Defence) Called Peace-keepers? Corroding the Concept of Peaceful Use," *Leiden Journal of International Law* 14, no. 4 (2001): 759–828.

66. "United States (U.S.)-Russian Federation: The Moscow Treaty (Treaty Between the United States of America and The Russian Federation on Strategic Offensive Reductions) [May 24, 2002]" 41 ILM 799 (2002). Also available at www.whitehouse.gov/news/releases/2002/05/20020524–3.html.

67. Patrick E. Tyler, "Pulling Russia Closer," *New York Times,* May 14, 2002, p. A1.

10

International Human Rights Law

Although it has ancient origins and there were some human rights–related mechanisms within the League of Nations system, international human rights law is primarily a post–World War II phenomenon. The development of a comprehensive system of human rights protection was given much impetus by the horrors of Nazi persecution of the Jews and other atrocities during World War II. Particularly as it operates at a global level, international human rights law is intimately related to the United Nations system. All the global instruments have their origins in the UN. The second-mentioned goal of the UN is to "reaffirm faith in fundamental human rights, in the dignity and worth of the human person, in the equal rights of men and women and of nations large and small." The most substantive human rights obligation in the UN Charter is found in article 56, by which members pledge to take "joint and separate action in cooperation with the Organization for the achievement of . . . universal respect for, and observance of, human rights and fundamental freedoms for all without distinction as to race, sex, language, or religion."[1]

This was to be done "with a view to the creation of conditions of stability and well-being which are necessary for peaceful and friendly relations among nations," illustrating the fact that the development of international human rights law, especially in its early days, was not as distinct from the more mainstream objectives of states as is often thought. As we saw in Chapter 3, the primary function attributed to the UN was the maintenance of world peace. Human rights abuse, especially on a large scale, was regarded as a potential threat to that peace. The violent treatment by the Nazis of their own population was considered ultimately inseparable from German aggression beyond its borders. The drafters of the UN Charter emphasized social justice and human rights as the foundations for a stable international order.[2] This notion is reiterated in the preamble to a number of human rights treaties. The Convention on the Rights of the Child, for example, states in its preamble that "recognition of the inherent dignity and of the equal and inalienable rights of all members of the human family is the foundation of freedom, justice and peace in the world." The International Convention on the Elimination of All Forms of Racial Discrimination "reaffirm[s] that discrimination between human beings on the grounds of race, colour or ethnic origin is an obstacle to friendly and peaceful relations among nations and is capable of disturbing peace and security among peoples and the harmony of persons living side by side even within one and the same State." See Figure 10.1.

The Universal Declaration of Human Rights, 1948

The UN Charter indicated the new interest in international human rights, but the 1948 Universal Declaration of Human Rights (UDHR)[3] is usually regarded as the foundation of international human rights law. As a declaration, it is not a legally binding instrument but rather is hortatory or recommendatory in nature. The UDHR has nevertheless been of great influence, both on national constitutions and case law, and as an impetus for the further development of human rights law at an international level. Some lawyers have sought to argue that it has become

Figure 10.1   Some Landmarks in the Evolution of Global International Human Rights Law

1948   Convention on the Prevention and Punishment of the Crime of Genocide
1948   Universal Declaration of Human Rights
1951   Convention Relating to the Status of Refugees
1965   International Convention on the Elimination of All Forms of Racial Discrimination
1966   International Covenant on Economic, Social, and Cultural Rights
1966   International Covenant on Civil and Political Rights
1973   International Convention on the Suppression and Punishment of the Crime of Apartheid
1979   Convention on the Elimination of All Forms of Discrimination Against Women
1984   Convention Against Torture and Other Cruel, Inhuman, or Degrading Treatment or Punishment
1989   Convention on the Rights of the Child

customary international law, but even though there may not be much opposition to its principles, and some of it may have been binding by custom, few would accept that the actual practice by states with the UDHR as a whole has been such as to satisfy the requirement of "general, uniform, and consistent practice." The UDHR was drafted by a committee chaired by Eleanor Roosevelt, which reported to the Commission on Human Rights, which in turn sent it to the UN General Assembly. There the UDHR was scrutinized by the Third Committee of the Assembly and adopted by the General Assembly, all in a remarkably short period. The Cold War, the women's lobby, and the tradition of Latin American socialism all influenced the wording of the UDHR, but the primary influence was the Holocaust; the UDHR was adopted to avoid any similar abomination.[4] In Nazi Germany there had been a breakdown in the dividing line between the persons and the state. The UDHR was an assertion that "the interests of the individual [come] before those of the State and that the State should not be allowed to deprive the individual of his dignity and his basic rights."[5] Rights set out in the UDHR include civil and political rights, such as those to life, liberty, and security of person, freedom from arbitrary arrest and the presumption of innocence, freedom of opinion and expression and of peaceful assembly and association; as well as economic, social, and cultural rights, including social security, forming and joining trade unions, rest and leisure, and participating in the cultural life of the community.

The twentieth anniversary of the adoption of the Universal Declaration of Human Rights was marked by the International Conference on Human Rights, held in Teheran, Iran, from April 22 to May 13, 1968. The Proclamation of Teheran affirmed the faith of the conference in the principles of the UDHR and urged all peoples and governments to dedicate themselves to those principles and to redouble their efforts to "provide for all human beings a life consonant with freedom and dignity and conducive to physical, mental, social and spiritual welfare." In referring to "new standards and obligations to which States should conform," the proclamation also made reference to the two recently concluded international covenants.

The International Covenant on Civil and Political Rights (ICCPR) and the International Covenant on Economic, Social, and Cultural Rights (ICESCR), 1966

The UDHR was the springboard for two treaties. The 1966 International Covenant on Civil and Political Rights[6] built on the civil and political rights found in the UDHR, although it did not include the right to property, nationality, or asylum. The 1966 International Covenant on Economic, Social, and Cultural Rights[7] built on the second group of rights found in the UDHR, although it did not include a right to property as had been found in article 17 of the UDHR. This pattern of a declaration, followed by a legally binding treaty, has been standard in international human rights law. The UDHR, together with the two covenants, are often referred to as the "International Bill of Rights." The covenants did not enter into force until 1976.

The two covenants contain some of the same or similar provisions. Article 1 of each is identical. It reaffirms the principle that the right of self-determination is universal and calls upon all states to respect and promote the realization of that right; it also provides that "all peoples may, for their own ends, freely dispose of their natural wealth and resources."[8] Article 3 of both covenants requires states to undertake to ensure the equal right of men and women to the enjoyment of all the rights set out in the covenant.

The ICCPR established the Human Rights Committee, to which states parties to the covenant submit reports on the measures they have adopted that give effect to the rights recognized in the covenant.[9] The committee studies the reports and makes "general comments."[10] There is also an optional procedure by which states may grant other states that have also accepted the provision the right to bring a complaint against them before the committee.[11] Should the matter referred to the committee not be resolved to the satisfaction of the states parties concerned, the committee may, with the prior consent of the parties concerned, appoint an ad hoc conciliation commission.[12] The First Optional Protocol to the ICCPR provides for individual complaints to the Human Rights Committee.[13] Several conditions must have been met:

- The state having jurisdiction over that individual is a party to the protocol (art. 1)
- The individual has exhausted all available domestic remedies (except where the application of the remedies has been unreasonably prolonged) (art. 5(2)(b))
- The communication must not be anonymous, or an abuse of the right of submission of such communications or be incompatible with the provisions of the Covenant (art. 3)
- The matter is not being examined under another procedure of international investigation or settlement (art. 5(2))

The committee's decisions are structured like court judgments, although they are not legally binding. The Second Optional Protocol to the ICCPR,[14] aimed at the abolition of the death penalty, was adopted by the General Assembly on December 15, 1989.

A state party to the International Covenant on Economic, Social, and Cultural Rights undertakes to take steps "to the maximum of its available resources, with a view to achieving progressively the full realization of the rights recognized in the . . . Covenant."[15] This obligation under the ICESCR is a much weaker legal obligation than that required of a state in relation to the ICCPR, by article 2(1) of which a state party undertakes to "respect and to ensure to all individuals within its territory and subject to its jurisdiction the rights recognized in the present Covenant"; the ICESCR contains no provision for interstate complaints or individual petitions. States are to submit reports, which since 1987 have been considered by the Committee on Economic, Social, and Cultural Rights, responsible to ECOSOC. The committee prepares "general comments" in response.

Apart from these two covenants, there are a large number of more specific global human rights treaties, some of which preceded, some of which paralleled, and some of which have followed, the negotiation of the covenants.

Convention on the Prevention and Punishment of the Crime of Genocide, 1948

The twentieth century has been referred to as the "century of genocide."[16] The Holocaust involved the systematic extermination of between 5 and 6 million Jews, as well as the murder of large numbers of Gypsies, Russian, and Polish prisoners of war, East European slave laborers, and Germans who were physically disabled or mentally retarded.[17] The term "genocide" was invented by a Polish lawyer, Raphael Lemkin, from the Greek *genos*, meaning "race," and the Latin *cide*, meaning "killing," to refer to the destruction of a nation or of an ethnic group.[18] In his 1944 book entitled *Axis Rule in Occupied Europe*, Lemkin detailed the techniques developed by the Germans to carry out political, social, economic, biological, physical, religious, and moral genocide, which he referred to as "one of the most complete and glaring illustrations of the violation of international law and the laws of humanity."

The decision of the Nuremberg Tribunal not to accept jurisdiction over crimes against humanity in times of peace prompted Lemkin to embark on an intensive campaign to draft and bring into force an international agreement that would define the crime of genocide and prevent the recurrence of Nazi atrocities.[19] The text of the convention was drawn up by an ad hoc committee of ECOSOC, drawing on preparatory work undertaken by the UN Secretariat, which drew on experts in the field as well as the comments of member states and the Commission on Human Rights. Not all members of the Sixth (Legal) Committee had agreed with the idea of drafting a multilateral treaty. The United Kingdom's representative, for example, argued that a convention would not deter state-initiated genocide and that if a significant number of states resisted ratifying such a convention it would cast doubt on the claim that genocide was an internationally recognized crime. The UK proposed that the General Assembly affirm that genocide was a crime entailing national and international responsibility and that member states should be urged to incorporate the principles of the Secretariat's draft into their domestic laws.[20] Of particular importance to bringing about the Genocide Convention was the "exceptional dedication" of several experts and appeals from many NGOs.[21] The General Assembly adopted the text of the Genocide Convention in 1948, and it entered into force in 1951.[22]

Article I of the Genocide Convention established genocide as an international crime, "whether committed in time of peace or in time of war." Genocide is defined in article II as:

> acts committed with the intent to destroy, in whole or in part, a national, ethnical, racial, or religious group and includes any of the following:
> (a) Killing members of the group;
> (b) Causing serious bodily or mental harm to members of the group;
> (c) Deliberately inflicting on the group conditions of life calculated to bring about its physical destruction in whole or in part;
> (d) Imposing measures intended to prevent births within the group;
> (e) Forcibly transferring children of the group to another group.

Notable about this definition is the element of intent and the breadth of actions encompassed by the term "genocide": it is not just about killing. In an article published in *The American Journal of International Law* in 1947, Lemkin explained:

> The crime of genocide involves a wide range of actions, including not only the deprivation of life but also the prevention of life (abortions, sterilizations) and also devices considerably endangering life and health (artificial infections, working to death in special camps, delib-

erate separation of families for depopulation purposes and so forth). All these actions are subordinated to the criminal intent to destroy or to cripple permanently a human group. The acts are directed against groups, as such, and individuals are selected for destruction only because they belong to these groups. In view of such a phenomenon the terms previously used to describe an attack upon nationhood were not adequate. Mass murder or extermination wouldn't apply in the case of sterilization because the victims of sterilizations were not murdered, rather a people was killed through delayed action by stopping propagation. Moreover mass murder does not convey the specific losses to civilization in the form of the cultural contributions which can be made only by groups of people united through national, racial or cultural characteristics.[23]

There have been proposals to amend the convention so as to include negligent as well as intentional genocide, and to include other types of groups omitted from this definition, including economic and political. Political groups were included in a 1946 General Assembly resolution, but the Soviets blocked attempts to include political groups in the convention's definition of genocide.[24]

By articles III and IV of the Genocide Convention, persons who commit genocide, conspire to commit genocide, directly and publicly incite others to commit genocide, attempt to commit genocide, or who are complicit in genocide are to be punished "whether they are constitutionally responsible rulers, public officials or private individuals." The war crimes trials at Nuremburg had established that subordinates were not able to plead "superior orders" but were individually responsible for their role in the Holocaust. By article V of the Genocide Convention contracting parties undertake to enact legislation to give effect to the provisions of the convention and to provide effective penalties for persons guilty of genocide or the related acts specified in article 3.

Many states have ratified the Genocide Convention with reservations, particularly to the compromissory clause. The United States ratified the convention only in 1986, and even then it made two reservations, five "understandings," and one "declaration."[25] One of the reservations requires the consent of the United States to the submission of any dispute to the International Court of Justice. A reservation by the United States to article IX can, on the basis of the principle of reciprocity, be drawn on by another state in the event the United States attempts to invoke ICJ jurisdiction against it on the basis of the Genocide Convention. Hence, the effect of the U.S. reservation is much broader than it appears.

Despite the existence of the Genocide Convention, the Nazi

Holocaust was not the last genocide of the twentieth century. Others included that of the Tutsi in Burundi from 1993 to 1998 and in Rwanda in 1994.[26]

During the 1990s, supporters of an international criminal court argued that, even if it is ultimately not possible to prevent genocide, the least we can do is to establish a permanent international criminal court so that potential perpetrators of genocide recognize that there is a good chance that they will be brought to justice.

Convention Relating to
the Status of Refugees, 1951

There have been mass migrations throughout human history. The World War II experience, including the Nazi attempt to exterminate the Jews, their invasion of other states, and the Sovietization of Eastern Europe, led to millions of displaced people. The Office of the United Nations High Commissioner for Refugees (UNHCR) was established by General Assembly Resolution 428(V) of December 14, 1950, and the Convention relating to the Status of Refugees[27] was concluded the following year. The regime founded on the 1951 Refugee Convention is generally classified as a human rights regime, but it is important to be aware that the treatment of refugees is an intensely political issue; international refugee law has been shaped by the perceived security implications of mass movements of people across borders.[28]

The United States, which after World War II took in many Eastern European immigrants, regarding them as examples of the failure of communism,[29] was the "principal architect" of the postwar refugee regime.[30] Article 1 of the 1951 Refugee Convention defined a refugee as a person who

> owing to [a] well-founded fear of being persecuted for reasons of race, religion, nationality, membership of a particular social group or political opinion, is outside the country of his nationality and is unable or, owing to such fear, is unwilling to avail himself of the protection of that country; or who, not having a nationality and being outside the country of his former habitual residence as a result of such events, is unable or, owing to such fear, is unwilling to return to it.

The 1951 definition began with the words "as a result of events occurring before 1 January 1951," and each contracting party was to make a declaration at the time of signature, ratification, or accession as to whether it was going to apply these words to "events occurring in Europe before 1 January 1951" or to "events occurring in Europe or elsewhere before 1 January 1951." Perhaps not surprisingly, the Soviet Union and Eastern bloc rejected the convention. "Indeed for at least the next three decades the Soviet Union perceived the UNHCR to be a tool of Western political ambitions."[31] The 1967 Protocol to the Convention[32] removed the temporal and geographical restrictions of the refugee definition.

The most important protection that the convention accords those qualifying as refugees under article 1 is contained in the convention's prohibition of expulsion or return (called refoulement). By article 33(1), no contracting state shall expel or return a refugee to the frontiers of territories where their life or freedom would be threatened on account of their race, religion, nationality, membership of a particular social group, or political opinion. No reservations are permitted to article 33.[33] By article 31(1), the contracting states are not to impose penalties, on account of illegal entry or presence, on refugees who, coming directly from a territory where their life or freedom was threatened in the sense of article 1, enter or are present in their territory without authorization, provided they present themselves without delay to the authorities and show good cause for their illegal entry or presence. Furthermore, by article 31(2), contracting states "shall not apply to the movements of such refugees restrictions other than those which are necessary and such restrictions shall only be applied until their status in the country is regularised or they obtain admission into another country."

Since the late 1960s, when a major proportion of the international refugee population began to come from the less developed world, Western governments have been less enthusiastic about welcoming refugees. Many countries began to practice deterrence policies by, for example, turning back potential asylum-seekers before they entered a country—and hence before they were able to apply for refugee status. Other deterrence tactics have included the denial or limitation of welfare benefits to asylum seekers, limited access to appeal procedures regarding the determination of their refugee status, and the use of negative propaganda and language.[34]

The Refugee Convention does not address the problem of internally displaced people. A 2002 global survey put the number of conflict-driven internally displaced people at 25 million, outnumbering conventional refugees by two-to-one.[35] In February 2001 the UNHCR began a series of global consultations on international protection with states and other interested parties aimed to revitalize the 1951 convention framework.[36]

A ministerial meeting of states parties to the 1951 convention and/or 1967 protocol held in Geneva in December 2001 adopted a declaration of states parties by which the contracting states reaffirmed their commitment to implement their obligations under the 1951 convention and/or its 1967 protocol "fully and effectively"[37] and expressed the belief that the regime should be developed further in a way that "complements and strengthens the 1951 Convention and its Protocol."[38]

International Convention on the Elimination of All Forms of Racial Discrimination, 1965

On November 20, 1963, the General Assembly adopted the United Nations Declaration on the Elimination of All Forms of Racial Discrimination.[39] Article 1 proclaims that

> discrimination between human beings on the grounds of race, colour or ethnic origin is an offence to human dignity and shall be condemned as a denial of the principles of the Charter of the United Nations, as a violation of the human rights and fundamental freedoms proclaimed in the Universal Declaration of Human Rights, as an obstacle to friendly and peaceful relations among nations and as a fact capable of disturbing peace and security among peoples.

The Human Rights Commission drafted the treaty at the request of the General Assembly. The Sub-Commission on the Prevention of Discrimination and Protection of Minorities began work on the convention, using a draft prepared by the U.S. member of the subcommission. The Commission on Human Rights dealt with the draft prepared by the subcommission and passed the draft on to the Third Committee, which passed on a final text to the General Assembly.[40] Racial discrimination is defined in article 1 as "any distinction, exclusion, restriction or preference based on race, colour, descent or national or ethnic origin which has the purpose or effect of nullifying or impairing the recognition, enjoyment or exercise, on an equal footing, of human rights and fundamental freedoms." By article 2, states parties "condemn racial discrimination and undertake to pursue by all appropriate means and without delay a policy of eliminating racial discrimination in all its forms and promoting understanding among all races." States are

> (a) to engage in no act or practice of racial discrimination against persons, groups of persons or institutions and to ensure that all public authorities and public institutions, national and local , shall act in conformity with this obligation. . . ;

(b) not to sponsor, defend or support racial discrimination by any persons or organizations. . . ;

(c) take effective measures to review governmental, national and local policies, and to amend, rescind or nullify any laws and regulations which have the effect of creating or perpetuating racial discrimination wherever it exists. . . ;

(d) prohibit and bring to an end, by all appropriate means, including legislation as required by circumstances, racial discrimination by any persons, group or organization. . . ;

(e) encourage, where appropriate, integrationist multiracial organizations and movements and other means of eliminating barriers between races, and to discourage anything which tends to strengthen racial division.

Other provisions intended to assist in the elimination of racial discrimination include preventing, prohibiting, and eradicating all racial segregation and apartheid (article 3), condemning all racial propaganda and dissemination of ideas based on racial superiority or hatred (article 4), guaranteeing the right of everyone to equality before the law (article 5), and adopting immediate and effective educational measures to promote understanding, tolerance, and friendship among nations and racial or ethnical groups (article 7).

CERD was the first UN human rights instrument to set up an international monitoring system, including a procedure for individual complaints. The details of this are set out in part II of the convention, which provided for the Committee on the Elimination of Racial Discrimination.[41] The committee was established in 1969. It consists of eighteen independent experts elected by the states parties after being nominated by states. The committee receives the periodic reports of states (article 9) and inquires into and helps settle complaints about one state by another (articles eleven to 13). Article 14 is an optional clause about individual complaints:

A State Party may at any time declare that it recognizes the competence of the Committee to receive and consider communications from individuals or groups of individuals within its jurisdiction claiming to be victims of a violation by that State Party of any of the rights set forth in this Convention. No communication shall be received by the Committee if it concerns a State Party which has not made such a declaration.

After exhausting available local remedies, an individual must first seek a review at the domestic level by a national body nominated by the state in its optional declaration. If unsatisfied with the outcome of that review the individual has six months to bring the matter before the committee. The committee must first find the complaint to be admissible (not be anonymous and to have exhausted local remedies unless the application of the remedies has been too prolonged) and, having received any written communications from the state concerned, will make "suggestions and recommendations" to that state.

Convention on the Elimination of All Forms of Discrimination Against Women, 1979

The Commission on the Status of Women laid the foundations for CEDAW[42] with a number of instruments to deal with specific political, social, and cultural concerns of women. Such early initiatives included the 1953 Convention on the Political Rights of Women, the 1957 Convention on the Nationality of Married Women, the 1962 Convention on Consent to Marriage, Minimum Age for Marriage, and Registration of Marriages, and the 1967 Declaration on the Elimination of Discrimination Against Women. These generated international interest in women's human rights: the scholarly literature on women's human rights increased as the number of legal instruments increased.[43] CEDAW was opened for signature on March 1, 1980, and entered into force only eighteen months later, on September 3, 1981.

Articles 2 and 3 contain the crux of the obligations assumed by states under this convention. By article 2, states parties "condemn discrimination against women in all its forms" and "agree to pursue by all appropriate means and without delay a policy of eliminating discrimination against women." Article 3 requires states to "take in all fields, in particular in the political, social, economic and cultural fields, all appropriate measures, including legislation, to ensure the full development and advancement of women." "Discrimination against women" is defined in the convention as "any distinction, exclusion or restriction made on the basis of sex which has the effect or purpose of impairing or nullifying the recognition, enjoyment or exercise by women, irrespective of their marital status, on a basis of equality of men and women, of human rights and fundamental freedoms in the political, economic, social, cultural, civil or any other field." "Temporary special measures aimed at accelerating de facto equality between men and women" and special measures aimed at protecting maternity (i.e., affirmative action measures) are not to be regarded as discrimination.[44]

The particular actions required of states are specified in more detail in the other substantive provisions. They include taking appropriate measures

- To suppress all forms of traffic in women and exploitation of prostitution of women (art. 6)
- To ensure to women, on equal terms with men and without any discrimination, the opportunity to represent their Governments at the international level and to participate in the work of international organizations (art. 8)
- To eliminate discrimination against women in order to ensure to them equal rights with men in the field of education (art. 10), in the field of employment (art. 11), in the field of health care (art. 12), and in other areas of economic and social life (art. 13); in rural areas (art. 14); in all matters relating to marriage and family relations (art. 16)
- To accord women equality with men before the law (art. 15)

Reservations have been an issue of major concern within the CEDAW regime, the convention having been subject to more substantive reservations than probably any other major human rights treaty.[45] Several states have reservations that indicate acceptance of major articles of the convention only to the extent that they are consistent with the requirements of Islamic *sharia* or traditional customs and practices. Critics say that the treaty cannot be effective in eliminating "all forms of discrimination" against women if it is subject to a large number of reservations, particularly those that are far-reaching.[46]

CEDAW established the Committee on the Elimination of Discrimination Against Women, whose main role is to receive and consider reports of state parties.[47] There was no provision in the convention for the consideration of complaints from states or from individuals.

The World Conference on Human Rights, held at Vienna in 1993, proposed the adoption of an optional protocol authorizing the committee to receive communications from individuals. An optional protocol to CEDAW was adopted by the Commission on the Status of Women on March 12, 1999, and by the General Assembly on October 6, 1999.[48] The optional protocol contains two procedures. The first allows individual women, or groups of women, under the jurisdiction of a state party to the protocol, to submit claims of violations of rights under CEDAW to the Committee on the Elimination of Discrimination Against Women; the second enables the committee to initiate inquiries into situations of grave or systematic violations of women's rights under CEDAW.

Convention Against Torture and Other Cruel, Inhuman, or Degrading Treatment or Punishment, 1984

The Convention Against Torture[49] followed the 1975 General Assembly Declaration on the Protection of All Persons from Being Subjected to Torture and Other Cruel, Inhuman, or Degrading Treatment or Punishment. The convention proved much more difficult to achieve than the declaration, particularly in regard to the implementation provisions.[50] The text was drafted by a working group set up by the Commission on Human Rights, which received a draft international convention proposed by Sweden as well as one from the International Association of Penal Law. NGOs, including the International Commission of Jurists, Amnesty International, and the International Association of Penal Law, had for some time been calling for an international convention on torture.[51] The General Assembly adopted the Convention on December 10, 1984.

"Torture" is defined in article 1 as

> any act by which severe pain or suffering, whether physical or mental, is intentionally inflicted on a person for such purposes as obtaining from him or a third person information or a confession, punishing him for an act he or a third person has committed or is suspected of having committed, or intimidating or coercing him or a third person, or for any reason based on discrimination of any kind, when such pain or suffering is inflicted by or at the instigation of or with the consent or acquiescence of a public official or other person acting in an official capacity. It does not include pain or suffering arising only from, inherent in or incidental to lawful sanctions.

Article 2 of the convention provides:

1. Each State Party shall take effective legislative, administrative, judicial or other measures to prevent acts of torture in any territory under its jurisdiction.
2. No exceptional circumstances whatsoever, whether a state of war or a threat of war, internal political instability or any other public emergency, may be invoked as a justification of torture.
3. An order from a superior officer or a public authority may not be invoked as a justification of torture.

The convention established the Committee Against Torture.[52] This consists of ten elected members, acting in their personal capacity. States parties are to submit a report on the measures they have taken to give effect to their undertakings under the convention within one year of entry into force of the convention for the state involved and thereafter submit supplementary reports every four years. The committee deals with complaints by one state party against another and, if the state involved has declared its acceptance, of communications from or on behalf of individuals subject to its jurisdiction.

In December 2002 the General Assembly adopted an Optional Protocol to the convention,[53] to establish a preventive system of regular visits to places of detention.

Convention on the Rights of the Child, 1989

The Convention on the Rights of the Child (CROC)[54] has been ratified by more countries than any other human rights instrument; it has almost universal membership.[55] Proposals for a global treaty on children's rights had been proposed as early as at a conference organized by the League of Nations in 1924. In 1959 the General Assembly adopted the Declaration on the Rights of the Child. But the 1979 UN Year of the Child was the final impetus for the Human Rights Commission, which sponsored a forum that met for one week each year to produce a convention on the rights of children. The General Assembly adopted the convention, without a formal vote, on November 20, 1989, and it entered into force on September 2, 1991.

A key phrase in the treaty is that of the "best interests of the child." "In all actions concerning children, whether undertaken by public or private social welfare institutions, courts of law, administrative authorities or legislative bodies, the best interests of the child shall be a primary consideration." (article 3(1)). The bulk of the text in the substantive part of the convention is devoted to specifying the various rights of the child. These include the right to life (article 6); the right to a name from birth, to acquire a nationality, and, as far as possible, to know and be cared for by his or her parents (article 7); the right of a child who is separated from one or both parents to maintain personal relations and direct contact with both parents on a regular basis, except if it is contrary to the child's best interests (article 9); the right to express his or her own views in all matters affecting the child, the views to be given due weight in accordance with the age and maturity of the child (article 12); the right to the enjoyment of the highest attainable standard of health and to facilities for the treatment of illness and rehabilitation of health (article 24); the right to education (article 28); the right to be protected from economic exploitation, hazardous work, or work that interferes with the child's education or is detrimental to the child's health or physical, mental, spiritual, moral, or social development (article 32); and the right to rest and leisure, play, and recreational activities and to participate fully in cultural and artistic life (article 31). The state is to implement the various rights included in the convention, by "all appropriate legislative, administrative, and other measures" (article 4).

CROC established the Committee on the Rights of the Child, which receives and examines state reports on the measures taken to implement the convention and the progress that has been made in furthering the enjoyment of rights under it.[56] The committee may make suggestions and general recommendations to any state party concerned and report to the General Assembly, together with comments, if any, from states parties. There are two optional protocols to CROC: on the involvement of children in armed conflict, and on the sale of children, child prostitution, and child pornography.[57] These protocols were adopted by the General Assembly in May 2000.

Vienna Declaration and Programme of Action, 1993

By General Assembly Resolution 45/155 of December 18, 1990, the United Nations decided to hold a world conference on human rights to review and assess the progress that had been made in the field of human rights and to identify potential future obstacles and ways to overcome them.[58] The resultant Vienna Declaration and Programme of Action[59] reaffirmed the commitment of all states to observe and protect human rights and fundamental freedoms for all. "Human rights and fundamental freedoms are the birthright of all human beings; their protection and promotion is the first responsibility of Governments" (section I(1). The Declaration and Programme of Action reiterated that enhancement of international cooperation in the field of human rights is essential for the full achievement of the purposes of the United Nations. The establishment of a UN high commissioner for human rights was discussed extensively at the conference; section II(18) of the declaration recommended that the General Assembly consider, as a matter of priority, the establishment of a high commissioner for human rights "for the promotion and protection of all human rights." The General Assembly created the position on December 20, 1993, by Resolution 48/151.[60]

Regional Human Rights Treaty Regimes

The global human rights treaties are complemented by regional treaty regimes in Europe, the Americas, and Africa. The most complex is the European system.[61] The European Convention for the Protection of Human Rights and Fundamental Freedoms[62] was drafted by the Council of Europe, opened for signature on November 4, 1950, and entered into force on September 3, 1953.[63] It was intended to enforce the rights contained in the Universal Declaration of Human Rights. Thirteen basic rights of individuals are contained in the original convention, including the right to life (article 2), the prohibition of torture (article 3), and the right to a fair trial (article 6). Other rights or freedoms have been added in a series of protocols; Protocol 13, for example, concerns "the abolition of the death penalty in all circumstances."[64] Under the 1950 convention, contracting states and, if the contracting states have accepted the right of individual petition, individual applicants (individuals, groups of individuals, or NGOs), can lodge complaints against contracting states for alleged violations of Convention rights. Protocol 11 of 1994[65] has meant that the right of individual petition has become mandatory for all member states. It also provides that the preexisting part-time institutions of the European Commission of Human Rights and the European Court of Human Rights were superseded by a single new full-time European Court of Human Rights.[66] The Committee of Ministers of the Council of Europe is tasked with supervising the enforcement of the Court's judgments. Although the rights covered in the European Convention are primarily civil and political rights, the European Social Charter of 1961 and its protocols address economic and social rights.[67] The revised Social Charter was opened for signature in 1996 and entered into force in 1999. The European Convention on Human Rights has had an increasing influence on the European Union,[68] which in the 1990s made being a party to the convention a condition for membership. The European convention was a strong influence on the text of the European Union Charter of Fundamental Rights, which was signed in 2000, setting out the whole range of civil, political, economic, and social rights of European citizens and all persons resident in the European Union.[69]

Although predecessor organizations dated from the nineteenth century, the Organization of American States was established at the Ninth International Conference of American States, held in Bogotá, Colombia, in 1948. As well as concluding the charter for the Organization of American States, the participants at Bogotá adopted the American

Declaration of the Rights and Duties of Man.[70] This is similar in content to, but preceded by several months, the Universal Declaration of Human Rights. This declaration includes ten articles setting out the duties of the citizen, including to "acquire at least an elementary education" and to "render whatever civil and military service his country may require for its defence and preservation, and, in case of public disaster, to render such services as may be in his power."

The next major step in establishing a regional human rights system was the establishment by the Organization of American States of the Inter-American Commission on Human Rights in 1959.[71] It was established by a resolution of the Fifth Meeting of Consultation of Ministers of Foreign Affairs, rather than by treaty, reflecting reluctance on the part of the countries involved to take legally binding obligations as regards human rights.[72] The commission began work the following year. In its early years it was concerned primarily with preparing country reports, for the preparation of which it conducted on-site investigations.[73] With the return of more countries to a democratic form of government and with the 1978 entry into force of the American Convention on Human Rights,[74] the individual complaint procedure became a more prominent part of its work in the 1980s.

The 1969 American Convention on Human Rights focuses on civil and political rights, although articles 26 and 42 are dedicated to the progressive development of economic, social, and cultural rights. The convention provided for a compulsory individual petition procedure (article 44) and created the Inter-American Court of Human Rights.[75] This court has an advisory and contentious jurisdiction. The right of individual petition to the commission is mandatory in the convention; by article 44 any person, group of persons, or nongovernmental entity legally recognized in one or more member states of the Organization of American States may lodge petitions with the commission containing denunciations or complaints of violation of the convention by a state party.[76] The commission also has jurisdiction over petitions filed by individuals from states not party to the convention, as they relate to the American Declaration. Once the commission's procedures have been completed, the commission or the state concerned can submit the matter to the court, as long as the state concerned has accepted the jurisdiction of the court. Compared to the European system, the issues that have been dealt with by both the commission and the court have concerned gross, rather than ordinary, violations of human rights, including forced disappearance, killing, torture, and the arbitrary detention of political opponents.[77]

The newest of the three regional systems is that of the African Union. Also known as the Banjul Charter, the African Charter on Human and Peoples' Rights[78] was adopted unanimously on June 17, 1981, by the Organization of African Unity and entered into force in 1986. The preamble takes into consideration "the virtues of [the African] historical tradition and the values of African civilization, which should inspire and characterize . . . reflection on the concept of human and peoples' rights." The charter covers civil and political rights and, by article 22(1), recognizes the right of all peoples "to their economic, social, and cultural development." African society is said to place more emphasis on the community than on the individuals within the community. This, together with a Marxist influence,[79] led to inclusion in the charter of "peoples'" rights.[80] Also notable is that it imposes duties on the individual;[81] article 27 provides that the individual has duties toward his family and society, the state and other legally recognized communities, and the international community. So-called clawback clauses do, however, serve to limit the rights provided for in the charter;[82] the profession and free practice of religion is, for example, "subject to law and order." Article 14 guarantees the right to property; the right "may only be encroached upon in the interest of public need and in accordance with the provisions of appropriate laws."

Chapter I of part II of the charter provides for the establishment within the Organization of African Unity of the African Commission on Human and Peoples' Rights whose primary role is to be a fact-finding and conciliatory body.[83] The Convention Governing the Specific Aspects of Refugee Problems in Africa[84] is one of some twenty regional treaties on refugees.[85] It is notable for its definition of "refugees," which is broader than that of the 1951 convention; it includes "every person who, owing to external aggression, occupation, foreign domination or events seriously disturbing public order in either part or the whole of his country of origin or nationality, is compelled to leave his place of habitual residence in order to seek refuge in another place outside his country of origin or nationality." On June 8, 1998, the Organization of African Unity adopted the Protocol to the African Charter on Human and Peoples' Rights on the Establishment of an African Court on Human and Peoples' Rights.[86] The African Charter on the Rights and Welfare of the Child entered into force in 1999, and in 2003 the African Union adopted the Protocol to the African Charter on Human and Peoples' Rights on the Rights of Women in Africa.

Human Rights in Sociopolitical Context

There have been critics of the human rights movement from within the movement itself. Feminists have critiqued the notion of "human" rights, pointing out that the supposed gender neutrality of human rights documents and rhetoric has disguised a masculine bias in the selective promotion and protection of human rights. If, for example, the original International Bill of Rights had really been addressed to all human beings, why was a separate women's convention required? Just how do human rights relate to women's rights?[87] Similarly, the 1948 UDHR "utterly failed to encompass the circumstances and worldviews of indigenous peoples, and . . . never considered their participation in the norm-creating processes as essential to establish the claim of universality."[88]

There has in recent year been considerable debate regarding the duty of states, regardless of their political, economic, and cultural systems, to promote rights versus the relativity of rights to a particular religious and cultural tradition.[89] Is it possible to elucidate rights that are truly universal, or has the development of international human rights law been a process of Western imperialism?[90] The Final Declaration and Programme of Action of the World Conference of Human Rights held in Vienna in 1993 proclaimed all human rights to be "universal, indivisible and interdependent and interrelated." Although it explicitly stipulated that "it is the duty of States, regardless of their political, economic and cultural systems, to promote and protect all human rights and fundamental freedoms," this was preceded by the qualification that "the significance of national and regional particularities and various historical, cultural and religious backgrounds must be borne in mind."[91]

The debate as to the universality of rights is not a new phenomenon arising from the globalizing of politics but has for centuries taken place within Western thought.[92] The particular rights that have been incorporated into international human rights law are historically contingent and may evolve in tandem with other strands of sociopolitical change. This is evident, in part, from the ongoing definitional debates that surround several human rights treaty regimes—how, for example, to define the terms "genocide"[93] or "refugees."[94]

The temporal relativity of rights is also evident in the notion of "generations" of human rights. Civil and political rights are sometimes referred to as "first generation" human rights; economic, social, and cultural rights are referred to as "second generation" rights. The importance of the 1993 conference declaring all human rights to be indivisible stemmed from the fact that civil and political rights are associated with the eighteenth-century Declaration on the Rights of Man, whereas economic, social, and cultural rights derived from the growth of socialist ideals in the late nineteenth and early twentieth centuries and the impact of the organized labor movement.[95] Whereas the former Soviet states believed in the supremacy of economic, social, and cultural rights, Western states have given priority to civil and political rights.

Third-generation rights are usually deemed those that will benefit groups and peoples rather than just individuals,[96] including the right to self-determination and the right to development. The right to development was declared by the General Assembly in its 1986 Declaration on the Right to Development[97] and recognized in the African Charter of Human and Peoples' Rights.[98] Article 24 of the African Charter on Human and Peoples' Rights refers to the right of peoples "to a general satisfactory environment favourable to their development." The right "to live in a healthy environment" was referred to in the Additional Protocol to the American Convention on Human Rights in the Area of Economic, Social, and Cultural Rights.[99]

The human rights of indigenous peoples are sometimes referred to as "fourth generation" rights.[100] Indigenous peoples were not expressly included in the text of any United Nations human rights instrument before the 1989 Convention on the Rights of the Child;[101] article 30 of that convention provides that a child "who is indigenous shall not be denied the right, in community with other members of his or her group, to enjoy his or her own culture, to profess and practise his or her own religions, or to use his or her own language." The International Labor Organization had, however, acted before this, its Convention 107 of 1957[102] having been primarily a response to reports of labor discrimination in Latin America.[103] Article 2 of the Convention Concerning the Protection and Integration of Indigenous and Other Tribal and Semi-Tribal Populations in Independent Countries accorded governments the "primary responsibility for developing co-ordinated and systematic action for the protection of the populations concerned and their progressive integration into the life of their respective communities."

The convention came to be criticized for having adopted a 1950s-style, paternalistic, or integrationist, approach toward indigenous peoples[104] and so was revised and replaced by ILO Convention 169 of 1989.[105] Article 2 of the Convention Concerning Indigenous and Tribal Peoples in Independent Countries recognized the responsibility of governments for "developing, with the participation of the peoples concerned, coordinated and systematic action to protect the rights of [indigenous and tribal peoples] and to guarantee respect for their integrity." Article 3(1) of ILO Convention 169 provides that indigenous and tribal peoples shall enjoy the full measure of human rights and fundamental freedoms "without hindrance or discrimination."

The Draft Declaration on the Rights of Indigenous Peoples was agreed upon by the members of the Working Group on Indigenous Populations in 1993, adopted by the Sub-Commission on the Prevention of Discrimination and Protection of Minorities in 1994, and received by governments in February 1995 at the fiftieth session of the Commission on Human Rights.[106] In March 1995 the Commission on Human Rights decided to establish an open-ended intersessional working group to consider the draft with a view to having the General Assembly adopt the declaration before the end of the International Decade of the World's Indigenous People in 2004.[107]

Conclusion

The evolution of international human rights law has been a momentous development. Although there undoubtedly remains an "enduring" gap between human rights principles and the practices of states,[108] international human rights norms appear to have had some effect on the behavior of states toward their citizens.[109] More work is needed, however, both of a practical and a scholarly nature. Oona Hathaway, for example, has undertaken empirical analysis that called into question the view that the human rights practices of a country that has ratified human rights treaties will be better than they would otherwise be.[110] We still do not know very much, for example, about how the process of change is brought about, and hence about what specific improvements are needed to existing law to bring about further change in the practice of states and other international actors.[111]

Notes

1. For background, see John P. Humphrey, "The UN Charter and the Universal Declaration of Human Rights," in Evan Luard, ed., *The International Protection of Human Rights* (London: Thames and Hudson, 1967), pp. 39–58, 39–46.

2. Ian Brownlie, ed., *Basic Documents on Human Rights* 3rd ed. (Oxford: Clarendon, 1993), p. 1. Reflecting in 1950 on the causes for international law coming to give individual rights, Sir Hersch Lauterpacht suggested that they included "the realisation of the dangers besetting international peace as the result of the denial of fundamental human rights." H. Lauterpacht, *International Law and Human Rights* (London: Stevens & Sons, 1950), p. 62.

3. General Assembly Resolution 217 A (III), December 10, 1948, UN Doc A/810, p. 71. See, inter alia, Gudmundur Alfredsson and Asbjørn Eide, eds., *The Universal Declaration of Human Rights: A Common Standard of Achievement* (The Hague: Martinus Nijhoff, 1999); and Asbjørn Eide et al., eds., *The Universal Declaration of Human Rights: A Commentary* (London: Scandinavian University Press, 1992).

4. Johannes Morsink, *The Universal Declaration of Human Rights: Origins, Drafting, and Intent* (Philadelphia: University of Pennsylvania Press, 1999), p. 37. See also Johannes van Aggelen, "The Preamble of the United Nations Declaration of Human Rights," *Denver Journal of International Law and Policy* 28, no. 2 (2000): 129–144; and Susan Waltz, "Universalising Human Rights: The Role of Small States in the Construction of the Universal Declaration of Human Rights," *Human Rights Quarterly* 23 (2001): 44–72.

5. Hernan Santa Cruz, Chilean delegate to the Third Committee, cited in Morsink, *The Universal Declaration of Human Rights*, p. 38.

6. 6 International Legal Materials (ILM) 368 (1967). See M. Bossuyt, *Guide to the Travaux Préparatoires of the International Covenant on Civil and Political Rights* (Dordrecht: M. Nijhoff, 1987), and Theodor Meron, *Human Rights Law-Making in the United Nations: A Critique of Instruments and Process* (Oxford: Clarendon, 1986), chap. 3.

7. 6 ILM 360 (1967).

8. See Sally Morphet, "Article 1 of the Human Rights Covenants: Its Development and Current Significance," in Dilys M. Hill, ed., *Human Rights and Foreign Policy: Principles and Practice* (Houndmills, Basingstoke: Macmillan, 1989), pp. 67–88.

9. Article 40(1). Individual Complaints, Decisions, Official Records, and Country Reports can be found at www.unhchr.ch/html/menu2/6/hrc.htm. General Comments, Decisions and Views, and Annual Reports can be accessed at www1.umn.edu/humanrts/hrcommittee/hrc-page.html. See also P. R. Ghandhi, *The Human Rights Committee and the Right of Individual Communication: Law and Practice* (Aldershot, UK: Ashgate 1998).

10. International Covenant on Civil and Political Rights, article 40(4).

11. International Covenant on Civil and Political Rights, article 41.

12. International Covenant on Civil and Political Rights, article 42.

13. 6 ILM 383 (1967).

14. 29 ILM 1465 (1990).

15. International Covenant on Economic, Social, and Cultural Rights, article 2(1).

16. Roger Smith, "Human Destructiveness and Politics: The Twentieth Century as an Age of Genocide," in Isidor Wallimann and Michael Dobkowski, eds., *Genocide and the Modern Age: Etiology and Case Studies of Mass Death* (Westport, CT: Greenwood, 1987), pp. 21–39; and Israel W. Charny, "The Study of Genocide," in Israel Charny, ed. *Genocide: A Critical Bibliographic Review* (New York: Facts on File, 1988), pp. 1–19. See also M. Levine, "Why Is the Twentieth Century the Century of Genocide?" *Journal of World History* 11, no. 2 (2000): 305–336; and Samuel Totten, William S. Parsons, and Israel Charny, eds., *Century of Genocide: Eyewitness Accounts and Critical Views* (New York and London: Garland, 1997).

17. Donald L. Niewyk, "Holocaust: The Jews," in Totten, Parsons, and Charny, *Century of Genocide*, pp. 136–170, 136.

18. Raphael Lemkin, *Axis Rule in Occupied Europe* (New York: Howard Fertig, 1973), p. 79.

19. Richard W. Edwards, "Contributions of the Genocide Convention to the Development of International Law," *Ohio Northern University Law Review* 8 (1981): 300–320.

20. Matthew Lippman, "The Convention on the Prevention and Punishment of the Crime of Genocide: Fifty Years Later," *Arizona Journal of International and Comparative Law* 15, no. 2 (1998): 427–428, 449.

21. *The United Nations and Human Rights, 1945–1995* (New York: United Nations, 1995), p. 20.

22. 78 UNTS (1951) 277.

23. Raphael Lemkin, "Genocide as a Crime Under International Law," *American Journal of International Law (AJIL)* 41, no. 1 (1947): 145–151, 147.

24. Lippman, "The Convention on the Prevention and Punishment of the Crime of Genocide," p. 452.

25. See "Counterpoint," *Case Western Reserve Journal of International Law* 18 (1986): 277–282.

26. Howard Ball, *Prosecuting War Crimes and Genocide: The Twentieth Century Experience* (Lawrence: University Press of Kansas, 1999), p. 219.

27. 189 UNTS 137.

28. Gil Loescher, "Refugee Movements and International Security," *Adelphi Papers* 268 (Summer 1992); and Gil Loescher, "Refugees and Foreign Policy," in Hill, *Human Rights and Foreign Policy*, pp. 130–139.

29. See James C. Hathaway, "A Reconsideration of the Underlying Premise of Refugee Law," *Harvard International Law Journal* 31, no. 1 (Winter 1990): 129–183; Dennis Gallagher, "The Evolution of the International Refugee System," *International Migration Review* 23, no. 3 (1989): 579–598, 594; Tom J. Farer, "How the International System Copes with Involuntary Migration: Norms, Institutions, and State Practice," *Human Rights Quarterly* 17 (1995): 72–100.

30. Gil Loescher, "The International Refugee Regime: Stretched to the Limit?" *Journal of International Affairs* 47, no. 2 (Winter 1994): 351–377, 356.

31. Alex Cunliffe, "The Refugee Crises: A Study of the United Nations High Commission for Refugees," *Political Studies* 43 (1995): 278–290, 281.

32. 606 UNTS 267.

33. Convention Relating to the Status of Refugees, article 42, and Protocol Relating to the Status of Refugees, article 7.

34. Lisa Hassan, "Deterrence Measures and the Preservation of Asylum in the United Kingdom and United States," *Journal of Refugee Studies* 13, no. 2 (2000): 184–204, 186. See also M. Fullerton, "Failing the Test: Germany Leads Europe in Dismantling Refugee Protection," *Texas International Law Journal* 36 (2001): 231–276; and P. Hyndman, "The 1951 Convention and Its Implications for Procedural Questions," *International Journal of Refugee Law* 6, no. 2 (1994): 245–252.

35. The Global IDP Project, *Internally Displaced People: Global Survey 2002* (London: Earthscan, 2002).

36. See Erika Feller, Volker Türk, and Frances Nicholson, eds., *Refugee Protection in International Law: UNHCR's Global Consultations on International Protection* (Cambridge: Cambridge University Press, 2003).

37. Article 1, "Declaration Reaffirming the Commitment of Signatory States to the 1951 Refugee Convention," available at www.unhcr.ch/cgi-bin/texis/vtx, accessed August 2, 2002.

38. Preamble, article 7, "Declaration Reaffirming the Commitment of , Signatory States to the 1951 Refugee Convention," available at www.unhcr.ch/cgi-bin/texis/vtx, accessed August 2, 2002.

39. 5 ILM 352 (1966).

40. See Egon Schwelb, "The International Convention on the Elimination of All Forms of Racial Discrimination," *International and Comparative Law Quarterly (ICLQ)* 15 (1966): 996–1059.

41. Individual complaints, selected decisions, country reports, and other documents are located at www.unhchr.ch/html/menu2/6/cerd.htm. General recommendations, opinions, country observations, decisions, and other documents can be accessed at www1.umn.edu/humanrts/country/cerd-page.html.

42. 19 ILM 33 (1980). See, inter alia, N. Burrows, "The 1979 Convention on the Elimination of all Forms of Discrimination Against Women," *Netherlands International Law Review* 32 (1985): 419–460; A. C. Byrnes, "The 'Other' Human Rights Treaty Body: The Work of the Committee on the Elimination of Discrimination Against Women," *Yale Journal of International Law* 14 (1989): 1–67; K. Engle, "International Human Rights and Feminism: When Two Discourses Meet," *Michigan Journal of International Law* 13, no. 515 (Spring 1992): 517–610; Elizabeth Evatt, "Finding a Voice for Women's Rights: The Early Days of CEDAW," *George Washington International Law Review* 34, no. 3 (2002): 515–553; M. Galey, "Promoting Nondiscrimination Against Women," *International Studies Quarterly* 23, no. 2 (June 1979); A. R. Lars, *Guide to the Travaux Préparatoires of the UN Convention on the Elimination of All Forms of Discrimination Against Women* (Dordrecht: Martinus Nijhoff, 1993); M. S. McDougal, H. D. Lasswell, and L. Chen, "Human Rights for Women and World Public Order: The Outlawing of Sex-Based Discrimination," *AJIL* 69 (1975): 497–533; Theodor Meron, *Human Rights Law-Making in the United Nations: A Critique of Instruments and Process* (Oxford: Clarendon, 1986), chap. 2; L. Reanda, "Human Rights and Women's Rights: The United Nations Approach," *Human Rights Quarterly* 3, no. 2 (Spring 1981): 11–31; S. Zearfoss, "Note: The Convention for the Elimination of All Forms of Discrimination Against Women: Radical, Reasonable, or Reactionary?" *Michigan Journal of International Law* 12, no. 4 (Summer 1991): 903–942.

43. K. Engle, "International Human Rights and Feminism: When Two Discourses Meet," *Michigan Journal of International Law* 13, no. 515 (Spring 1992): 517–610, 521.

44. Convention on the Elimination of All Forms of Discrimination Against Women, article 4.

45. Byrnes, "The 'Other' Human Rights Treaty Body," p. 52.

46. Cook, "Reservations to the Convention," p. 644. See also Jennifer Riddle, "Making CEDAW Universal: A Critique of CEDAW's Reservation

Regime Under Article 28 and the Effectiveness of the Reporting Process," *George Washington International Law Review* 34, no. 3 (2002): 605–638.

47. For country reports and other documents, see www.unhchr.ch/html/menu2/6/cedw.htm. For reports and documentation of the CEDAW Committee, see www.un.org/womenwatch/daw/cedaw/committ.htm.

48. "United Nations General Assembly: Optional Protocol to the Convention on the Elimination of All Forms of Discrimination Against Women," October 15, 1999, 39 ILM 281 (2000). See Laboni Amena Hoq, "The Women's Convention and Its Optional Protocol: Empowering Women to Claim Their Internationally Protected Rights," *Columbia Human Rights Law Review* 32, no. 3 (Summer 2001): 677–726; and Emilia Della Torre, "Women's Business: The Development of an Optional Protocol to the United Nations Women's Convention," *Australian Journal of Human Rights* 6, no. 2 (2000): 181–193.

49. 23 ILM 1027 (1984). See, inter alia, Peter R. Baehr, "The General Assembly: Negotiating the Convention on Torture," in David P. Forsythe, ed., *The United Nations in the World Political Economy: Essays in Honour of Leon Gordenker* (Basingstoke, UK: Macmillan, 1989), pp. 36–53; J. Herman Burgers and Hans Danelius, *The United Nations Convention Against Torture: A Handbook on the Convention Against Torture and Other Cruel, Inhuman, or Degrading Treatment or Punishment* (Dordrecht and Boston: M. Nijhoff, 1988); Matthew Lippman, "The Development and Drafting of the United Nations Convention Against Torture and Other Cruel, Inhuman, or Degrading Treatment or Punishment," *Boston College International and Comparative Law Review* 17, no. 2 (1994): 275–335; Winston P. Nagan and Lucie Atkins, "The International Law of Torture: From Universal Proscription to Effective Application and Enforcement," *Harvard Human Rights Journal* 14 (Spring 2001): 87–121; Nigel S. Rodley, *The Treatment of Prisoners Under International Law,* 2nd ed. (Oxford: Clarendon, 1999); and Aaron Solomon, "The Politics of Prosecutions Under The Convention Against Torture," *Chicago Journal of International Law* 2, no. 1 (Spring 2001): 309–313.

50. J. Herman Burgers, "An Arduous Delivery: The United Nations Convention Against Torture (1984)," in Johan Kaufmann, ed., *Effective Negotiation: Case Studies in Conference Diplomacy* (The Hague: Martinus Nijhoff, 1989), pp. 45–52, 46.

51. *Review of the Multilateral Treaty-Making Process* (New York: United Nations, 1985), p. 206.

52. For individual complaints, decisions, and country reports, see www.unhchr.ch/html/menu2/6/cat.htm. Consideration of reports and decisions and views can be accessed at www1.umn.edu/humanrts/cat/cat-page.html. See Chris Ingelese, *The UN Committee Against Torture: An Assessment* (The Hague: Kluwer Law International, 2001).

53. 42 ILM 26 (2003).

54. 28 ILM 1448 (1989). See, inter alia, Sharon Detrick, *A Commentary on the United Nations Convention on the Rights of the Child* (The Hague: M. Nijhoff, 1999); and A. Glenn Mower Jr., *The Convention on the Rights of the Child: International Law Support for Children* (Westport, CT: Greenwood, 1997).

55. *The United Nations and Human Rights, 1945–1995*, p. 84.

56. For country reports and other documents, see www.unhchr.ch/html/ menu2/6/crc.htm. Comments on country reports and other documents are located at www1.umn.edu/humanrts/crc/crc-page.html.

57. 39 ILM 1285 (2000).

58. For an overview of the conference, see that prepared by the Centre for Human Rights in Geneva for the *Human Rights Law Journal* 14, nos. 9–10 (November 30, 1993): 346–352. See also Adama Dieng, "Introduction," *International Commission of Jurists Review* 50 (June 1993): 3–7.

59. A/CONF.157/24, June 25, 1993. Reproduced in the *Human Rights Law Journal* 14, nos. 9–10 (November 30, 1993): 352–363.

60. See Andrew Clapham, "Creating the High Commissioner for Human Rights: The Outside Story," *European Journal of International Law (EJIL)* 5 (1994): 556–568.

61. See, inter alia, Robert Blackburn and Jørg Polakiewicz, eds., *Fundamental Rights in Europe: The European Convention on Human Rights and Its Member States, 1950–2000* (Oxford: Oxford University Press, 2001); and Mark Janis, Richard Kay, and Anthony Bradley, *European Human Rights Law: Text and Materials,* 2nd ed. (Oxford: Oxford University Press, 2000).

62. European Convention on Human Rights and Fundamental Freedoms (1953), 213 UNTS 221.

63. On the negotiation of the European Convention on Human Rights, see G. Marston, "The UK's Part in the Preparation of the European Convention on Human Rights," *ICLQ* 42 (1993): 796–826; and A. H. Robertson and J. G. Merrills, *Human Rights in Europe*, 3rd ed. (Manchester, UK: Manchester University Press, 1993), chap. 1.

64. 41 ILM 515 (2002).

65. Protocol No. 11 to the Convention, adopted by the Council of Europe on May 11, 1994, 33 ILM 943 (1994). See, inter alia, Laurence R. Helfer and Anne-Marie Slaughter, "Toward a Theory of Effective Supranational Adjudication," *Yale Law Journal* 107 (1997): 273–391; and the special issue on Protocol No. 11 in *Human Rights Law Journal* (1994).

66. The website of the Court of Human Rights is at www.echr.coe.int.

67. See Règis Brillat, "The European Social Charter," in G. Alfredsson et al., eds., *International Human Rights Monitoring Mechanisms* (The Hague: Martinus Nijhoff, 2001), pp. 601–606; and Donna Gomien, David Harris, and Leo Zwaak, *Law and Practice of the European Convention on Human Rights and the European Social Charter* (Strasbourg: Council of Europe, 1996).

68. Blackburn and Polakiewicz, *Fundamental Rights in Europe*, p. 89.

69. See Philip Alston, ed., *The EU and Human Rights* (Oxford: Oxford University Press, 1999); and Thomas Von Danwitz, "The Charter of Fundamental Rights of the European Union between Political Symbolism and Legal Realism," *Denver Journal of International Law and Policy* 29 (2001): 289–304.

70. Organization of American States Resolution XXX, OAS Off. Rec. OEA/Ser.L/V/I.4 Rev. (1965).

71. On the creation of the commission, see C. Medina Quiroga, *The Battle*

of Human Rights, Gross Systematic Violations, and the Inter-American System (Dordrecht: Martinus Nijhoff, 1988).

72. Christina Cerna, "The Inter-American Commission on Human Rights: Its Organization and Examination of Petitions and Communications," in David J. Harris and Stephen Livingstone, eds., *The Inter-American System of Human Rights* (Oxford: Clarendon, 1998), pp. 65–114, 66.

73. See ibid.

74. 9 ILM 673 (1970).

75. The website of the Inter-American Court of Human Rights can be found at www.corteidh.or.cr/index-ingles.html.

76. For more detail, see Cecilia Medina, "The Inter-American Commission on Human Rights and the Inter-American Court of Human Rights: Reflections on a Joint Venture," *Human Rights Quarterly* 12, no. 4 (1990): 439–464.

77. See David Harris, "Regional Protection of Human Rights: The Inter-American Achievement," in Harris and Livingstone, *The Inter-American System of Human Rights,* pp. 1–29.

78. 21 ILM 58 (1982). For background and commentary, see Theo van Boven, "The Relations Between Peoples' Rights and Human Rights in the African Charter," *Human Rights Journal* 7, no. 2–4 (1986): 183–194; Malcolm D. Evans and Rachel Murray, eds., *The African Charter on Human and Peoples' Rights: The System in Practice, 1986–2000* (Cambridge: Cambridge University Press, 2002); Michelo Hansungule, "The African Charter on Human and Peoples' Rights: A Critical Review," *African Yearbook of International Law* 8 (2000): 265–331; Isaac Nguema, "Human Rights Perspectives in Africa: The Roots of a Constant Challenge," *Human Rights Law Journal* 11, nos. 3–4 (1990): 261–283; B. Obinna Okere, "The Protection of Human Rights in Africa and the African Charter on Human and Peoples' Rights: A Comparative Analysis with the European and American Systems," *Human Rights Quarterly* 6, no. 2 (1984): 141–159; U. O. Umozurike, "The African Charter on Human and Peoples' Rights," *AJIL* 77 (1983): 902–912.

79. Hansungule, "The African Charter on Human and Peoples' Rights," pp. 265–331, 273.

80. For discussion of how to define "peoples" see Yoram Dinstein, "Collective Human Rights of Peoples and Minorities," *ICLQ* 25 (January 1976): 102–120.

81. Part 1, chapter II, articles 27–29.

82. Cees Flinterman and Catherine Henderson, "The African Charter on Human and Peoples' Rights," in R. Hanski and M. Suksi, eds., *An Introduction to the International Protection of Human Rights. A Textbook* (Turku: Abo Akademi University Institute for Human Rights, 1997). See also N. Udombana, "Toward the African Court on Human and Peoples' Rights: Better Late Than Never," *Yale Human Rights and Development Law Journal* 3, no. 1 (2000): 45–111.

83. The Mandate of the commission is set out in article 45. See, inter alia, Evelyn Ama Ankumah, *The African Commission on Human and Peoples' Rights: Practice and Procedures* (The Hague: Martinus Nijhoff, 1996); Oji Umozurike, "The Complaint Procedures of the African Commission on Human

and People's Rights," in Gudmundur Alfredsson, Jonas Grimheden, Bertram G. Ramcharan, and Alfred de Zayas, eds., *International Human Rights Monitoring Mechanisms: Essays in Honour of Jakob Th. Möller* (The Hague, Boston, London: Martinus Nijhoff, 2001), pp. 707–712; and Claude E. Welch Jr., "The African Commission on Human and Peoples' Rights: A Five-Year Report and Assessment," *Human Rights Quarterly* 14:1 (1992), 43–61.

84. 1001 UNTS 45. Also available at http://heiwww.unige.ch/humanrts/instree/z2arcon.htm. The convention entered into force on June 20, 1974. For the background to the convention, see Ivor Jackson, *The Refugee Concept in Group Situations* (The Hague: Martinus Nijhoff, 1999). For discussion, see Eduardo Arboleda, "Refugee Definition in Africa and Latin America: The Lessons of Pragmatism," *International Journal of Refugee Law* 3, no. 2 (1991): 185–205; and George Okoth-Obbo, "Thirty Years On: A Legal Review of the 1969 OAU Refugee Convention," *African Yearbook of International Law* (2001): 3–69.

85. Dennis Gallagher, "The Evolution of the International Refugee System," *International Migration Review* 23, no. 3 (1989): 579–598, 584.

86. Protocol to the African Charter of Human and Peoples' Rights, OAU Doc. OAU/LEG/EXP/AFCHPRPROT (2). See, inter alia, Makau Mutua, "The African Human Rights Court: A Two-Legged Stool?" *Human Rights Quarterly* 21, no. 2 (1999): 342–363; and Gino J. Naldi and Konstantinos Magliveras, "Reinforcing the African System of Human Rights: The Protocol on the Establishment of a Regional Court of Human and Peoples' Rights," *Netherlands Quarterly Human Rights* 16 (1998): 431–456.

87. See, inter alia, C. Bunch, "Women's Rights as Human Rights: Toward a Re-Vision of Human Rights," *Human Rights Quarterly* 12 (1990): 486–498; Rebecca J. Cook, ed., *Human Rights of Women: National and International Perspectives* (Philadelphia: University of Pennsylvania Press, 1994); K. Engle, "International Human Rights and Feminism: When Discourses Meet," *Michigan Journal of International Law* 13 (Spring 1992): 517–610; and V. Spike Peterson and Laura Parisi, "Are Women Human? It's Not an Academic Question," in Tony Evans, ed., *Human Rights Fifty Years On: A Reappraisal* (Manchester and New York: Manchester University Press, 1998), pp. 132–160.

88. Richard Falk, *Human Rights Horizons* (New York: Routledge, 2000), p. 51.

89. See, inter alia, Christina Cerna, "Universality of Human Rights and Cultural Diversity: Implementation of Human Rights in Different Socio-Cultural Contexts," *Human Rights Quarterly* 16, no. 4 (1994): 740–752; J. Donnelly, "Cultural Relativism and Universal Human Rights," in Jack Donnelly, ed., *Universal Human Rights in Theory and Practice* (Ithaca: Cornell University Press, 1989), pp. 109–124; Neil Englehart, "Rights and Culture in the Asian Values Argument: The Rise and Fall of Confucian Ethics in Singapore" *Human Rights Quarterly* 22, no. 2 (2000): 548–568; Makau Mutua, "Savages, Victims, and Saviors: The Metaphor of Human Rights," *Harvard International Law Journal* 42 (2001): 201; Fali S. Nariman, "The Universality of Human Rights," *International Commission of Jurists Review* 50 (June 1993): 8–22; A. Pollis, "Cultural Relativism Revisited: Through a State Prism" *Human Rights Quarterly* 18, no. 2 (1996): 316–344; Alison Dundes Renteln,

International Human Rights: Universalism Versus Relativism (Newbury Park: Sage, 1990); Ferdinand Teson, "International Human Rights and Cultural Relativity," *Virginia Journal of International Law* 25 (1985): 869–898; G. J. H. van Hoof, "Asian Challenges to the Concept of Universality: Afterthoughts on the Vienna Conference on Human Rights," in Peter R. Baehr, Fried van Hoof, Liu Nanlai, Tao Zhenghua, and Jacqueline Smith, eds., *Human Rights: Chinese and Dutch Perspectives* (The Hague: Martinus Nijhoff, 1996), pp. 1–15.

90. For discussion of this and other challenges to the universality of human rights, see D. Otto, "Everything Is Dangerous: Some Post-Structural Tools for Rethinking the Universal Knowledge Claims of Human Rights Law," *Australian Journal of Human Rights* 5, no. 1 (1998): 17–47.

91. Vienna Declaration and Programme of Action adopted at the World Conference on Human Rights, A/CONF.157/24, June 25, 1993, sec. I, para. 5.

92. See, for example, Chris Brown, "Universal Human Rights: A Critique," in Tim Dunne and Nicholas J. Wheeler, eds., *Human Rights in Global Politics* (Cambridge: Cambridge University Press, 1999), p. 103.

93. See, for example, George J. Andreopoulos, ed., *Genocide: Conceptual and Historical Dimensions* (Philadelphia: University of Pennsylvania Press, 1994).

94. See, for example, E. Arboleda and I. Hoy, "The Convention Refugee Definition in the West: Disharmony of Interpretation and Application," *International Journal of Refugee Law* 5, no. 1 (1993): 66–90.

95. Matthew C. R. Craven, *The International Covenant on Economic, Social, and Cultural Rights: A Perspective on its Development* (Oxford: Clarendon, 1995), p. 8.

96. See, inter alia, P. H. Kooijmans, "Human Rights Universal Panacea? Some Reflections on the So-called Human Rights of the Third Generation," *Netherlands International Law Review* 37 (1990): 315–329; and Stephen P. Marks, "Emerging Human Rights: A New Generation for the 1980s," *Rutgers Law Review* 33, no. 2 (1981): 435–452.

97. UN General Assembly Resolution 41/128, December 4, 1986.

98. For literature on the right to development, see, inter alia, P. Alston, "Making Space for New Human Rights: The Case of the Right to Development," *Human Rights Yearbook* 1 (1988): 3–40; R. L. Barsh, "The Right to Development as a Human Right: Results of the Global Consultation," *Human Rights Quarterly* 13 (1991): 322–338; S. R. Chowdhury, E. M. G. Denters, and P. J. I. M. de Waart, eds., *The Right to Development in International Law* (Dordrecht: Martinus Nijhoff, 1992); J. Donnelly, "In Search of the Unicorn: The Jurisprudence and Politics of the Right to Development," *California Western International Law Journal* 15 (1985): 473–509; J. O'Manique, "Human Rights and Development," *Human Rights Quarterly* 14, no. 1 (February 1992): 78–103; W. Mansell, "Why Bother About a Right to Development?" *Journal of Law and Society* 21, no. 2 (June 1994): 171–192; "The Right to Development: A North-South Divide?" *UN Chronicle* 30, no. 1 (1993): 96(2); A. Rosas, "The Right to Development," in A. Eide, C. Krause, and A. Rosas, *Economic, Social, and Cultural Rights: A Textbook* (Dordrecht: Martinus Nijhoff, 2001), pp. 247–255; and Argun Sengupta, "On the Theory and Practice of the Right to Development," *Human Rights Quarterly* 24 (2002): 837–889.

99. OAS Treaty Series, no. 69 (1988).

100. See, inter alia, S. James Anaya, *Indigenous Peoples in International Law* (New York: Oxford University Press, 1996), and the collection of essays in S. James Anaya, ed., *International Law and Indigenous Peoples* (Abingdon, Oxon: Ashgate, 2003).

101. *The United Nations and Human Rights 1945–1995*, p. 102.

102. Convention No. 107, "Convention Concerning the Protection and Integration of Indigenous Populations and Other Tribal and Semi-Tribal Populations in Independent Countries," International Labour Organization, *Conventions and Recommendations Adopted by the International Labour Conference 1919–1966* (Geneva: International Labour Office, 1966), pp. 901–908.

103. Russel Lawrence Barsh, "Indigenous Peoples: An Emerging Object of International Law," *AJIL* 80 (1986): 369–385, 370.

104. Convention No. 169, "Convention Concerning Indigenous and Tribal Peoples in Independent Countries," *Conventions and Recommendations 1919–1937: International Labour Conference* (Geneva: International Labour Office, 1937), pp. 1436–1447. Julian Burger and Paul Hunt, "Towards the International Protection of Indigenous Peoples' Rights," *Netherlands Quarterly of Human Rights* 12, no. 1 (1994): 405–423, 406.

105. ILO Convention Concerning Indigenous and Tribal Peoples in Independent Countries (No. 169), 72 ILO Official Bull. 59. See S. James Anaya, "Indigenous Peoples and Their Demands Within the Modern Human Rights Movement," in Yael Danieli, Elsa Stamatopoulou, and Clarence J. Dias, *The Universal Declaration of Human Rights: Fifty Years and Beyond* (New York: Baywood, 1999), pp. 149–161, 156–158; L. Swepston, "The Indigenous and Tribal Peoples Convention (No. 169): Eight Years after Adoption," in C. Price Cohen, ed., *The Human Rights of Indigenous Peoples* (Ardsley, NY: Transnational, 1998), pp. 17–36.

106. 34 ILM 541 (1995); UN Doc. E/CN.4/SUB.2/1994/2/Add.1 (1994), at www.unhchr.ch. See, inter alia, Sarah Pritchard, "United Nations and the Making of a Declaration on Indigenous Rights," *Aboriginal Law Bulletin* 3, no. 89 (February 1997); Elsa Stamatopoulou, "Indigenous Peoples and the United Nations: Human Rights as a Developing Dynamic," *Human Rights Quarterly* 16 (1994): 58–81; and Robert A. Williams Jr., "Encounters on the Frontiers of International Human Rights Law: Redefining the Terms of Indigenous Peoples' Survival in the World," *Duke Law Journal* (1990): 676–683.

107. See, inter alia, Russel Lawrence Barsh, "Indigenous Peoples and the UN Commission on Human Rights: A Case of the Immovable Object and the Irresistible Force," *Human Rights Quarterly* 18, no. 4 (1996): 782–813; and Siegfried Wiessner, "Rights and Status of Indigenous Peoples: A Global Comparative and International Legal Analysis," *Harvard Human Rights Journal* 12 (1999): 57–128.

108. David P. Stewart, "Human Rights at the Millennium," *AJIL* 95, no. 1 (2001): 227–235.

109. See Thomas Risse, Stephen C. Ropp, and Kathryn Sikkink, eds., *The Power of Human Rights: International Norms and Domestic Change* (New York: Cambridge University Press, 1999).

110. See Oona A. Hathaway, "Do Human Rights Treaties Make a

Difference?" *Yale Law Journal* 111, no. 8 (2002): 1935–2043. See also the response from Goodman and Jinks, "Measuring the Effects of Human Rights Treaties," *EJIL* 14, no. 3 (2003): 171–183; and the reply by Hathaway, "Testing Conventional Wisdom," *EJIL* 14, no. 1 (2003): 185–200.

111. David P. Stewart, "Human Rights at the Millennium," *AJIL* 95, no. 1 (2001): 227–235, 234.

11

International Humanitarian Law

The phrase "international humanitarian law" (IHL) denotes "all those rules of international law which are designed to regulate the treatment of the individual—civilian or military, wounded or active—in international armed conflicts."[1] Here we reach the *jus in bello*, the laws of war, that we set aside in Chapter 5 when examining the *jus ad bellum*. International humanitarian law is now regarded largely as a field of international law separate from that of arms control, which establishes controls over the production, testing, stockpiling, transfer, and deployment of weaponry by which conflict might be conducted.[2] There is nevertheless some overlap; even though arms control treaties do not directly address what happens when there is armed conflict, treaties relating to international humanitarian law that limit or prohibit weaponry could also be classified as arms control treaties. The Ottawa Convention on landmines, for example, could be classified either as an addition to international humanitarian law or to the treaties on arms control.[3] See Figure 11.1.

Laws governing the conduct of war are much older than those seeking to prevent states from initiating war; ancient societies of various civilizations had legal codes with humanitarian provisions similar to those found in the modern laws of war. Wars between Egypt and Sumeria in the second millennium B.C., for example, were governed by a complex set of rules obligating belligerents to distinguish combatants from civilians.[4] The Laws of Manu, the greatest of the ancient Hindu codes, prohibited Hindus from using poisoned arrows.[5] In the nineteenth century there began a process of codifying what we now refer to as "international humanitarian law." Modern international humanitarian law has two streams: that pertaining to limitations or prohibitions of

Figure 11.1   Some Landmarks in the Codification and Development of International Humanitarian Law

1856 Paris Declaration on Maritime War
1864 Geneva Convention on Wounded and Sick
1868 Declaration Renouncing the Use, in Time of War, of Explosive Projectiles Under 400 Grammes Weight (St. Petersburg Declaration)
1899 Hague Conventions and Declarations
1907 Hague Conventions and Declaration
1929 Geneva Convention for the Amelioration of the Condition of the Wounded and Sick in Armies in the Field
1949 The Geneva Conventions
1954 Hague Convention for the Protection of Cultural Property in the Event of Armed Conflict
1976 Convention on the Prohibition of Military or Any Other Hostile Use of Environmental Modification Techniques
1977 Protocols Additional to the Geneva Conventions
1980 Convention on Prohibitions or Restrictions on the Use of Certain Conventional Weapons Which May Be Deemed to Be Excessively Injurious or to Have Indiscriminate Effects (CCW)
1997 Convention on the Prohibition of the Use, Stockpiling, Production, and Transfer of Anti-Personnel Mines and Their Destruction
1998 Rome Statute of the International Criminal Court

specific means and methods of warfare (the Hague Laws), and that regarding the protection of civilians and those no longer fighting (the Geneva laws). This distinction has been less useful since the 1977 Protocols Additional to the Geneva Conventions, which address both issues.

Perhaps more so than in any other issue area of international law, the relevant treaty regimes in international humanitarian law need to be understood in the context of customary international law on the subject. This was expressly recognized in the so-called *Martens Clause,* which first appeared in the preamble to the 1899 Hague Convention II and has appeared in similar wording in other treaties. The preamble to the 1907 Hague Convention IV stated that:

> Until a more complete code of the laws of war has been issued, the high contracting parties deem it expedient to declare that, in cases not included in the Regulations adopted by them, the inhabitants and the belligerents remain under the protection and the rule of the principles of the law of nations, as they result from the usages established among civilized peoples, from the laws of humanity, and the dictates of the public conscience.

Another fundamental principle underpinning international humanitarian law stipulates that parties to a conflict and members of their armed forces do not have an unlimited choice of methods and means of warfare.[6] The *principle of military necessity* stipulates that "only that degree and kind of force, not otherwise prohibited by the law of armed conflict, required for the partial or complete submission of the enemy with a minimum expenditure of time, life, and physical resources may be applied."[7]

The first modern effort to ban weapons that caused unnecessary suffering was the St. Petersburg Declaration of 1868, a response to the development of a bullet that exploded on contact with a hard surface. The preamble stated what became known as the *principle of unnecessary suffering*, which has underpinned attempts at limiting battlefield armaments:

> Considering . . . [t]hat the only legitimate object which States should endeavour to accomplish during war is to weaken the military forces of the enemy;
>
> That for this purpose it is sufficient to disable the greatest possible number of men;
>
> That this object would be exceeded by the employment of arms which uselessly aggravate the sufferings of disabled men, or render their death inevitable;
>
> That the employment of such arms would, therefore, be contrary to the laws of humanity.[8]

The 1899 and 1907 Hague Conventions and Declarations

The first Hague Conference was held at the initiative of Czar Nicholas II of Russia, with the aim of limiting armaments.[9] Representatives of twenty-six states concluded conventions relating to the peaceful settlement of disputes, the laws and customs of war on land, and maritime warfare; as well as declarations prohibiting the launching of projectiles and explosives from balloons, using projectiles diffusing asphyxiating gases, and using expanding bullets.

The second Hague Conference, aimed at limiting armaments, was attended by representatives of forty-four states. This conference adopted thirteen conventions and one declaration. Those relevant to international humanitarian law are:

- Hague Convention III Concerning the Opening of Hostilities
- Hague Convention IV Concerning the Laws and Customs of War

on Land and Annex to the Convention: Regulations Concerning
the Laws and Customs of War on Land

- Hague Convention V Concerning the Rights and Duties of
  Neutral Powers and Persons in Case of War on Land
- Hague Convention VI Concerning the Status of Enemy
  Merchant Ships at the Outbreak of Hostilities
- Hague Convention VII Concerning the Conversion of Merchant
  Ships into Warships
- Hague Convention VIII Concerning the Laying of Automatic
  Submarine Contact Mines
- Hague Convention IX Concerning Bombardment by Naval
  Forces in Times of War
- Hague Convention XI Concerning Certain Restrictions with
  Regard to the Exercise of the Right of Capture in Naval War
- Hague Convention XIII Concerning the Rights and Duties of
  Neutral Powers in Naval War

The conventions vary in their contemporary importance.
Convention III has been completely disregarded, for example, but
Hague Convention IV and annexed regulations, which revised the laws
of land warfare embodied in the Second Hague Convention of 1899,
remains of importance.[10] Article 23(e) of the regulations annexed to
the Fourth Hague Convention of 1907 reiterated the principle of
unnecessary suffering that had been expressed in the preamble to the
1868 St. Petersberg Declaration, forbidding the employment of "arms,
projectiles, or material calculated to cause unnecessary suffering."
Because it was recognized that the convention did not represent a complete code of the law of land warfare, the Martens Clause was included
in its preamble. The military tribunal at Nuremberg in 1946 recognized
the 1907 Hague Convention IV as declaratory of customary international law.[11]

The Geneva Conventions of 1949

The well-known Geneva Conventions are identified below:

- Geneva Convention I for the Amelioration of the Condition of
  the Wounded and Sick in Armed Forces in the Field[12]
- Geneva Convention II for the Amelioration of the Condition of
  the Wounded, Sick, and Shipwrecked Members of Armed Forces
  at Sea[13]

- Geneva Convention III Concerning the Treatment of Prisoners of War[14]
- Geneva Convention IV Concerning the Protection of Civilian Persons in Time of War[15]

The focus of these conventions was the protection of victims of war. Sponsored by the ICRC, they grew out of prewar efforts to draft new conventions as well as the experience of the war in demonstrating inadequacies in the existing law. The First Geneva Convention was a new and enlarged version of a 1929 Geneva Convention on the wounded and sick. It provides, inter alia, that members of the armed forces and other categories provided for in article 13, who are wounded or sick, "shall be respected and protected in all circumstances." The Third Geneva Convention defines "prisoners of war" and specifies how they are to be treated. Article 13 provides:

> Prisoners of war must at all times be humanely treated. Any unlawful act or omission by the Detaining Power causing death or seriously endangering the health of a prisoner of war in its custody is prohibited, and will be regarded as a serious breach of the present Convention. In particular, no prisoner of war may be subjected to physical mutilation or to medical or scientific experiments of any kind which are not justified by the medical, dental or hospital treatment of the prisoner concerned and carried out in his interest.
>
> Likewise, prisoners or war must at all times be protected, particularly against acts of violence or intimidation and against insults and public curiosity.
>
> Measures of reprisal against prisoners of war are prohibited.

Article 17 provides that prisoners of war, when questioned on the subject, are required to give only their surname, first names and rank, date of birth, and army, regimental, personal or serial number, or failing this, equivalent information. They are, by article 118, to be released and repatriated without delay after the cessation of active hostilities.

The Fourth Geneva Convention was the first international agreement in the laws of war to exclusively address the treatment of civilians—those who "find themselves, in case of a conflict or occupation, in the hands of a Party to the conflict or Occupying Power of which they are not nationals."[16] It provides, inter alia, that such

> protected persons are entitled, in all circumstances, to respect for their persons, their honour, their family rights, their religious convictions

and practices, and their manners and customs. They shall at all times
be humanely treated, and shall be protected especially against all acts
of violence or threats thereof and against insults and public curiosi-
ty.[17]

Some consideration was given to the laws of war for internal conflicts. This resulted in a common article 3 in the 1949 Geneva
Conventions, which extended some fundamental humanitarian protec-
tions to noncombatants "in the case of armed conflict not of an international character." The 1949 Geneva Conventions entered into force in
1954 and now have virtually universal participation. It is likely that
most, if not all, of their provisions have attained the status of customary
international law.[18]

The 1977 Protocols Additional to the Geneva Conventions are:

* Protocol Additional to the Geneva Conventions of 12 August
  1949, and Relating to the Protection of Victims of International
  Arms Conflicts[19]
* Protocol Additional to the Geneva Conventions of 12 August
  1949, and Relating to the Protection of Victims of Non-
  International Armed Conflicts[20]

These two protocols to the Geneva Conventions, again sponsored
by the ICRC, were an attempt to respond to issues that had become
increasingly apparent since the conclusion of the Geneva Conventions,
both in terms of reaffirming some customary international humanitarian law and further developing international humanitarian law.[21] One
major problem was that war had increasingly become an intrastate
rather than interstate phenomenon in the years since World War II, and
only the common article 3 of the 1949 Geneva Conventions had
applied specifically to civil wars. A second problem was that, even
though the 1949 Geneva Conventions had updated international law
regarding the protection of civilians and those no longer fighting, limitations or prohibitions of specific means and methods of warfare were
becoming increasingly dated. Much of the preparatory work for the
protocols was undertaken by the ICRC, which presented the
Diplomatic Conference on the Reaffirmation and Development of
International Humanitarian Law with two draft protocols from which
to work. The conference held four sessions in Geneva between 1974
and 1977.

The two protocols represent some merging of the Hague and

Geneva streams of international humanitarian law. The first protocol deals with international conflict. It is divided into several parts, addressing the wounded, sick, and shipwrecked; medical transportation; missing and dead persons; methods and means of warfare; combatant and prisoner-of-war status; and the civilian population. Article 48 codifies the *principle of distinction*:

> In order to ensure respect for and protection of the civilian population and civilian objects, the Parties to the conflict shall at all times distinguish between the civilian population and combatants and between civilian objects and military objectives and accordingly shall direct their operations only against military objectives.

Military objectives were defined in article 52(2). Article 51(5) prohibits "an attack which may be expected to cause incidental loss of civilian life, injury to civilians, damage to civilian objects, or a combination thereof, which would be excessive in relation to the concrete and direct military advantage anticipated," thereby codifying the *principle of proportionality*. "When a choice is possible between several military objectives for obtaining a similar military advantage, the objective to be selected shall be that the attack on which may be expected to cause the least danger to civilian lives and to civilian objects."[22]

Chapter II of section III (Treatment of Persons in the Power of a Party to the Conflict) provides measures relating to women and children. Article 76(1) provides that "women shall be the object of special respect and shall be protected against rape, forced prostitution and any other form of indecent assault." Critics have claimed that women can still be regarded as the "forgotten victims of armed conflict" and suggest the need for an additional protocol to the Geneva Conventions directed to the needs of women in armed conflict.[23] The conference also discussed the question of the legality of nuclear weapons but left it unresolved. Resolution 22(IV) recommended that a separate conference be convened with a view toward reaching agreements on prohibitions or restrictions on the use of specific conventional weapons.[24]

The second protocol (Protection of Victims of Non-International Armed Conflicts) builds on the common article 3 in the Geneva Conventions. It was the first international treaty devoted exclusively to the protection of persons affected by noninternational armed conflict. Strongest support for the protocol came from Europe and North America, while the struggle for independence on the part of national liberation movements led to much Third World opposition.[25] The difficulty of reaching agreement produced a much shorter document than the first protocol. It has separate parts on humane treatment (of all persons who do not take a direct part or who have ceased to take part in hostilities); wounded, sick, and shipwrecked; and the civilian population.

Convention on Prohibitions or Restrictions on the Use of Certain Conventional Weapons Which May Be Deemed to Be Excessively Injurious or to Have Indiscriminate Effects (CCW), 1980

The CCW[26] resulted from the efforts of the ICRC and was adopted at a conference convened by the United Nations. The CCW bans or restricts the use of specific weapons or means of warfare that pose special risks of causing indiscriminate damage to civilians or unnecessary suffering. Annexed protocols each deal with a specific type of conventional weapon: fragmentation weapons undetectable by X-ray (protocol I); mines, booby-traps, and other devices (protocol II, which was amended in 1996); incendiary weapons (protocol III); and blinding laser weapons (protocol IV, adopted in 1995). Article 8 provides for the review of the CCW, for amendments, and for the addition of further annexed protocols. The second review conference, held in December 2001, amended the framework convention to make all existing protocols applicable to noninternational armed conflict.

Convention on the Prohibition of the Use, Stockpiling, Production, and Transfer of Anti-Personnel Mines and Their Destruction (Ottawa Convention), 1997

The first widespread use of landmines as a means of curtailing attack occurred in World War I. Driven by improvements in landmine technology, which made them much cheaper to produce, use expanded greatly. By far the majority of victims are civilians, and it is usually after the conflict that they are killed or injured.

It was in the 1970s that landmines were placed on the international policy agenda. Protocol II of the 1980 CCW dealt with landmines but stopped short of actually banning them and had no impact on countries using them during internal conflicts.[27] The 1996 review conference of the CCW amended protocol II to further tighten restrictions on the production, use, and transfer of antipersonnel mines but stopped short of a ban. Disappointed by this outcome, Canada took the lead in efforts to have a total ban on antipersonnel mines. A conference in Ottawa in October 1996 attended by NGOs and representatives of seventy-four countries set in motion the so-called Ottawa process, which led to the Ottawa Convention.[28] It is notable because it was not brought about through the efforts of a superpower or coalition of great powers. It was brought to fruition by a coalition of states led by Canada as well as NGOs led by the International Campaign to Ban Landmines (ICBL), with the strong support of the UN Secretary-General.[29]

Article 1 lists the general obligations:

1. Each State Party undertakes never under any circumstances:
   a. To use anti-personnel mines;
   b. To develop, produce, otherwise acquire, stockpile, retain or transfer to anyone, directly or indirectly, anti-personnel mines;
   c. To assist, encourage or induce, in any way, anyone to engage in any activity prohibited to a State Party under this Convention.
2. Each State Party undertakes to destroy or ensure the destruction of all anti-personnel mines in accordance with the provisions of this Convention.

Article 7 of the Ottawa Convention requires states parties to submit an annual report to the UN Secretary-General on the measures taken to meet its obligations. At the first meeting of the states parties in Mozambique, it was decided to make these reports publicly available, including on the Internet.[30] The state-based reporting system is complemented by the work of the ICBL, which in June 1998 established the "Landmine Monitor" reporting network to monitor and document compliance with the convention.[31]

The Ottawa Convention appears to be a success. By September 2002, there was a reduced rate of new mine victims, reduced use of the weapon in key countries, a dramatic drop in production, and an almost complete halt in trade.[32] Such success has been tempered by the fact that the United States, Russia, and China—three of the major users of landmines—did not become parties. President Bill Clinton gave two reasons. First, the United States would have to remove its antipersonnel landmines from the Demilitarized Zone along the border between North Korea and South Korea; and second, the convention would have banned U.S. antitank mines as well as antipersonnel mines.[33] There are indications, however, that the

United States is actively looking for alternatives to its military reliance on landmines.

The Rome Statute of the
International Criminal Court, 1998

The earliest recorded precedent for an international criminal court or tribunal was the 1474 trial of the Burgundian governor of Breisach, Peter von Hagenback. He was brought before a court made up of twenty-eight judges from Alsace, Switzerland, and other states within the Holy Roman Empire when it was found that his troops had raped and killed innocent civilians and pillaged their property during the occupation of Breisach. Hagenback argued that he had been following the orders of his superiors, but his defense was rejected and he was sentenced to death. There appears then to have been a gap of nearly four centuries before the first proposal to set up a permanent international criminal court was made by Gustave Moynier, a founder of the Red Cross.[34]

Although some commentators have reservations about the criminal prosecution of the perpetrators of mass atrocity,[35] the mainstream view is that trying war criminals can further the goals of justice by assigning specific, individual guilt and avoiding collective guilt. Crimes are acknowledged, and many believe that seeing justice done facilitates a society's healing and enables it to move forward. It is through the trial process that records are made of the nature of, and responsibility for, the crimes committed. "Without the thousands of pages of documents and tribunal judgments, the victims' suffering and the horrid deeds of the killers will in part rest in the hands of the 'revisionists,' persons who say that the Jewish Holocaust never occurred. And the perpetrators will have accomplished one of their goals: to erase all memory of the victims."[36]

Attempts to create an international criminal court were made in the aftermath of World War I.[37] Sections 227–230 of the Versailles Treaty mandated the establishment of an international war crimes tribunal, and war crimes clauses were included in the various peace treaties. But the political will to push for strict enforcement of these provisions was weak, and the victorious Western allies allowed Germany to try its alleged war criminals in Germany's Supreme Court; of the 900 Germans identified by the allies, 888 were acquitted or had the charges dismissed without trial.[38] In 1937 the League of Nations finalized the text of a convention to establish an international criminal court in which to try persons accused of crimes defined in the Convention for the Prevention and Punishment of Terrorism, but the treaty never entered into force.[39]

After World War II, the Nuremberg International Military Tribunal and the International Military Tribunal for the Far East were established as ad hoc tribunals, the Tokyo Charter being based largely on the Nuremberg Charter. These tribunals were controversial because they were sometimes seen as "victors' justice": the victorious Allies were the judges, and the defendants were citizens of the defeated Axis powers. The tribunals appeared to be judging people for crimes that had not existed as legal crimes at the time of the actions.[40] The vital legacy of Nuremberg, however, is the principle that individuals, whether government officials or otherwise, are accountable for acts deemed unacceptable to common standards of international law and morality.

In 1946 the UN General Assembly decided that the important principles and precedents created by the Nuremberg charter and the judgments of the Nuremberg Tribunal should serve as the basis for the further codification of international law,[41] and in 1948 the General Assembly asked the International Law Commission to examine the possibility of creating a permanent international criminal court. The ILC decided in 1950 "that the establishment of an international judicial organ for the trial of persons charged with genocide or other crimes over which jurisdiction will be conferred upon that organ by international conventions is desirable."[42] On December 12, 1950, the General Assembly by resolution 489(V) established a committee to prepare one or more preliminary draft conventions and proposals relating to the establishment and the statute of an international criminal court. A second committee, established two years later, prepared a revised draft statute. A major stumbling block in the 1953 draft statute was the absence of an internationally accepted definition of the crime of aggression.

No further action was taken during the Cold War years; an international criminal court whose goals included the punishment of aggressive warfare was seen during these years as a threat to national sovereignty.[43] The end of the Cold War provided an opportunity for the United Nations to resume its work toward an international criminal court. In 1989 Trinidad and Tobago proposed that efforts at drafting a statute be resumed so as to create an international judicial institution capable of dealing with the increase in international drug trafficking.

The General Assembly requested the ILC to do so and, prompted by the widespread atrocities being committed in the war in the former Yugoslavia, asked that the ILC complete the drafting as a matter of priority.

In 1993 the Security Council, acting under Chapter VII of the UN Charter, passed Resolution 827,[44] adopting the Secretary-General's report on the establishment of a criminal tribunal for the former Yugoslavia, to which the Statute of the International Tribunal was annexed. The Statute of the International Tribunal for the Prosecution of Persons Responsible for Serious Violations of International Humanitarian Law Committed in the Territory of the Former Yugoslavia Since 1991 (ICTY) gives the tribunal jurisdiction to prosecute individuals who, in the territory of the former Yugoslavia, have committed grave breaches of the 1949 Geneva Conventions (article 2), violations of the laws or customs of war (article 3), genocide (article 4), or crimes against humanity (article 5).[45] By Resolution 827 the Security Council decided "that all States shall cooperate fully with the International Tribunal and its organs in accordance with the present resolution and the Statute of the International Tribunal." Sixty-six alleged war criminals appeared before the ICTY during its first eight years, the most notable of which was Slobodan Milosevic, the former Yugoslav president, whose trial began in 2002. He faced a total of sixty-six counts of crimes against humanity, genocide, and violating the laws and regulations of war, relating to activities in Croatia (1991), Bosnia (1995), and Kosovo (1999). Most of his alleged crimes carry a life sentence, the most serious penalty the tribunal may impose.

By Resolution 955 of November 8, 1994,[46] the Security Council established the International Criminal Tribunal for Rwanda "for the sole purpose of prosecuting persons responsible for genocide and other serious violations of international humanitarian law committed in the territory of Rwanda and Rwandan citizens responsible for genocide and other such violations committed in the territory of neighbouring States, between 1 January 1994 and 31 December 1994." By Resolution 977 of February 22, 1995, the Security Council decided that the seat of the ICTR would be Arusha in the United Republic of Tanzania. The ICTR began work in 1998, in which year the trial chamber convicted a former mayor, Jean-Paul Akayesu, of genocide and crimes against humanity for his encouragement of the rape of Tutsi women in Rwanda; the conviction was upheld by the Appeals Chamber in 2001.[47] This case represented the first time that rape had been found to be an act of genocide,[48] and it laid a foundation for later prosecutions for sexual crimes, both by the

ICTR and the ICTY.[49] The ICTY case against Kunarac, Kovac, and Vukovic was the first by an international tribunal to focus entirely on war-time crimes of sexual violence and gave rise to the first convictions for sexual enslavement as a crime against humanity. Jean Kambanda, the prime minister of Rwanda during the genocide, was the first head of government to have been indicted and subsequently convicted for genocide.[50]

Meanwhile, in 1993 the ILC submitted a draft statute for an international criminal court to the General Assembly; after comments by governments, a revised draft statute was submitted by the ILC to the General Assembly in 1994. The ILC recommended that the General Assembly "convene an international conference of plenipotentiaries to study the draft Statute and to conclude a convention on the establishment of an International Criminal Court." The General Assembly created a PrepCom to achieve a draft treaty that a diplomatic conference would be able to negotiate into a final text in a matter of weeks. The PrepCom met for six difficult sessions, in 1996–1998. The key political issues involved in the negotiation of the court were to include its relation to national courts and to the Security Council, the powers of the prosecutor, the scope of the subject-matter jurisdiction of the court, and state cooperation with the court.[51]

A five-week diplomatic conference was held in Rome in mid-1998, on the final day of which the Rome Statute[52] was adopted. During negotiations, states tended to group into three: the "like-minded group," which had promoted the establishment of an ICC and generally favored a strong and independent court. It was composed of middle powers and developing states. The second group consisted of the permanent members of the Security Council, which wanted a strong role for the Council vis-à-vis the Court and the exclusion of nuclear weapons from the types of weapons prohibited by the Rome Statute. The third group of states—including India, Mexico, and Egypt—insisted that nuclear weapons be included among those prohibited by the Rome Statute. NGOs generally pressed for a strong court, an independent prosecutor, sensitivity to gender concerns, and jurisdiction over internal armed conflict.[53]

The relationship of national courts and processes to that of the ICC was, naturally, one of the most sensitive issues during the negotiations. The solution to the sovereignty concerns raised by this issue had been conceived by the ILC in its draft statute and incorporated into preambular paragraph 10, as well as articles 1, 17, and 18 of the Rome Statute. This was the principle of *complementarity*, by which the Court operates only if a national jurisdiction is unwilling or unable genuinely to carry out an investigation or prosecution. The Rome Statute makes clear that the Court is not intended to have primacy over national courts but rather to be complementary to national criminal jurisdictions.[54]

The Court has jurisdiction over individuals, not states, with respect to four crimes: *genocide*; *crimes against humanity* (including murder, extermination, enslavement, deportation or forcible transfer of the population, imprisonment or other severe deprivation of physical liberty in violation of fundamental rules of international law, torture, sexual violence, and so on, when committed as part of a widespread or systematic attack directed against any civilian population); *war crimes* (including most of the serious violations of international humanitarian law mentioned in the 1949 Geneva Conventions and their protocols such as rape, sexual slavery, enforced prostitution, forced pregnancy, and other forms of sexual violence, whether committed during an international or internal conflict); and *aggression* (once a provision defining this crime and setting out the conditions for the exercise of such jurisdiction is adopted).[55]

Drug trafficking, which had provided the impetus for the renewed efforts to create an international criminal court, was not included because most delegations took the view that it was not of the same nature as the other crimes to be included, that the Court would not have the resources to undertake the necessary investigations, and that it could eventually flood the Court.[56] Similarly, whereas some states were particularly keen to have terrorism included within the jurisdiction of the Court, it could have unduly politicized the Court, particularly because there was no widely accepted definition of the crime.[57]

Article 13 provides for three "trigger mechanisms" by which a case can come before the Court: (1) if referred to the prosecutor by a state party; (2) on the initiative of the prosecutor with the authorization of a pretrial chamber; or (3) if referred to the prosecutor by the Security Council acting under Chapter VII of the UN Charter. But article 12 contains preconditions to the exercise of jurisdiction by the ICC in a case initiated by either of the first two triggers. The state on the territory of which the crime was committed and/or the state of which the person accused of the crime is a national must be a party to the statute or have accepted the jurisdiction of the Court.

The Court does not have retrospective jurisdiction (article 11). On becoming a party to the Rome Statute a state may declare that, for a period of seven years, it does not accept the jurisdiction of the Court with respect to war crimes when a crime is alleged to have been committed by its nationals or on its territory. States parties are obliged to cooperate with a request for assistance from the Court in relation to its investigation and prosecution of crimes (article 86). Such assistance may involve, for example, the taking of evidence, the provision of records, the protection of victims and witness, or the arrest and surrender of an individual on its territory. The Court, which is situated in The Hague, may order imprisonment for up to thirty years, fines, and forfeiture of the proceeds of a crime.

The Rome Statute was adopted by the United Nations Diplomatic Conference of Plenipotentiaries on the Establishment of an International Criminal Court on July 17, 1998, by a vote of 120-7 with twenty-one abstentions. The United States, despite having been active in the preparation of the treaty text, voted against its adoption, together with Israel, China, Iraq, Yemen, Libya, and Qatar. The primary sticking point for the United States was that the Court would be able to assume jurisdiction without the express permission of the Security Council.[58] The United States argued that the Security Council has prime responsibility for the maintenance of the peace and that an independent court might interfere with Security Council efforts to contain threats to the peace. The United States has also argued that the ICC is taking jurisdiction over nonstates parties in violation of article 34 of the Vienna Convention on the Law of Treaties, since the ICC has jurisdiction over a listed crime if it is committed on the territory of a state party to the statute even if the state of which the accused is a national is not a party.[59] Defenders of the Rome Statute respond by saying that when an alien commits a crime on the territory of another state, prosecution of that person is never dependent on the consent of the state of nationality.[60] Territorial jurisdiction over crimes is firmly established in international law.[61] The United States is party to a number of antiterrorism treaties that empower states parties to investigate and prosecute perpetrators of any nationality found within their territory. The United States expressed concern that the Rome Statute would allow politicized prosecutions of its peacekeepers and hence inhibit its involvement in multinational operations.[62]

Despite voting against adoption of the treaty text, the United States signed just before the December 31, 2000, deadline for doing so. President Bill Clinton was quoted as saying that "with signature, we will be in a position to influence the evolution of the court. Without signature, we will not."[63] Then, by letter to the UN Secretary-General of April 27, 2002, the U.S. undersecretary of state for arms control and international security, John Bolton, briefly stated the intention of the United States not to become a party to the treaty. "Accordingly, the

United States has no legal obligations arising from its signature on December 31, 2000. The United States requests that its intention not to become a party, as expressed in this letter, be reflected in the depositary's status lists relating to this treaty."[64]

General Assembly Resolution 53/105 of December 8, 1999, established the PrepCom tasked with finalizing the draft texts of the rules of procedure and evidence and of the elements of crimes.[65] The Rome Statute entered into force on July 1, 2002. Following entry into force of the statute, the United States came under criticism for its efforts to negotiate "impunity agreements" to prevent U.S. nationals accused of crimes within the jurisdiction of the ICC from being surrendered to the International Criminal Court.

The creation of the International Criminal Court has been one of the most significant developments not only in international humanitarian law but also in public international law as a whole for over fifty years.

Notes

1. Dieter Fleck, ed., *The Handbook of Humanitarian Law in Armed Conflicts* (Oxford: Oxford University Press, 1995), p. 9.

2. Adam Roberts and Richard Guelff, eds., *Documents on the Laws of War*, 2nd ed. (Oxford: Clarendon, 1989), p. 17.

3. See Ramesh Thakur and William Maley, "The Ottawa Convention on Landmines: A Landmark Humanitarian Treaty in Arms Control?" *Global Governance* 5 (1992): 273–302.

4. Chris af Jochnick and Roger Normand, "The Legitimation of Violence: A Critical History of the Laws of War," *Harvard International Law Journal* 35, no. 1 (Winter 1994): 49–95, 60.

5. Roberts and Guelff, *Documents on the Laws of War*, p. 29.

6. This is number six in the "Fundamental Rules of International Humanitarian Law Applicable in Armed Conflicts," reprinted in ibid., p. 470.

7. Ibid., p. 5.

8. "Declaration Renouncing the Use, in Time of War, of Explosive Projectiles Under 400 Grammes Weight," in ibid., pp. 30–31.

9. For texts and commentary on the conventions and declarations, see J. B. Scott, ed., *The Hague Conventions and Declarations of 1899 and 1907*, 3rd ed. (New York: Oxford University Press, 1918).

10. Fleck, *The Handbook of Humanitarian Law in Armed Conflicts*, pp. 24–25.

11. Roberts and Guelff, *Documents on the Laws of War*, p. 44.

12. 75 United Nations Treaty Series (UNTS) 31.

13. 75 UNTS 85.

14. 75 UNTS 135.

15. 75 UNTS 267.

16. Geneva Convention IV Concerning the Protection of Civilian Persons in Time of War, article 4.

17. Geneva Convention IV Concerning the Protection of Civilian Persons in Time of War, article 27.

18. Fleck, *The Handbook of Humanitarian Law in Armed Conflicts,* p. 24.

19. 1125 UNTS 3.

20. 1125 UNTS 609.

21. See Y. Sandoz, C. Swinarski, and B. Zimmermann, eds., *Commentary on the Additional Protocols of 8 June 1977 to the Geneva Conventions of 12 August 1949* (Geneva: ICRC and Martinus Nijhoff, 1987).

22. Protocol of 8 June 1977 Additional to the Geneva Conventions of 12 August 1949, and Concerning the Protection of Victims of International Armed Conflicts, article 57(3).

23. Christine Chinkin, "Women: The Forgotten Victims of Armed Conflict?" in Helen Durham and Timothy L. H. McCormack, eds., *The Changing Face of Conflict and the Efficacy of International Humanitarian Law* (The Hague: Martinus Nijhoff, 1999), pp. 23–44. See also J. G. Gardam, "Women and the Law of Armed Conflict: Why the Silence?" *International and Comparative Law Quarterly* 46 (1997): 55–80.

24. Roberts and Guelff, *Documents on the Laws of War*, p. 471.

25. For the negotiating history of the Protocol see D. Forsythe, "Legal Management of International War: The 1977 Protocol on Non-International Armed Conflicts," *American Journal of International Law* 72 (1978): 272–295.

26. 1342 UNTS 137.

27. The inadequacies of the protocol are canvassed in Yvette Politis, "The Regulation of an Invisible Enemy: The International Community's Response to Land Mine Proliferation," *Boston College International & Comparative Law Review* 22, no. 2 (1999): 465–493, 472–475.

28. 36 ILM 1509 (1997).

29. See Shawn Roberts, "No Exceptions, No Reservations, No Loopholes: The Campaign for the 1997 Convention on the Prohibition of the Development, Production, Stockpiling, Transfer, and Use of Anti-Personnel Mines and on Their Destruction," *Colorado Journal of International Environmental Law and Policy* 9, no. 2 (Summer 1998): 371–391. See also Stephen Biddle, J. Klare, J. Wallis, and I. Oelrich, "Controlling Anti-personnel Landmines," *Contemporary Security Policy* 19, no. 3 (December 1998): 27–71.

30. "Mine Ban Treaty Transparency Reporting," *Landmine Monitor*, at www.icbl.org/lm/factsheets/transprep2000.php3.

31. The website for the Landmine Monitor can be found at www. icbl.org/lm.

32. "Major Findings of the *Landmine Monitor Report 2002: Towards a Mine-Free World*," at www.icbl.org/lm/2002/findings.html.

33. Christian M. Capece, "The Ottawa Treaty and Its Impact on US Military Policy and Planning," *Brooklyn Journal of International Law* 25, no. 1 (1999): 183–204, 183–184. See also Lynn Sellers Bickley, "U.S. Resistance to the International Criminal Court: Is the Sword Mightier Than the Law?" *Emory*

International Law Review 14 (2000): 213–276; Jodi Preusser Mustoe, "The 1997 Treaty to Ban the Use of Landmines: Was President Clinton's Refusal to Become a Signatory Warranted?" *Georgia Journal of International and Comparative Law* 27, no. 3 (1999): 541–569.

34. See Christopher Keith Hall, "The First Proposal for a Permanent International Criminal Court," *International Review of the Red Cross* 322 (March 1998): 57–74.

35. See Mark J. Osiel, "Why Prosecute? Critics of Punishment for Mass Atrocity," *Human Rights Quarterly* 22, no. 1 (2000): 118–147.

36. Howard Ball, *Prosecuting War Crimes and Genocide: The Twentieth Century Experience* (Lawrence: University Press of Kansas, 1999), p. 225.

37. Benjamin B. Ferencz, "An International Criminal Code and Court: Where They Stand and Where They're Going," *Columbia Journal of Transnational Law* 30 (1992): 375–399, 382.

38. Ball, *Prosecuting War Crimes and Genocide*, p. 24. See also James F. Willis, *Prologue to Nuremberg: The Politics and Diplomacy of Punishing War Criminals of the First World War* (Westport, CT: Greenwood, 1982).

39. Michael P. Scharf, "The Jury Is Still Out on the Need for an International Criminal Court," *Duke Journal of Comparative and International Law* 1 (1991): 135–168, 137.

40. See Arnold C. Brackman, *The Other Nuremberg* (New York: Morrow, 1987); Robert E. Conot, *Justice at Nuremberg* (New York: Harper & Row, 1983); and Richard H. Minear, *Victor's Justice: The Tokyo War Crimes Trial* (Princeton, NJ: Princeton University Press, 1971).

41. General Assembly Resolution 95(I), UN Doc. A/236 (1946).

42. The vote was 8-1 with two abstentions. The 43rd Meeting of the International Law Commission, Friday, June 9, 1950, *Yearbook of the International Law Commission, 1950*, vol. 1, p. 23.

43. Robert Rosenstock, "Symposium: Should There Be an International Tribunal for Crimes Against Humanity?" *Pace International Law Review* 6 (1984): 84. See also Ferencz, "An International Criminal Code and Court," 383–384.

44. S/RES/827 (1993), May 25, 1993.

45. Statute of the International Tribunal, adopted May 25, 1993, at www.un.org/icty/basic/statut/statute.htm.

46. S/RES/955 (1994), November 8, 1994.

47 James R. McHenry III, "The Prosecution of Rape Under International Law: Justice That Is Long Overdue," *Vanderbilt Journal of Transnational Law* 35, no. 4 (October 2002): 1269–1312.

48. "Human Rights Watch Applauds Rwanda Rape Verdict," Press Release, September 1998, at www.hrw.org/press98/sept/rrape902.htm, accessed August 16, 2002.

49. McHenry, "The Prosecution of Rape."

50. The website of the tribunal is www.ictr.org.

51. Fanny Benedetti and John L. Washburn, "Drafting the International Criminal Court Treaty: Two Years to Rome and an Afterword on the Rome Diplomatic Conference," *Global Governance* 5, no. 1 (January–March 1999): 1–37.

52. 37 ILM 999 (1998). See, inter alia, M. Cherif Bassiouni, *The Statute of the International Criminal Court* (Ardsley, NY: Transnational, 2002); Yves Beigbeder, *Judging War Criminals* (New York: St. Martin's, 1999); and Leila Nadya Sadat, *The International Criminal Court and the transformation of international law* (Ardsley, NY: Transnational, 2002).

53. Cited in Philippe Kirsch and John T. Holmes, "The Rome Conference on an International Criminal Court: The Negotiating Process," *American Journal of International Law (AJIL)* 93, no. 2 (1999): 2–12, 4–5.

54. See John T. Holmes, "The Principle of Complementarity," in Roy S. Lee, ed., *The International Criminal Court: The Making of the Rome Statute* (1999), p. 41; and Sharon A. Williams, "Article 17 Issues of Admissibility," in Otto Trifftterer, ed., *Commentary on the Rome Statute of the International Criminal Court: Observers' Notes, Article by Article* (Baden-Baden: Nomos Verlagsgesellschaft, 1999), pp. 383–394.

55. The Rome Statute of the International Criminal Court, articles 5–8.

56. Andreas Zimmermann, "Article 5 Crimes Within the Jurisdiction of the Court," in Trifftterer, *Commentary on the Rome Statute of the International Criminal Court*, pp. 97–106, 99.

57. Ibid.

58. For a succinct explanation as to why the United States voted "no," see Michael P. Scharf, "Results of the Rome Conference for an International Criminal Court," *ASIL Insight*, at www.asil.org/insigh23.htm. See also Marcella David, "Grotius Repudiated: The American Objections to the International Criminal Court and the Commitment to International Law," *Michigan Journal of International Law* 20 (1999): 337–412; David J. Scheffer, "The United States and the International Criminal Court," *AJIL* 93 (1999): 12–22; and Sarah B. Sewall and Carl Kaysen, eds., *The United States and the International Criminal Court: National Security and International Law* (Lanham, MD: Rowman & Littlefield, 2000).

59. Sharon A. Williams, "Article 12 Preconditions to the Exercise of Jurisdiction," in Trifftterer, *Commentary on the Rome Statute of the International Criminal Court*, pp. 329–342, 340.

60. Ibid., p. 340.

61. Although this is not to the exclusion of the active and passive personality principles. Antonio Cassese, "The Statute of the International Criminal Court: Some Preliminary Reflections," *European Journal of International Law (EJIL)* 10 (1999): 144–171, 160.

62. For analysis of this objection see Marten Zwanenburg, "The Statute for an International Criminal Court and the United States: Peacekeepers Under Fire?" *EJIL* 10 (1999): 124–143.

63. "U.S. President 'Makes History' in Last-minute Assent to War Crimes Court," *Sydney Morning Herald,* January 2, 2001, p. 9.

64. 41 ILM 1014 (2002). For discussion, see Curtis A. Bradley, "US Announces Intent Not to Ratify International Criminal Court Treaty," *ASIL Insight*, May 2002, available at www.asil.org/insights.htm.

65. A/RES/53/105, January 26, 1999.

12

International Law
and the Environment

As with international human rights law, international environmental law is primarily a product of the post–World War II years. Two of the legal documents vitally important to the evolution of international environmental law are not treaties but declarations: nonbinding statements of agreed principles and intent. These are the Stockholm Declaration of 1972,[1] which was one of three nonbinding instruments adopted by the first Conference on the Human Environment held in Stockholm, Sweden;[2] and the Rio Declaration on Environment and Development.[3] Principle 21 of the Stockholm Declaration has become a principle of customary international law. It states:

> States have, in accordance with the Charter of the United Nations and the principles of international law, the sovereign right to exploit their own resources pursuant to their own environmental policies, and the responsibility to ensure that activities within their jurisdiction or control do not cause damage to the environment of other States or of areas beyond the limits of national jurisdiction.

The 1992 Rio Conference produced a suite of documents, including the 800-page Agenda 21, intended to provide a global framework for environmental and developmental policies, and the Rio Declaration on Environment and Development — a counterpart to the Stockholm Declaration on the Human Environment. The Rio Declaration is a statement of twenty-seven key environmental principles, Principle 7 being the *principle of common but differentiated responsibility to the environment.* Building on the concept of the "common heritage of mankind," this principle specifies that, even though all countries are responsible for global environmental problems, some countries are more responsible than others:[4]

> States shall cooperate in a spirit of global partnership to conserve, protect and restore the health and integrity of the Earth's ecosystem. In view of the different contributions to global environmental degradation, States have common but differentiated responsibilities. The developed countries acknowledge the responsibility that they bear in the international pursuit of sustainable development in view of the pressures their societies place on the global environment and of the technologies and financial resources they command.

As the examples of regime development in this chapter will show, North-South issues have been central to the development of international environmental law.[5]

Principle 15 of the Rio Declaration expresses a widely accepted definition of the *precautionary principle*, the essence of which is the idea of taking action to address an environmental threat ahead of a disaster:[6]

> In order to protect the environment, the precautionary approach shall be widely applied by States according to their capabilities. Where there are threats of serious or irreversible damage, lack of full scientific certainty shall not be used as a reason for postponing cost-effective measures to prevent environmental degradation.

Figure 12.1   Some Key Global Treaties Establishing Environmental Treaty Regimes

1972 Convention for the Protection of the World Cultural and Natural Heritage
1973 Convention on International Trade in Endangered Species of Wild Fauna and Flora
1979 Convention on the Conservation of Migratory Species of Wild Animals
1979 Convention on Long Range Transboundary Air Pollution
1982 Third United Nations Convention on the Law of the Sea, Part XII
1985 Convention for the Protection of the Ozone Layer
1986 Convention on Early Notification of a Nuclear Accident
1989 Convention on the Control of Transboundary Movements of Hazardous Wastes and Their Disposal
1992 Framework Convention on Climate Change
1992 Convention on the Protection and Use of Transboundary Watercourses and Lakes
1992 Convention on Biological Diversity
2001 Stockholm Convention on Persistent Organic Pollutants

Principle 4 of the Rio Declaration endorses the concept of *sustainable development*, which had been enunciated by the 1987 Brundtland Report, *Our Common Future*: "In order to achieve sustainable development, environmental protection shall constitute an integral part of the development process and cannot be considered in isolation from it." In accordance with chapter 38 of Agenda 21, the Commission on Sustainable Development was created in December 1992 as a functional commission of the UN Economic and Social Council, not as a forum for the negotiation of multilateral environmental agreements[7] but to monitor and report on implementation of the 1992 Rio agreements.[8]

Thirty years after Stockholm, and ten years after the Rio Earth Summit, the World Summit on Sustainable Development was held in Johannesburg to review progress since Rio. In addition to the 10,000 delegates, some 8,000 representatives of major organizations (representing women, children and youth, indigenous people, NGOs, local authorities, workers and trade unions, business and industry, scientific and technological communities, and farmers) were accredited to the summit; the Civil Society Global Forum ran parallel to the summit. The summit produced the Johannesburg Declaration on Sustainable Development, by which the "representatives of the peoples of the world" reaffirmed the commitment to sustainable development, as well as the more detailed Johannesburg Plan of Implementation, which set out a number of specific targets by which to make sustainable development a reality. Under "poverty eradication," for example, governments agreed to halve, by 2015, the proportion of the world's people whose income is less than $1 a day and the proportion of people who suffer from hunger; and, by the same date, to halve the proportion of people without access to safe drinking water.[9] These agreements were complemented by the commitment by governments and other stakeholders to a broad range of partnership activities and initiatives to implement sustainable development at the national, regional, and international levels; businesses became involved in more than ninety partnership initiatives launched at the summit in a range of sectors, including energy, water, agriculture, and biodiversity.[10]

Although there had been some international agreements relating to the environment prior to Stockholm, they were comparatively few. Stockholm was the springboard for the development of international environmental law. By the time of the United Nations Conference on Environment and Development in June 1992, there were more than 870 legal instruments in which at least some provisions are concerned with environmental issues.[11] (See Figure 12.1.) It was partly in reaction to the years of negotiating the detailed and comprehensive Law of the Sea Convention that was ultimately rejected by the United States, and partly due to the difficulties of getting far-reaching commitments to environmental action, that the standard in environmental negotiations has become that of negotiating a framework convention followed by one or more protocols.[12] The Framework Convention on Climate Change was followed by the Kyoto Protocol; the Vienna Convention for the Protection of the Ozone Layer was followed by the Montreal Protocol; and so on. Most of the environmental treaty regimes have established at least two institutions: a Conference of the Parties (COP) and a secretariat, though the precise role played by each varies between regimes.

The Ozone Depletion Regime

This treaty regime was founded on the Vienna Convention for the Protection of the Ozone Layer[13] and the Montreal Protocol on Substances That Deplete the Ozone Layer.[14] The ozone depletion regime has been described as "the most successful example of international environmental cooperation to date"[15] and "a milestone in the field of international co-operation."[16] Aspects of the regime—including its application of the precautionary approach, financial mechanisms, and institutional arrangements—have influenced other regimes. The stratospheric ozone layer first became a subject of concern in 1970 when it was feared that supersonic transportation may cause it damage. Concern reappeared in 1974 when two scientists suggested that the chlorine in CFCs could destroy ozone molecules and deplete the ozone layer.[17] CFCs were invented in 1928 by DuPont and General Motors chemists who were seeking a nontoxic heat transfer fluid for refrigeration. CFCs came to be widely used not only in refrigeration and air conditioning but also as blowing foams, solvents, sterilants, freezing agents, surface treatment agents, and propellants for aerosol spray cans. Ozone destruction permits increased levels of UV-B radiation to reach the Earth's surface, causing increases in skin cancers and other damaging health and environmental effects. The strength of the scientific evidence against CFCs was a factor that contributed to the success of the treaty-making efforts.[18]

In response to the scientific findings the United States and several other countries, including Canada and Sweden, took unilateral action in the 1970s to control aerosol emissions of CFCs. Several international organizations also became involved in the CFC/ozone issue, including the World Meteorological Organization and the Organization for

Economic Cooperation and Development. And in response to growing concern the United Nations Environment Programme established in 1981 an ad hoc working group of legal and technical experts, charged with the task of drafting the Global Framework Convention for the Protection of the Ozone Layer. By article 2 of the 1985 Vienna Convention, the parties agreed to "take appropriate measures in accordance with the provisions of this Convention and of those protocols in force to which they are party to protect human health and the environment against adverse effects resulting or likely to result from human activities which modify or are likely to modify the ozone layer." No specific controls on production and use could be agreed at Vienna, but the convention legitimized stratospheric ozone depletion as an international environmental issue and provided a framework—including an agreement to cooperate in scientific research and to exchange information—within which further negotiation could take place.[19]

Scientific understanding of stratospheric ozone continued to evolve, and by 1987 there was much stronger evidence of the ozone-depleting role of CFCs and other ozone-depleting substances (ODS) and hence greater public concern and international consensus on the need to take decisive action. Although the two largest manufacturers of CFCs were initially opposed to international restrictions on CFCs, Imperial Chemical Industries (ICI) and DuPont came to favor controls once they saw the opportunity for increased profits through the marketing of new, more profitable substitutes.[20] The Montreal Protocol, adopted and opened for signature on September 16, 1987, provided for the production and consumption of the controlled chemicals to be limited to 80 percent of 1986 levels by July 1, 1993, and to 50 percent of 1986 levels by July 1, 1998.[21] Scientific findings released soon after Montreal indicated not only that these reductions would be inadequate to eliminate the existing hole in the ozone layer but also that they would not even reduce ozone depletion.[22] Both the convention and the protocol provide that there shall be regular meetings of the parties to the respective instruments,[23] and at the 1990 London meeting[24] the parties amended the protocol to strengthen existing measures for the control of substances covered by the original protocol and agreed on controls for additional substances.[25]

Ozone depletion had initially been an issue of concern to certain developed countries that manufactured and used CFCs. But by the time of London, developed countries realized that their efforts would be to no avail if the large, highly populated, developing countries were not actively involved in the treaty regime. The realization that any regime relating to protection of the ozone layer must include highly populated states, whether or not they were significant consumers or producers of ozone-depleting substances, was particularly important "because it marked one of the few times that the industrialized world needed the cooperation and participation of the Third World."[26] It was not clear at this stage whether some of the largest developing countries would come on board. India and China argued strongly that it was unfair for industrialized countries to expect developing countries to forego CFC-containing technologies or to pay more for substitutes and thereby enrich the chemical industries that had created the problem in the first place.[27] Developing countries wanted to retain access to CFCs or to get assistance to acquire substitutes.

Article 5(1) of the Montreal Protocol allows developing countries to delay for ten years their compliance with the control measures, as well as to exceed the target percentage reductions at any point if such action is deemed necessary in order to satisfy basic domestic needs. Concerned at the precedent it would set, the United States and other industrialized states were at first strongly opposed to establishing a fund to assist the developing countries in their transitions from CFC technologies.[28] But after intense bargaining at the London conference, key developing states became parties to the protocol; in return developed states agreed to provide financial incentives and technical cooperation through a multilateral fund. This was the first time that the national governments of developed countries voted to provide developing countries with financial assistance for reaching environmental goals.[29] The Interim Multilateral Fund was established in London, and in December 1992 it became permanent. The Multilateral Fund pays the agreed incremental costs incurred by developing countries in phasing out their consumption and production of ozone-depleting substances.[30] Azerbaijan, the Czech Republic, Hungary, the Russian Federation, and other Central and East European states with "economies in transition" are not eligible for assistance from the Multilateral Fund but have received assistance from the Global Environmental Facility, an institution established to provide funding to help developing countries meet the costs associated with implementing Agenda 21.[31]

Parties to the protocol are required to "take every practicable step, consistent with the programmes supported by the financial mechanism, to ensure . . . that the best available, environmentally safe substitutes and related technologies" are expeditiously transferred to certain developing countries. Important to the success of the London conference was the work of NGOs, which sought to influence national policy in countries with responsive political systems and participated at the meeting itself.[32] The protocol has been further adjusted and amended at several meetings of the parties since London. Details of adjustments, amendments, and other decisions of the parties to the Montreal Protocol and the Vienna Convention can be found in the *Handbook for the International Treaties for the Protection of the Ozone Layer*, available over the Internet from the UNEP Ozone Secretariat.[33]

The Climate Change Regime

The phrase "greenhouse effect" refers to the gradual warming of the Earth's atmosphere.[34] Carbon dioxide, water vapor, methane, and nitrous oxide act as a blanket around the Earth; their increased emission and the steady reduction in the number of trees to absorb carbon dioxide means that heat has been increasingly less able to escape the atmosphere, thereby raising the Earth's temperature. Scientists believe that even a warming of two degrees could have dramatic effects on the Earth's climate, affecting rainfall, wind, cloud cover, ocean currents, sea levels, growing seasons, and polar ice caps. Although there might be an occasional positive effect from such change, the overall impact is negative. The solution to the greenhouse effect appears clear, although it is not easy to achieve: "(1) stop the burning of fossil fuels, (2) stop the destruction of the world's rain forests, and (3) replant those areas that have already been destroyed."[35]

The success of the Montreal Protocol encouraged international negotiations on the larger concern of global climate change.[36] The climate change regime was one of the most quickly established of all international regimes. In December 1988 the UN General Assembly passed a resolution calling for the adoption of a framework convention on climate change.[37] The World Meteorological Organization and the United Nations Environment Programme then established the Intergovernmental Panel on Climate Change (IPCC) in 1988 to assess the scientific basis and impact of climate change and to make recommendations. Its first scientific report was published in 1990. In the same year the General Assembly established the Intergovernmental Negotiating Committee to draft a framework treaty. The United Nations Framework Convention on Climate Change[38] was opened for signature at the UN Conference on Environment and Development and entered into force on March 21, 1994.[39]

The Climate Change Convention incorporated the principle of common but differentiated responsibility: although all parties share certain common responsibilities in the context of global warming, developed countries have a particular onus to act. Articles 4(2)(a) and 4(2)(b) oblige developed states (annex 1 countries) to adopt national policies that "will demonstrate that developed countries are taking the lead in modifying longer-term trends in anthropogenic emissions consistent with the objective of the convention," and to provide detailed reports on such policies "with the aim of returning individually or jointly to their 1990 levels . . . of carbon dioxide and other greenhouse gases not controlled by the Montreal Protocol." The Alliance of Small Island States, Australia, Canada, and New Zealand supported the inclusion of time-tabled emission reductions in the treaty text, but the United States and some oil-producing countries argued that any introduction of specific emission reductions would be premature.[40] The convention left the negotiation of the limits on emission standards and implementation procedure to the Conference of the Parties. The convention included a financial mechanism as well as an implementation and dispute settlement mechanism.

By the mid-1990s it was becoming clear that developed countries, in particular the United States, would not meet their emission reduction targets of 1990 levels by the year 2000;[41] scientific opinion also indicated that earlier agreed targets would not be enough to significantly reduce climate change. Business NGOs became more active in the regime and were quite influential, particularly in the United States, in discouraging any move on the part of governments toward controlled emission standards.[42] No protocol was negotiated at the First Conference of the Parties at Berlin in 1995, but the parties did adopt the so-called Berlin Mandate, a decision that they would adopt a protocol or another legal instrument to strengthen the commitments of the annex 1 parties.[43]

In the lead-up to the Third Conference of the Parties, the United States, with 4 percent of the world's population, more than 20 percent of the world's wealth, and producing more than 20 percent of greenhouse emissions,[44] made it known that it expected the developing nations, as well as the industrialized nations, to participate in setting "realistic and binding goals." The European Union took a strong line, proposing uniform binding targets of a 15 percent reduction in greenhouse gas emissions by 2010 (based on 1990 levels). The European Union planned to meet its proposed target of a net 10 percent decrease by averaging emission levels across the whole EU "bubble." Thus Greece, Ireland, Portugal, Spain, and Sweden were to be permitted to increase their emission levels, but this would be countered by the closing of East Germany's outdated heavy industry and Britain's change from coal-fired to natural gas power stations. The Group of 77 accepted the European target as appropriate for the industrialized nations, but the developing countries made it quite clear that they would not commit themselves to reduce their own emissions of greenhouse gases.

The Kyoto Protocol to the United Nations Framework Convention on Climate Change[45] was adopted by the Third Conference of the Parties on December 11, 1997. The individual emission targets of states were tailored in a way to meet a global outcome of a 5.2 percent reduction below 1990 levels in greenhouse gases by 2008–2012. Three non-EU annex 1 (developed) countries were to be allowed emissions growth above their 1990 levels: Australia (+8 percent), Iceland (+10 percent), and Norway (+1 percent), and the EU received a collective emissions target of –8 percent, the United States –7 percent, and Japan –6 percent. In addition to individual emission targets, the protocol also allowed for other mechanisms to help reduce emissions, including the clean development mechanism (CDM), joint implementation, and emissions trading. These were designed to help annex 1 countries achieve their reductions more cheaply than they could at home by doing so in other countries. Emissions trading, for example, would allow companies to be able to sell excess permits on the open market, where they could be bought by companies that failed to meet emission targets. The Kyoto Protocol also included stronger reporting obligations and a system to address noncompliance.[46]

The Kyoto Protocol was to enter into force "on the ninetieth day after the date on which not less than 55 Parties to the Convention, incorporating Parties included in Annex I which accounted in total for at least 55 per cent of the total carbon dioxide emissions for 1990 of the Parties included in Annex I, have deposited their instruments of ratification, acceptance, approval or accession."[47] U.S. president Bill Clinton signed the protocol but said that he would not submit it to the Senate for ratification unless several changes were made. The administration of President George W. Bush reaffirmed U.S. opposition to the protocol, insisting that developing countries make "meaningful" contributions to future reductions in greenhouse gas emissions. To critics, this position appears to reject the principle of common but differentiated responsibility.[48] EU members ratified the Kyoto Protocol in June 2002.[49]

The Basel Regime

One reason sometimes given for the success of the ozone depletion regime was that the United States campaigned so strongly for it, having already introduced its own domestic legislation, which could then be used as a blueprint for an international agreement. The Basel regime provides an interesting contrast to the ozone depletion regime in this respect, because the major impetus for its creation was concern on the part of the developing world and environmental NGOs.

The Basel Convention on the Control of Transboundary Movements of Hazardous Wastes and Their Disposal[50] was concluded in 1989 and entered into force in 1992. It was the first global attempt to deal with the problem of toxic trade and was negotiated under the auspices of the United Nations Environment Programme. Between the 1940s and the 1980s there was an enormous increase in the volume of hazardous waste generated annually worldwide, particularly by the United States and Western Europe. And because more stringent environmental regulations increased costs of local disposal, producers increasingly looked elsewhere to dispose of waste. Some was exported to other industrialized countries but was sent increasingly to the developing world. Africa was particularly targeted in the mid-1980s, as was the South Pacific, the Caribbean, and Latin America. As opposition to the trade in these countries increased by the early 1990s, Asia and Eastern and Central Europe were increasingly targeted.[51] Although the receipt of considerable foreign exchange was an obvious attraction, the trade caused many problems. The developing countries often had inadequate or no means by which to safeguard the dump. Waste could easily cause considerable environmental damage and endanger health. This was particularly so if the waste was mislabeled and the recipient misinformed or deceived regarding the product. For example, the European Community sent radioactive milk to Jamaica in 1987, and a U.S. company sold fertilizer mixed with copper smelter dust containing high levels of lead to Bangladeshi farmers.[52]

In the early 1980s UNEP began drafting guidelines on the waste trade. The work was completed in 1985, and the Cairo Guidelines were adopted by the UNEP Governing Council in 1987[53] and endorsed by the General Assembly in December 1987. In 1987 UNEP began work on what became the Basel Convention. The text was negotiated during five working sessions between late 1987 and early 1989 by an ad hoc working group of legal and technical experts, with the mandate to prepare a global convention on the control of transboundary movements of hazardous wastes. Informal negotiations conducted by the executive director with governments, IGOs, NGOs, and industry also played an important part in the success of the preparatory process.[54] The three main types of actors involved in the negotiations were developed countries, developing countries, and a grouping of environmental NGOs, the International Toxic Waste Action Network. Developing countries were opposed to the trade, which they regarded as environmentally damaging and in the longer term damaging to their economies.

The Basel Convention does not ban all transboundary movement of hazardous waste, but it does impose controls and limitations on the trade. A party is not to permit hazardous or other wastes to be exported to, or imported from, a nonparty and, by article 4, may elect to prohibit the import of hazardous wastes for disposal; other parties are then to prohibit the export of wastes to that party. If a party has not prohibited the import of wastes, its written consent to a specific import must be obtained. By article 9, parties are to ensure that the transboundary movement of hazardous wastes and other wastes only be allowed if: (1) the state of export does not have the technical capacity and the necessary facilities, capacity, or suitable disposal sites in order to dispose of the wastes in an environmentally sound and efficient manner; (2) the wastes are required as a raw material for recycling or recovery industries in the state of import; or (3) the transboundary movement in question is in accordance with other criteria to be decided by the parties.

In the belief that the Basel Convention had not gone far enough, the Organization of African Unity provided in the 1991 Bamako Convention that "all Parties shall take appropriate legal, administrative and other measures within the area under their jurisdiction to prohibit the import of all hazardous wastes, for any reason, into Africa from non-Contracting Parties. Such import shall be deemed illegal and a criminal act."[55]

In December 1992 Costa Rica, Honduras, El Salvador, Guatemala, and Nicaragua signed a regional agreement requiring parties to prohibit the import and transit of hazardous wastes to Central America.[56] Individual countries, including Poland, the Ukraine, and the Philippines, have imposed national bans on hazardous waste imports.[57]

In September 1995 the Basel Convention was amended to ban hazardous waste exports for final disposal and recycling from what are known as annex VII countries (members of the Organization for Economic Cooperation and Development, the EU, and Liechtenstein) to non–annex VII countries. This was a major breakthrough for environmentalists but has to be ratified by sixty-two of the parties present at its adoption in order to enter into force. In December 1999 parties adopted the Basel Protocol on Liability and Compensation for Damage Resulting from Transboundary Movements of Hazardous Waste and Their Disposal.

Convention on Biological Diversity, 1992

The Convention on Biological Diversity,[58] the first global agreement specifically devoted to the conservation and sustainable use of biological diversity, was negotiated between 1987 and 1992 under the auspices of the United Nations Environment Programme. The convention was adopted on May 22, 1992, in Nairobi and opened for signature at UNCED. *Biodiversity* means the variability within and among living organisms and the systems they inhabit. Biodiversity supports the ecosystem functions essential for life on Earth, such as the provision of fresh water, soil conservation, and climate stability, as well as providing products such as food, medicines, and materials for industry. The rate of biodiversity loss has been increasing at an unprecedented rate. The Convention on Biological Diversity does not focus on saving specific species facing extinction but takes a holistic approach to maintaining genetic diversity. *Diversity* is understood to include diversity within species, among species, and of ecosystems. The convention incorporates the precautionary principle in that it is a step toward lessening harmful impacts of human activity despite the fact that scientists recognize that they do not yet know all the scientific implications of reduced diversity or the extent to which diversity has already been reduced, particularly in the oceans.

As a framework convention it does not go far in setting out substantive rules. Primary responsibility remains at the national level; each state party is "in accordance with its particular conditions and capabilities" to "develop national strategies, plans or programmes for the conservation and sustainable use of biological diversity" and to "integrate, as far as possible and as appropriate, the conservation and sustainable use of biological diversity into relevant sectoral or cross-sectoral plans, programmes and policies" (article 6). Areas beyond national jurisdiction are to be addressed, as appropriate, either by states acting individually or through "competent international organizations." The Convention on Biological Diversity entered into force in late 1993. The Conference of the Parties to the Convention on Biological Diversity adopted the Cartagena Protocol on Biosafety on January 29, 2000.[59] The protocol provides an international regulatory framework for the safe transfer, handling, and use of any living modified organisms resulting from modern biotechnology.

Stockholm Convention on
Persistent Organic Pollutants (POPs), 2001

The Stockholm Convention on Persistent Organic Pollutants,[60] which came about as a result of the 1992 Earth Summit, is designed to eliminate or severely restrict the production and use of certain toxic pesticides and industrial chemicals such as aldrin, chlordane, DDT, dieldrin, endrin, and dioxins. Such chemicals are termed "persistent" because they do not break down in the environment; they accumulate in the body fat of people and animals and can travel great distances on wind and water currents. The treaty reflected a precautionary approach to these chemicals. It is believed that many people around the world may now carry enough persistent organic pollutants (POPs) in their body fat to cause serious health problems, including reproductive and developmental problems, cancer, and immune system disruption, although the exact nature and extent of toxic chemical threats remains unknown. Article 1 states:

> Mindful of the precautionary approach as set forth in Principle 15 of the Rio Declaration on Environment and Development, the objective of this Convention is to protect human health and the environment from persistent organic pollutants.

Chemicals are listed in annexes to the convention. Some are to be immediately banned, the use of others to be significantly curtailed. Developed countries commit to providing additional financing to assist in the implementation of the convention by developing countries. The treaty text was finalized by consensus in December 2000 and opened for signature on May 22, 2001. It establishes a scientific POPs review committee to evaluate additional chemicals.

As with other environmental treaties, a network of NGOs played an active role in the negotiations. In early 1998 a small group of NGOs formed the International POPs Elimination Network.[61] The network grew to include more than 300 NGOs and coordinated NGO conferences and workshops at the five negotiating sessions: Montreal (June 1998), Nairobi (January 1999), Geneva (September 1999), Bonn (March 2000), and Johannesburg (December 2000). The treaty requires at least fifty ratifications in order to enter into force.

The Law of the Sea and Protection of the Marine Environment

In Chapters 9–12 we have considered separately some of the key treaties in several fields of international law. In practice, however, legal instruments rarely function as discrete entities but as part of a network of interrelated treaties. To get some sense of that, we will survey a group of treaties that bear on the subject of the marine environment. The 1982 Law of the Sea Convention is the starting point for considering any aspect of existing oceans law. Although comprehensive in the sense of dealing with all areas of marine protection, the 1982 convention is supplemented by many other more detailed agreements, some of which predated it and some of which are more recent than the convention. We begin by looking briefly at the background to the 1982 convention before moving on to the treaty itself and then to other treaties that address the protection of the marine environment.

The 1930, 1958, and 1960 Conferences on the Law of the Sea

The law of the sea was unsettled between the end of the fifteenth century and the beginning of the nineteenth. There were two contending schools of thought. The first, Mare Clausum (Closed Sea), held that the sea and its resources are capable of being subject to appropriation and dominion. The second school of thought, expounded by Hugo Grotius, argued that things that cannot be seized or enclosed cannot become property. It was the Grotian view, by which no one can claim exclusive rights over fisheries or navigation on the high seas, that came gradually to predominate in the eighteenth century.[62] By the beginning of the nineteenth century Britain was the champion of the idea of the "freedom of the seas," subject only to a coastal state's right to claim a narrow belt of the sea offshore its coast for the purpose of fishing and protecting its neutrality.[63] Foreign vessels retained a right of "innocent passage" through those waters. The only accepted extensions of these rights were some claims to exclusive fishing rights beyond territorial waters, made on the basis of long uninterrupted usage. The principle of freedom of the seas was clearly in the interests of a major trading and colonial power.

By 1930 the international law of the sea was nearing the end of two centuries of relative stability. The Hague Codification Conference in 1930, which followed years of work by a committee of experts, sought to clarify a standard width for territorial waters, but its participants were unable to agree on the exact extent of the territorial sea. The fact that only ten of the participating states accepted the three-mile limit, favored by Britain, was evidence of the challenge to its supremacy. The "traditional" law of the sea had developed primarily in response to issues of transport, communications, and fisheries. Following World War II, these issues were transformed; new fishing methods increased markedly the total volume of fishing, necessitating new conservation measures. It also became technically possible and economically feasible to exploit other resources of the sea and to use the oceans for military deployment and the dumping of waste materials, also raising a number of new management issues. One of the first postwar changes to the traditional law of the sea was the emergence of the continental shelf doctrine. The *continental shelf* was a term used by geologists and geographers to refer to the area of comparatively shallow water bordering a continent and separating it from the deep drop to the ocean floor. The depth and width of the shelf and its surface range considerably. In the first of two "Truman Proclamations" in September 1945, President Harry Truman asserted sovereign rights of jurisdiction and control over the natural resources of the subsoil and seabed of its continental shelf.[64] Although the wording of the proclamation included all "natural resources," there is little doubt that the motivation for Truman's action was the emerging offshore oil industry.[65] The declaration was to in no way affect the legal status of the high seas above the continental shelf. In the second proclamation, Truman provided for the establishment of conservation zones for the protection of fisheries in "certain areas of the high seas contiguous to the United States." In those areas fished by nationals of other countries as well as the United States, zones were to be established by agreement, and joint regulations and controls put into effect.

Although it was the relative shallowness of the water over the continental shelf that facilitated the exploitation of oil reserves and prompted the Truman Proclamations, the geographical phenomenon of a shelf became the convenient basis for a general extension of coastal state's rights beyond the territorial limit. More than twenty nations followed suit during the next eight years, many of which had no immediate interest in mining developments, and some of which did not even have a continental shelf in the geological sense.[66] The precise nature of the claims varied according to motivations, from mere jurisdiction over resources of the seabed, to actual ownership of the bed and the seas above the shelf. The first country to claim a 200-mile zone was Chile, which on June 23, 1947, proclaimed national sovereignty over the continental shelf off its coasts and islands and over the seas above the shelf to a distance of 200 miles.[67] The Chilean proclamation was motivated primarily by the perceived needs of its new offshore whaling operations. Peru promulgated its declaration of a 200-mile zone on August 1, 1947, in an effort to protect its fisheries; a number of other declarations followed. The Truman Proclamation, claiming to be based solely on that which was "reasonable and just," met little opposition,[68] but the more extensive claims of the South American states prompted international protest.

Preparatory work for the 1958 Law of the Sea Conference had been undertaken by the International Law Commission, which had prepared seventy-three draft articles that the conference transformed into four treaties: the Convention on the High Seas, the Convention on Fishing and Conservation of the Living Resources of the High Seas, the Convention on the Territorial Sea, and the Convention on the Continental Shelf. Neither the 1958 conference nor the Second Conference on the Law of the Sea held two years later was able to agree on the limits of the territorial sea or on the coastal states' exclusive fishing rights.

With the decolonization process of the 1960s and 1970s, many newly independent states became dissatisfied with the existing law of the sea, which they believed to be the product of European experience.[69] On November 1, 1967, Arvid Pardo, the Maltese ambassador to the United Nations, made a landmark speech to the First Committee of the UN General Assembly. Ambassador Pardo drew attention to the immense resources of the seabed and ocean floor beyond the limits of national jurisdiction and proposed that the seabed and ocean floor be used exclusively for peaceful purposes and that the area and its resources be considered the "common heritage of mankind." He suggested that a constitution or charter be adopted dealing with ocean space as an organic and ecological whole.[70] The United Nations responded by establishing the Seabed Committee to develop a legal regime for the exploration and exploitation of the resources of the ocean floor area.

The 1982 Law of the Sea Convention

The Third UN Law of the Sea Conference was a vast diplomatic and legal undertaking. By the time negotiations began in December 1973, only twenty-seven out of 111 coastal states still claimed a three-mile territorial sea; fifty-two claimed a territorial sea of twelve miles. The Third United Nations Convention of the Law of the Sea (UNCLOS III)[71] established the right of every state to a twelve-mile territorial sea and also included the right of ships of all states to innocent passage through the territorial sea. UNCLOS III established that, adjacent to the territorial sea there be an exclusive economic zone (EEZ) of not more than 200 nautical miles from the baselines from which the breadth of the territorial sea is measured. All states retained high seas freedom of navigation within the EEZ while coastal states acquired jurisdiction over vessels only to apply international rules for enforcement purposes. The coastal state has sovereign rights over living and mineral resources within this zone, as well as jurisdiction with regard to the protection and preservation of the marine environment. The coastal state was to fix a total allowable catch of different species within the EEZ and, if unable to harvest that entire catch, allocate the surplus to third states (article 62). The first priority was to go to landlocked and geographically disadvantaged states, second to developing countries, and third to other countries, including the traditional fishing nations (articles 62, 69, 70).

The Convention consists of the following parts:

Part I:	Introduction
Part II:	Territorial Sea and Contiguous Zone
Part III:	Straits Used for International Navigation
Part IV:	Archipelagic States
Part V:	Exclusive Economic Zone
Part VI:	Continental Shelf
Part VII:	High Seas
Part VIII:	Regime of Islands
Part IX:	Enclosed or Semi-Enclosed Seas
Part X:	Right of Access of Land-Locked States to and from the Sea and Freedom of Transit
Part XI:	The Area
Part XII:	Protection and Preservation of the Marine Environment
Part XIII:	Marine Scientific Research
Part XIV:	Development and Transfer of Marine Technology
Part XV:	Settlement of Disputes
Part XVI:	General Provisions
Part XVII:	Final Provisions

There are also nine annexes:

Annex I:	Highly Migratory Species
Annex II:	Commission on the Limits of the Continental Shelf
Annex III:	Basic Conditions of Prospecting, Exploration and Exploitation
Annex IV:	Statute of the Enterprise
Annex V:	Conciliation
Annex VI:	Statute of the International Tribunal for the Law of the Sea
Annex VII:	Arbitration
Annex VIII:	Special Arbitration
Annex IX:	Participation by International Organizations

UNCLOS III entered into force on November 16, 1994, one year after the deposit of the sixtieth instrument of ratification of or accession to the convention. Several key Western states had not become parties to the convention, however, because they were not happy with the provisions in part XI relating to exploitation of the deep seabed. Consultations initiated by the UN Secretary-General with the objective of increasing regime participation resulted in the 1994 Agreement Relating to the Implementation of Part XI of the Convention.[72]

UNCLOS III and Protection of the Marine Environment

The most fundamental environmental obligation states accept under the UNCLOS regime is to "protect and preserve" the marine environment. To this end states are to take, individually or jointly as appropriate, all measures consistent with the convention necessary to prevent, reduce, and control pollution of the marine environment from any source.[73] Part XII focuses on the protection and preservation of the marine environment, although provisions relating to protection of the marine environment are scattered throughout the convention. The principle that states have the responsibility to ensure that activities within their jurisdiction or control do not cause damage to the environment of other states, or of areas beyond the limits of national jurisdiction, is reiterated in the 1982 convention as it relates to pollution of the marine environment.[74]

In providing for international rules and national legislation to prevent, reduce, and control pollution of the marine environment within zones of national jurisdiction and on the high seas, UNCLOS III distinguishes between flag states, port states, and coastal states, although in practice a state may fall into more than one category. The 1982 convention leaves no doubt that the freedom of the high seas no longer includes the freedom to pollute the high seas. Flag states are to ensure that vessels flying their flag or of their registry are prohibited from sailing until they comply with relevant international rules and standards; they are to provide the vessels with a certificate to that effect.[75] The 1982 convention marked a major change from customary international law, in that it also accorded jurisdiction to port states and coastal states. A port state—a state whose ports are visited by a vessel—may under article 211(3) establish particular requirements for the prevention, reduction, and control of pollution of the marine environment as a condition for the entry of foreign vessels into its ports. Coastal states may adopt laws and regulations for the prevention, reduction, and control of marine pollution from foreign vessels operating in their territorial waters and EEZs as long as the rules do not hamper the right of innocent passage through the territorial sea. Under article 211(6)(a) a coastal state may apply to the International Maritime Organization to have a certain area designated a special marine area protected from shipping. Two such sensitive areas that have been approved by the IMO are the Great Barrier Reef in Australia and the archipelago of Sabana-Camaguey in Cuba. Under the UNCLOS III provisions on the marine environment, the flag state retains primary enforcement responsibility, but port states and coastal states are also given powers of inspection, detention, and institution of proceedings against a vessel in violation of marine pollution laws.

Despite the fact that land-based sources of marine pollution contribute about 77 percent of marine pollution,[76] UNCLOS III provides a weak framework for the prevention of pollution from land-based sources; the negotiating states wanted latitude to weigh environmental objectives against the needs of their economies.[77] Whereas the convention requires states to adhere to minimum international standards established by international organizations as regards pollution from ships, dumping, and seabed installations, they are only required to "take into account" internationally agreed rules, standards, and recommended practices and procedures in adopting laws and regulations to prevent, reduce, and control pollution of the environment from land-based sources.[78] They are also to "take other measures as may be necessary to prevent, reduce and control such pollution."[79]

The IMO and Global Treaties to Protect the Marine Environment

Part XII of UNCLOS III reinforced, and in some instances effectively superseded, the 1958 Geneva Conventions on the Law of the Sea and the 1972 Action Plan resulting from the Stockholm Conference. UNCLOS III deals with the broad spectrum of ocean issues, but most provisions are of a very general nature. In this sense the treaty provides a framework for a complex web of more detailed treaty law, some of which predated, and some of which is more recent than, the 1982 convention. The bulk of the instruments that fill in the UNCLOS framework for the marine environment have been sponsored by one of the two major institutions working to protect and preserve the marine environment: the International Maritime Organization, formerly called the Intergovernmental Maritime Consultative Organization (IMCO), and the United Nations Environment Programme.

In the late 1960s there were several major tanker accidents, such as the 1967 incident in which the *Torrey Canyon* ran aground at the entrance to the English Channel, spilling its entire cargo of 120,000 tons of crude oil. This was the biggest oil pollution incident ever recorded up to that time.[80] Such accidents posed major questions regarding their prevention and management and prompted the IMO to conclude a number of conventions relating to accidental pollution of the seas by ships. Some related directly to protection of the marine environment, whereas others, such as the 1974 International Convention for the Safety of Life at Sea,[81] did so indirectly by addressing shipping safety concerns.

In terms of tonnage of oil entering the oceans, routine operations such as the cleaning of oil cargo tanks and the disposal of engine room wastes posed an even bigger threat to the marine environment than accidents; at the time when IMCO first began operations it was normal practice simply to wash cargo tanks out with water and pump the resulting mixture of oil and water into the sea.[82] The IMCO assumed responsibility for the administration of the 1954 Convention for the Prevention of Pollution of the Sea by Oil (OILPOL)[83] and went on to sponsor a number of global and regional single-issue treaties designed to minimize ocean pollution from ships. OILPOL prohibited the dumping of oily wastes within a certain distance of land and in "special areas" where the danger to the environment was especially acute. The 1973 International Convention for the Prevention of Pollution from Ships (MARPOL 73/78)[84] superseded an earlier 1954 convention that had dealt only with oil pollution from ships, to encompass also vessel-source pollution by chemicals, sewage, garbage, and other harmful substances. It applies to ships of all types except naval vessels or other state-owned ships used only on government noncommercial service. The 1978 MARPOL Protocol, which entered into force in 1983, effectively absorbs the 1973 agreement. In 1996 IMO members concluded the International Convention on Liability and Compensation for Damage in Connection with the Carriage of Hazardous and Noxious Substances by Sea.[85]

The 1969 International Convention for Civil Liability for Oil Pollution Damage and the 1971 International Convention on the Establishment of an International Fund for Compensation for Oil Pollution Damage established a system of liability and compensation for oil pollution damage caused by ships. In 1989 the International Convention on Salvage was adopted under IMO auspices; it was designed to create an incentive for salvors to take measures to protect the environment, even if those measures may have no useful result. The 1990 London International Convention on Oil Pollution Preparedness, Response, and Cooperation (OPRC) is designed to facilitate international cooperation in the event of a major oil pollution incident. The OPRC requires states to take certain precautionary measures, such as having oil pollution emergency plans on ships, as well as national and regional systems for preparedness and response. It upholds the widely, though not universally, accepted principle of "polluter pays," that is, the costs of pollution should be borne by the person responsible for causing the pollution and consequential costs.[86]

Other Global Instruments That "Fill in" the UNCLOS III Framework

The Convention on the Control of Transboundary Movements of Hazardous Wastes and Their Disposal (the Basel Convention) of 1989 helps protect the marine environment by regulating the transboundary movement of hazardous wastes. Agenda 21 devotes its longest chapter to ocean management. The ozone depletion and climate change regimes are also significant to the marine environment because stratospheric ozone depletion and global warming can harm plankton growth in ocean surface waters; a significant loss of phytoplankton could in turn deprive the world of a key carbon sink and perhaps even accelerate climate change.[87] Warming of the atmosphere will lead to a concomitant rise in ocean temperature; an increase of only one or two degrees in the ocean temperature will have a dramatic impact on biological communities.[88]

The Convention on Biological Diversity is also of significance because fifteen of the thirty-three types of animal life (phyla) are found only in the oceans;[89] even the deep seabed is high in biodiversity.[90] The importance of marine biodiversity extends beyond the loss of specific species or genetic diversity; losses of marine biological diversity may lead to damaging environmental change elsewhere.[91] One of the difficulties in protecting marine biodiversity is that the level of knowledge of our marine biodiversity is significantly less than that of terrestrial environments. Under the Biodiversity Convention states are to promote research for the identification, conservation, and sustainable use of marine biology and to promote scientific cooperation in biodiversity matters.

The UNEP Regional Seas Programme and Other Regional Agreements

Although many environmental problems such as climate change are truly global, their particular nature and relative importance tends to vary from region to region; each sea has its own special characteristics. Under the Regional Seas Programme of the United Nations Environment Programme, launched in 1974, states in a particular region formulate a region-specific "action plan" that identifies areas of cooperation. In most cases a regional seas convention has been concluded to provide the legal framework for a regional action plan; technical protocols address specific problems such as oil spills or conservation of a specific habitat. The Regional Seas Programme has been considered a great success. There are other regional treaties and programs for marine environmental protection, such as the OSPAR Commission for the North Atlantic and North Sea, not formally part of the Regional Seas Programme. The first international convention specifically concerned with land-based marine pollution was the 1974 Paris Convention on the Prevention of Marine Pollution from Land-Based Sources, concluded by states bordering the North Sea and the Northern Atlantic.

Current Issues and Trends in the Body of International Law Aimed to Protect the Marine Environment

The body of international law designed to protect the marine environment has evolved into an extensive web of multilateral treaties, which has witnessed some notable successes. Operational discharges of oil from ships have been greatly reduced, in many cases sewage and industrial discharges have been controlled, and a ban on ocean disposal of radioactive waste has reduced radionuclide contamination of the marine environment. Despite these successes, however, gaps remain. Although land-based sources of marine pollution are the most serious, there is as yet no legally binding global treaty on the subject. There is also a need for greater linkage between the law relating to the marine environment and that pertaining to living resources, including fisheries.

Most of the early developments in the international law to protect the marine environment came about in reaction to specific incidents such as those involving the *Torrey Canyon* in 1967 and the *Exxon Valdez* in 1989. There is now a perceived need to, and trend toward, having provisions in place ahead of disasters. Of particular concern in recent years has been the process of unrestrained coastal development, as well as the introduction, through the discharge of a ship's ballast water, of unwanted organisms, including dormant stages of toxic aquatic organisms, which can sometimes flourish to the detriment of indigenous marine life; the pathogens, including cholera, may cause illness in humans. It is to be hoped that current moves to strengthen the body of law aimed to protect the marine environment will be adequate to provide for "sustainable ocean development."

Notes

1. 11 International Legal Materials (ILM) 1416 (1972).

2. The other two were a resolution on institutional and financial arrangements, and an action plan.

3. 31 ILM 876 (1992).

4. Paul G. Harris, "Common but Differentiated Responsibility: The Kyoto Protocol and United States Policy," *New York University Environmental Law Journal* 7 (1999): 27–48, 30. See also Duncan French, "Developing States and International Environmental Law: The Importance of Differentiated Responsibilities," *International and Comparative Law Quarterly (ICLQ)* 49 (January 2000): 35–60; and panel discussion on common but differentiated responsibility in the American Society of International Law, *Proceedings of the 96th Annual Meeting*, March 13–16, 2002, pp. 358–368.

5. See, inter alia, C. K. Mensah, "The Role of Developing Countries," in L. Campiglio, *The Environment After Rio: International Law and Economics* (The Hague: Graham & Trotman/N. Nijhoff, 1994), pp. 33–52; M. A. L. Miller, *The Third World in Global Environmental Politics* (Boulder: Lynne Rienner, 1995); N. Middleton, P. O'Keefe, and S. Moyo, *The Tears of the Crocodile: From Rio to Reality in the Developing World* (London: Pluto, 1993); and John Ntambirweki, "The Developing Countries in the Evolution of an International Environmental Law," *Hastings International & Comparative Law Review* 14 (1991): 905–928.

6. See, inter alia, D. Freestone and Ellen Key, eds., *The Precautionary Principle and International Law: The Challenge of Implementation* (The Hague: Kluwer, 1996); Arie Trouwborst, *Evolution and Status of the Precautionary Principle in International Law* (The Hague: Kluwer Law International, 2002); and David VanderZwaag, "The Precautionary Principle in Environmental Law and Policy: Elusive Rhetoric and First Embraces," *Journal of Environmental Law and Practice* 8 (1999): 355–375.

7. For discussion of the relationship between the United Nations Environment Programme and the Commission on Sustainable Development, see Gerhard Loibl, "The Proliferation of International Institutions Dealing with International Environmental Matters," in N. M. Blokker and H. G. Schermers, eds., *Proliferation of International Organizations* (The Hague: Kluwer, 2001), pp. 151–175.

8. It was created by General Assembly Resolution 47/191, dated December 22, 1992. For further information, see www.un.org/esa/sustdev/csd-gen.htm.

9. This is available at the official website: www.johannesburgsummit.org.

10. For details, see www.basd-action.net.

11. Edith Brown Weiss, "Introductory Note," 31 ILM 814 (1992), 814.

12. James K. Sebenius, "Designing Negotiations Toward a New Regime: The Case of Global Warming," *International Security* 15, no. 4 (Spring 1991): 110–148, 114.

13. Vienna Convention for the Protection of the Ozone Layer, March 22, 1985, 26 ILM 1541 (1987).

14. Montreal Protocol on Substances that Deplete the Ozone Layer, September 16, 1987, 26 ILM 1541 (1987).

15. Edward A. Parson, "Protecting the Ozone Layer," in Peter M. Haas, Robert O. Keohane, and Marc A. Levy, eds., *Institutions for the Earth: Sources of Effective International Environmental Protection* (Cambridge: MIT Press, 1993), p. 29.

16. B. Blegen, "International Co-operation in Protection of the Atmospheric Ozone: The Montreal Protocol on Substances That Deplete the Ozone Layer," *Denver Journal of International Law and Policy* 16, nos. 2–3 (1988): 413–428, 413.

17. A pathfinding study by Mario Molina and Sherwood Rowland in 1974 suggested that the release of CFCs might be leading to the depletion of the ozone layer. See M. J. Molina and F. S. Rowland, "Stratospheric Sink for Chlorofluoromethanes: Chlorine Atom Catalyzed Destruction of Ozone," *Nature* 249 (1974): 810.

18. Edward A. Parson, "Protecting the Ozone Layer," in Haas, Keohane, and Levy, *Institutions for the Earth*, p. 29.

19. Peter M. Morrisette, "The Evolution of Policy Responses to Stratospheric Ozone Depletion," *Natural Resources Journal* 29 (1989): 793–820.

20. D. Bryk, "The Montreal Protocol and Recent Developments to Protect the Ozone Layer," *Harvard Environmental Law Review* 15 (1995): 275–298, 293.

21. For discussion and analysis, see James T. B. Tripp, "The Montreal Protocol: Industrialised and Developing Countries Sharing the Responsibility for Protecting the Stratospheric Ozone Layer," *International Law and Politics* 20 (1988): 733–752.

22. Lori B. Talbot, "Recent Developments in the Montreal Protocol on Substances That Deplete the Ozone Layer: The June 1990 Meeting and Beyond," *International Lawyer* (Spring 1992): 145–181, 147.

23. Article 6 of the convention; Article 11 of the protocol.

24. Amendment to the Montreal Protocol on the Substances That Deplete the Ozone Layer, 29 ILM 537 (1991).

25. For the story and analysis of the London negotiations, see, inter alia, R. E. Benedick, *Ozone Diplomacy: New Directions in Safeguarding the Planet* (Cambridge: Harvard University Press, 1991), chap. 3; and J. A. Mintz, "Progress Toward a Healthy Sky: An Assessment of the London Amendments to the Montreal Protocol on Substances That Deplete the Ozone Layer," *Yale Journal of International Law* 16, no. 2 (Summer 1991): 571–582.

26. David D. Caron, "Protection of the Stratospheric Ozone Layer and the Structure of International Environmental Lawmaking," *Hastings International & Comparative Law Review* 14 (1991), p. 761.

27. E. R. DeSombre and J. Kauffman, "The Montreal Protocol Multilateral Fund: Partial Success Story," in Robert O. Keohane and Marc A. Levy, eds, *Institutions for Environmental Aid: Pitfalls and Promises* (Cambridge: MIT Press, 1996), pp. 89–126, 95.

28. Miller, *The Third World in Global Environmental Politic*, p. 79.

29. "The Ozone Layer: The Lady Turned," *Economist,* July 7, 1990, p. 43.

30. "Backgrounder: Basic Facts and Data on the Science and Politics of

Ozone Protection." United Nations Environment Programme, October 5, 2001, p. 8.

31. See, inter alia, J. C. Dernbach, "The Global Environment Facility: Financing the Treaty Obligations of Developing Nations," *Environmental Law Reporter* 23, no. 3 (March 1993): 10124–10132; and S. A. Silard, "The Global Environment Facility: A New Development in International Law and Organization," *George Washington Journal of International Law and Economics* 28, no. 3 (Summer 1995): 607–654.

32. E. P. Barratt-Brown, "Building a Monitoring and Compliance Regime Under the Montreal Protocol," *Yale Journal of International Law* 16 (1991): 519–570, 531.

33. For information on the regime, see the website of the Ozone Secretariat, at www.unep.ch/ozone/index.shtml.

34. Margot B. Peters, "An International Approach to the Greenhouse Effect: The Problem of Increased Atmospheric Carbon Dioxide Can Be Approached by an Innovative International Agreement," *California Western International Law Journal* 20, no. 1 (1989–1990): 67–89, 68.

35. Ibid., p. 70.

36. Talbot, "Recent Developments in the Montreal Protocol," p. 181. The ozone depletion regime is still looked at as a useful model. See, e.g., J. Abdel-Khalik, "Prescriptive Treaties in Global Warming: Applying the Factors Leading to the Montreal Protocol," *Michigan Journal of International Law* 22 (Spring 2001): 489–521.

37. United Nations General Assembly, "Resolution on the Protection of the Global Climate," GA Res. 43/53, A/RES/43/53 (January 27, 1989).

38. 31 ILM 849 (1992).

39. The homepage of the Secretariat can be found at http://unfccc.int.

40. Peter G. G. Davies, "Global Warming and the Kyoto Protocol," *ICLQ* 47 (1998): 446–461, 448.

41. David Driesen, "Free Lunch or Cheap Fix? The Emissions Trading Idea and the Climate Change Convention," *Boston College Environmental Affairs Law Review* 26, no. 1 (1998): 1–88, 18.

42. Tony Brenton, *The Greening of Machiavelli: The Evolution of International Environmental Politics* (London: Royal Institute of International Affairs and Earthscan, 1994), p. 168.

43. Decision 1/CP.1 (UN Doc.Fccc/CP/1995/7/Add.1). For an account and evaluation of the First Conference of the Parties, see S. Oberthür and H. Ott, "The First Conference of the Parties," *Environmental Law and Policy* 25, nos. 4/5 (1995), 144–156.

44. "US Plays Greenhouse Game Hard as Possible," *The Australian*, October 8, 1997.

45. UN Doc.FCCC/CP/1997/L.7/Add.1.

46. See O. Yoshida, "Soft Enforcement of Treaties: The Montreal Protocol's Noncompliance Procedure and the Functions of Internal International Institutions," *Colorado Journal of International Environmental Law and Policy* 10, no. 1 (1999): 95–141.

47. Kyoto Protocol to the United Nations Framework Convention on Climate Change, article 25 (1).

48. See discussion in Paul G. Harris, "Common but Differentiated Responsibility: The Kyoto Protocol and United States Policy," *New York University Environmental Law Journal* 7 (1999): 27–48.

49. "US Attacked as EU Ratifies Kyoto," CNN.com, June 1, 2002, at www.cnn.com/2002/WORLD/europe/06/01/kyoto.ed, accessed July 18, 2002.

50. 28 ILM 657 (1989). The website address of the Secretariat is www.basel.int/index.html.

51. J. Clapp, "The Toxic Waste Trade with Less-industrialised Countries: Economic Linkages and Political Alliances," *Third World Quarterly* 15, no. 3 (1994): 505–518, 507.

52. Ibid., p. 507.

53. Iwona Rummel-Bulsa, "The Basel Convention: A Global Approach for the Management of Hazardous Wastes," *Environmental Policy and Law* 24, no. 1 (1994): 13–18, 13.

54. Ibid., p. 14.

55. Bamako Convention on the Ban of the Import into Africa and the Control of Transboundary Movement and Management of Hazardous Wastes within Africa, at www.tufts.edu/fletcher/multi/texts/BH984.txt.

56. Jennifer R. Kitt, "Waste Exports to the Developing World: A Global Response," *Georgetown International Environmental Law Review* 7 (1995): 485–514, 504.

57. Ibid., p. 504.

58. 31 ILM 818 (1992). The website for the Convention on Biological Diversity is located at www.biodiv.org.

59. 39 ILM 1027 (2000).

60. 40 ILM 532 (2001).

61. Its website is located at www.ipen.org.

62. T. T. B. Koh, "Negotiating a New World Order for the Sea," in Alan K. Henrikson, ed., *Negotiating World Order: The Artisanship and Architecture of Global Diplomacy* (Wilmington, DE: Scholarly Resources, 1986), pp. 33–45, 33–34.

63. For discussion of the origins of the three-mile territorial waters, see Wyndham L. Walker, "Territorial Waters: The Cannon Shot Rule," *British Year Book of International Law 1945*, pp. 210–231; and H. S. K. Kent, "The Historical Origins of the Three-Mile Limit," *American Journal of International Law* 48 (1954): 537–553.

64. Proclamations No. 2667 and No. 2668, "Policy of the United States with Respect to the Natural Resources of the Subsoil and Sea Bed of the Continental Shelf," September 28, 1945, 10 *Federal Register* 12303–12304.

65. A. L. Hollick, "United States Oceans Policy: The Truman Proclamations," *Virginia Journal of International Law* 17, no. 1 (1976): 23–55, 23.

66. Only four states were actually engaged in offshore drilling operations by 1954. R. Cullen, *Australian Federalism Offshore* (Melbourne: University of Melbourne Press, 1985), p. 7.

67. M. Whiteman, *Digest of International Law* 14 (Washington, DC: U.S. Department of State, 1965), pp. 794–796.

68. B. A. Helmore, "The Continental Shelf," *Australian Law Review* 27 (1954): 732–734, 732.

69. Koh, "Negotiating a New World Order for the Sea," p. 36.

70. See also Arvid Pardo, "Who Will Control the Seabed?" *Foreign Affairs* 47, no. 1 (October 1968): 123–137.

71. United Nations Convention on the Law of the Sea, 21 ILM 1261 (1982).

72. 33 ILM 1309.

73. United Nations Convention on the Law of the Sea, article 194 (1).

74. United Nations Convention on the Law of the Sea, article 194(2).

75. United Nations Convention on the Law of the Sea, article 217.

76. Independent World Commission on the Oceans, *The Ocean Our Future: The Report of the Independent World Commission on the Oceans* (Cambridge: Cambridge University Press: 1998), p. 27.

77. P. W. Birnie and A. E. Boyle, *International Law and the Environment* (Oxford: Clarendon, 1992), p. 307.

78. United Nations Convention on the Law of the Sea, article 207(1).

79. United Nations Convention on the Law of the Sea, article 207(2).

80. International Maritime Organization, "IMO: The First Fifty Years," at www.imo.org/imo/50ann/history3.htm, accessed September 10, 2000.

81. "International Convention for the Safety of Life at Sea," November 1, 1974, 1184 United Nations Treaty Series (UNTS) 2.

82. International Maritime Organization, "IMO: The First Fifty Years."

83. International Convention for the Prevention of Pollution of the Sea by Oil, May 12, 1954, 327 UNTS 3.

84. International Convention for the Prevention of Pollution from Ships, November 2, 1973, 12 ILM 1319 (1973).

85. 35 ILM 1406 (1996).

86. See discussion in P. Sands, *Principles of International Environmental Law, Volume 1: Frameworks, Standards, and Implementation* (Manchester: Manchester University Press, 1995), pp. 213–217.

87. Donald K. Anton, "Law for the Sea's Biological Diversity," *Columbia Journal of Transnational Law* 36 (1997): 341–371, 350.

88. Christopher C. Joyner, "Biodiversity in the Marine Environment: Resource Implications for the Law of the Sea," *Vanderbilt Journal of Transnational Law* 28 (1995): 635–687, 643.

89. *The Ocean Our Future: The Report of the Independent World Commission on the Oceans* (Cambridge: Cambridge University Press, 1998), p. 99.

90. Lyle Glowka, "Beyond the Deepest of Ironies: Genetic Resources, Marine Scientific Research and International Seabed Area," in Jean-Pierre Beurier, Alexandre Kiss, and Said Mahmoudi, *New Technologies and Law of the Marine Environment* (The Hague: Kluwer, 2000), p. 77. On the relationship of the Convention on Biological Diversity to the Law of the Sea Convention, see Rüdiger Wolfrum and Nele Matz, "The Interplay of the United Nations Convention on the Law of the Sea and the Convention on Biological Diversity," *Max Planck Yearbook of United Nations Law* 4 (2000): 445–480.

91. Joyner, "Biodiversity in the Marine Environment."

13

The Future Role of International Law in World Politics

I n this book we have examined the operation of the system of international law, viewed as a largely autonomous subsystem within world politics. We will begin this chapter by reviewing briefly some of the major themes that have surfaced during this discussion. We will then be ready to consider some of the questions international lawyers are currently asking about the future role of international law in world politics.

Five Themes Concerning the Current Operation of the System of International Law

A System of Interrelated Ideas
International law is, in essence, a system of interrelated ideas. In Chapter 1 we defined international law as a system of interrelated rules, principles, and concepts that governs relations among states and, increasingly, international organizations, individuals, and other actors in world politics. In defining "international law," we could have chosen to emphasize that international law is a process more than a static entity,[1] or that the system of international law incorporates international institutions such as the International Court of Justice. Although it is true that international law is dynamic and that it does incorporate institutional structures, the essence of international law is its *ideas*. What is interesting from a political perspective is how political actors draw on the intangible components of international law as a medium of interaction and as a mechanism by which to mediate their power relationships. The vast majority of disputes between political actors in world politics are settled peacefully; international law facilitates the reconciliation of otherwise conflicting policy agendas.

A State-Based System of Law

International law is a primarily state-based system of law. The two most important sources of international law are *treaties* and *custom.* Both of these emerge through the actions of states. The vast majority of the content of international law accords rights and responsibilities to states. The International Court of Justice decides contentious cases between states only, and states are the primary enforcement agents of international law, although they sometimes act through intergovernmental organizations. This is not to say that nonstate actors, such as nongovernmental organizations, multinational corporations, and individuals, do not influence the creation, implementation, enforcement, and dispute resolution processes in international law. But in terms of the formal operation of the system of international law, states and IGOs with states as members retain a preeminent position.

Entwined with World Politics

International law is entwined with world politics. International law is closely related to the broader political system in which it functions. This could not help but be the case when there is such a strong degree of overlap among the major actors in world politics and those in international law, and when some of the most basic concepts in international law, notably sovereignty, are also political concepts. International law is a medium of political interaction and negotiation as well as a source of authority and legitimacy. Political actors draw on the rules, concepts, and principles of international law to justify their actions and to persuade other actors to behave in certain ways favorable to themselves. The relative power of states and the policy goals that each is pursuing thus cannot help but influence the content of international law and its implementation. The fact that the rules, principles, and concepts of international law are evolving in a logical relationship with each other and that lawyers constantly seek to distinguish the meanings of those terms from those of their political or moral counterparts nevertheless acts as a force for stability both within international law and, beyond that, in world politics more generally.

An Autonomous System of Interrelated Rules, Principles, and Concepts

Although international law is entwined with world politics, it has a considerable degree of autonomy as a system of interrelated rules, principles, and concepts. Thinking of international law as a system of interrelated rules, principles, and concepts can facilitate our recognition of the considerable autonomy enjoyed by the system of international law. It is the specific definition attributed to concepts such as sovereignty and statehood within a relatively autonomous system of interrelated ideas that gives them authority as legal concepts and so allows them to function as a mechanism of interaction in world politics. If international law did not enjoy internal coherence it would all too easily merge into its political surroundings and its influence be dissipated.

In Chapter 5 the system of ideas that constitutes international law was represented as a pyramid to emphasize the importance to the unity of the system of its foundation philosophy. One of the key functions fulfilled by the underpinning philosophy is explaining why states should comply with international law. Internal to international law must be an explanation of the basis of legal obligation: why it is that a state must do as international law dictates. We have seen that, according to legal positivism, a state must comply because it has consented to the relevant law; consent is the source of legal obligation.

If the system is to retain coherence, the notion that international law derives from the will of states must also underpin other rules in the system. Thus, for example, the International Court of Justice has jurisdiction over a case only if it believes that the states involved have given consent. Of course, it is not always clear-cut as to when a state has given consent. It sometimes suits one party to a dispute to have a case heard by the Court, in which case it is likely to attempt to demonstrate consent by the other party. International law remains at every stage entwined with world politics.

Expansion Since 1945

A characteristic feature of world politics since 1945 has been the rapid expansion of the system of public international law. This expansion of international law has more than one dimension. There has been an increase in the breadth of subject matters addressed by international law. Most notable in this regard has been the growth of a distinguishable body of law known as *international human rights law* and another known as *international environmental law*. International criminal law is also an expanding field, in which the entry into force of the Rome Statute for an International Criminal Court was a landmark development.

International law has also expanded in terms of the sheer quantity of rules, principles, and concepts found within the system. The multilateral treaty has been the primary vehicle for such expansion. Also, there has been an increase in the number of actors involved in international law. The number of states has increased due to the process of decolonization and, more recently, the dissolution of the Soviet Union and Yugoslavia; nonstate actors are also playing an active role in the system of international law, albeit often an informal one.

The period of rapid growth of the system of international law is now being followed by one in which there is greater emphasis on enhancing the effectiveness of existing treaty regimes. Pick up a book on recent developments in any field of public international law and one is likely to find a comment to the effect that it is now time to consolidate the international law in this field, to find ways of making specific treaty regimes more effective rather than to continually negotiate new treaties. If we take as an example the field of international law that we have examined most recently—protection of the marine environment—there has already been some shift in focus, both within the regime itself and within scholarly commentary on the regime, away from treaty-making and toward treaty implementation.[2] This is true in other fields of international law as well. In relation to human rights, for example, "the conceptual battle is over, and the focus has shifted to . . . implementation."[3]

Five Questions About the Future of International Law

We are now ready to take an informed position on some of the questions that lawyers are currently asking about the future of international law.

QUESTION 1: Can international law meet the challenge posed by the increased role being played in world politics by multinational corporations and other nonstate actors?

We have noted the centrality of states to the formal workings of the system of international law. It is thus not surprising that international lawyers are currently exploring the question of the adequacy of the system to cater to the increased role in world politics of nonstate actors. There may be many abuses of human rights, such as against refugees at a UN refugee camp, for example, which do not give rise to a breach of international human rights law because the violator is not a state or an agent of a state.[4] Multinational corporations have been accused of violating human rights, including the right to life; the right to freedom from torture and cruel, inhumane, or degrading treatment; freedom from forced or slave labor; and freedom from discrimination.[5] Expectations of acceptable conduct by MNCs are increasingly being couched in human rights terms.[6] The spotlight on human rights violations has thus been moving to MNCs.[7]

Often spurred to action by the campaigns of NGOs and moving only when fearful of the effect of those campaigns on profits,[8] a number of large corporations as well as industry bodies have adopted codes of conduct.[9] The UN has also adopted a voluntaristic, cooperative approach to the regulation of MNC behavior.[10] But there is a growing view that existing methods have been inadequate and that new ways forward must be found. A report by the International Council on Human Rights Policy concluded that there was no theoretical obstacle to states imposing international human rights obligations much more clearly onto companies.[11] There are now calls to move beyond voluntary self-regulation and for international law to tackle head-on the issue of how to regulate the human rights actions, labor standards, and environmental behavior of MNCs.

The issue of the regulation by international law of nonstate actors goes beyond MNCs to include the applicability of international humanitarian law to conflicts in which at least one party is a nonstate actor, an issue that rose to greater prominence during the war against Al-Qaida and Taliban forces in Afghanistan. Along similar lines, questions have been asked as to whether the international law of arms control remains relevant in an era of potential "catastrophic terrorism"[12] involving the use of weapons of mass destruction by nonstate terrorist actors that cannot be parties to treaties on arms control. In February 2002 the U.S. Senate Subcommittee on International Security, Proliferation, and Federal Services held hearings to examine the usefulness of an international management system of weapons of mass destruction run by and for states. In her testimony, Amy Smithson, director of the Chemical and Biological Weapons Nonproliferation Project, cited three ways in which multilateral arms control treaties help with the threat by nonstate actors. First, the fewer the governments that maintain chemical or biological weapons programs, the fewer places terrorists will have to turn for technical assistance in the form of weapons materials, information, and human expertise. Second, participating states pass legislation to implement the treaties, and individuals are responsible to their governments. Third, many arms control treaties incorporate export controls on proliferation risk items, which diminishes one avenue whereby terrorists might acquire the materials and/or expertise to make weapons of mass destruction.[13] Although the security landscape has changed since the end of the Cold War, multilateral arms control agreements still play a central role in the international management of weapons of mass destruction.

Although the focus of concern in relation to nonstate actors has been on multinational corporations and nonstate security threats, the considerable discrepancy between the active role NGOs play in world politics and international law and their formal role within the system of international law has also prompted calls to formalize the role of NGOs in international lawmaking as well as to increase their accountability.[14] An example here is that of the Greenpeace boycott campaign conducted in response to the plan of Shell UK to scuttle the Brent Spar oilrig on the floor of the North Sea. Shell had received the necessary approvals from national and international agencies for its planned course of action, but the consumer boycott went ahead and was highly effective in terms of lost sales; Greenpeace should, according to one perspective, be accountable for the impact of its actions.[15]

The obvious means to ameliorate the discrepancy between the state-centric paradigm of international law and the globalized world is to accord nonstate actors a greater formal role within the legal system. But it is not necessarily just a case of states giving NGOs and MNCs equivalent legal personality to that of states. It is unlikely that they would want to assume equivalent governance responsibilities. NGOs and MNCs play a unique role because of their single-issue focus and their positioning primarily external to the formal system of international lawmaking, implementation, and enforcement. There is a huge difference between challenging a system from without and doing so from within. Were MNCs and NGOs suddenly to find themselves with governance responsibilities equivalent to those of states, they would inevitably change the way that they function. Neither is it likely that states would want to give away their capacity to change policy direction via law. Although much has been made of the "loss of sovereignty" issue, states have for the most part retained the lawmaking capacity that allows them to change policy direction should they, for example, decide against nuclear nonproliferation or free trade. The political power balance may have altered to a certain extent over the years, but if the lawmaking power of states were relinquished we would see political change of a truly revolutionary character.

QUESTION 2: Are we likely to witness the "triumph" of international human rights law over national sovereignty?

The decision of a state to be bound by a treaty is itself an expression of sovereign statehood. Nevertheless, reference is often made in political debate to the rhetoric of a "loss of sovereignty," particularly in a domestic context regarding, for example, a negative report from a UN human rights treaty committee or regional body. Loss of sovereignty rhetoric generally disguises opposition, not to the loss of sovereignty per se but to the pursuit by others of a political agenda with which one does not agree. The same politician may oppose strengthening international human rights law but accept the loss of sovereignty associated with the regulation of international trade.

It should, nevertheless, be remembered that all international law has a political dimension. This is not easy to see when one agrees with the agenda in question, whether human rights or environmental protection. Following the Pinochet decision by the House of Lords in 1999 there was a broad international campaign to bring to justice heads of state and other leaders accused of human rights abuses. Although it easy to criticize those who would oppose such a campaign, advocates of universal jurisdiction for human rights abuses tend to overlook the fact that, at a global level, even justice remains inseparable from the dynamics of power politics. It is still difficult to imagine the former head of state of a major power being required to stand trial in a developing country for alleged abuses of human rights or international humanitarian law.[16] And while international human rights law and sovereignty may often seem to be juxtaposed, in practice the implementation of effective human rights policies is not possible in a weak state. Those who advocate the more stringent regulation of multinational corporations generally assume that states will in some way be the creators and enforcers of the relevant law.

No doubt prompted by events that included the intervention of NATO in the Kosovo crisis and the proceedings against Pinochet in the United Kingdom, Kenneth Roth, executive director of Human Rights Watch, commented, "We will remember 1999 as the year in which sovereignty gave way in places where crimes against humanity were being committed." But he went on to acknowledge the inherent complexities involved: "Ordinarily we depend on sovereign states to defend human rights."[17] The relationship between human rights and sovereignty is in a process of evolution. At present it is not possible, or even desirable, to foresee how one might "defeat" the other.

QUESTION 3: Should international law require states to be democratic?
We have seen that sovereign equality is one of the most important principles in the current system of international law. The principle suggests that all states are to be treated equally by international law. But in a key article published in the *American Journal of International Law* in the aftermath of the end of the Cold War, Thomas Franck claimed that democracy was on the way to becoming a global entitlement, "one that increasingly will be promoted and protected by collective international processes."[18] According to Franck, the entitlement to democracy in

international law has gone through both a normative and a customary evolution in three phases. The first was the normative entitlement to self-determination. Second, free expression became a human right. Third and most recently, there has emerged a normative entitlement to a participatory electoral process. Franck's article was not an objective empirical analysis of recent history, although he was obviously basing it on post–Cold War trends, as much as an intentionally normative piece of writing; he concluded that "the task is to perfect what has been so wondrously begun."

Other writers took up where Franck left off, their opinions differing as to whether the norm of democratic governance is emerging or has already been firmly established.[19] The answer to this question may, of course, vary from region to region. Steven Wheatley has argued, for example, that an obligation to introduce and maintain democratic government already exists in Europe but not at a universal level.[20] Wheatley also sought to outline the scope and content of the norm, considering it to consist of the right to free and fair elections, to freedom of association, political expression, and the right to seek to influence political decisions. Set out in this way, the possibly emergent right of democratic governance is undeniably closely aligned with the Western ideal of liberal democracy. Noting this, Makau Mutua has posited that the norm of democratic governance is merely an extension of the human rights agenda, which he regards as the globalization of Western liberalism.[21]

International law, as it emerged from World War II through the United Nations system, recognized the sovereign equality of ideologically diverse states, avoiding discussion of the domestic constitution of individual states. Since the end of the Cold War a marked change in attitude has been observable within international law and the United Nations. It is a change that has been noted critically by those who reject Francis Fukuyama's celebrated interpretation of the end of the Cold War as the triumph of Western liberal democracy and the end of history.[22]

QUESTION 4: Is legal positivism still adequate as a philosophy of international law?

Some observers of the contemporary system of international law consider that legal positivism is inadequate as the foundation of a complex system of international law and that the internal coherence of the system is being weakened by inconsistencies between the underlying philosophy of the system and other constituent elements. J. L. Brierly expounded on this several decades ago:

> The assumption that international law consists of nothing save what States have consented to is an inadequate account of the system as it can be seen in actual operation, and even if it were a complete account of the contents of the law, it would fail to explain why the law is binding. . . . [C]onsent cannot of itself create an obligation: it can do so only within a system of law which declares that consent duly given, as in a treaty or a contract, shall be binding on the party consenting.[23]

Opinions differ as to what should be done to rectify the inconsistencies. One school of thought advocates a return, or partial return, to theories of natural law. Stephen Hall has reminded us that before Enlightenment naturalism took hold in the seventeenth century, naturalism was not an exclusionary philosophy; it permitted elements of positive law. Hall appears to advocate reincorporating elements of a natural law philosophy into the current positivist philosophy of international law.[24] According to another view, the principle of consent must be modified to include a principle of obligation. It is thought by some theorists that the principle of consent has been left behind by changes to the law on the use of force, by international human rights law, international environmental law, and by acceptance of the concept of *jus cogens*. *Jus cogens*, or "peremptory norms" of international law, are those rules—widely considered to include the prohibition against the use of force in article 2(4) of the UN Charter as well as those against aggression, genocide, and slavery—that have come to be accepted so widely that they are considered to be compulsory for all states.[25] The concept of *jus cogens* is therefore incompatible with an absolutist acceptance of the principle of consent. The fact that the concept has become increasingly accepted[26] suggests to some that it is legal positivism that must either evolve to make room for such a notion or be replaced.

A concept related to *jus cogens* is that of obligations *erga omnes*—obligations binding on all states. Such obligations may, but need not, derive from rules of *jus cogens*.[27] According to John Perkins, the "world is [already] acting on the pragmatic insight that the binding obligation of international law can arise out of a State's perceived responsibilities, as well as by its consent. . . . [W]hat has come to drive and must drive the development of much of international law is not the sovereign consent of States but the recognition that fundamental interests of the international community give rise to necessary obligations."[28]

It is not clear whether legal positivism, in its current form, will continue to underpin the system of international law. But as this book has endeavored to highlight, the practical importance to the system of international law of its underlying philosophy cannot be overemphasized.

QUESTION 5: Is it possible to have too much international law—to "overlegalize" world politics?
We have noted the rapid expansion of the system of international law that has taken place in tandem with the globalization of world politics. We have also noted that there is now a discernible shift in focus toward the better enforcement of existing international law, and the refinement of existing legal instruments, rather than a continuation of the rapid expansion in the number of treaty regimes. Noting that a number of political processes, including, for example, the resolution of international trade disputes, have been transformed into legal processes, one can rightly ask whether there are limits to legalization, whether it is possible to "overlegalize" world politics.[29]

This is a question that a pure legal positivist would be unlikely to ask, because the assumption is that the more law the better. But the long-standing divide between the perspectives of the political scientist and the international lawyer has broken down in recent years, and a number of attempts have been made to bridge the realist-positivist divide to better understand the complex relationship between international law and world politics.[30]

Although it is true that there may be unexpected consequences of legalizing political processes, research on this question is still in the early stages. It is worth noting that the suggestion that we may already have too much international law tends to overlook possible gaps in the current system. Although it is possible that some subject areas have been "overlegalized," there may well be substantive issue areas that remain neglected by international law, and/or certain actors that to date have not received sufficient recognition from the system of international law. What about the ongoing concerns of minorities, women, and indigenous peoples? And as we have already considered, what place should there be for the responsibilities of multinational corporations and NGOs? It may be that it is primarily the silences of international law that have been overlegalized.[31] There is much still to be done in the twenty-first century to refine the existing body of international law to manage effectively the conduct of relations among powerful states, as well as to further develop international law to provide a political voice for previously silenced peoples.

Notes

1. See, for example, R. Higgins, *Problems and Process: International Law and How We Use It* (New York: Oxford University Press, 1994).

2. Emeka Duruigbo, "Reforming the International Law and Policy on Marine Oil Pollution," *Journal of Maritime Law and Commerce* 31, no. 1 (January 2000): 65–87, 85. See also David S. Ardia, "Does the Emperor Have No Clothes? Enforcement of International Laws Protecting the Marine Environment," *Michigan Journal of International Law* 19 (Winter 1998): 497–567.

3. Christof Heyns and Frans Viljoen, "The Impact of the United Nations Human Rights Treaties on the Domestic Level," *Human Rights Quarterly* 23 (2001): 483–535, 483.

4. See Robert McCorquodale, "Overlegalizing Silences: Human Rights and Nonstate Actors," 96 *American Society of International Law Proceedings* (2002): 384–388.

5. Jordan J. Paust, "Human Rights Responsibilities of Private Corporations," *Vanderbilt Journal of Transnational Law* 35, no. 3 (May 2002): 801–826, 801.

6. International Council on Human Rights Policy, *Beyond Voluntarism: Human Rights and the Developing International Legal Obligations of Companies* (Versoix, Switzerland: International Council on Human Rights Policy, 2002), p. 1.

7. Jennifer Duke, "Enforcement of Human Rights on Multi-national Corporations: Global Climate, Strategies, and Trends for Compliance," *Denver Journal of International Law and Policy* 28, no. 4 (2000): 339–363, 355.

8. Deborah Spar, "The Spotlight and the Bottom Line: How Multinationals Export Human Rights," *Foreign Affairs* 77, no. 2 (March/April 1998): 7–12.

9. See, inter alia, Mark B. Baker, "Tightening the Toothless Vise: Codes of Conduct and the American Multinational Enterprises," *Wisconsin International Law Journal* 20, no. 1 (Winter 2001): 89–142; Adelle Blackett, "Global Governance, Legal Pluralism, and the Decentered State: A Labor Critique of Codes of Corporate Conduct," *Indiana Journal of Global Legal Studies* 8, no. 2 (Spring 2001): 401–447; Stephanie F. Dyson, "The Clash Between Corruption and Codes of Conduct: The Corporate Role in Forging a Human Rights Standard," *Connecticut Journal of International Law* 17, no. 2 (Spring 2002): 335–360; and Elisa Westfield, "Globalization, Governance, and Multinational Enterprises Responsibility: Corporate Codes of Conduct in the Twenty-first Century," *Virginia Journal of International Law* 42, no. 4 (Summer 2002): 1075–1108.

10. See Meaghan Shaughnessy, "The United Nations Global Compact and the Continuing Debate About the Effectiveness of Corporate Voluntary Codes of Conduct," *Colorado Journal of International Environmental Law and Policy* (Fall 2000): 159–172. See also the UN websites on the Global Compact, at www.unglobalcompact.org, and on the United Nations and Business, at www.un.org/partners/business.

11. International Council on Human Rights Policy, *Beyond Voluntarism*, p. 160.

12. A. Carter, J. Deutch, and P. Zelikow, "Catastrophic Terrorism: Tackling the New Danger," *Foreign Affairs* 77, no. 6 (November–December 1998): 80–94.

13. Amy E. Smithson, director, Chemical and Biological Weapons Nonproliferation Project, "Prepared Statement Before the Senate Committee on Governmental Affairs Subcommittee on International Security, Proliferation, and Federal Services," February 12, 2002, available at www.stimson.org/cbw/?SN=CB20020219314.

14. Comments by Dr. Jost Delbrück, in Rainer Hofmann, ed., *Non-State Actors as New Subjects of International Law. International Law: From the Traditional State Order Towards the Law of the Global Community*, proceedings of an international symposium of the Kiel Walther-Schücking Institute of International Law, March 25–28, 1998 (Berlin: Ducker & Humblot, 1999), p. 67.

15. Ruth Wedgwood, "Legal Personality and the Role of Non-Governmental Organizations and Non-State Political Entities in the United Nations System," in Hofmann, *Non-State Actors*, pp. 21–36, 31–32.

16. See Christopher Hitchens, *The Trial of Henry Kissinger* (London and New York: Verso, 2001); and Sarah C. Rispin, "Implications of *Democratic Republic of the Congo v. Belgium* on the *Pinochet* Precedent: A Setback for International Human Rights Litigation?" *Chicago Journal of International Law* 3, no. 2 (Fall 2002): 527–536.

17. Kenneth Roth, executive director of Human Rights Watch, cited at www.hrw.org/press/1999/dec/wr2keng.htm.

18. Thomas M. Franck, "The Emerging Right to Democratic Governance," *American Journal of International Law (AJIL)* 86 (1992): 46–91.

19. See the range of views expressed in Gregory H. Fox and Brad R. Roth, eds., *Democratic Governance and International Law* (Cambridge: Cambridge University Press, 2000). See also James Crawford, *Democracy in International Law* (Cambridge: Cambridge University Press, 1994).

20. Steven Wheatley, "Democracy in International Law: A European Perspective," *International and Comparative Law Quarterly* 51 (April 2002): 225–247.

21. Makau wa Mutua, "The Ideology of Human Rights," *Virginia Journal of International Law* 36 (1996): 589–657.

22. Francis Fukuyama, "The End of History," *National Interest* 16 (Summer 1989): 3–16; and Francis Fukuyama, *The End of History and the Last Man* (New York: Free Press, 1992). See also the discussion in Susan Marks, "International Law, Democracy and the End of History," in Fox and Roth, *Democratic Governance and International Law*.

23. J. L. Brierly, *The Law of Nations: An Introduction to the International Law of Peace,* 5th ed. (Oxford: Clarendon, 1955), pp. 52, 54.

24. Stephen Hall, "The Persistent Spectre: Natural Law, International Order, and the Limits of Legal Positivism," *European Journal of International Law* 12, no. 2 (2001): 269–307.

25. It is arguable that natural law elements are evident in the concept of *jus cogens,* which seems to suggest an "overriding system of law to which state laws are subject." Sam Blay, Ryszard Piotrowicz, and B. Martin Tsamenyi, eds., *Public International Law: An Australian Perspective* (Melbourne: Oxford University Press, 1997), p. 20.

26. It was used in the Vienna Convention on the Law of Treaties (1969). Article 53 states that a treaty is void "if, at the time of its conclusion, it conflicts with a peremptory norm of general international law. For the purposes of the present Convention, a peremptory norm of general international law is a norm accepted and recognised by the international community of States as a whole as a norm from which no derogation is permitted and which can be modified only by a subsequent norm of general international law having the same character." Article 64 provides that, if a new peremptory norm of general international law emerges, any existing treaty that is in conflict with that norm becomes void and terminates.

27. Maurizio Ragazzi, *The Concept of International Obligations Erga Omnes* (Oxford: Clarendon, 1997), pp. 189ff.

28. John A. Perkins, "Essay: The Changing Foundations of International Law: From State Consent to State Responsibility," *Boston University International Law Journal* 15 (1997): 433–509, 509.

29. See remarks by Anne-Marie Slaughter, in *American Society of International Law Proceedings* 96 (2002): 294–296. On the study of legalization more generally, see Judith Goldstein, Miles Kahler, Robert O. Keohane, and Anne-Marie Slaughter, eds., "Legalization and World Politics: A Special Issue of International Organization," *International Organization* 54 (2000).

30. See, inter alia, Kenneth W. Abbott, "Modern International Relations Theory: A Prospectus for International Lawyers," *Yale Journal of International Law* 14 (1989): 335–411; Kenneth W. Abbott, "International Law and International Relations Theory: Building Bridges—Elements of a Joint Discipline," *Proceedings of the American Society of International Law* 86 (1992): 167–172; J. Craig Barker, *International Law and International Relations* (London: Continuum, 2000); Robert J. Beck, "International Law and International Relations: The Prospects of Interdisciplinary Collaboration," in Robert J. Beck et al., eds., *International Rules: Approaches from International Law and International Relations* (Oxford: Oxford University Press, 1986); Michael Byers, *Custom, Power, and the Power of Rules* (Cambridge: Cambridge University Press, 1999); Robert O. Keohane, "International Relations and International Law: Two Optics," *Harvard International Law Journal* 38 (1997): 487–502; Charlotte Ku et al., "Exploring International Law: Opportunities and Challenges for Political Science Research: A Roundtable," *International Studies Review* 3, no. 1 (2001): 3–23; Anne-Marie Slaughter, "International Law and International Relations Theory: A Dual Agenda," *AJIL* 87 (1993): 205–239; Anne-Marie Slaughter et al., "International Law and International Relations Theory: A New Generation of Interdisciplinary Scholarship," *AJIL* 92 (1998): 367–397.

31. McCorquodale, "Overlegalizing Silences."

Acronyms

ABM	antiballistic missile
ATS	Antarctic Treaty System
BWC	Convention on the Prohibition of the Development, Production, and Stockpiling of Bacteriological (Biological) and Toxin Weapons and on Their Destruction
CAT	Convention Against Torture and Other Cruel, Inhuman, or Degrading Treatment or Punishment
CCW	Convention on Prohibitions or Restrictions on the Use of Certain Conventional Weapons Which May Be Deemed to Be Excessively Injurious or to Have Indiscriminate Effects
CD	Conference on Disarmament
CDM	clean development mechanism
CEDAW	Convention on the Elimination of All Forms of Discrimination Against Women
CERD	International Convention on the Elimination of All Forms of Racial Discrimination
CFC	chlorofluorocarbon
CICC	Coalition for an International Criminal Court
COP	Conference of the Parties
COPUOS	Committee on the Peaceful Uses of Outer Space
CRAMRA	Convention for the Regulation of Antarctic Mineral Resources
CRC	Convention on the Rights of the Child
CROC	Convention on the Rights of the Child
CTBT	Comprehensive Nuclear Test-Ban Treaty

CWC	Convention on the Prohibition of the Development, Production, Stockpiling, and Use of Chemical Weapons and on Their Destruction
DPRK	Democratic People's Republic of Korea
DSB	Dispute Settlement Body
ECOSOC	Economic and Social Council
EEZ	exclusive economic zone
FMCT	Fissile Material Cut-Off Treaty
FRY	Federal Republic of Yugoslavia
GA	General Assembly
GATT	General Agreement on Tariffs and Trade
GEMS	Global Environmental Monitoring System
IAEA	International Atomic Energy Agency
ICBL	International Campaign to Ban Landmines
ICC	International Criminal Court
ICCPR	International Covenant on Civil and Political Rights
ICESCR	International Covenant on Economic, Social, and Cultural Rights
ICJ	International Court of Justice
ICRC	International Committee of the Red Cross
ICRW	International Convention for the Regulation of Whaling
ICTR	International Criminal Tribunal for Rwanda
ICTY	International Criminal Tribunal for the Former Yugoslavia
IGO	intergovernmental organization
IHL	international humanitarian law
ILC	International Law Commission
ILM	International Legal Materials
ILO	International Labor Organization
IMCO	Intergovernmental Maritime Consultative Organization
IMO	International Maritime Organization
INF	Intermediate-Range Nuclear Forces (Treaty)
INGO	international nongovernmental organization
IPB	International Peace Bureau
IPCC	Intergovernmental Panel on Climate Change
IPPNW	International Physicians for the Prevention of Nuclear War
ITLOS	International Tribunal for the Law of the Sea
IWC	International Whaling Commission
KEDO	Korean Peninsula Energy Development Organization
MAD	mutually assured destruction

MARPOL	International Convention for the Prevention of Pollution from Ships
MNC	multinational corporation
MNE	multinational enterprise
MOU	memorandum of understanding
NATO	North Atlantic Treaty Organization
NGO	nongovernmental organization
NNWS	non-nuclear-weapon state
NPT	Treaty on the Non-Proliferation of Nuclear Weapons
NWFZs	nuclear-weapon-free zones
NWS	nuclear-weapon state
OAS	Organization of American States
ODS	ozone-depleting substances
OILPOL	Convention for the Prevention of Pollution of the Sea by Oil
ONUC	United Nations Operation in the Congo
OPCW	Organization for the Prohibition of Chemical Weapons
OPRC	International Convention on Oil Pollution Preparedness, Response, and Cooperation
PCIJ	Permanent Court of International Justice
POPs	persistent organic pollutants
PTBT	Treaty Banning Nuclear Weapon Tests in the Atmosphere, in Outer Space, and Under Water (Partial Test-Ban Treaty)
ROK	Democratic Republic of Korea
SALT	Strategic Arms Limitation Talks
SOFA	status of forces agreement
SOLAS	International Convention for the Safety of Life at Sea
START	Strategic Arms Reduction Talks
TRIPS	Trade-Related Aspects of Intellectual Property Rights
TWAIL	Third World Approaches to International Law
UDHR	Universal Declaration of Human Rights
UN	United Nations
UNCED	United Nations Conference on Environment and Development
UNCLOS	United Nations Convention on the Law of the Sea
UNEF	United Nations Emergency Force
UNEP	United Nations Environment Programme
UNESCO	United Nations Educational, Scientific, and Cultural Organization

UNHCR	United Nations High Commissioner for Human Rights
UNITAF	Unified Task Force
UNMISET	United Nations Mission of Support in East Timor
UNMOVIC	United Nations Monitoring, Verification, and Inspection Commission
UNOSOM	United Nations Operation in Somalia
UNSCOM	United Nations Special Commission
UNTAG	United Nations Transition Assistance Group
UNTS	United Nations Treaty Series
UNTSO	United Nations Truce Supervision Organization
WHO	World Health Organization
WTO	World Trade Organization

For Further Reference

Websites

www.eisil.org
The Electronic Information System for International Law is a collaborative project created by the American Society of International Law with useful information, documents, and links to a vast array of online sources of information in the various subfields of international law.

www.ppl.nl
This will give you access to the online catalog of the Peace Palace Library in The Hague as well as much up-to-the-minute reference information.

www.un.org
The United Nations website is the starting point for exploring any aspect of international law related to the work of the United Nations.

http://fletcher.tufts.edu/multilaterals.html
The Multilaterals Project, begun in 1992, is an ongoing project at the Fletcher School of Law and Diplomacy, Tufts University. It is an ideal starting point for locating the text of any multilateral treaty.

Books

Anaya, S. James. *Indigenous Peoples in International Law* (New York/Oxford: Oxford University Press, 1996).

Aust, A. *Modern Treaty Law and Practice* (Cambridge: Cambridge University Press, 2000).

Barker, J. Craig. *International Law and International Relations* (London: Continuum, 2000).

Beck, Robert J., Anthony Clark Arend, and Robert D. Vander Lugt, eds. *International Rules: Approaches from International Law and International Relations* (New York/Oxford: Oxford University Press, 1996).

Bernhardt, Rudolf, ed. *Encyclopedia of Public International Law* (Amsterdam/New York: North-Holland, 1992–2000).

311

Birnie, P. W., and A. E. Boyle. *International Law and the Environment,* 2nd ed. (Oxford: Oxford University Press, 2002).

Bröhmer, J. *State Immunity and the Violation of Human Rights* (The Hague/Boston/London: Martinus Nijhoff, 1997).

Byers, M. *Custom, Power, and the Power of Rules: International Relations and Customary International Law* (Cambridge: Cambridge University Press, 1999).

Charlesworth, H., and C. Chinkin. *The Boundaries of International Law: A Feminist Analysis* (Manchester: Manchester University Press, 2000).

Chayes, A., and A. H. Chayes. *The New Sovereignty: Compliance with International Regulatory Agreements* (Cambridge: Harvard University Press, 1995).

Dinstein, Y. *War, Aggression, and Self-Defence,* 3rd ed. (Cambridge: Cambridge University Press, 2001).

Durham, Helen, and Timothy L. H. McCormack, eds. *The Changing Face of Conflict and the Efficacy of International Humanitarian Law* (The Hague: Martinus Nijhoff, 1999).

Evans, Malcolm D., ed. *Blackstone's International Law Documents,* 6th ed. (London: Blackstone, 2003).

Fleck, Dieter, ed. *The Handbook of Humanitarian Law in Armed Conflict* (Oxford: Oxford University Press, 1995).

Goldblat, Jozef. *Arms Control: A Guide to Negotiations and Agreements* (London: Sage, 1994).

Grant, Thomas D. *The Recognition of States: Law and Practice in Debate and Evolution* (London: Praeger, 1999).

Harris, D. J. *Cases and Materials on International Law*, 5th ed. (London: Sweet & Maxwell, 1998).

Henkin, Louis. *How Nations Behave: Law and Foreign Policy* (New York: Published for the Council on Foreign Relations by Columbia University Press, 1979).

Higgins, R. *Problems and Process: International Law and How We Use It* (Oxford: Clarendon, 1994).

Janis, Mark W. *An Introduction to International Law,* 3rd ed. (Gaithersburg, NY: Aspen, 1999).

Klabbers, J. *An Introduction to International Institutional Law* (Cambridge: Cambridge University Press, 2002).

Ku, Charlotte, and Paul F. Diehl, eds. *International Law: Classic and Contemporary Readings,* 2nd ed. (Boulder: Lynne Rienner, 2003).

Merrills, J. G. *International Dispute Settlement,* 3rd ed. (Cambridge: Cambridge University Press, 1998).

Mrak, M., ed. *Succession of States* (The Hague: Martinus Nijhoff, 1999).

Philipp, C., and Rüdiger Wolfrum, eds. *United Nations: Law, Policies, and Practice,* 2 vols. (Dordrecht/London/Boston: Martinus Nijhoff, 1995).

Sabel, R. *Procedure at International Conferences: A Study of the Rules of Procedure of Conferences and Assemblies of International Intergovernmental Organisations* (Cambridge: Cambridge University Press, 1997).

Sarooshi, Danesh. *The United Nations and the Development of Collective*

Security: The Delegation by the UN Security Council of Its Chapter VII Powers (Oxford: Clarendon, 1999).

Schacter, O., and C. C. Joyner, eds. *United Nations Legal Order,* 2 vols. (Cambridge: Cambridge University Press and American Society of International Law, 1995).

Schermers, Henry G., and Niels M. Blokker. *International Institutional Law: Unity Within Diversity,* 3rd rev. ed. (The Hague/London/Boston: Martinus Nijhoff, 1995).

Simma, B., ed. *The Charter of the United Nations: A Commentary* (Oxford: Oxford University Press, 1994).

Steiner, Henry J., and Philip Alston. *International Human Rights in Context: Law, Politics, Morals,* 2nd ed. (Oxford: Oxford University Press, 2000).

Index

State jurisdiction: active personality principle and, 27; in criminal cases, 27–28; objective territorial principle and, 27; passive personality principle and, 27; protective principle and, 27; sovereignty equality and, 28; state immunity and, 28; and universal jurisdiction, 27–28

Statehood, international criteria for, 22–23

Status of forces agreement (SOFA), 4

Statute, defined, 144*fig7.2*

Stockholm Convention on Persistent Organic Pollutants, 276–277

Stockholm Declaration of 1972, 265, 267

Strategic Arms Limitation Talks (SALT), 206–207

Strategic Arms Reduction Talks (START), 206–208

Sub-Commission on the Prevention of Discrimination and the Protection of Minorities, 49

Sub-Commission on the Promotion and Protection of Human Rights, 80

Territorial acquisition, international law of, 127

Terrorism: attempts to define, 108; and International Criminal Court jurisdiction, 258; passive personality principle and, 27; and right to use force, 8–9*fig1.1*; September 2001 attacks on U.S., 38; treaties, 108, 180

Third United Nations Convention on the Law of the Sea (UNCLOS III), 5, 280–283; dispute settlement in, 152

Third World Approaches to International Law (TWAIL), 132–133

Threshold Test-Ban Treaty, 203

Tokyo Charter, 255

Torrey Canyon incident, 283–284

Torture Victim Protection Act of 1991, 10–11. *See also See* Convention Against Torture

Toxic chemicals threats, Stockholm Convention on, 276–277

Toxic trade, 274–275

Trade Related Aspects of Intellectual Property Rights (TRIPS), 133

Treaty(ies): bilateral, 36; characteristics of, 5–6; compromissory clause in, 96; disarmament, 47; extradition, 4; grouped by subject, 141–142; and intergovernmental organizations (IGOs), 36–37; law of, 141; obligations, 6; reservations, 98; sources, 5; terrorism, 108, 180; types of, 3–5. *See also* Multilateral treaties

Treaty of Anaya, 134

Treaty Banning Nuclear Weapon Tests in the Atmosphere, in Outer Space, and Under Water. *See* Partial Test-Ban Treaty

Treaty on Further Reduction and Limitation of Strategic Offensive Arms (START II), 207

Treaty on the Limitation of Anti-Ballistic Missile Systems. See ABM Treaty

Treaty on the Limitation of Strategic Offensive Arms (SALT II), 206

Treaty negotiations, 164–170; consensus decisionmaking in, 173; hegemon influence in, 165–166; lowest-common-denominator factor in, 172–173; middle-power leadership in, 166–167; public interest NGOs influence in, 169, 176; rules of procedure in, 172; subject-matter experts in, 169; and *travaux préparatoires*, 171–172

Treaty on the Nonproliferation of Nuclear Weapons (NPT), 62, 65, 192–198, 203; challenges to, 175; duration, withdrawal, and termination of, 149; extension of, 197; inequity in, 193–194, 196–197; verification of, 181

Treaty on Principles Governing the Activities of States in the Exploration and Use of Outer Space, Including the Moon and Other Celestial Bodies, 46

Treaty on the Reduction and Limitation of Strategic Offensive Arms (START I), 207

Treaty regime: compliance in, 177–180; dispute resolution in, 150–152,

About the Book

Terrorist attacks. UN sanctions. The creation of the International Criminal Court. The war on Iraq. In each of these headline events, the complex relationship of international law and world politics comes into play. *International Law in World Politics* introduces the concepts, the rules, and the functioning of international law in a way that is accessible to students of political science.

Scott covers such core topics as the nature of legal argument, the negotiation and implementation of multilateral treaties, and the place of the United Nations, other intergovernmental organizations, and nonstate actors in the international legal system. Equally important, she connects the actual content of laws dealing with, for example, human rights, the use of force, the environment, and genocide to current issues and problems. Case studies within the chapters bring the real world of world politics to life.

Covering the full range of this essential subfield of IR, this new text effectively explains the role that international law plays in the changing arena of world politics.

Shirley V. Scott is senior lecturer in international relations at the University of New South Wales.